LEAVES OF GRASS

LEAVES OF GRASS

Walt Whitman

HarperLargePrint Classics
An Imprint of HarperCollins*Publishers*

HarperCollins books may be purchased for educational, business, or sales promotional use. For information please write: Special Markets Department, HarperCollins Publishers, Inc., 10 East 53rd Street, New York, NY 10022.

First HarperLargePrint Classics edition published 2000.

HarperLargePrint Classics are published by HarperLargePrint, an imprint of HarperCollins Publishers.

Library of Congress Cataloging-in-Publication Data is available.

ISBN 0-06-095697-6

00 01 02 03 04 ❖/RRD 10 9 8 7 6 5 4 3 2 1

This Large Print Book carries the Seal of Approval of N.A.V.H.

Table of Contents

COME, said my Soul,
Such verses for my Body let us write, (for we are
    one,)
That should I after death invisibly return,
Or, long, long hence, in other spheres,
There to some group of mates the chants
    resuming,
(Tallying Earth's soil, trees, winds, tumultous
    waves,)
Ever with pleas'd smile I may keep on,
Ever and ever yet the verses owning—as, first, I
    here and now,
Signing for Soul and Body, set to them my
    name,

Walt Whitman

One's-Self I Sing

ONE'S-SELF I sing, a simple separate person,
Yet utter the word Democratic, the word
      En-Masse.

Of physiology from top to toe I sing,
Not physiognomy alone nor brain alone is
      worthy for the Muse, I say the Form
      complete is worthier far,
The Female equally with the Male I sing.

Of Life immense in passion, pulse, and power,
Cheerful, for freest action form'd under the laws
      divine,
The Modern Man I sing.

As I Ponder'd in Silence

AS I ponder'd in silence,
Returning upon my poems, considering,
      lingering long,
A Phantom arose before me with distrustful
      aspect,
Terrible in beauty, age, and power,
The genius of poets of old lands,
As to me directing like flame its eyes,
With finger pointing to many immortal songs,

And menacing voice, What singest thou? it said,
Know'st thou not there is hut one theme for
    ever-enduring bards?
And that is the theme of War, the fortune of
    battles,
The making of perfect soldiers.

Be it so, then I answer'd,
I too haughty Shade also sing war, and a longer
    and greater one than any,
Waged in my book with varying fortune, with
    flight, advance and retreat, victory deferr'd
    and wavering,
(Yet methinks certain, or as good as certain, at
    the last,) the field the world,
For life and death, for the Body and for the
    eternal Soul,
Lo, I too am come, chanting the chant of
    battles,
I above all promote brave soldiers.

In Cabin'd Ships at Sea

IN cabin'd ships at sea,
The boundless blue on every side expanding,
With whistling winds and music of the waves,
    the large imperious waves,
Or some lone bark buoy'd on the dense marine,

Where joyous full of faith, spreading white
   sails,
She cleaves the ether mid the sparkle and the
   foam of day, or under many a star at night,
By sailors young and old haply will I, a
   reminiscence of the land, be read,
In full rapport at last.

Here are our thoughts, voyagers' thoughts,
Here not the land, firm land, alone appears, may
   then by them be said,
The sky o'erarches here, we feel the undulating
   deck beneath our feet,
We feel the long pulsation, ebb and flow of
   endless motion,
The tones of unseen mystery, the vague and vast
   suggestions of the briny world, the liquid-
   flowing syllables,
The perfume, the faint creaking of the cordage,
   the melancholy rhythm,
The boundless vista and the horizon far and dim
   are all here,
And this is ocean's poem.

Then falter not O book, fulfil your destiny,
You not a reminiscence of the land alone,
You too as a lone bark cleaving the ether,
   purpos'd I know not whither, yet ever full of
   faith,
Consort to every ship that sails, sail you!

Bear forth to them folded my love, (dear
    mariners, for you I fold it here in every leaf;)
Speed on my book! spread your white sails my
    little bark athwart the imperious waves,
Chant on, sail on, bear o'er the boundless blue
    from me to every sea,
This song for mariners and all their ships.

To Foreign Lands

I HEARD that you ask'd for something to
    prove this puzzle the New World,
And to define America, her athletic Democracy,
Therefore I send you my poems that you behold
    in them what you wanted.

To a Historian

YOU who celebrate bygones,
Who have explored the outward, the surfaces of
    the races, the life that has exhibited itself,
Who have treated of man as the creature of
    politics, aggregates, rulers and priests,
I, habitan of the Alleghanies, treating of him as
    he is in himself in his own rights,
Pressing the pulse of the life that has seldom
    exhibited itself, (the great pride of man in
    himself,)

Chanter of Personality, outlining what is yet to be,
I project the history of the future.

To Thee Old Cause

To thee old cause!
Thou peerless, passionate, good cause,
Thou stern, remorseless, sweet idea,
Deathless throughout the ages, races, lands,
After a strange sad war, great war for thee,
(I think all war through time was really fought,
    and ever will be really fought, for thee,)
These chants for thee, the eternal march of thee.

(A war O soldiers not for itself alone,
Far, far more stood silently waiting behind, now
    to advance in this book.)

Thou orb of many orbs!
Thou seething principle! thou well-kept, latent
    germ! thou centre!
Around the idea of thee the war revolving,
With all its angry and vehement play of causes,
(With vast results to come for thrice a thousand
    years,)
These recitatives for thee,—my book and the
    war are one,
Merged in its spirit I and mine, as the contest
    hinged on thee,

As a wheel on its axis turns, this book unwitting
   to itself,
Around the idea of thee.

EIDOLONS

I MET a seer,
Passing the hues and objects of the world,
The fields of art and learning, pleasure, sense,
To glean eidolons.

Put in thy chants said he,
No more the puzzling hour nor day, nor
   segments, parts, put in,
Put first before the rest as light for all and
   entrance-song of all,
That of eidolons.

Ever the dim beginning,
Ever the growth, the rounding of the circle,
Ever the summit and the merge at last, (to
   surely start again,)
Eidolons! eidolons!

Ever the mutable,
Ever materials, changing, crumbling,
   re-cohering,
Ever the ateliers, the factories divine,
Issuing eidolons.

Lo, I or you,
Or woman, man, or state, known or unknown,
We seeming solid wealth, strength, beauty
    build,
But really build eidolons.

The ostent evanescent,
The substance of an artist's mood or savan's
    studies long,
Or warrior's, martyr's, hero's toils,
To fashion his eidolon.

Of every human life,
(The units gather'd, posted, not a thought,
    emotion, deed, left out,)
The whole or large or small summ'd, added up,
In its eidolon.

The old, old urge,
Based on the ancient pinnacles, lo, newer, higher
    pinnacles,
From science and the modern still impell'd,
The old, old urge, eidolons.

The present now and here,
America's busy, teeming, intricate whirl,
Of aggregate and segregate for only thence
    releasing,
To-day's eidolons.

These with the past,
Of vanish'd lands, of all the reigns of kings
    across the sea,
Old conquerors, old campaigns, old sailors'
    voyages,
Joining eidolons.

Densities, growth, facades,
Strata of mountains, soils, rocks, giant trees,
Far-born, far-dying, living long, to leave,
Eidolons everlasting.

Exalte, rapt, ecstatic,
The visible but their womb of birth,
Of orbic tendencies to shape and shape and
    shape,
The mighty earth-eidolon.

All space, all time,
(The stars, the terrible perturbations of the suns,
Swelling, collapsing, ending, serving their
    longer, shorter use,)
Fill'd with eidolons only.

The noiseless myriads,
The infinite oceans where the rivers empty,
The separate countless free identities, like
    eyesight,
The true realities, eidolons.

Not this the world,
Nor these the universes, they the universes,
Purport and end, ever the permanent life of life,
Eidolons, eidolons.

Beyond thy lectures learn'd professor,
Beyond thy telescope or spectroscope observer
    keen, beyond all mathematics,
Beyond the doctor's surgery, anatomy, beyond
    the chemist with his chemistry,
The entities of entities, eidolons.

Unfix'd yet fix'd,
Ever shall be, ever have been and are,
Sweeping the present to the infinite future,
Eidolons, eidolons, eidolons.

The prophet and the bard,
Shall yet maintain themselves, in higher stages
    yet,
Shall mediate to the Modern, to Democracy,
    interpret yet to them,
God and eidolons.

And thee my soul,
Joys, ceaseless exercises, exaltations,
Thy yearning amply fed at last, prepared to
    meet,
Thy mates, eidolons.

Thy body permanent,
The body lurking there within thy body,
The only purport of the form thou art, the real I
  myself,
An image, an eidolon.

Thy very songs not in thy songs,
No special strains to sing, none for itself,
But from the whole resulting, rising at last and
  floating,
A round full-orb'd eidolon.
For Him I Sing

FOR him I sing,
I raise the present on the past,
(As some perennial tree out of its roots, the
  present on the past,)
With time and space I him dilate and fuse the
  immortal laws,
To make himself by them the law unto himself.

WHEN I READ THE BOOK

WHEN I read the book, the biography famous,
And is this then (said I) what the author calls a
  man's life?
And so will some one when I am dead and gone
  write my life?

(As if any man really knew aught of my life,
Why even I myself I often think know little or
  nothing of my real life,
Only a few hints, a few diffused faint clews and
  indirections
I seek for my own use to trace out here.)

BEGINNING MY STUDIES

BEGINNING my studies the first step pleas'd
  me so much,
The mere fact consciousness, these forms, the
  power of motion,
The least insect or animal, the senses, eyesight,
  love,
The first step I say awed me and pleas'd me so
  much,
I have hardly gone and hardly wish'd to go any
  farther,
But stop and loiter all the time to sing it in
  ecstatic songs.

BEGINNERS

HOW they are provided for upon the earth,
  (appearing at intervals,)
How dear and dreadful they are to the earth,

How they inure to themselves as much as to
    any—what a paradox appears their age,
How people respond to them, yet know them
    not,
How there is something relentless in their fate
    all times,
How all times mischoose the objects of their
    adulation and reward,
And how the same inexorable price must still be
    paid for the same great purchase.

TO THE STATES

To the States or any one of them, or any city of
    the States, Resist much, obey little,
Once unquestioning obedience, once fully
    enslaved,
Once fully enslaved, no nation, state, city of this
    earth, ever afterward resumes its liberty.

ON JOURNEYS THROUGH THE STATES

ON journeys through the States we start,
(Ay through the world, urged by these songs,
Sailing henceforth to every land, to every sea,)
We willing learners of all, teachers of all, and
    lovers of all.

We have watch'd the seasons dispensing
    themselves and passing on,
And have said, Why should not a man or woman
    do as much as the seasons, and effuse as much?

We dwell a while in every city and town,
We pass through Kanada, the North-east, the
    vast valley of the Mississippi, and the
    Southern States,
We confer on equal terms with each of the
    States,
We make trial of ourselves and invite men and
    women to hear,
We say to ourselves, Remember, fear not, be
    candid, promulge the body and the soul,
Dwell a while and pass on, be copious,
    temperate, chaste, magnetic,
And what you effuse may then return as the
    seasons return,
And may be just as much as the seasons.

To a Certain Cantatrice

HERE, take this gift,
I was reserving it for some hero, speaker, or
    general,
One who should serve the good old cause, the
    great idea, the progress and freedom of the
    race,

Some brave confronter of despots, some daring
    rebel;
But I see that what I was reserving belongs to
    you just as much as to any.

ME IMPERTURBE

ME imperturbe, standing at ease in Nature,
Master of all or mistress of all, aplomb in the
    midst of irrational things,
Imbued as they, passive, receptive, silent as they,
Finding my occupation, poverty, notoriety,
    foibles, crimes, less important than I thought,
Me toward the Mexican sea, or in the
    Mannahatta or the Tennessee, or far north or
    inland,
A river man, or a man of the woods or of any
    farm-life of these States or of the coast, or the
    lakes or Kanada,
Me wherever my life is lived, O to be self-
    balanced for contingencies,
To confront night, storms, hunger, ridicule,
    accidents, rebuffs, as the trees and animals do.

SAVANTISM

THITHER as I look I see each result and glory
    retracing itself and nestling close, always
    obligated,
Thither hours, months, years—thither trades,
    compacts, establishments, even the most
    minute,
Thither every-day life, speech, utensils, politics,
    persons, estates;
Thither we also, I with my leaves and songs,
    trustful, admirant,
As a father to his father going takes his children
    along with him.

THE SHIP STARTING

LO, the unbounded sea,
On its breast a ship starting, spreading all sails,
    carrying even her moonsails.
The pennant is flying aloft as she speeds she
    speeds so stately—below emulous waves press
    forward,
They surround the ship with shining curving
    motions and foam.

I HEAR AMERICA SINGING

I HEAR America singing, the varied carols I
　　hear,
Those of mechanics, each one singing his as it
　　should be blithe and strong,
The carpenter singing his as he measures his
　　plank or beam,
The mason singing his as he makes ready for
　　work, or leaves off work,
The boatman singing what belongs to him in his
　　boat, the deckhand singing on the steamboat
　　deck,
The shoemaker singing as he sits on his bench,
　　the hatter singing as he stands,
The wood-cutter's song, the ploughboy's on his
　　way in the morning, or at noon intermission
　　or at sundown,
The delicious singing of the mother, or of the
　　young wife at work, or of the girl sewing or
　　washing,
Each singing what belongs to him or her and to
　　none else,
The day what belongs to the day—at night the
　　party of young fellows, robust, friendly,
Singing with open mouths their strong
　　melodious songs.

What Place Is Besieged?

WHAT place is besieged, and vainly tries to raise
    the siege?
Lo, I send to that place a commander, swift,
    brave, immortal,
And with him horse and foot, and parks of
    artillery,
And artillery-men, the deadliest that ever fired
    gun.

Still Though the One I Sing

STILL though the one I sing,
(One, yet of contradictions made,) I dedicate to
    Nationality,
I leave in him revolt, (O latent right of
    insurrection! O quenchless, indispensable
    fire!)

Shut Not Your Doors

SHUT not your doors to me proud libraries,
For that which was lacking on all your well-fill'd
    shelves, yet needed most, I bring,
Forth from the war emerging, a book I have
    made,

The words of my book nothing, the drift of it
  every thing,
A book separate, not link'd with the rest nor felt
  by the intellect,
But you ye untold latencies will thrill to every
  page.

POETS TO COME

POETS to come! orators, singers, musicians to
  come!
Not to-day is to justify me and answer what I
  am for,
But you, a new brood, native, athletic,
  continental, greater than before known,
Arouse! for you must justify me.

I myself but write one or two indicative words
  for the future,
I but advance a moment only to wheel and
  hurry back in the darkness.

I am a man who, sauntering along without fully
  stopping, turns a casual look upon you and
  then averts his face,
Leaving it to you to prove and define it,
Expecting the main things from you.

To You

STRANGER, if you passing meet me and desire
    to speak to me, why should you not speak to
    me?
And why should I not speak to you?

Thou Reader

THOU reader throbbest life and pride and love
    the same as I,
Therefore for thee the following chants.

Starting from Paumanok

STARTING from fish-shape Paumanok where I
    was born,
Well-begotten, and rais'd by a perfect mother,
After roaming many lands, lover of populous
    pavements,
Dweller in Mannahatta my city, or on southern
    savannas,
Or a soldier camp'd or carrying my knapsack
    and gun, or a miner in California,
Or rude in my home in Dakota's woods, my
    diet meat, my drink from the spring,
Or withdrawn to muse and meditate in some
    deep recess,
Far from the clank of crowds intervals passing
    rapt and happy,
Aware of the fresh free giver the flowing
    Missouri, aware of mighty Niagara,
Aware of the buffalo herds grazing the plains,
    the hirsute and strong-breasted bull,
Of earth, rocks, Fifth-month flowers
    experienced, stars, rain, snow, my amaze,
Having studied the mocking-bird's tones and
    the flight of the mountain-hawk,
And heard at dawn the unrivall'd one, the
    hermit thrush from the swamp-cedars,

Solitary, singing in the West, I strike up for a
    New World.

2

Victory, union, faith, identity, time,
The indissoluble compacts, riches, mystery,
Eternal progress, the kosmos, and the modern
    reports.
This then is life,
Here is what has come to the surface after so
    many throes and convulsions.

How curious! how real!
Underfoot the divine soil, overhead the sun.

See revolving the globe,
The ancestor—continents away group'd
    together,
The present and future continents north and
    south, with the isthmus between.

See, vast trackless spaces,
As in a dream they change, they swiftly fill,
Countless masses debouch upon them,
They are now cover'd with the foremost people,
    arts, institutions, known.

See, projected through time,
For me an audience interminable.

With firm and regular step they wend, they
  never stop,
Successions of men, Americanos, a hundred
  millions,
One generation playing its part and passing on,
Another generation playing its part and passing
  on in its turn,
With faces turn'd sideways or backward towards
  me to listen,
With eyes retrospective towards me.

3

Americanos! conquerors! marches
  humanitarian!
Foremost! century marches! Libertad! masses!
For you a programme of chants.

Chants of the prairies,
Chants of the long-running Mississippi, and
  down to the Mexican sea,
Chants of Ohio, Indiana, Illinois, Iowa,
  Wisconsin and Minnesota,
Chants going forth from the centre from
  Kansas, and thence equidistant,
Shooting in pulses of fire ceaseless to vivify all.

4

Take my leaves America, take them South and
  take them North,

Make welcome for them everywhere, for they
    are your own off-spring,
Surround them East and West, for they would
    surround you,
And you precedents, connect lovingly with
    them, for they connect lovingly with you.

I conn'd old times,
I sat studying at the feet of the great masters,
Now if eligible O that the great masters might
    return and study me.

In the name of these States shall I scorn the
    antique?
Why these are the children of the antique to
    justify it.

5

Dead poets, philosophs, priests,
Martyrs, artists, inventors, governments long
    since,
Language-shapers on other shores,
Nations once powerful, now reduced,
    withdrawn, or desolate,
I dare not proceed till I respectfully credit what
    you have left waited hither,
I have perused it, own it is admirable, (moving
    awhile among it,)
Think nothing can ever be greater, nothing can
    ever deserve more than it deserves,

Regarding it all intently a long while, then
  dismissing it,
I stand in my place with my own day here.

Here lands female and male,
Here the heir-ship and heiress-ship of the world,
  here the flame of materials,
Here spirituality the translatress, the openly-
  avow'd,
The ever-tending, the finale of visible forms,
The satisfier, after due long-waiting now
  advancing,
Yes here comes my mistress the soul.

6

The soul,
Forever and forever—longer than soil is brown
  and solid—longer than water ebbs and
  flows.
I will make the poems of materials, for I
  think they are to be the most spiritual
  poems,
And I will make the poems of my body and of
  mortality,
For I think I shall then supply myself with the
  poems of my soul and of immortality.

I will make a song for these States that no one
  State may under any circumstances be
  subjected to another State,

And I will make a song that there shall be
    comity by day and by night between all the
    States, and between any two of them,
And I will make a song for the ears of the
    President, full of weapons with menacing
    points,
And behind the weapons countless dissatisfied
    faces;
And a song make I of the One form'd out of all,
The fang'd and glittering One whose head is
    over all,
Resolute warlike One including and over all,
(However high the head of any else that head is
    over all.)

I will acknowledge contemporary lands,
I will trail the whole geography of the globe and
    salute courteously every city large and small,
And employments! I will put in my poems that
    with you is heroism upon land and sea,
And I will report all heroism from an American
    point of view.

I will sing the song of companionship,
I will show what alone must finally compact
    these,
I believe these are to found their own ideal of
    manly love, indicating it in me,
I will therefore let flame from me the burning
    fires that were threatening to consume me,

I will lift what has too long kept down those
    smouldering fires,
I will give them complete abandonment,
I will write the evangel-poem of comrades and
    of love,
For who but I should understand love with all
    its sorrow and joy?
And who but I should be the poet of comrades?

7

I am the credulous man of qualities, ages,
    races,
I advance from the people in their own spirit,
Here is what sings unrestricted faith.

Omnes! omnes! let others ignore what they may,
I make the poem of evil also, I commemorate
    that part also,
I am myself just as much evil as good, and my
    nation is—and I say there is in fact no evil,
(Or if there is I say it is just as important to you,
    to the land or to me, as any thing else.)

I too, following many and follow'd by many,
    inaugurate a religion, I descend into the
    arena,
(It may be I am destin'd to utter the loudest
    cries there, the winner's pealing shouts,
Who knows? they may rise from me yet, and
    soar above every thing.)

Each is not for its own sake,
I say the whole earth and all the stars in the sky
   are forreligion's sake.

I say no man has ever yet been half devout
   enough,
None has ever yet adored or worship'd half
   enough,
None has begun to think how divine he himself
   is, and how certain the future is.

I say that the real and permanent grandeur of
   these States must be their religion,
Otherwise there is just no real and permanent
   grandeur;
(Nor character nor life worthy the name without
   religion,
Nor land nor man or woman without religion.)

8

What are you doing young man?
Are you so earnest, so given up to literature,
   science, art, amours?
These ostensible realities, politics, points?
Your ambition or business whatever it may be?

It is well—against such I say not a word, I am
   their poet also,
But behold! such swiftly subside, burnt up for
   religion's sake,

For not all matter is fuel to heat, impalpable
    flame, the essential life of the earth,
Any more than such are to religion.

9

What do you seek so pensive and silent?
What do you need camerado?
Dear son do you think it is love?

Listen dear son—listen America, daughter
    or son,
It is a painful thing to love a man or woman to
    excess, and yet it satisfies, it is great,
But there is something else very great, it makes
    the whole coincide,
It, magnificent, beyond materials, with
    continuous hands sweeps and provides
    for all.

10

Know you, solely to drop in the earth the germs
    of a greater religion,
The following chants each for its kind I sing.

My comrade!
For you to share with me two greatnesses, and a
    third one rising inclusive and more
    resplendent,
The greatness of Love and Democracy, and the
    greatness of Religion.

Melange mine own, the unseen and the
    seen,
Mysterious ocean where the streams empty,
Prophetic spirit of materials shifting and
    flickering around me,
Living beings, identities now doubtless near us
    in the air that we know not of,
Contact daily and hourly that will not release
    me,
These selecting, these in hints demanded
    of me.

Not he with a daily kiss onward from childhood
    kissing me,
Has winded and twisted around me that which
    holds me to him,
Any more than I am held to the heavens and all
    the spiritual world,
After what they have done to me, suggesting
    themes.

O such themes—equalities! O divine average!
Warblings under the sun, usher'd as now, or at
    noon, or setting,
Strains musical flowing through ages, now
    reaching hither,
I take to your reckless and composite chords,
    add to them, and cheerfully pass them
    forward.

11

As I have walk'd in Alabama my morning
    walk,
I have seen where the she-bird the mocking-bird
    sat on her nest in the briers hatching her
    brood.

I have seen the he-bird also,
I have paus'd to hear him near at hand inflating
    his throat and joyfully singing.

And while I paus'd it came to me that what he
    really sang for was not there only,
Nor for his mate nor himself only, nor all sent
    back by the echoes,
But subtle, clandestine, away beyond,
A charge transmitted and gift occult for those
    being born.

12

Democracy! near at hand to you a throat is now
    inflating itself and joyfully singing.

Ma femme! for the brood beyond us and
    of us,
For those who belong here and those to come,
I exultant to be ready for them will now shake
    out carols stronger and haughtier than have
    ever yet been heard upon earth.

I will make the songs of passion to give them
  their way,
And your songs outlaw'd offenders, for I scan
  you with kindred eyes, and carry you with me
  the same as any.

I will make the true poem of riches,
To earn for the body and the mind whatever
  adheres and goes forward and is not dropt by
  death;
I will effuse egotism and show it underlying all,
  and I will be the bard of personality,
And I will show of male and female that either is
  but the equal of the other,
And sexual organs and acts! Do you concentrate
  in me, for I am determin'd to tell you with
  courageous clear voice to prove you
  illustrious,
And I will show that there is no imperfection
  in the present, and can be none in the
  future,
And I will show that whatever happens to
  anybody it may be turn'd to beautiful
  results,
And I will show that nothing can happen more
  beautiful than death,
And I will thread a thread through my poems
  that time and events are compact,
And that all the things of the universe are
  perfect miracles, each as profound as any.

I will not make poems with reference to parts,
But I will make poems, songs, thoughts, with
    reference to ensemble,
And I will not sing with reference to a day, but
    with reference to all days,
And I will not make a poem nor the least part of
    a poem but has reference to the soul,
Because having look'd at the objects of the
    universe, I find there is no one nor any
    particle of one but has reference to the soul.

13

Was somebody asking to see the soul?
See, your own shape and countenance, persons,
    substances, beasts, the trees, the running
    rivers, the rocks and sands.

All hold spiritual joys and afterwards loosen
    them;
How can the real body ever die and be buried?

Of your real body and any man's or woman's
    real body,
Item for item it will elude the hands of the
    corpse-cleaners and pass to fitting spheres,
Carrying what has accrued to it from the
    moment of birth to the moment of death.

Not the types set up by the printer return their
    impression, the meaning, the main concern,

Any more than a man's substance and life or a
    woman's substance and life return in the body
    and the soul,
Indifferently before death and after death.

Behold, the body includes and is the meaning,
    the main concern and includes and is the
    soul;
Whoever you are, how superb and how divine is
    your body, or any part of it!

14

Whoever you are, to you endless
    announcements!

Daughter of the lands did you wait for your Did
    you wait for one with a flowing mouth and
    indicative hand?
Toward the male of the States, and toward the
    female of the States,
Exulting words, words to Democracy's lands.

Interlink'd, food-yielding lands!
Land of coal and iron! land of gold! land of
    cotton, sugar, rice!
Land of wheat, beef, pork! land of wool and
    hemp! land of the apple and the grape!
Land of the pastoral plains, the grass-fields of
    the world! land of those sweet-air'd
    interminable plateaus!

Land of the herd, the garden, the healthy house
of adobie!
Lands where the north-west Columbia winds,
and where the south-west Colorado winds!
Land of the eastern Chesapeake! land of the
Delaware!
Land of Ontario, Erie, Huron, Michigan!
Land of the Old Thirteen! Massachusetts land!
land of Vermont and Connecticut!
Land of the ocean shores! land of sierras and
peaks!
Land of boatmen and sailors! fishermen's land!
Inextricable lands! the clutch'd together! the
passionate ones!
The side by side! the elder and younger
brothers! the bony-limb'd!
The great women's land! the feminine! the
experienced sisters and the inexperienced
sisters!
Far breath'd land! Arctic braced! Mexican
breez'd! the diverse! the compact!
The Pennsylvanian! the Virginian! the double
Carolinian!
O all and each well-loved by me! my intrepid
nations! O I at any rate include you all with
perfect love!
I cannot be discharged from you! not from one
any sooner than another!
O death! O for all that, I am yet of you unseen
this hour with irrepressible love,

Walking New England, a friend, a traveler,
Splashing my bare feet in the edge of the
   summer ripples on Paumanok's sands,
Crossing the prairies, dwelling again in Chicago,
   dwelling in every town,
Observing shows, births, improvements,
   structures, arts,
Listening to orators and oratresses in public
   halls,
Of and through the States as during life, each
   man and woman my neighbor,
The Louisianian, the Georgian, as near to me,
   and I as near to him and her,
The Mississippian and Arkansian yet with me,
   and I yet with any of them,
Yet upon the plains west of the spinal river, yet
   in my house of adobie,
Yet returning eastward, yet in the Seaside State
   or in Maryland,
Yet Kanadian cheerily braving the winter, the
   snow and ice welcome to me,
Yet a true son either of Maine or of the Granite
   State, or the Narragansett Bay State, or the
   Empire State,
Yet sailing to other shores to annex the same,
   yet welcoming every new brother,
Hereby applying these leaves to the new
   ones from the hour they unite with the old
   ones,

Coming among the new ones myself to be their
    companion and equal, coming personally to
    you now,
Enjoining you to acts, characters, spectacles,
    with me.

15
With me with firm holding, yet haste, haste on.
For your life adhere to me,
(I may have to be persuaded many times before
    I consent to give myself really to you, but
    what of that?
Must not Nature be persuaded many times?)

No dainty dolce affettuoso I,
Bearded, sun-burnt, gray-neck'd, forbidding, I
    have arrived,
To be wrestled with as I pass for the solid prizes
    of the universe,
For such I afford whoever can persevere to win
    them.

16
On my way a moment I pause,
for you! and here for America!
Still the present I raise aloft, still the future of
    the States I harbinge glad and sublime,
And for the past I pronounce what the air holds
    of the red aborigines.

The red aborigines,
Leaving natural breaths, sounds of rain and
    winds, calls as of birds and animals in the
    woods, syllabled to us for names,
Okonee, Koosa, Ottawa, Monongahela,
    Sauk, Natchez, Chattahoochee, Kaqueta,
    Oronoco,
Wabash, Miami, Saginaw, Chippewa, Oshkosh,
    Walla-Walla,
Leaving such to the States they melt, they
    depart, charging the water and the land with
    names.

17

Expanding and swift, henceforth,
Elements, breeds, adjustments, turbulent, quick
    and audacious,
A world primal again, vistas of glory incessant
    and branching,
A new race dominating previous ones and
    grander far, with new contests,
New politics, new literatures and religions, new
    inventions and arts.

These, my voice announcing—I will sleep no
    more but arise,
You oceans that have been calm within me! how
    I feel you, fathomless, stirring, preparing
    unprecedented waves and storms.

18

See, steamers steaming through my poems,

See, in my poems immigrants continually
coming and landing,

See, in arriere, the wigwam, the trail, the
hunter's hut, the flat-boat, the maize-leaf, the
claim, the rude fence, and the backwoods
village,

See, on the one side the Western Sea and on the
other the Eastern Sea, how they advance and
retreat upon my poems as upon their own
shores,

See, pastures and forests in my poems—see,
animals wild and tame—see, beyond the Kaw,
countless herds of buffalo feeding on short
curly grass,

See, in my poems, cities, solid, vast, inland, with
paved streets, with iron and stone edifices,
ceaseless vehicles, and commerce,

See, the many-cylinder'd steam printing-press—
see, the electric telegraph stretching across the
continent,

See, through Atlantica's depths pulses American
Europe reaching, pulses of Europe duly
return'd,

See, the strong and quick locomotive as it
departs, panting, blowing the steam-whistle,

See, ploughmen ploughing farms—see, miners
digging mines—see, the numberless factories,

See, mechanics busy at their benches with tools-
    see from among them superior judges,
    philosophs, Presidents, emerge, drest in
    working dresses,
See, lounging through the shops and fields of
    the States, me well-belov'd, close-held by day
    and night,
Hear the loud echoes of my songs there—read
    the hints come at last.

19

O camerado close! O you and me at last, and us
    two only.
O a word to clear one's path ahead endlessly!
O something ecstatic and undemonstrable! O
    music wild!
O now I triumph—and you shall also;
O hand in hand—O wholesome pleasure—O
    one more desirer and lover!
O to haste firm holding—to haste, haste on
    with me.

Song of Myself

1

I CELEBRATE myself, and sing myself,
And what I assume you shall assume,
For every atom belonging to me as good
    belongs to you.

I loafe and invite my soul,
I lean and loafe at my ease observing a spear of
    summer grass.

My tongue, every atom of my blood, form'd
    from this soil, this air,
Born here of parents born here from parents the
    same, and their parents the same,
I, now thirty-seven years old in perfect health
    begin,
Hoping to cease not till death.

Creeds and schools in abeyance,
Retiring back a while sufficed at what they are,
    but never forgotten,
I harbor for good or bad, I permit to speak at
    every hazard,
Nature without check with original energy.

2

Houses and rooms are full of perfumes, the
  shelves are crowded with perfumes,
I breathe the fragrance myself and know it and
  like it,
The distillation would intoxicate me also, but I
  shall not let it.

The atmosphere is not a perfume, it has no taste
  of the distillation, it is odorless,
It is for my mouth forever, I am in love
  with it,
I will go to the bank by the wood and become
  undisguised and naked,
I am mad for it to be in contact with me.

The smoke of my own breath,
Echoes, ripples, buzz'd whispers, love-root, silk-
  thread, crotch and vine,
My respiration and inspiration, the beating of
  my heart, the passing of blood and air
  through my lungs,
The sniff of green leaves and dry leaves, and of
  the shore and dark-color'd sea-rocks, and of
  hay in the barn,

The sound of the belch'd words of my voice
  loos'd to the eddies of the wind,
A few light kisses, a few embraces, a reaching
  around of arms,

The play of shine and shade on the trees as the
    supple boughs wag,
The delight alone or in the rush of the streets,
    or along the fields and hill-sides,
The feeling of health, the full-noon trill, the
    song of me rising from bed and meeting the
    sun.

Have you reckon'd a thousand acres much? have
    you reckon'd the earth much?
Have you practis'd so long to learn to read?
you felt so proud to get at the meaning of
    poems?

Stop this day and night with me and you shall
    possess the origin of all poems,
You shall possess the good of the earth and sun,
    (there are millions of suns left,)
You shall no longer take things at second or
    third hand, nor look through the eyes of the
    dead, nor feed on the spectres in books,You
    shall not look through my eyes either, nor
    take things from me,
You shall listen to all sides and filter them from
    your self.

3

I have heard what the talkers were talking, the
    talk of the beginning and the end,
But I do not talk of the beginning or the end.

There was never any more inception than there
    is now,
Nor any more youth or age than there is now,
And will never be any more perfection than
    there is now,
Nor any more heaven or hell than there is now.

Urge and urge and urge,
Always the procreant urge of the world.

Out of the dimness opposite equals advance,
    always substance and increase, always sex,
Always a knit of identity, always distinction,
    always a breed of life.
To elaborate is no avail, learn'd and unlearn'd
    feel that it is so.

Sure as the most certain sure, plumb in the
    uprights, well entretied, braced in the
    beams,
Stout as a horse, affectionate, haughty, electrical,
I and this mystery here we stand.

Clear and sweet is my soul, and clear and sweet
    is all that is not my soul.

Lack one lacks both, and the unseen is proved
    by the seen,
Till that becomes unseen and receives proof in
    its turn.

Showing the best and dividing it from the worst
    age vexes age,
Knowing the perfect fitness and equanimity of
    things, while they discuss I am silent, and go
    bathe and admire myself.

Welcome is every organ and attribute of me, and
    of any man hearty and clean,
Not an inch nor a particle of an inch is vile, and
    none shall be less familiar than the rest.

I am satisfied—I see, dance, laugh, sing;
As the hugging and loving bed-fellow sleeps at
    my side through the night, and withdraws at
    the peep of the day with stealthy tread,
Leaving me baskets cover'd with white towels
    swelling the house with their plenty,
Shall I postpone my acceptation and realization
    and scream at my eyes,
That they turn from gazing after and down the
    road,
And forthwith cipher and show me to a cent,
Exactly the value of one and exactly the value of
    two, and which is ahead?

4

Trippers and askers surround me,
People I meet, the effect upon me of my early
    life or the ward and city I live in, or the
    nation,

The latest dates, discoveries, inventions,
    societies, authors old and new,
My dinner, dress, associates, looks, compliments,
    dues,
The real or fancied indifference of some man or
    woman I love,
The sickness of one of my folks or of myself, or
    ill-doing or loss or lack of money, or
    depressions or exaltations,
Battles, the horrors of fratricidal war, the fever
    of doubtful news, the fitful events;
These come to me days and nights and go from
    me again,
But they are not the Me myself.

Apart from the pulling and hauling stands what
    I am,
Stands amused, complacent, compassionating,
    idle, unitary,
Looks down, is erect, or bends an arm on an
    impalpable certain rest,
Looking with side-curved head curious what will
    come next,
Both in and out of the game and watching and
    wondering at it.

Backward I see in my own days where I sweated
    through fog with linguists and contenders,
I have no mockings or arguments, I witness and
    wait.

5

I believe in you my soul, the other I am must
not abase itself to you,
And you must not be abased to the other.

Loafe with me on the grass, loose the stop from
your throat,
Not words, not music or rhyme I want, not
custom or lecture, not even the best,
Only the lull I like, the hum of your valved voice.

I mind how once we lay such a transparent
summer morning,
How you settled your head athwart my hips and
gently turn'd over upon me,
And parted the shirt from my bosom-bone,
and plunged your tongue to my bare-stript
heart,
And reach'd till you felt my beard, and reach'd
till you held my feet.

Swiftly arose and spread around me the peace
and knowledge that pass all the argument of
the earth,
And I know that the hand of God is the promise
of my own,
And I know that the spirit of God is the brother
of my own,
And that all the men ever born are also my
brothers, and the women my sisters and lovers,

And that a kelson of the creation is love,
And limitless are leaves stiff or drooping in the
 fields,
And brown ants in the little wells beneath them,
And mossy scabs of the worm fence, heap'd
 stones, elder, mullein, and poke-weed.

6

A child said What is the grass? fetching it to me
 with full hands;
How could I answer the child? I do not know
 what it is any more than he.

I guess it must be the flag of my disposition, out
 of hopeful green stuff woven.

Or I guess it is the handkerchief of the Lord,
A scented gift and remembrancer designedly
 dropt,
Bearing the owner's name someway in the
 corners, that we may see and remark, and say
 Whose?

Or I guess the grass is itself a child, the
 produced babe of the vegetation.

Or I guess it is a uniform hieroglyphic,
And it means,
Sprouting alike in broad zones and narrow zones,
Growing among black folks as among white,

Kanuck, Tuckahoe, Congressman, Cuff, I give
 them the same, I receive them the same.

And now it seems to me the beautiful uncut hair
 of graves.

Tenderly will I use you curling grass,
It may be you transpire from the breasts of
 young men,
It may be if I had known them I would have
 loved them,
It may be you are from old people, or from
 offspring taken soon out of their mothers'
 laps,
And here you are the mothers' laps.

This grass is very dark to be from the white
 heads of old mothers,
Darker than the colorless beards of old men,
Dark to come from under the faint red roofs of
 mouths.

O I perceive after all so many uttering tongues,
And I perceive they do not come from the roofs
 of mouths for nothing.

I wish I could translate the hints about the dead
 young men and women,
And the hints about old men and mothers, and
 the offspring taken soon out of their laps.

What do you think has become of the young
    and old men?
And what do you think has become of the
    women and children?

They are alive and well somewhere,
The smallest sprout shows there is really no
    death,
And if ever there was it led forward life, and
    does not wait at the end to arrest it,
And ceas'd the moment life appear'd.

All goes onward and outward, nothing
    collapses,
And to die is different from what any one
    supposed, and luckier.

7

Has any one supposed it lucky to be born?
I hasten to inform him or her it is just as lucky
    to die, and I know it.

I pass death with the dying and birth with the
    new-wash'd babe, and am not contain'd
    between my hat and boots,
And peruse manifold objects, no two alike and
    every one good,
The earth good and the stars good, and their
    adjuncts all good.

I am not an earth nor an adjunct of an earth,
I am the mate and companion of people, all just
    as immortal and fathomless as myself,
(They do not know how immortal, but I
    know.)

Every kind for itself and its own, for me mine
    male and female,
For me those that have been boys and that love
    women,
For me the man that is proud and feels how it
    stings to be slighted,
For me the sweet-heart and the old maid, for
    me mothers and the mothers of mothers,
For me lips that have smiled, eyes that have shed
    tears,
For me children and the begetters of children.

Undrape! you are not guilty to me, nor stale nor
    discarded,
I see through the broadcloth and gingham
    whether or no,
And am around, tenacious, acquisitive, tireless,
    and cannot be shaken away.

8

The little one sleeps in its cradle,
I lift the gauze and look a long time, and silently
    brush away flies with my hand.

The youngster and the red-faced girl turn aside
    up the bushy hill,
I peeringly view them from the top.

The suicide sprawls on the bloody floor of the
    bedroom,
I witness the corpse with its dabbled hair, I note
    where the pistol has fallen.

The blab of the pave, tires of carts, sluff of boot-
    soles, talk of the promenaders,
The heavy omnibus, the driver with his
    interrogating thumb, the clank of the shod
    horses on the granite floor,
The snow-sleighs, clinking, shouted jokes, pelts
    of snow-balls,
The hurrahs for popular favorites, the fury of
    rous'd mobs,
The flap of the curtain'd litter, a sick man inside
    borne to the hospital,
The meeting of enemies, the sudden oath, the
    blows and fall,
The excited crowd, the policeman with his star
    quickly working his passage to the center of
    the crowd,
The impassive stones that receive and return so
    many echoes,
What groans of over-fed or half-starv'd who fall
    sunstruck or in fits,

What exclamations of women taken suddenly
who hurry home and give birth to babes,
What living and buried speech is always vibrating
here, what howls restrain'd by decorum,
Arrests of criminals, slights, adulterous offers
made, acceptances, rejections with convex
lips,
I mind them or the show or resonance of them-
I come and I depart.

9

The big doors of the country barn stand open
and ready,
The dried grass of the harvest-time loads the
slow-drawn wagon,
The clear light plays on the brown gray and
green intertinged,
The armfuls are pack'd to the sagging mow.

I am there, I help, I came stretch'd atop of the
load,
I felt its soft jolts, one leg reclined on the
other,
I jump from the cross-beams and seize the
clover and timothy,
And roll head over heels and tangle my hair full
of wisps.

10

Alone far in the wilds and mountains I hunt,
Wandering amazed at my own lightness and
    glee,
In the late afternoon choosing a safe spot to pass
    the night,
Kindling a fire and broiling the fresh-kill'd
    game,
Falling asleep on the gather'd leaves with my
    dog and gun by my side.

The Yankee clipper is under her sky-sails, she
    cuts the sparkle and scud,
My eyes settle the land, I bend at her prow or
    shout joyously from the deck.

The boatmen and clam-diggers arose early and
    stopt for me,
I tuck'd my trowser-ends in my boots and went
    and had a good time;
You should have been with us that day round
    the chowder-kettle.

I saw the marriage of the trapper in the open air
    in the far west, the bride was a red girl,
Her father and his friends sat near cross-legged
    and dumbly smoking, they had moccasins to
    their feet and large thick blankets hanging
    from their shoulders,

On a bank lounged the trapper, he was drest
    mostly in skins, his luxuriant beard and curls
    protected his neck, he held his bride by the
    hand,
She had long eyelashes, her head was bare, her
    coarse straight locks descended upon her
    voluptuous limbs and reach'd to her feet.

The runaway slave came to my house and stopt
    outside,
I heard his motions crackling the twigs of the
    woodpile,
Through the swung half-door of the kitchen I
    saw him limpsy and weak,
And went where he sat on a log and led him in
    and assured him,
And brought water and fill'd a tub for his
    sweated body and bruis'd feet,
And gave him a room that enter'd from my
    own, and gave him some coarse clean clothes,
And remember perfectly well his revolving eyes
    and his awkwardness,
And remember putting piasters on the galls of
    his neck and ankles;
He staid with me a week before he was
    recuperated and pass'd north,
I had him sit next me at table, my fire-lock
    lean'd in the corner.

11

Twenty-eight young men bathe by the shore,
Twenty-eight young men and all so friendly;
Twenty-eight years of womanly life and all so
  lonesome.

She owns the fine house by the rise of the
  bank,
She hides handsome and richly drest aft the
  blinds of the window.

Which of the young men does she like the best?
Ah the homeliest of them is beautiful to her.

Where are you off to, lady? for I see you,
You splash in the water there, yet stay stock still
  in your room.

Dancing and laughing along the beach came the
  twenty-ninth bather,
The rest did not see her, but she saw them and
  loved them.

The beards of the young men glisten'd with wet,
  it ran from their long hair,
Little streams pass'd all over their bodies.

An unseen hand also pass'd over their bodies,
It descended tremblingly from their temples and
  ribs.

The young men float on their backs, their white
    bellies bulge to the sun, they do not ask who
    seizes fast to them,
They do not know who puffs and declines with
    pendant and bending arch,
They do not think whom they souse with spray.

12

The butcher-boy puts off his killing-clothes, or
    sharpens his knife at the stall in the market,
I loiter enjoying his repartee and his shuffle and
    break-down.

Blacksmiths with grimed and hairy chests
    environ the anvil,
Each has his main-sledge, they are all out, there
    is a great heat in the fire.

From the cinder-strew'd threshold I follow their
    movements,
The lithe sheer of their waists plays even with
    their massive arms,
Overhand the hammers swing, overhand so slow,
    overhand so sure,
They do not hasten, each man hits in his place.

13

The negro holds firmly the reins of his four
    horses, the block swags underneath on its
    tied-over chain,

The negro that drives the long dray of the
    stone-yard, steady and tall he stands pois'd on
    one leg on the string-piece,
His blue shirt exposes his ample neck and breast
    and loosens over his hip-band,
His glance is calm and commanding, he tosses
    the slouch of his hat away from his forehead,
The sun falls on his crispy hair and mustache,
    falls on the black of his polish'd and perfect
    limbs.

I behold the picturesque giant and love him,
    and I do not stop there,
I go with the team also.

In me the caresser of life wherever moving,
    backward as well as forward sluing,
To niches aside and junior bending, not a person
    or object missing,
Absorbing all to myself and for this song.

Oxen that rattle the yoke and chain or halt in
    the leafy shade, what is that you express in
    your eyes?
It seems to me more than all the print I have
    read in my life.

My tread scares the wood-drake and wood-duck
    on my distant and day-long ramble,
They rise together, they slowly circle around.

I believe in those wing'd purposes,
And acknowledge red, yellow, white, playing
within me,
And consider green and violet and the tufted
crown intentional,
And do not call the tortoise unworthy because
she is not something else,
And the in the woods never studied the gamut,
yet trills pretty well to me,
And the look of the bay mare shames silliness
out of me.

14

The wild gander leads his flock through the cool
night,
Ya-honk he says, and sounds it down to me like
an invitation,
The pert may suppose it meaningless, but I
listening close,
Find its purpose and place up there toward the
wintry sky.

The sharp-hoof'd moose of the north, the cat
on the house-sill, the chickadee, the prairie-
dog,
The litter of the grunting sow as they tug at her
teats,
The brood of the turkey-hen and she with her
half-spread wings,
I see in them and myself the same old law.

The press of my foot to the earth springs a
    hundred affections,
They scorn the best I can do to relate them.

I am enamour'd of growing out-doors,
Of men that live among cattle or taste of the
    ocean or woods,
Of the builders and steerers of ships and the
    wielders of axes and mauls, and the drivers of
    horses,
I can eat and sleep with them week in and week
    out.

What is commonest, cheapest, nearest, easiest, is
    me,
Me going in for my chances, spending for vast
    returns,
Adorning myself to bestow myself on the first
    that will take me,
Not asking the sky to come down to my good
    will,
Scattering it freely forever.

15

The pure contralto sings in the organ loft,
The carpenter dresses his plank, the tongue
    of his foreplane whistles its wild ascending
    lisp,
The married and unmarried children ride home
    to their Thanksgiving dinner,

The pilot seizes the king-pin, he heaves down
  with a strong arm,
The mate stands braced in the whale-boat, lance
  and harpoon are ready,
The duck-shooter walks by silent and cautious
  stretches,
The deacons are ordain'd with cross'd hands at
  the altar,
The spinning-girl retreats and advances to the
  hum of the big wheel,
The farmer stops by the bars as he walks on a
  First-day loafe and looks at the oats and rye,
The lunatic is carried at last to the asylum a
  confirm'd case,
(He will never sleep any more as he did in the
  cot in his mother's bed-room;)
The jour printer with gray head and gaunt jaws
  works at his case,
He turns his quid of tobacco while his eyes blurr
  with the manuscript;
The malform'd limbs are tied to the surgeon's
  table,
What is removed drops horribly in a pail;
The quadroon girl is sold at the auction-stand,
  the drunkard nods by the bar-room stove,
The machinist rolls up his sleeves, the policeman
  travels his beat, the gate-keeper marks who
  pass,
The young fellow drives the express-wagon,
  (I love him, though I do not know him;)

The half-breed straps on his light boots to
    compete in the race,
The western turkey-shooting draws old and
    young, some lean on their rifles, some sit on
    logs,
Out from the crowd steps the marksman, takes
    his position, levels his piece;
The groups of newly-come immigrants cover the
    wharf or levee,
As the woolly-pates hoe in the sugar-field, the
    overseer views them from his saddle,
The bugle calls in the ball-room, the gentlemen
    run for their partners, the dancers bow to
    each other,
The youth lies awake in the cedar-roof'd garret
    and harks to the musical rain,
The Wolverine sets traps on the creek that helps
    fill the Huron,
The squaw wrapt in her yellow-hemm'd cloth is
    offering moccasins and bead-bags for sale,
The connoisseur peers along the exhibition-
    gallery with half-shut eyes bent sideways,
As the deck-hands make fast the steamboat the
    plank is thrown for the shore-going
    passengers,
The young sister holds out the skein while the
    elder sister winds it off in a ball, and stops
    now and then for the knots,
The one-year wife is recovering and happy
    having a week ago borne her first child,

The clean-hair'd Yankee girl works with her
  sewing-machine or in the factory or mill,
The paving-man leans on his two-handed
  rammer, the reporter's lead flies swiftly over
  the note-book, the sign-painter is lettering
  with blue and gold,
The canal boy trots on the tow-path, the book-
  keeper counts at his desk, the shoemaker
  waxes his thread,
The conductor beats time for the band and all
  the performers follow him,
The child is baptized, the convert is making his
  first professions,
The regatta is spread on the bay, the race is
  begun, (how the white sails sparkle!)
The drover watching his drove sings out to
  them that would stray,
The pedler sweats with his pack on his back,
  (the purchaser higgling about the odd
  cent;)
The bride unrumples her white dress, the
  minute-hand of the clock moves slowly,
The opium-eater reclines with rigid head and
  just-open'd lips,
The prostitute draggles her shawl, her bonnet
  bobs on her tipsy and pimpled neck,
The crowd laugh at her blackguard oaths, the
  men jeer and wink to each other,
(Miserable! I do not laugh at your oaths nor jeer
  you;)

The President holding a cabinet council is
    surrounded by the great Secretaries,
On the piazza walk three matrons stately and
    friendly with twined arms,
The crew of the fish-smack pack repeated layers
    of halibut in the hold,
The Missourian crosses the plains toting his
    wares and his cattle,
As the fare-collector goes through the train he
    gives notice by the jingling of loose change,
The floor-men are laying the floor, the tinners
    are tinning the roof, the masons are calling
    for mortar,
In single file each shouldering his hod pass
    onward the laborers;
Seasons pursuing each other the indescribable
    crowd is gather'd, it is the fourth of Seventh-
    month, (what salutes of cannon and small arms!)
Seasons pursuing each other the plougher
    ploughs, the mower mows, and the winter-
    grain falls in the ground;
Off on the lakes the pike-fisher watches and
    waits by the hole in the frozen surface,
The stumps stand thick round the clearing, the
    squatter strikes deep with his axe,
Flatboatmen make fast towards dusk near the
    cotton-wood or pecan-trees,
Coon-seekers go through the regions of the Red
    river or through those drain'd by the
    Tennessee, or through those of the Arkansas,

Torches shine in the dark that hangs on the
    Chattahooche or Altamahaw,
Patriarchs sit at supper with sons and grandsons
    and great-grandsons around them,
In walls of adobie, in canvas tents, rest hunters
    and trappers after their day's sport,
The city sleeps and the country sleeps,
The living sleep for their time, the dead sleep for
    their time,
The old husband sleeps by his wife and the
    young husband sleeps by his wife;
And these tend inward to me, and I tend
    outward to them,
And such as it is to be of these more or less I am,
And of these one and all I weave the song of
    myself.

16

I am of old and young, of the foolish as much as
    the wise,
Regardless of others, ever regardful of others,
Maternal as well as paternal, a child as well as a
    man,
Stuff'd with the stuff that is coarse and stuff'd
    with the stuff that is fine,
One of the Nation of many nations, the smallest
    the same and the largest the same,
A Southerner soon as a Northerner, a planter
    nonchalant and hospitable down by the
    Oconee I live,

A Yankee bound my own way ready for trade,
my joints the limberest joints on earth and
the sternest joints on earth,
A Kentuckian walking the vale of the Elkhorn in
my deer-skin leggings, a Louisianian or
Georgian,
A boatman over lakes or bays or along coasts, a
Hoosier, Badger, Buckeye;
At home on Kanadian snow-shoes or up in the
bush, or with fishermen off Newfoundland,
At home in the fleet of ice-boats, sailing with
the rest and tacking,
At home on the hills of Vermont or in the
woods of Maine, or the Texan ranch,
Comrade of Californians, comrade of free
North-Westerners, (loving their big
proportions,)
Comrade of raftsmen and coalmen, comrade of
all who shake hands and welcome to drink
and meat,
A learner with the simplest, a teacher of the
thoughtfullest,
A novice beginning yet experient of myriads of
seasons,
Of every hue and caste am I, of every rank and
religion,
A farmer, mechanic, artist, gentleman, sailor,
quaker,
Prisoner, fancy-man, rowdy, lawyer, physician,
priest.

I resist any thing better than my own diversity,
Breathe the air but leave plenty after me,
And am not stuck up, and am in my place.

(The moth and the fish-eggs are in their place,
The bright suns I see and the dark suns I cannot
    see are in their place,
The palpable is in its place and the impalpable is
    in its place.)

17

These are really the thoughts of all men in
    all ages and lands, they are not original
    with me,
If they are not yours as much as mine they are
    nothing, or next to nothing,
If they are not the riddle and the untying of the
    riddle they are nothing,
If they are not just as close as they are distant
    they are nothing.

This is the grass that grows wherever the land is
    and the water is,
This the common air that bathes the globe.

18

With music strong I come, with my cornets and
    my drums,
I play not marches for accepted victors only, I
    play marches for conquer'd and slain persons.

Have you heard that it was good to gain the
    day?
I also say it is good to fall, battles are lost in the
    same spirit in which they are won.

I beat and pound for the dead,
I blow through my embouchures my loudest
    and gayest for them.

Vivas to those who have fail'd!
And to those whose war-vessels sank in the sea!
And to those themselves who sank in the sea!
And to all generals that lost engagements, and
    all overcome heroes!
And the numberless unknown heroes equal to
    the greatest heroes known!

19

This is the meal equally set, this the meat for
    natural hunger,
It is for the wicked just same as the righteous, I
    make appointments with all,
I will not have a single person slighted or left
    away,
The kept-woman, sponger, thief, are hereby
    invited,
The heavy-lipp'd slave is invited, the venerealee
    is invited;
There shall be no difference between them and
    the rest.

This is the press of a bashful hand, this the float
    and odor of hair,
This the touch of my lips to yours, this the
    murmur of yearning,
This the far-off depth and height reflecting my
    own face,
This the thoughtful merge of myself, and the
    outlet again.

Do you guess I have some intricate purpose?
Well I have, for the Fourth-month showers have,
    and the mica on the side of a rock has.

Do you take it I would astonish?
Does the daylight astonish? does the early
    redstart twittering through the woods?
Do I astonish more than they?

This hour I tell things in confidence,
I might not tell everybody, but I will tell
    you.

20

Who goes there? hankering, gross, mystical,
    nude;
How is it I extract strength from the beef
    I eat?

What is a man anyhow? what am I? what are
    you?

All I mark as my own you shall offset it with
    your own,
Else it were time lost listening to me.

I do not snivel that snivel the world over,
That months are vacuums and the ground but
    wallow and filth.

Whimpering and truckling fold with powders for
    invalids, conformity goes to the fourth-
    remov'd,
I wear my hat as I please indoors or out.

Why should I pray? why should I venerate and
    be ceremonious?

Having pried through the strata, analyzed to a
    hair, counsel'd with doctors and calculated
    close,
I find no sweeter fat than sticks to my own
    bones.

In all people I see myself, none more and not
    one a barley-corn less,
And the good or bad I say of myself I say of
    them.

I know I am solid and sound,
To me the converging objects of the universe
    perpetually flow,

All are written to me, and I must get what the
    writing means.

I know I am deathless,
I know this orbit of mine cannot be swept by a
    carpenter's compass,
I know I shall not pass like a child's carlacue cut
    with a burnt stick at night.

I know I am august,
I do not trouble my spirit to vindicate itself or
    be understood,
I see that the elementary laws never apologize,
(I reckon I behave no prouder than the level I
    plant my house by, after all.)

I exist as I am, that is enough,
If no other in the world be aware I sit content,
And if each and all be aware I sit content.

One world is aware and by far the largest to me,
    and that is myself,
And whether I come to my own to-day or in ten
    thousand or ten million years,
I can cheerfully take it now, or with equal
    cheerfulness I can wait.

My foothold is tenon'd and mortis'd in granite,
I laugh at what you call dissolution,
And I know the amplitude of time.

21

I am the poet of the Body and I am the poet of
the Soul,
The pleasures of heaven are with me and the
pains of hell are with me,
The first I graft and increase upon myself, the
latter I translate into new tongue.

I am the poet of the woman the same as the
man,
And I say it is as great to be a woman as to be a
man,
And I say there is nothing greater than the
mother of men.

I chant the chant of dilation or pride,
We have had ducking and deprecating about
enough,
I show that size is only development.

Have you outstript the rest? are you the
President?
It is a trifle, they will more than arrive there
every one, and still pass on.

I am he that walks with the tender and growing
night,
I call to the earth and sea half-held by the
night.

Press close bare-bosom'd night—press close
magnetic nourishing night!
Night of south winds—night of the large few stars!
Still nodding night—mad naked summer night.

Smile O voluptuous cool-breath'd earth!
Earth of the slumbering and liquid trees!
Earth of departed sunset—earth of the
mountains misty-topt!
Earth of the vitreous pour of the full moon just
tinged with blue!
Earth of shine and dark mottling the tide of the
river!
Earth of the limpid gray of clouds brighter and
clearer for my sake!
Far-swooping elbow'd earth—rich apple-
blossom'd earth!
Smile, for your lover comes.

Prodigal, you have given me love—therefore I
to you give love!
O unspeakable passionate love.

22

You sea! I resign myself to you also—I guess
what you mean,
I behold from the beach your crooked fingers,
I believe you refuse to go back without feeling
of me,

We must have a turn together, I undress, hurry
    me out of sight of the land,
Cushion me soft, rock me in billowy drowse,
Dash me with amorous wet, I can repay you.

Sea of stretch'd ground-swells,
Sea breathing broad and convulsive breaths,
Sea of the brine of life and of unshovell'd yet
    always-ready graves,
Howler and scooper of storms, capricious and
    dainty sea,
I am integral with you, I too am of one phase
    and of all phases.

Partaker of influx and efflux I, extoller of hate
    and conciliation,
Extoller of amies and those that sleep in each
    others' arms.

I am he attesting sympathy,
(Shall I make my list of things in the house and
    skip the house that supports them?)

I am not the poet of goodness only, I do not
    decline to be the poet of wickedness also.

What blurt is this about virtue and about vice?
Evil propels me and reform of evil propels me, I
    stand indifferent,

My gait is no fault-finder's or rejecter's
  gait,
I moisten the roots of all that has grown.

Did you fear some scrofula out of the unflagging
  pregnancy?
Did you guess the celestial laws are yet to be
  work'd over and rectified?

I find one side a balance and the antipedal side a
  balance,
Soft doctrine as steady help as stable
  doctrine,
Thoughts and deeds of the present our rouse
  and early start.

This minute that comes to me over the past
  decillions,
There is no better than it and now.

What behaved well in the past or behaves well
  to-day is not such wonder,
The wonder is always and always how there can
  be a mean man or an infidel.

23

Endless unfolding of words of ages!
And mine a word of the modern, the word
  En-Masse.

A word of the faith that never balks,
Here or henceforward it is all the same to me, I
  accept Time absolutely.

It alone is without flaw, it alone rounds and
  completes all,
That mystic baffling wonder alone completes all.

I accept Reality and dare not question it,
Materialism first and last imbuing.

Hurrah for positive science! long live exact
  demonstration!
Fetch stonecrop mixt with cedar and branches of
  lilac,
This is the lexicographer, this the chemist, this
  made a grammar of the old cartouches,
These mariners put the ship through dangerous
  unknown seas.
This is the geologist, this works with the scalper,
  and this is a mathematician.

Gentlemen, to you the first honors always!
Your facts are useful, and yet they are not my
  dwelling,
I but enter by them to an area of my dwelling.

Less the reminders of properties told my words,
And more the reminders they of life untold, and
  of freedom and extrication,

And make short account of neuters and
    geldings, and favor men and women fully
    equipt,
And beat the gong of revolt, and stop with
    fugitives and them that plot and conspire.

24

Walt Whitman, a kosmos, of Manhattan the son,
Turbulent, fleshy, sensual, eating, drinking and
    breeding,
No sentimentalist, no stander above men and
    women or apart from them,
No more modest than immodest.

Unscrew the locks from the doors!
Unscrew the doors themselves from their
    jambs!

Whoever degrades another degrades me,
And whatever is done or said returns at last to
    me.

Through me the afflatus surging and surging,
    through me the current and index.

I speak the pass-word primeval, I give the sign
    of democracy,
By God! I will accept nothing which all
    cannot have their counterpart of on the same
    terms.

Through me many long dumb voices,
Voices of the interminable generations of
    prisoners and slaves,
Voices of the diseas'd and despairing and of
    thieves and dwarfs,
Voices of cycles of preparation and accretion,
And of the threads that connect the stars, and of
    wombs and of the father-stuff,
And of the rights of them the others are down
    upon,
Of the deform'd, trivial, flat, foolish, despised,
Fog in the air, beetles rolling balls of dung.

Through me forbidden voices,
Voices of sexes and lusts, voices veil'd and I
    remove the veil,
Voices indecent by me clarified and transfigur'd.

I do not press my fingers across my mouth,
I keep as delicate around the bowels as around
    the head and heart,
Copulation is no more rank to me than death is.

I believe in the flesh and the appetites,
Seeing, hearing, feeling, are miracles, and each
    part and tag of me is a miracle.

Divine am I inside and out, and I make holy
    whatever I touch or am touch'd from,

The scent of these arm-pits aroma finer than
   prayer,
This head more than churches, bibles, and all
   the creeds.

If I worship one thing more than another it
   shall be the spread of my own body, or any
   part of it,
Translucent mould of me it shall be you!
Shaded ledges and rests it shall be you!
Firm masculine colter it shall be you!
Whatever goes to the tilth of me it shall be
   you!
You my rich blood! your milky stream pale
   strippings of my life!
Breast that presses against other breasts it shall
   be you!
My brain it shall be your occult convolutions!
Root of wash'd sweet-flag! timorous pond-snipe!
   nest of guarded duplicate eggs! it shall be
   you!
Mix'd tussled hay of head, beard, brawn, it shall
   be you!
Trickling sap of maple, fiber of manly wheat, it
   shall be you!
Sun so generous it shall be you!
Vapors lighting and shading my face it shall be
   you!
You sweaty brooks and dews it shall be you!

Winds whose soft-tickling genitals rub against
    me it shall be you!
Broad muscular fields, branches of live oak,
    loving lounger in my winding paths, it shall
    be you!
Hands I have taken, face I have kiss'd, mortal I
    have ever touch'd, it shall be you.

I dote on myself, there is that lot of me and all
    so luscious,
Each moment and whatever happens thrills me
    with joy,
I cannot tell how my ankles bend, nor whence
    the cause of my faintest wish,
Nor the cause of the friendship I emit, nor the
    cause of the friendship I take again.

That I walk up my stoop, I pause to consider if
    it really be,
A morning-glory at my window satisfies me
    more than the metaphysics of books.

To behold the day-break!
The little light fades the immense and
    diaphanous shadows,
The air tastes good to my palate.

Hefts of the moving world at innocent gambols
    silently rising freshly exuding,
Scooting obliquely high and low.

Something I cannot see puts upward libidinous
    prongs,
Seas of bright juice suffuse heaven.

The earth by the sky staid with, the daily close
    of their junction,
The heav'd challenge from the east that moment
    over my head,
The mocking taunt, See then whether you shall
    be master!

25

Dazzling and tremendous how quick the sun-
    rise would kill me,
If I could not now and always send sun-rise out
    of me.

We also ascend dazzling and tremendous as the
    sun,
We found our own O my soul in the calm and
    cool of the daybreak.

My voice goes after what my eyes cannot
    reach,
With the twirl of my tongue I encompass worlds
    and volumes of worlds.

Speech is the twin of my vision, it is unequal to
    measure itself,
It provokes me forever, it says sarcastically,

Walt you contain enough, why don't you let it
    out then?

Come now I will not be tantalized, you conceive
    too much of articulation,
Do you not know O speech how the buds
    beneath you are folded?
Waiting in gloom, protected by frost,
The dirt receding before my prophetical
    screams,
I underlying causes to balance them at last,
My knowledge my live parts, it keeping tally
    with the meaning of all things,
Happiness, (which whoever hears me let him or
    her set out in search of this day.)

My final merit I refuse you, I refuse putting
    from me what I really am,
Encompass worlds, but never try to encompass
    me,
I crowd your sleekest and best by simply looking
    toward you.

Writing and talk do not prove me,
I carry the plenum of proof and every thing else
    in my face,
With the hush of my lips I wholly confound the
    skeptic.

26

Now I will do nothing but listen,
To accrue what I hear into this song, to let
   sounds contribute toward it.

I hear bravuras of birds, bustle of growing
   wheat, gossip of flames, clack of sticks
   cooking my meals,
I hear the sound I love, the sound of the human
   voice,
I hear all sounds running together, combined,
   fused or following,
Sounds of the city and sounds out of the city,
   sounds of the day and night,
Talkative young ones to those that like them,
   the loud laugh of work-people at their meals,
The angry base of disjointed friendship, the faint
   tones of the sick,
The judge with hands tight to the desk, his
   pallid lips pronouncing a death-sentence,
The heave'e'yo of stevedores unlading ships by
   the wharves, the refrain of the anchor-lifters,
The ring of alarm-bells, the cry of fire, the whirr
   of swift-streaking engines and hose-carts with
   premonitory tinkles and color'd lights,
The steam-whistle, the solid roll of the train of
   approaching cars,
The slow march play'd at the head of the
   association marching two and two,

(They go to guard some corpse, the flag-tops are
    draped with black muslin.)

I hear the violoncello, ('tis the young man's
    heart's complaint,)
I hear the key'd cornet, it glides quickly in
    through my ears,
It shakes mad-sweet pangs through my belly and
    breast.

I hear the chorus, it is a grand opera,
Ah this indeed is music—this suits me.

A tenor large and fresh as the creation fills me,
The orbic flex of his mouth is pouring and
    filling me full.

I hear the train'd soprano (what work with hers
    is this?)
The orchestra whirls me wider than Uranus flies,
It wrenches such ardors from me I did not know
    I possess'd them,
It sails me, I dab with bare feet, they are lick'd
    by the indolent waves,
I am cut by bitter and angry hail, I lose my breath,
Steep'd amid honey'd morphine, my windpipe
    throttled in fakes of death,
At length let up again to feel the puzzle of
    puzzles,
And that we call Being.

27

To be in any form, what is that?
(Round and round we go, all of us, and ever
   come back thither,)
If nothing lay more develop'd the quahaug in its
   callous shell were enough.

Mine is no callous shell,
I have instant conductors all over me whether I
   pass or stop,
They seize every object and lead it harmlessly
   through me.

I merely stir, press, feel with my fingers, and am
   happy,
To touch my person to some one else's is about
   as much as I can stand.

28

Is this then a touch? quivering me to a new
   identity,
Flames and ether making a rush for my veins,
Treacherous tip of me reaching and crowding to
   help them,
My flesh and blood playing out lightning to
   strike what is hardly different from myself,
On all sides prurient provokers stiffening my
   limbs,
Straining the udder of my heart for its withheld
   drip,

Behaving licentious toward me, taking no denial,
Depriving me of my best as for a purpose,
Unbuttoning my clothes, holding me by the
    bare waist,
Deluding my confusion with the calm of the
    sunlight and pasture-fields,
Immodestly sliding the fellow-senses away,
They bribed to swap off with touch and go and
    graze at the edges of me,
No consideration, no regard for my draining
    strength or my anger,
Fetching the rest of the herd around to enjoy
    them a while,
Then all uniting to stand on a headland and
    worry me.

The sentries desert every other part of me,
They have left me helpless to a red marauder,
They all come to the headland to witness and
    assist against me.

I am given up by traitors,
I talk wildly, I have lost my wits, I and nobody
    else am the greatest traitor,
I went myself first to the headland, my own
    hands carried me there.

You villain touch! what are you doing? my
    breath is tight in its throat,

Unclench your floodgates, you are too much
    for me.

29

Blind loving wrestling touch, sheath'd hooded
    sharp-tooth'd touch!
Did it make you ache so, leaving me?

Parting track'd by arriving, perpetual payment of
    perpetual loan,
Rich showering rain, and recompense richer
    afterward.

Sprouts take and accumulate, stand by the curb
    prolific and vital,
Landscapes projected masculine, full-sized, and
    golden.

30

All truths wait in all things,
They neither hasten their own delivery nor
    resist it,
They do not need the obstetric forceps of the
    surgeon,
The insignificant is as big to me as any,
(What is less or more than a touch?)

Logic and sermons never convince,
The damp of the night drives deeper into my soul.

(Only what proves itself to every man and
　　woman is so,
Only what nobody denies is so.)

A minute and a drop of me settle my brain,
I believe the soggy clods shall become lovers and
　　lamps,
And a compend of compends is the meat of a
　　man or woman,
And a summit and flower there is the feeling
　　they have for each other,
　And they are to branch boundlessly out of that
　　lesson until it becomes omnific,
And until one and all shall delight us, and we
　　them.

31

I believe a leaf of grass is no less than the
　　journey work of the stars,
And the pismire is equally perfect, and a grain of
　　sand, and the egg of the wren,
And the tree-toad is a chef-d'oeuvre for the
　　highest,
And the running blackberry would adorn the
　　parlors of heaven,
And the narrowest hinge in my hand puts to
　　scorn all machinery,
And the cow crunching with depress'd head
　　surpasses any statue,

And a mouse is miracle enough to stagger
    sextillions of infidels.

I find I incorporate gneiss, coal, long-threaded
    moss, fruits, grains, esculent roots,
And am stucco'd with quadrupeds and birds all
    over,
And have distanced what is behind me for good
    reasons,
But call any thing back again when I desire it.

In vain the speeding or shyness,
In vain the plutonic rocks send their old heat
    against my approach,
In vain the mastodon retreats beneath its own
    powder'd bones,
In vain objects stand leagues off and assume
    manifold shapes,
In vain the ocean settling in hollows and the
    great monsters lying low,
In vain the buzzard houses herself with the sky,
In vain the snake slides through the creepers and
    logs,
In vain the elk takes to the inner passes of the
    woods,
In vain the razor-bill'd auk sails far north to
    Labrador,
I follow quickly, I ascend to the nest in the
    fissure of the cliff.

32

I think I could turn and live with animals, they
    are so placid and self-contain'd,
I stand and look at them long and long.

They do not sweat and whine about their
    condition,
They do not lie awake in the dark and weep for
    their sins,
They do not make me sick discussing their duty
    to God,
Not one is dissatisfied, not one is demented with
    the mania of owning things,
Not one kneels to another, nor to his kind that
    lived thousands of years ago,
Not one is respectable or unhappy over the
    whole earth.

So they show their relations to me and I accept
    them,
They bring me tokens of myself, they evince
    them plainly in their possession.

I wonder where they get those tokens,
Did I pass that way huge times ago and
    negligently drop them?

Myself moving forward then and now and
    forever,

Gathering and showing more always and with
   velocity,
Infinite and omnigenous, and the like of these
   among them,
Not too exclusive toward the reachers of my
   remembrancers,
Picking out here one that I love, and now go
   with him on brotherly terms.

A gigantic beauty of a stallion, fresh and
   responsive to my caresses,
Head high in the forehead, wide between the
   ears,
Limbs glossy and supple, tail dusting the
   ground,
Eyes full of sparkling wickedness, ears finely cut,
   flexibly moving.

His nostrils dilate as my heels embrace him,
His well-built limbs tremble with pleasure as we
   race around and return.

I but use you a minute, then I resign you,
   stallion,
Why do I need your paces when I myself out-
   gallop them?
Even as I stand or sit passing faster than
   you.

33

Space and Time! now I see it is true, what I
  guess'd at,
What I guess'd when I loaf'd on the grass,
What I guess'd while I lay alone in my bed,
And again as I walk'd the beach under the
  paling stars of the morning.

My ties and ballasts leave me, my elbows rest in
  sea-gaps,
I skirt sierras, my palms cover continents,
I am afoot with my vision.

By the city's quadrangular houses—in log huts,
  camping with lumber-men,
Along the ruts of the turnpike, along the dry
  gulch and rivulet bed,
Weeding my onion-patch or hosing rows of
  carrots and parsnips, crossing savannas,
  trailing in forests,
Prospecting, gold-digging, girdling the trees of a
  new purchase,
Scorch'd ankle-deep by the hot sand, hauling
  my boat down the shallow river,
Where the panther walks to and fro on a limb
  overhead, where the buck turns furiously at
  the hunter,
Where the rattlesnake suns his flabby length
  on a rock, where the otter is feeding on
  fish,

Where the alligator in his tough pimples sleeps
    by the bayou,
Where the black bear is searching for roots or
    honey, where the beaver pats the mud with
    his paddle-shaped tall;
Over the growing sugar, over the yellow-
    flower'd cotton plant, over the rice in its low
    moist field,
Over the sharp-peak'd farm house, with its
    scallop'd scum and slender shoots from the
    gutters,
Over the western persimmon, over the long-
    leav'd corn, over the delicate blue-flower flax,
Over the white and brown buckwheat, a
    hummer and buzzer there with the rest,
Over the dusky green of the rye as it ripples and
    shades in the breeze;
Scaling mountains, pulling myself cautiously up,
    holding on by low scragged limbs,
Walking the path worn in the grass and beat
    through the leaves of the brush,
Where the quail is whistling betwixt the woods
    and the wheat-lot,
Where the bat flies in the Seventh-month eve,
    where the great goldbug drops through the
    dark,
Where the brook puts out of the roots of the
    old tree and flows to the meadow,
Where cattle stand and shake away flies with the
    tremulous shuddering of their hides,

Where the cheese-cloth hangs in the kitchen,
   where andirons straddle the hearth-slab,
   where cobwebs fall in festoons from the
   rafters;
Where trip-hammers crash, where the press is
   whirling its cylinders,
Wherever the human heart beats with terrible
   throes under its ribs,
Where the pear-shaped balloon is floating aloft,
   (floating in it myself and looking composedly
   down,)
Where the life-car is drawn on the slip-noose,
   where the heat hatches pale-green eggs in the
   dented sand,
Where the she-whale swims with her calf and
   never forsakes it,
Where the steam-ship trails hind-ways its long
   pennant of smoke,
Where the fin of the shark cuts like a black chip
   out of the water,
Where the half-burn'd brig is riding on
   unknown currents,
Where shells grow to her slimy deck, where the
   dead are corrupting below;
Where the dense-starr'd flag is borne at the head
   of the regiments,
Approaching Manhattan up by the long-
   stretching island,
Under Niagara, the cataract falling like a veil
   over my countenance,

Upon a door-step, upon the horse-block of hard
  wood outside,
Upon the race-course, or enjoying picnics or jigs
  or a good game of base-ball,
At he-festivals, with blackguard gibes, ironical
  license, bull-dances, drinking, laughter,
At the cider-mill tasting the sweets of the
  brown mash, sucking the juice through a
  straw,
At apple-peelings wanting kisses for all the red
  fruit I find,
At musters, beach-parties, friendly bees,
  huskings, house-raisings;
Where the mocking-bird sounds his delicious
  gurgles, cackles, screams, weeps,
Where the hay-rick stands in the barn-yard,
  where the dry-stalks are scatter'd, where the
  brood-cow waits in the hovel,
Where the bull advances to do his masculine
  work, where the stud to the mare, where the
  cock is treading the hen,
Where the heifers browse, where geese nip their
  food with short jerks,
Where sun-down shadows lengthen over the
  limitless and lonesome prairie,
Where herds of buffalo make a crawling spread
  of the square miles far and near,
Where the humming-bird shimmers, where the
  neck of the long-lived swan is curving and
  winding,

Where the laughing-gull scoots by the shore,
    where she laughs her near-human laugh,
Where bee-hives range on a gray bench in the
    garden half hid by the high weeds,
Where band-neck'd partridges roost in a ring on
    the ground with their heads out,
Where burial coaches enter the arch'd gates of a
    cemetery,
Where winter wolves bark amid wastes of snow
    and icicled trees,
Where the yellow-crown'd heron comes to the
    edge of the marsh at night and feeds upon
    small crabs,
Where the splash of swimmers and divers cools
    the warm noon,
Where the katy-did works her chromatic reed on
    the walnut-tree over the well,
Through patches of citrons and cucumbers with
    silver-wired leaves,
Through the salt-lick or orange glade, or under
    conical firs,
Through the gymnasium, through the
    curtain'd saloon, through the office or public
    hall;
Pleas'd with the native and pleas'd with the
    foreign, pleas'd with the new and old,
Pleas'd with the homely woman as well as the
    handsome,
Pleas'd with the quakeress as she puts off her
    bonnet and talks melodiously,

Pleas'd with the tune of the choir of the
    whitewash'd church,
Pleas'd with the earnest words of the sweating
    Methodist preacher, impress'd seriously at the
    camp-meeting;
Looking in at the shop-windows of Broadway
    the whole forenoon, flatting the flesh of my
    nose on the thick plate glass,
Wandering the same afternoon with my face
    turn'd up to the clouds, or down a lane or
    along the beach,
My right and left arms round the sides of two
    friends, and I in the middle;
Coming home with the silent and dark-cheek'd
    bush-boy, (behind me he rides at the drape of
    the day,)
Far from the settlements studying the print of
    animals' feet, or the moccasin print,
By the cot in the hospital reaching lemonade to
    a feverish patient,
Nigh the coffin'd corpse when all is still,
    examining with a candle;
Voyaging to every port to dicker and
    adventure,
Hurrying with the modern crowd as eager and
    fickle as any,
Hot toward one I hate, ready in my madness to
    knife him,
Solitary at midnight in my back yard, my
    thoughts gone from me a long while,

Walking the old hills of Judaea with the
    beautiful gentle God by my side,
Speeding through space, speeding through
    heaven and the stars,
Speeding amid the seven satellites and the broad
    ring, and the diameter of eighty thousand
    miles,
Speeding with tail'd meteors, throwing fire-balls
    like the rest,
Carrying the crescent child that carries its own
    full mother in its belly,
Storming, enjoying, planning, loving,
    cautioning,
Backing and filling, appearing and disappearing,
I tread day and night such roads.

I visit the orchards of spheres and look at the
    product,
And look at quintillions ripen'd and look at
    quintillions green.

I fly those flights of a fluid and swallowing soul,
My course runs below the soundings of plummets.

I help myself to material and immaterial,
No guard can shut me off, no law prevent me.

I anchor my ship for a little while only,
My messengers continually cruise away or bring
    their returns to me.

I go hunting polar furs and the seal, leaping
    chasms with a pike-pointed staff, clinging to
    topples of brittle and blue.

I ascend to the foretruck,
I take my place late at night in the crow's-
    nest,
We sail the arctic sea, it is plenty light enough,
Through the clear atmosphere I stretch around
    on the wonderful beauty,
The enormous masses of ice pass me and I
    pass them, the scenery is plain in all
    directions,
The white-topt mountains show in the distance,
    I fling out my fancies toward them,
We are approaching some great battle-field in
    which we are soon to be engaged,
We pass the colossal outposts of the
    encampment, we pass with still feet and
    caution,
Or we are entering by the suburbs some vast
    and ruin'd city,
The blocks and fallen architecture more than all
    the living cities of the globe.

I am a free companion, I bivouac by invading
    watchfires,
I turn the bridgroom out of bed and stay with
    the bride myself,
I tighten her all night to my thighs and lips.

My voice is the wife's voice, the screech by the
    rail of the stairs,
They fetch my man's body up dripping and
    drown'd.

I understand the large hearts of heroes,
The courage of present times and all times,
How the skipper saw the crowded and
    rudderless wreck of the steamship, and Death
    chasing it up and down the storm,
How he knuckled tight and gave not back an
    inch, and was faithful of days and faithful of
    nights,
And chalk'd in large letters on a board, Be of
    good cheer, we will not desert you;
How he follow'd with them and tack'd with
    them three days and would not give it up,
How he saved the drifting company at last,
How the lank loose-gown'd women look'd
    when boated from the side of their prepared
    graves,
How the silent old-faced infants and the lifted
    sick, and the sharp-lipp'd unshaved men;
All this I swallow, it tastes good, I like it well, it
    becomes mine,
I am the man, I suffer'd, I was there.

The disdain and calmness of martyrs,
The mother of old, condemn'd for a witch,
    burnt with dry wood, her children gazing on,

The hounded slave that flags in the race, leans
  by the fence, blowing, cover'd with sweat,
The twinges that sting like needles his legs and
  neck, the murderous buckshot and the
  bullets,
All these I feel or am.

I am the hounded slave, I wince at the bite of
  the dogs,
Hell and despair are upon me, crack and again
  crack the marksmen,
I clutch the rails of the fence, my gore dribs,
  thinn'd with the ooze of my skin,
I fall on the weeds and stones,
The riders spur their unwilling horses, haul
  close,
Taunt my dizzy ears and beat me violently over
  the head with whip-stocks.

Agonies are one of my changes of garments,
I do not ask the wounded person how he feels, I
  myself become the wounded person,
My hurts turn livid upon me as I lean on a cane
  and observe.

I am the mash'd fireman with breast-bone
  broken,
Tumbling walls buried me in their debris,
Heat and smoke I inspired, I heard the yelling
  shouts of my comrades,

I heard the distant click of their picks and
    shovels,
They have clear'd the beams away, they tenderly
    lift me forth.

I lie in the night air in my red shirt, the
    pervading hush is for my sake,
Painless after all I lie exhausted but not so
    unhappy,
White and beautiful are the faces around me, the
    heads are bared of their fire-caps,
The kneeling crowd fades with the light of the
    torches.

Distant and dead resuscitate,
They show as the dial or move as the hands of
    me, I am the clock myself.

I am an old artillerist, I tell of my fort's
    bombardment,
I am there again.

Again the long roll of the drummers,
Again the attacking cannon, mortars,
Again to my listening ears the cannon
    responsive.

I take part, I see and hear the whole,
The cries, curses, roar, the plaudits for well-
    aim'd shots,

The ambulanza slowly passing trailing its red
    drip,
Workmen searching after damages, making
    indispensable repairs,
The fall of grenades through the rent roof, the
    fan-shaped explosion,
The whizz of limbs, heads, stone, wood, iron,
    high in the air.

Again gurgles the mouth of my dying general,
    he furiously waves with his hand,
He gasps through the clot Mind not me—
    mind—the entrenchments.

34

Now I tell what I knew in Texas in my early
    youth,
(I tell not the fall of Alamo,
Not one escaped to tell the fall of Alamo,
The hundred and fifty are dumb yet at Alamo,)
'Tis the tale of the murder in cold blood of four
    hundred and twelve young men.

Retreating they had form'd in a hollow square
    with their baggage for breastworks,
Nine hundred lives out of the surrounding
    enemies, nine times their number, was the
    price they took in advance,
Their colonel was wounded and their
    ammunition gone,

They treated for an honorable capitulation,
   receiv'd writing and seal, gave up their arms
   and march'd back prisoners of war.

They were the glory of the race of rangers,
Matchless with horse, rifle, song, supper,
   courtship,
Large, turbulent, generous, handsome, proud,
   and affectionate,
Bearded, sunburnt, drest in the free costume of
   hunters,
Not a single one over thirty years of age.

The second First-day morning they were
   brought out in squads and massacred, it was
   beautiful early summer,
The work commenced about five o'clock and
   was over by eight.

None obey'd the command to kneel,
Some made a mad and helpless rush, some stood
   stark and straight,
A few fell at once, shot in the temple or heart,
   the living and dead lay together,
The maim'd and mangled dug in the dirt, the
   new-comers saw them there,
Some half-kill'd attempted to crawl away,
These were despatch'd with bayonets or batter'd
   with the blunts of muskets,

A youth not seventeen years old seiz'd his
    assassin till two more came to release
    him,
The three were all torn and cover'd with the
    boy's blood.

At eleven o'clock began the burning of the
    bodies;
That is the tale of the murder of the four
    hundred and twelve young men.

35

Would you hear of an old-time sea-fight?
Would you learn who won by the light of the
    moon and stars?
List to the yarn, as my grandmother's father the
    sailor told it to me.

Our foe was no sulk in his ship I tell you, (said
    he,)
His was the surly English pluck, and there is no
    tougher or truer, and never was, and never
    will be;
Along the lower'd eve he came horribly raking
    us.

We closed with him, the yards entangled, the
    cannon touch'd,
My captain lash'd fast with his own hands.

We had receiv'd some eighteen pound shots
    under the water,
On our lower-gun-deck two large pieces had
    burst at the first fire, killing all around and
    blowing up overhead.

Fighting at sun-down, fighting at dark,
Ten o'clock at night, the full moon well up, our
    leaks on the gain, and five feet of water reported,
The master-at-arms loosing the prisoners
    confined in the after-hold to give them a
    chance for themselves.

The transit to and from the magazine is now
    stopt by the sentinels,
They see so many strange faces they do not
    know whom to trust.

Our frigate takes fire,
The other asks if we demand quarter?
If our colors are struck and the fighting done?

Now I laugh content, for I hear the voice of my
    little captain,
We have not struck, he composedly cries, we
    have just begun our part of the fighting.

Only three guns are in use,
One is directed by the captain himself against
    the enemy's main-mast,

Two well serv'd with grape and canister silence
  his musketry and
clear his decks.

The tops alone second the fire of this little
  battery, especially the main-top,
They hold out bravely during the whole of the
  action.

Not a moment's cease,
The leaks gain fast on the pumps, the fire eats
  toward the powder-magazine.

One of the pumps has been shot away, it is
  generally thought we are sinking.

Serene stands the little captain,
He is not hurried, his voice is neither high nor
  low,
His eyes give more light to us than our battle-
  lanterns.

Toward twelve there in the beams of the moon
  they surrender to us.

36

Stretch'd and still lies the midnight,
Two great hulls motionless on the breast of the
  darkness,
Our vessel riddled and slowly sinking,

preparations to pass to the one we have
conquer'd,
The captain on the quarter-deck coldly giving
his orders through a countenance white as a
sheet,
Near by the corpse of the child that serv'd in the
cabin,
The dead face of an old salt with long white hair
and carefully curl'd whiskers,
The flames spite of all that can be done
flickering aloft and below,
The husky voices of the two or three officers yet
fit for duty,
Formless stacks of bodies and bodies by
themselves, dabs of flesh upon the masts and
spars,
Cut of cordage, dangle of rigging, slight shock
of the soothe of waves,
Black and impassive guns, litter of powder-
parcels, strong scent,
A few large stars overhead, silent and mournful
shining,
Delicate sniffs of sea-breeze, smells of sedgy
grass and fields by the shore, death-messages
given in charge to survivors,
The hiss of the surgeon's knife, the gnawing
teeth of his saw,
Wheeze, cluck, swash of falling blood, short wild
scream, and long, dull, tapering groan,
These so, these irretrievable.

37

You laggards there on guard! look to your arms!
In at the conquer'd doors they crowd! I am
   possess'd!
Embody all presences outlaw'd or suffering,
See myself in prison shaped like another man,
And feel the dull unintermitted pain.

For me the keepers of convicts shoulder their
   carbines and keep watch,
It is I let out in the morning and barr'd at
   night.

Not a mutineer walks handcuff'd to jail but
   I am handcuff'd to him and walk by his
   side,
(I am less the jolly one there, and more the
   silent one with sweat on my twitching lips.)

Not a youngster is taken for larceny but I go up
   too, and am tried and sentenced.

Not a cholera patient lies at the last gasp but I
   also lie at the last gasp,
My face is ash-color'd, my sinews gnarl, away
   from me people retreat.

Askers embody themselves in me and I am
   embodied in them,
I project my hat, sit shame-faced, and beg.

38

Enough! enough! enough!
Somehow I have been stunn'd. Stand back!
Give me a little time beyond my cuff'd head,
    slumbers, dreams, gaping,
I discover myself on the verge of a usual
    mistake.

That I could forget the mockers and insults!
That I could forget the trickling tears and the
    blows of the bludgeons and hammers!
That I could look with a separate look on my
    own crucifixion and bloody crowning.

I remember now,
I resume the overstaid fraction,
The grave of rock multiplies what has been
    confided to it, or to any graves,
Corpses rise, gashes heal, fastenings roll from
    me.

I troop forth replenish'd with supreme power,
    one of an average unending procession,
Inland and sea-coast we go, and pass all
    boundary lines,
Our swift ordinances on their way over the
    whole earth,
The blossoms we wear in our hats the growth of
    thousands of years.

Eleves, I salute you! come forward!
Continue your annotations, continue your
  questionings.

39

The friendly and flowing savage, who is he?
Is he waiting for civilization, or past it and
  mastering it?

Is he some Southwesterner rais'd out-doors? is
  he Kanadian?
Is he from the Mississippi country? Iowa,
  Oregon, California?
The mountains? prairie-life, bush-life? or sailor
  from the sea?

Wherever he goes men and women accept and
  desire him,
They desire he should like them, touch them,
  speak to them, stay with them.

Behavior lawless as snow-flakes, words simple as
  grass, uncomb'd head, laughter, and naivete,
Slow-stepping feet, common features, common
  modes and emanations,
They descend in new forms from the tips of his
  fingers,
They are waited with the odor of his body or
  breath, they fly out of the glance of his eyes.

40

Flaunt of the sunshine I need not your bask—
   lie over!
You light surfaces only, I force surfaces and
   depths also.

Earth! you seem to look for something at my
   hands,
Say, old top-knot, what do you want?

Man or woman, I might tell how I like you, but
   cannot,
And might tell what it is in me and what it is in
   you, but cannot,
And might tell that pining I have, that pulse of
   my nights and days.

Behold, I do not give lectures or a little
   charity,
When I give I give myself.

You there, impotent, loose in the knees,
Open your scarf'd chops till I blow grit within
   you,
Spread your palms and lift the flaps of your
   pockets,
I am not to be denied, I compel, I have stores
   plenty and to spare,
And any thing I have I bestow.

I do not ask who you are, that is not important
    to me,
You can do nothing and be nothing but what I
    will infold you.

To cotton-field drudge or cleaner of privies I
    lean,
On his right cheek I put the family kiss,
And in my soul I swear I never will deny him.

On women fit for conception I start bigger and
    nimbler babes.
(This day I am jetting the stuff of far more
    arrogant republics.)

To any one dying, thither I speed and twist the
    knob of the door.
Turn the bed-clothes toward the foot of the
    bed,
Let the physician and the priest go home.

I seize the descending man and raise him with
    resistless will,
O despairer, here is my neck,
By God, you shall not go down! hang your
    whole weight upon me.

I dilate you with tremendous breath, I buoy
    you up,

Every room of the house do I fill with an arm'd
    force,
Lovers of me, bafflers of graves.

Sleep—I and they keep guard all night,
Not doubt, not decease shall dare to lay finger
    upon you,
I have embraced you, and henceforth possess
    you to myself,
And when you rise in the morning you will find
    what I tell you is so.

41

I am he bringing help for the sick as they pant
    on their backs,
And for strong upright men I bring yet more
    needed help.

I heard what was said of the universe,
Heard it and heard it of several thousand years;
It is middling well as far as it goes—but is that all?

Magnifying and applying come I,
Outbidding at the start the old cautious
    hucksters,
Taking myself the exact dimensions of Jehovah,
Lithographing Kronos, Zeus his son, and
    Hercules his grandson,
Buying drafts of Osiris, Isis, Belus, Brahma,
    Buddha,

In my portfolio placing Manito loose, Allah on a
  leaf, the crucifix engraved,
With Odin and the hideous-faced Mexitli and
  every idol and image,
Taking them all for what they are worth and not
  a cent more,
Admitting they were alive and did the work of
  their days,
(They bore mites as for unfledg'd birds who
  have now to rise and fly and sing for
  themselves,)
Accepting the rough deific sketches to fill out
  better in myself, bestowing them freely on
  each man and woman I see,
Discovering as much or more in a framer
  framing a house,
Putting higher claims for him there with his
  roll'd-up sleeves driving the mallet and
  chisel,
Not objecting to special revelations, considering
  a curl of smoke or a hair on the back of my
  hand just as curious as any revelation,
Lads ahold of fire-engines and hook-and-ladder
  ropes no less to me than the gods of the
  antique wars,
Minding their voices peal through the crash of
  destruction,
Their brawny limbs passing safe over charr'd
  laths, their white foreheads whole and unhurt
  out of the flames;

By the mechanic's wife with her babe at her
    nipple interceding for every person born,
Three scythes at harvest whizzing in a row from
    three lusty angels with shirts bagg'd out at
    their waists,
The snag-tooth'd hostler with red hair
    redeeming sins past and to come,
Selling all he possesses, traveling on foot to fee
    lawyers for his brother and sit by him while
    he is tried for forgery;
What was strewn in the amplest strewing the
    square rod about me, and not filling the
    square rod then,
The bull and the bug never worshipp'd half
    enough,
Dung and dirt more admirable than was
    dream'd,
The supernatural of no account, myself waiting
    my time to be one of the supremes,
The day getting ready for me when I shall do
    as much good as the best, and be as
    prodigious;
By my life-lumps! becoming already a creator,
Putting myself here and now to the ambush'd
    womb of the shadows.

42

A call in the midst of the crowd,
My own voice, orotund sweeping and final.

Come my children,
Come my boys and girls, my women, household
    and intimates,
Now the performer launches his nerve, he has
    pass'd his prelude on the reeds within.

Easily written loose-finger'd chords—I feel the
    thrum of your climax and close.

My head slues round on my neck,
Music rolls, but not from the organ,
Folks are around me, but they are no household
    of mine.

Ever the hard unsunk ground,
Ever the eaters and drinkers, ever the upward
    and downward sun, ever the air and the
    ceaseless tides,
Ever myself and my neighbors, refreshing,
    wicked, real,
Ever the old inexplicable query, ever that
    thorn'd thumb, that breath of itches and
    thirsts,
Ever the vexer's hoot! hoot! till we find
    where the sly one hides and bring him
    forth,
Ever love, ever the sobbing liquid of life,
Ever the bandage under the chin, ever the
    trestles of death.

Here and there with dimes on the eyes walking,
To feed the greed of the belly the brains liberally
    spooning,
Tickets buying, taking, selling, but in to the
    feast never once going,
Many sweating, ploughing, thrashing, and then
    the chaff for payment receiving,
A few idly owning, and they the wheat
    continually claiming.

This is the city and I am one of the citizens,
Whatever interests the rest interests me, politics,
    wars, markets, newspapers, schools,
The mayor and councils, banks, tariffs,
    steamships, factories, stocks, stores, real
    estate, and personal estate.

The little plentiful manikins skipping around in
    collars and tail'd coats
I am aware who they are, (they are positively not
    worms or fleas,)
I acknowledge the duplicates of myself, the
    weakest and shallowest is deathless with me,
What I do and say the same waits for them,
Every thought that flounders in me the same
    flounders in them.

I know perfectly well my own egotism,
Know my omnivorous lines and must not write
    any less,

And would fetch you whoever you are flush with
   myself.

Not words of routine this song of mine,
But abruptly to question, to leap beyond yet
   nearer bring;
This printed and bound book—but the printer
   and the printing-office boy?
The well-taken photographs—but your wife or
   friend close and solid in your arms?
The black ship mail'd with iron, her mighty
   guns in her turrets—but the pluck of the
   captain and engineers?
In the houses the dishes and fare and furniture-
   but the host and hostess, and the look out of
   their eyes?
The sky up there—yet here or next door, or
   across the way?
The saints and sages in history—but you
   yourself?
Sermons, creeds, theology—but the fathomless
   human brain,
And what is reason? and what is love? and what
   is life?

43

I do not despise you priests, all time, the world
   over,
My faith is the greatest of faiths and the least of
   faiths,

Enclosing worship ancient and modern and all
    between ancient and modern,
Believing I shall come again upon the earth after
    five thousand years,
Waiting responses from oracles, honoring the
    gods, saluting the sun,
Making a fetich of the first rock or stump,
    powowing with sticks in the circle of obis,
Helping the llama or brahmin as he trims the
    lamps of the idols,
Dancing yet through the streets in a phallic
    procession, rapt and austere in the woods a
    gymnosophist,
Drinking mead from the skull-cap, to Shastas
    and Vedas admirant, minding the Koran,
Walking the teokallis, spotted with gore from
    the stone and knife, beating the serpent-skin
    drum,
Accepting the Gospels, accepting him that
    was crucified, knowing assuredly that he is
    divine,
To the mass kneeling or the puritan's prayer
    rising, or sitting patiently in a pew,
Ranting and frothing in my insane crisis, or
    waiting dead-like till my spirit arouses me,
Looking forth on pavement and land, or outside
    of pavement and land,
Belonging to the winders of the circuit of
    circuits.

One of that centripetal and centrifugal gang I
turn and talk like man leaving charges before
a journey.

Down-hearted doubters dull and excluded,
Frivolous, sullen, moping, angry, affected,
dishearten'd, atheistical,
I know every one of you, I know the sea of
torment, doubt, despair and unbelief.

How the flukes splash!
How they contort rapid as lightning, with
spasms and spouts of blood!

Be at peace bloody flukes of doubters and sullen
mopers,
I take my place among you as much as among
any,
The past is the push of you, me, all, precisely the
same,
And what is yet untried and afterward is for you,
me, all, precisely the same.

I do not know what is untried and afterward,
But I know it will in its turn prove sufficient,
and cannot fail.

Each who passes is consider'd, each who stops is
consider'd, not single one can it fall.

It cannot fall the young man who died and was
    buried,
Nor the young woman who died and was put by
    his side,
Nor the little child that peep'd in at the door,
    and then drew back and was never seen again,
Nor the old man who has lived without purpose,
    and feels it with bitterness worse than gall,
Nor him in the poor house tubercled by rum
    and the bad disorder,
Nor the numberless slaughter'd and wreck'd,
    nor the brutish koboo call'd the ordure of
    humanity,
Nor the sacs merely floating with open mouths
    for food to slip in,
Nor any thing in the earth, or down in the
    oldest graves of the earth,
Nor any thing in the myriads of spheres, nor the
    myriads of myriads that inhabit them,
Nor the present, nor the least wisp that is known.

44

It is time to explain myself—let us stand up.

What is known I strip away,
I launch all men and women forward with me
    into the Unknown.

The clock indicates the moment—but what does
    eternity indicate?

We have thus far exhausted trillions of winters
    and summers,
There are trillions ahead, and trillions ahead of
    them.

Births have brought us richness and variety,
And other births will bring us richness and
    variety.

I do not call one greater and one smaller,
That which fills its period and place is equal to
    any.

Were mankind murderous or jealous upon you,
    my brother, my sister?
I am sorry for you, they are not murderous or
    jealous upon me,
All has been gentle with me, I keep no account
    with lamentation,
(What have I to do with lamentation?)

I am an acme of things accomplish'd, and I an
    encloser of things to be.

My feet strike an apex of the apices of the
    stairs,
On every step bunches of ages, and larger
    bunches between the steps,
All below duly travel'd, and still I mount and
    mount.

Rise after rise bow the phantoms behind me,
Afar down I see the huge first Nothing, I know
    I was even there,
I waited unseen and always, and slept through
    the lethargic mist,
And took my time, and took no hurt from the
    fetid carbon.

Long I was hugg'd close—long and long.

Immense have been the preparations for me,
Faithful and friendly the arms that have help'd
    me.

Cycles ferried my cradle, rowing and rowing like
    cheerful boatmen,
For room to me stars kept aside in their own
    rings,
They sent influences to look after what was to
    hold me.

Before I was born out of my mother generations
    guided me,
My embryo has never been torpid, nothing
    could overlay it.

For it the nebula cohered to an orb,
The long slow strata piled to rest it on,
Vast vegetables gave it sustenance,

Monstrous sauroids transported it in their
  mouths and deposited it with care.

All forces have been steadily employ'd to
  complete and delight me,
Now on this spot I stand with my robust soul.

45

O span of youth! ever-push'd elasticity!
O manhood, balanced, florid and full.

My lovers suffocate me,
Crowding my lips, thick in the pores of my skin,
Jostling me through streets and public halls,
  coming naked to me at night,
Crying by day, Ahoy! from the rocks of the
  river, swinging and chirping over my head,
Calling my name from flower-beds, vines,
  tangled underbrush,
Lighting on every moment of my life,
Bussing my body with soft balsamic busses,
Noiselessly passing handfuls out of their hearts
  and giving them to be mine.

Old age superbly rising! O welcome, ineffable
  grace of dying days!

Every condition promulges not only itself, it
  promulges what grows after and out of itself,
And the dark hush promulges as much as any.

I open my scuttle at night and see the far-
    sprinkled systems,
And all I see multiplied as high as I can cipher
    edge but the rim of the farther systems.

Wider and wider they spread, expanding, always
    expanding,
Outward and outward and forever outward.

My sun has his sun and round him obediently
    wheels,
He joins with his partners a group of superior
    circuit,
And greater sets follow, making specks of the
    greatest inside them.

There is no stoppage and never can be stoppage,
If I, you, and the worlds, and all beneath or
    upon their surfaces, were this moment
    reduced back to a pallid float, it would not
    avail the long run,
We should surely bring up again where we now
    stand,
And surely go as much farther, and then farther
    and farther.

A few quadrillions of eras, a few octillions of
    cubic leagues, do not hazard the span or
    make it impatient,
They are but parts, any thing is but a part.

See ever so far, there is limitless space outside of
 that,
Count ever so much, there is limitless time
 around that.

My rendezvous is appointed, it is certain,
The Lord will be there and wait till I come on
 perfect terms,
The great Camerado, the lover true for whom I
 pine will be there.

46

I know I have the best of time and space, and was
 never measured and never will be measured.

I tramp a perpetual journey, (come listen all!)
My signs are a rain-proof coat, good shoes, and
 a staff cut from the woods,
No friend of mine takes his ease in my chair,
I have no chair, no church, no philosophy,
I lead no man to a dinner-table, library, exchange,
But each man and each woman of you I lead
 upon a knoll,
My left hand hooking you round the waist,
My right hand pointing to landscapes of
 continents and the public road.

Not I, not any one else can travel that road for
 you,
You must travel it for yourself.

It is not far, it is within reach,
Perhaps you have been on it since you were
  born and did not know,
Perhaps it is everywhere on water and on
  land.

Shoulder your duds dear son, and I will mine,
  and let us hasten forth,
Wonderful cities and free nations we shall fetch
  as we go.

If you tire, give me both burdens, and rest the
  chuff of your hand on my hip,
And in due time you shall repay the same service
  to me,
For after we start we never lie by again.

This day before dawn I ascended a hill and
  look'd at the crowded heaven,
And I said to my spirit When we become the
  enfolders of those orbs, and the pleasure and
  knowledge of every thing in them, shall we be
  fill'd and satisfied then?
And my spirit said No, we but level that lift to
  pass and continue beyond.

You are also asking me questions and I hear you,
I answer that I cannot answer, you must find out
  for yourself.

Sit a while dear son,
Here are biscuits to eat and here is milk to
    drink,
But as soon as you sleep and renew yourself in
    sweet clothes, I kiss you with a good-by kiss
    and open the gate for your egress hence.

Long enough have you dream'd contemptible
    dreams,
Now I wash the gum from your eyes,
You must habit yourself to the dazzle of the
    light and of every moment of your life.

Long have you timidly waded holding a plank
    by the shore,
Now I will you to be a bold swimmer,
To jump off in the midst of the sea, rise again,
    nod to me, shout, and laughingly dash with
    your hair.

47

I am the teacher of athletes,
He that by me spreads a wider breast than my
    own proves the width of my own,
He most honors my style who learns under it to
    destroy the teacher.

The boy I love, the same becomes a man not
    through derived power, but in his own right,

Wicked rather than virtuous out of conformity
   or fear,
Fond of his sweetheart, relishing well his
   steak,
Unrequited love or a slight cutting him worse
   than sharp steel cuts,
First-rate to ride, to fight, to hit the bull's eye,
   to sail a skiff, to sing a song or play on the
   banjo,
Preferring scars and the beard and faces pitted
   with small-pox over all latherers,
And those well-tann'd to those that keep out of
   the sun.

I teach straying from me, yet who can stray from
   me?
I follow you whoever you are from the present
   hour,
My words itch at your ears till you understand
   them.

I do not say these things for a dollar or to fill up
   the time while I wait for a boat,
(It is you talking just as much as myself, I act as
   the tongue of you,
Tied in your mouth, in mine it begins to be
   loosen'd.)

I swear I will never again mention love or death
   inside a house,

And I swear I will never translate myself at all,
only to him or her who privately stays with
me in the open air.

If you would understand me go to the heights
or water-shore,
The nearest gnat is an explanation, and a drop
or motion of waves key,
The maul, the oar, the hand-saw, second my
words.

No shutter'd room or school can commune
with me,
But roughs and little children better than they.

The young mechanic is closest to me, he knows
me well,
The woodman that takes his axe and jug with
him shall take me with him all day,
The farm-boy ploughing in the field feels good
at the sound of my voice,
In vessels that sail my words sail, I go with
fishermen and seamen and love them.

The soldier camp'd or upon the march is
mine,
On the night ere the pending battle many seek
me, and I do not fail them,
that solemn night (it may be their last) those
that know me seek me.

My face rubs to the hunter's face when he lies
    down alone in his blanket,
The driver thinking of me does not mind the
    jolt of his wagon,
The young mother and old mother comprehend
    me,
The girl and the wife rest the needle a moment
    and forget where they are,
They and all would resume what I have told them.

48

I have said that the soul is not more than the
    body,
And I have said that the body is not more than
    the soul,
And nothing, not God, is greater to one than
    one's self is,
And whoever walks a furlong without sympathy
    walks to his own funeral drest in his shroud,
And I or you pocketless of a dime may purchase
    the pick of the earth,
And to glance with an eye or show a bean in its
    pod confounds the learning of all times,
And there is no trade or employment but the
    young man following it may become a hero,
And there is no object so soft but it makes a hub
    for the wheel'd universe,
And I say to any man or woman, Let your soul
    stand cool and composed before a million
    universes.

And I say to mankind, Be not curious about
 God,
For I who am curious about each am not
 curious about God,
(No array of terms can say how much I am at
 peace about God and about death.)

I hear and behold God in every object, yet
 understand God not in the least,
Nor do I understand who there can be more
 wonderful than myself.

Why should I wish to see God better than this
 day?
I see something of God each hour of the
 twenty-four, and each moment then,
In the faces of men and women I see God, and
 in my own face in the glass,
I find letters from God dropt in the street, and
 every one is sign'd by God's name,
And I leave them where they are, for I know
 that wheresoe'er I go,
Others will punctually come for ever and ever.

49

And as to you Death, and you bitter hug of
 mortality, it is idle to try to alarm me.

To his work without flinching the accoucheur
 comes,

I see the elder-hand pressing receiving
   supporting,
I recline by the sills of the exquisite flexible
   doors,
And mark the outlet, and mark the relief and
   escape.

And as to you Corpse I think you are good
   manure, but that does not offend me,
I smell the white roses sweet-scented and growing,
I reach to the leafy lips, I reach to the polish'd
   breasts of melons.

And as to you Life I reckon you are the leavings
   of many deaths,
(No doubt I have died myself ten thousand
   times before.)

I hear you whispering there O stars of heaven,
O suns—O grass of graves—O perpetual
   transfers and promotions,
If you do not say any thing how can I say any
   thing?

Of the turbid pool that lies in the autumn forest,
Of the moon that descends the steeps of the
   soughing twilight,
Toss, sparkles of day and dusk—toss on the
   black stems that decay in the muck,
Toss to the moaning gibberish of the dry limbs.

I ascend from the moon, I ascend from the
  night,
I perceive that the ghastly glimmer is noonday
  sunbeams reflected,
And debouch to the steady and central from the
  offspring great or small.

50

There is that in me—I do not know what it is—
  but I know it is in me.

Wrench'd and sweaty—calm and cool then my
  body becomes,
I sleep—I sleep long.

I do not know it—it is without name—it is a
  word unsaid,
It is not in any dictionary, utterance, symbol.

Something it swings on more than the earth I
  swing on,
To it the creation is the friend whose embracing
  awakes me.

Perhaps I might tell more. Outlines! I plead for
  my brothers and sisters.

Do you see O my brothers and sisters?
It is not chaos or death—it is form, union,
  plan—it is eternal life—it is Happiness.

51

The past and present wilt—I have fill'd them,
emptied them.
And proceed to fill my next fold of the future.

Listener up there! what have you to confide to
me?
Look in my face while I snuff the sidle of
evening,
(Talk honestly, no one else hears you, and I stay
only a minute longer.)

Do I contradict myself?
Very well then I contradict myself,
(I am large, I contain multitudes.)

I concentrate toward them that are nigh, I wait
on the door-slab.

Who has done his day's work? who will soonest
be through with his supper?
Who wishes to walk with me?

Will you speak before I am gone? will you prove
already too late?

52

The spotted hawk swoops by and accuses me, he
complains of my gab and my loitering.

I too am not a bit tamed, I too am
    untranslatable,
I sound my barbaric yaws over the roofs of the
    world.

The last scud of day holds back for me,
It flings my likeness after the rest and true as any
    on the shadow'd wilds,
It coaxes me to the vapor and the dusk.

I depart as air, I shake my white locks at the
    runaway sun,
I effuse my flesh in eddies, and drift it in lacy
    jags.

I bequeath myself to the dirt to grow from the
    grass I love,
If you want me again look for me under your
    boot-soles.

You will hardly know who I am or what I mean,
But I shall be good health to you nevertheless,
And filter and fibre your blood.

Failing to fetch me at first keep encouraged,
Missing me one place search another,
I stop somewhere waiting for you.

To the Garden the World

TO the garden the world anew ascending,
Potent mates, daughters, sons, preluding,
The love, the life of their bodies, meaning and
    being,
Curious here behold my resurrection after
    slumber,
The revolving cycles in their wide sweep having
    brought me again,
Amorous, mature, all beautiful to me, all
    wondrous,
My limbs and the quivering fire that ever plays
    through them, for reasons, most wondrous,
Existing I peer and penetrate still,
Content with the present, content with the past,
By my side or back of me Eve following,
Or in front, and I following her just the same.

From Pent-Up Aching Rivers

FROM pent-up aching rivers,
From that of myself without which I were
    nothing,
From what I am determin'd to make illustrious,
    even if I stand sole among men,
From my own voice resonant, singing the
    phallus,
Singing the song of procreation,

Singing the need of superb children and therein
    superb grown people,
Singing the muscular urge and the blending,
Singing the bedfellow's song, (O resistless
    yearning!
O for any and each the body correlative
    attracting!
O for you whoever you are your correlative
    body! O it, more than all else, you
    delighting!)
From the hungry gnaw that eats me night and
    day,
From native moments, from bashful pains,
    singing them,
Seeking something yet unfound though I have
    diligently sought it many a long year,
Singing the true song of the soul fitful at
    random,
Renascent with grossest Nature or among
    animals,
Of that, of them and what goes with them my
    poems informing,
Of the smell of apples and lemons, of the
    pairing of birds,
Of the wet of woods, of the lapping of
    waves,
Of the mad pushes of waves upon the land, I
    them chanting,
The overture lightly sounding, the strain
    anticipating,

The welcome nearness, the sight of the perfect
    body,
The swimmer swimming naked in the bath, or
    motionless on his back lying and floating,
The female form approaching, I pensive, love-
    flesh tremulous aching,
The divine list for myself or you or for any one
    making,
The face, the limbs, the index from head to
    foot, and what it arouses,
The mystic deliria, the madness amorous, the
    utter abandonment,
(Hark close and still what I now whisper to you,
I love you, O you entirely possess me,
O that you and I escape from the rest and go
    utterly off, free and lawless,
Two hawks in the air, two fishes swimming in
    the sea not more lawless than we;)
The furious storm through me careering, I
    passionately trembling.
The oath of the inseparableness of two together,
    of the woman that loves me and whom I love
    more than my life, that oath swearing,
(O I willingly stake all for you,
O let me be lost if it must be so!
O you and I! what is it to us what the rest do or
    think?
What is all else to us? only that we enjoy each
    other and exhaust each other if it must be so;)
From the master, the pilot I yield the vessel to,

The general commanding me, commanding all,
    from him permission taking,
From time the programme hastening, (I have
    loiter'd too long as it is,)
From sex, from the warp and from the woof,
From privacy, from frequent repinings alone,
From plenty of persons near and yet the right
    person not near,
From the soft sliding of hands over me and
    thrusting of fingers through my hair and
    beard,
From the long sustain'd kiss upon the mouth or
    bosom,
From the close pressure that makes me or any
    man drunk, fainting with excess,
From what the divine husband knows, from the
    work of fatherhood,
From exultation, victory and relief, from the
    bedfellow's embrace in the night,
From the act-poems of eyes, hands, hips and
    bosoms,
From the cling of the trembling arm,
From the bending curve and the clinch,
From side by side the pliant coverlet off-
    throwing,
From the one so unwilling to have me leave, and
    me just as unwilling to leave,
(Yet a moment O tender waiter, and I return,)
From the hour of shining stars and dropping
    dews,

From the night a moment I emerging flitting
   out,
Celebrate you act divine and you children
   prepared for,
And you stalwart loins.

Children of Adam

I SING THE BODY ELECTRIC

1

I SING the body electric,
The armies of those I love engirth me and I
   engirth them,
They will not let me off till I go with them,
   respond to them,
And discorrupt them, and charge them full with
   the charge of the soul.

Was it doubted that those who corrupt their
   own bodies conceal themselves?
And if those who defile the living are as bad as
   they who defile the dead?
And if the body does not do fully as much as the
   soul?
And if the body were not the soul, what is the
   soul?

2

The love of the body of man or woman balks
   account, the body itself balks account,
That of the male is perfect, and that of the
   female is perfect.

The expression of the face balks account,
But the expression of a well-made man appears
   not only in his face,
It is in his limbs and joints also, it is curiously in
   the joints of his hips and wrists,
It is in his walk, the carriage of his neck, the flex
   of his waist and knees, dress does not hide
   him,
The strong sweet quality he has strikes through
   the cotton and broadcloth,
To see him pass conveys as much as the best
   poem, perhaps more,
You linger to see his back, and the back of his
   neck and shoulder-side.

The sprawl and fulness of babes, the bosoms and
   heads of women, the folds of their dress, their
   style as we pass in the street, the contour of
   their shape downwards,
The swimmer naked in the swimming-bath, seen
   as he swims through the transparent green-
   shine, or lies with his face up and rolls silently
   to and from the heave of the water,
The bending forward and backward of rowers in
   row-boats, the horse-man in his saddle,
Girls, mothers, house-keepers, in all their
   performances,
The group of laborers seated at noon-time with
   their open dinner-kettles, and their wives
   waiting,

The female soothing a child, the farmer's
    daughter in the garden or cow-yard,
The young fellow hosing corn, the sleigh-driver
    driving his six horses through the crowd,
The wrestle of wrestlers, two apprentice-boys,
    quite grown, lusty, good-natured, native-born,
    out on the vacant lot at sundown after work,
The coats and caps thrown down, the embrace
    of love and resistance,
The upper-hold and under-hold, the hair
    rumpled over and blinding the eyes;
The march of firemen in their own costumes,
    the play of masculine muscle through clean-
    setting trowsers and waist-straps,
The slow return from the fire, the pause when
    the bell strikes suddenly again, and the
    listening on the alert,
The natural, perfect, varied attitudes, the bent
    head, the curv'd neck and the counting;
Such-like I love—I loosen myself, pass freely, am
    at the mother's breast with the little child,
Swim with the swimmers, wrestle with wrestlers,
    march in line with the firemen, and pause,
    listen, count.

3

I knew a man, a common farmer, the father of
    five sons,
And in them the fathers of sons, and in them the
    fathers of sons.

This man was a wonderful vigor, calmness,
    beauty of person,
The shape of his head, the pale yellow and white
    of his hair and beard, the immeasurable
    meaning of his black eyes, the richness and
    breadth of his manners,
These I used to go and visit him to see, he was
    wise also,
He was six feet tall, he was over eighty years old,
    his sons were massive, clean, bearded, tan-
    faced, handsome,
They and his daughters loved him, all who saw
    him loved him,
They did not love him by allowance, they loved
    him with personal love,
He drank water only, the blood show'd like
    scarlet through the clear-brown skin of his
    face,
He was a frequent gunner and fisher, he sail'd
    his boat himself, he had a fine one presented
    to him by a ship-joiner, he had fowling-pieces
    presented to him by men that loved him,
When he went with his five sons and many
    grand-sons to hunt or fish, you would pick
    him out as the most beautiful and vigorous of
    the gang,
You would wish long and long to be with him,
    you would wish to sit by him in the boat that
    you and he might touch each other.

4

I have perceiv'd that to be with those I like is
enough,
To stop in company with the rest at evening is
enough,
To be surrounded by beautiful, curious,
breathing, laughing flesh is enough,
To pass among them or touch any one, or
rest my arm ever so lightly round his or
her neck for a moment, what is this
then?
I do not ask any more delight, I swim in it
as in a sea.

There is something in staying close to men and
women and looking on them, and in the
contact and odor of them, that pleases the
soul well,
All things please the soul, but these please the
soul well.

5

This is the female form,
A divine nimbus exhales from it from head to
foot,
It attracts with fierce undeniable attraction,
I am drawn by its breath as if I were no more
than a helpless vapor, all falls aside but
myself and it,

Books, art, religion, time, the visible and solid
    earth, and what was expected of heaven or
    fear'd of hell, are now consumed,
Mad filaments, ungovernable shoots play out of
    it, the response likewise ungovernable,
Hair, bosom, hips, bend of legs, negligent falling
    hands all diffused, mine too diffused,
Ebb stung by the flow and flow stung by the ebb,
    love-flesh swelling and deliciously aching,
Limitless limpid jets of love hot and enormous,
    quivering jelly of love, white-blow and
    delirious nice,
Bridegroom night of love working surely and
    softly into the prostrate dawn,
Undulating into the willing and yielding day,
Lost in the cleave of the clasping and sweet-
    flesh'd day.

This the nucleus—after the child is born of
    woman, man is born of woman,
This the bath of birth, this the merge of small
    and large, and the outlet again.

Be not ashamed women, your privilege encloses
    the rest, and is the exit of the rest,
You are the gates of the body, and you are the
    gates of the soul.

The female contains all qualities and tempers
    them,

She is in her place and moves with perfect
 balance,
She is all things duly veil'd, she is both passive
 and active,
She is to conceive daughters as well as sons, and
 sons as well as daughters.

As I see my soul reflected in Nature,
As I see through a mist, One with inexpressible
 completeness, sanity, beauty,
See the bent head and arms folded over the
 breast, the Female I see.

6

The male is not less the soul nor more, he too is
 in his place,
He too is all qualities, he is action and power,
The flush of the known universe is in him,
Scorn becomes him well, and appetite and
 defiance become him well,
The wildest largest passions, bliss that is utmost,
 sorrow that is utmost become him well, pride
 is for him,
The full-spread pride of man is calming and
 excellent to the soul,
Knowledge becomes him, he likes it always,
 he brings every thing to the test of
 himself,
Whatever the survey, whatever the sea and the
 sail he strikes soundings at last only here,

(Where else does he strike soundings except
   here?)

The man's body is sacred and the woman's body
   is sacred,
No matter who it is, it is sacred—is it the
   meanest one in the laborers' gang?
Is it one of the dull-faced immigrants just landed
   on the wharf?
Each belongs here or anywhere just as much as
   the well-off, just as much as you,
Each has his or her place in the procession.

(All is a procession,
The universe is a procession with measured and
   perfect motion.)

Do you know so much yourself that you call the
   meanest ignorant?
Do you suppose you have a right to a good
   sight, and he or she has no right to a sight?
Do you think matter has cohered together from
   its diffuse float, and the soil is on the surface,
   and water runs and vegetation sprouts,
For you only, and not for him and her?

7

A man's body at auction,
(For before the war I often go to the slave-mart
   and watch the sale,)

I help the auctioneer, the sloven does not half
    know his business.

Gentlemen look on this wonder,
Whatever the bids of the bidders they cannot be
    high enough for it,
For it the globe lay preparing quintillions of
    years without one animal or plant,
For it the revolving cycles truly and steadily
    roll'd.

In this head the all-baffling brain,
In it and below it the makings of heroes.

Examine these limbs, red, black, or white, they
    are cunning in tendon and nerve,
They shall be stript that you may see them.

Exquisite senses, life-lit eyes, pluck,
        volition,
Flakes of breast-muscle, pliant backbone and
    neck, flesh not flabby, good-sized arms and
    legs,
And wonders within there yet.

Within there runs blood,
The same old blood! the same red-running
    blood!
There swells and jets a heart, there all passions,
    desires, reachings, aspirations,

(Do you think they are not there because they
   are not express'd in parlors and lecture-
   rooms?)

This is not only one man, this the father of
   those who shall be fathers in their turns,
In him the start of populous states and rich
   republics,
Of him countless immortal lives with countless
   embodiments and enjoyments.

How do you know who shall come from the
   offspring of his offspring through the
   centuries?
(Who might you find you have come from
   yourself, if you could trace back through the
   centuries?)

8

A woman's body at auction,
She too is not only herself, she is the teeming
   mother of mothers,
She is the bearer of them that shall grow and be
   mates to the mothers.

Have you ever loved the body of a woman?
Have you ever loved the body of a man?
Do you not see that these are exactly the same
   to all in all nations and times all over the
   earth?

If any thing is sacred the human body is sacred,
And the glory and sweet of a man is the token
    of manhood untainted,
And in man or woman a clean, strong, firm-
    fiberd body, is more beautiful than the most
    beautiful face.

Have you seen the fool that corrupted his own
    live body? or the fool that corrupted her own
    live body?
For they do not conceal themselves, and cannot
    conceal themselves.

9

O my body! I dare not desert the likes of you in
    other men and women, nor the likes of the
    parts of you,
I believe the likes of you are to stand or fall with
    the likes of the soul, (and that they are the
    soul,)
I believe the likes of you shall stand or fall
    with my poems, and that they are my
    poems,
Man's, woman's, child, youth's, wife's,
    husband's, mother's, father's, young man's,
    young woman's poems,
Head, neck, hair, ears, drop and tympan of the
    ears,
Eyes, eye-fringes, iris of the eye, eyebrows, and
    the waking or sleeping of the lids,

Mouth, tongue, lips, teeth, roof of the mouth,
jaws, and the jaw-hinges,
Nose, nostrils of the nose, and the partition,
Cheeks, temples, forehead, chin, throat, back of
the neck, neck-slue,
Strong shoulders, manly beard, scapula, hind-
shoulders, and the ample side-round of the
chest,
Upper-arm, armpit, elbow-socket, lower-arm,
arm-sinews, arm-bones,
Wrist and wrist-joints, hand, palm, knuckles,
thumb, forefinger, finger-joints, finger-nails,
Broad breast-front, curling hair of the breast,
breast-bone, breast-side,
Ribs, belly, backbone, joints of the backbone,
Hips, hip-sockets, hip-strength, inward and
outward round, man-balls, man-root,
Strong set of thighs, well carrying the trunk
above,
Leg-fibres, knee, knee-pan, upper-leg, under-leg,
Ankles, instep, foot-ball, toes, toe-joints, the
heel;
All attitudes, all the shapeliness, all the
belongings of my or your body or of any
one's body, male or female,
The lung-sponges, the stomach-sac, the bowels
sweet and clean,
The brain in its folds inside the skull-frame,
Sympathies, heart-valves, palate-valves, sexuality,
maternity,

Womanhood, and all that is a woman, and the
  man that comes from woman,
The womb, the teats, nipples, breast-milk, tears,
  laughter, weeping, love-looks, love-
  perturbations and risings,
The voice, articulation, language, whispering,
  shouting aloud,
Food, drink, pulse, digestion, sweat, sleep,
  walking, swimming,
Poise on the hips, leaping, reclining, embracing,
  arm-curving and tightening,
The continual changes of the flex of the mouth,
  and around the eyes,
The skin, the sunburnt shade, freckles, hair,
The curious sympathy one feels when feeling
  with the hand the naked meat of the body,
The circling rivers the breath, and breathing it in
  and out,
The beauty of the waist, and thence of the hips,
  and thence downward toward the knees,
The thin red jellies within you or within me, the
  bones and the marrow in the bones,
The exquisite realization of health;
O I say these are not the parts and poems of the
  body only, but of the soul,
O I say now these are the soul!

A Woman Waits for Me

A WOMAN waits for me, she contains all,
   nothing is lacking,
Yet all were lacking if sex were lacking, or if the
   moisture of the right man were lacking.

Sex contains all, bodies, souls,
Meanings, proofs, purities, delicacies, results,
   promulgations,
Songs, commands, health, pride, the maternal
   mystery, the seminal milk,
All hopes, benefactions, bestowals, all the
   passions, loves, beauties, delights of the earth,
All the governments, judges, gods, follow'd
   persons of the earth,
These are contain'd in sex as parts of itself and
   justifications of itself.

Without shame the man I like knows and avows
   the deliciousness of his sex,
Without shame the woman I like knows and
   avows hers.

Now I will dismiss myself from impassive
   women,
I will go stay with her who waits for me, and
   with those women that are warm-blooded
   and sufficient for me,

I see that they understand me and do not deny
   me,
I see that they are worthy of me, I will be the
   robust husband of those women.

They are not one jot less than I am,
They are tann'd in the face by shining suns and
   blowing winds,
Their flesh has the old divine suppleness and
   strength,
They know how to swim, row, ride, wrestle,
   shoot, run, strike, retreat, advance, resist,
   defend themselves,
They are ultimate in their own right—they are
   calm, clear, well-possess'd of themselves.

I draw you close to me, you women,
I cannot let you go, I would do you good,
I am for you, and you are for me, not only for
   our own sake, but for others' sakes,
Envelop'd in you sleep greater heroes and bards,
They refuse to awake at the touch of any man
   but me.

It is I, you women, I make my way,
I am stern, acrid, large, undissuadable, but I
   love you,
I do not hurt you any more than is necessary for
   you,

I pour the stuff to start sons and daughters fit
   for these States, I press with slow rude
   muscle,
I brace myself effectually, I listen to no
   entreaties,
I dare not withdraw till I deposit what has so
   long accumulated within me.

Through you I drain the pent-up rivers of
   myself,
In you I wrap a thousand onward years,
On you I graft the grafts of the best-beloved of
   me and America,
The drops I distil upon you shall grow fierce and
   athletic girls, new artists, musicians, and
   singers,
The babes I beget upon you are to beget babes
   in their turn,
I shall demand perfect men and women out of
   my love-spendings,
I shall expect them to interpenetrate with others,
   as I and you inter-penetrate now,
I shall count on the fruits of the gushing
   showers of them, as I count on the fruits of
   the gushing showers I give now,
I shall look for loving crops from the birth, life,
   death, immortality, I plant so lovingly now.

SPONTANEOUS ME

SPONTANEOUS me, Nature,
The loving day, the mounting sun, the friend I
    am happy with,
The arm of my friend hanging idly over my
    shoulder,
The hillside whiten'd with blossoms of the
    mountain ash,
The same late in autumn, the hues of red,
    yellow, drab, purple, and light and dark green,
The rich coverlet of the grass, animals and birds,
    the private untrimm'd bank, the primitive
    apples, the pebble-stones,
Beautiful dripping fragments, the negligent list
    of one after another as I happen to call them
    to me or think of them,
The real poems, (what we call poems being
    merely pictures,)
The poems of the privacy of the night, and of
    men like me,
This poem drooping shy and unseen that I
    always carry, and that all men carry,
(Know once for all, avow'd on purpose,
    wherever are men like me, are our lusty
    lurking masculine poems,)
Love-thoughts, love-juice, love-odor, love-
    yielding, love-climbers, and the climbing
    sap,

Arms and hands of love, lips of love, phallic
thumb of love, breasts of love, bellies press'd
and glued together with love,
Earth of chaste love, life that is only life after
love,
The body of my love, the body of the woman I
love, the body of the man, the body of the
earth,
Soft forenoon airs that blow from the south-
west,
The hairy wild-bee that murmurs and hankers
up and down, that gripes the full-grown lady-
flower, curves upon her with amorous firm
legs, takes his will of her, and holds himself
tremulous and tight till he is satisfied;
The wet of woods through the early hours,
Two sleepers at night lying close together
as they sleep, one with an arm slanting
down across and below the waist of the
other,
The smell of apples, aromas from crush'd sage-
plant, mint, birch-bark,
The boy's longings, the glow and pressure as he
confides to me what he was dreaming,
The dead leaf whirling its spiral whirl and falling
still and content to the ground,
The no-form'd stings that sights, people,
objects, sting me with,
The hubb'd sting of myself, stinging me as
much as it ever can any one,

The sensitive, orbic, underlapp'd brothers, that
  only privileged feelers may be intimate where
  they are,
The curious roamer the hand roaming all over
  the body, the bashful withdrawing of flesh
  where the fingers soothingly pause and edge
  themselves,
The limpid liquid within the young man,
The vex'd corrosion so pensive and so painful,
The torment, the irritable tide that will not be at
  rest,
The like of the same I feel, the like of the same
  in others,
The young man that flushes and flushes, and the
  young woman that flushes and flushes,
The young man that wakes deep at night, the
  hot hand seeking to repress what would
  master him,
The mystic amorous night, the strange half-
  welcome pangs, visions, sweats,
The pulse pounding through palms and
  trembling encircling fingers, the young man
  all color'd, red, ashamed, angry;
The souse upon me of my lover the sea, as I lie
  willing and naked,
The merriment of the twin babes that crawl over
  the grass in the sun, the mother never turning
  her vigilant eyes from them,
The walnut-trunk, the walnut-husks, and the
  ripening or ripen'd long-round walnuts,

The continence of vegetables, birds, animals,
The consequent meanness of me should I skulk
  or find myself indecent, while birds and
  animals never once skulk or find themselves
  indecent,
The great chastity of paternity, to match the
  great chastity of maternity,
The oath of procreation I have sworn, my
  Adamic and fresh daughters,
The greed that eats me day and night with
  hungry gnaw, till I saturate what shall
  produce boys to fill my place when I am
  through,
The wholesome relief, repose, content,
And this bunch pluck'd at random from myself,
It has done its work—I toss it carelessly to fall
  where it may.

One Hour to Madness and Joy

ONE hour to madness and joy! O furious! O
  confine me not!
(What is this that frees me so in storms?
What do my shouts amid lightnings and raging
  winds mean?)
O to drink the mystic deliria deeper than any
  other man!
O savage and tender achings! (I bequeath them
  to you my children,

I tell them to you, for reasons, O bridegroom
    and bride.)

O to be yielded to you whoever you are, and
    you to be yielded to me in defiance of the
    world!
O to return to Paradise! O bashful and
    feminine!
O to draw you to me, to plant on you for the
    first time the lips of a determin'd man.

O the puzzle, the thrice-tied knot, the deep and
    dark pool, all untied and illumin'd!
O to speed where there is space enough and air
    enough at last!
To be absolv'd from previous ties and
    conventions, I from mine and you from
    yours!
To find a new unthought-of nonchalance with
    the best of Nature!
To have the gag remov'd from one's mouth!
To have the feeling to-day or any day I am
    sufficient as I am.

O something unprov'd! something in a
    trance!
To escape utterly from others' anchors and
    holds!
To drive free! to love free! to dash reckless and
    dangerous!

To court destruction with taunts, with
    invitations!
To ascend, to leap to the heavens of the love
    indicated to me!
To rise thither with my inebriate soul!
To be lost if it must be so!
To feed the remainder of life with one hour of
    fulness and freedom!
With one brief hour of madness and joy.

OUT OF THE ROLLING OCEAN THE CROWD

OUT of the rolling ocean the crowd came a
    drop gently to me,
Whispering I love you, before long I die,
I have travel'd a long way merely to look on you
    to touch you,
For I could not die till I once look'd on you,
For I fear'd I might afterward lose you.

Now we have met, we have look'd, we are
    safe,
Return in peace to the ocean my love,
I too am part of that ocean my love, we are not
    so much separated,
Behold the great rondure, the cohesion of all,
    how perfect!
But as for me, for you, the irresistible sea is to
    separate us,

As for an hour carrying us diverse, yet cannot
    carry us diverse forever;
Be not impatient—a little space—know you I
    salute the air, the ocean and the land,
Every day at sundown for your dear sake my
    love.

Ages and Ages Returning at Intervals

AGES and ages returning at intervals,
Undestroy'd, wandering immortal,
Lusty, phallic, with the potent original loins,
    perfectly sweet,
I, chanter of Adamic songs,
Through the new garden the West, the great
    cities calling,
Deliriate, thus prelude what is generated,
    offering these, offering myself,
Bathing myself, bathing my songs in Sex,
Offspring of my loins.

We Two, How Long We Were Fool'd

WE two, how long we were fool'd,
Now transmuted, we swiftly escape as Nature
    escapes,
We are Nature, long have we been absent, but
    now we return,
We become plants, trunks, foliage, roots, bark,
We are bedded in the ground, we are rocks,

We are oaks, we grow in the openings side by
    side,
We browse, we are two among the wild herds
    spontaneous as any,
We are two fishes swimming in the sea together,
We are what locust blossoms are, we drop scent
    around lanes mornings and evenings,
We are also the coarse smut of beasts,
    vegetables, minerals,
We are two predatory hawks, we soar above and
    look down,
We are two resplendent suns, we it is who
    balance ourselves orbic and stellar, we are as
    two comets,
We prowl fang'd and four-footed in the woods,
    we spring on prey,
We are two clouds forenoons and afternoons
    driving overhead,
We are seas mingling, we are two of those
    cheerful waves rolling over each other and
    interwetting each other,
We are what the atmosphere is, transparent,
    receptive, pervious, impervious,
We are snow, rain, cold, darkness, we are each
    product and influence of the globe,
We have circled and circled till we have arrived
    home again, we two,
We have voided all but freedom and all but our
    own joy.

O Hymen! O Hymenee!

O HYMEN! O hymenee! why do you tantalize
    me thus?
O why sting me for a swift moment only?
Why can you not continue? O why do you now
    cease?
Is it because if you continued beyond the swift
    moment you would soon certainly kill me?

I Am He that Aches with Love

I AM he that aches with amorous love;
Does the earth gravitate? does not all matter,
    aching, attract all matter?
So the body of me to all I meet or know.

Native Moments

NATIVE moments—when you come upon
    me—ah you are here now,
Give me now libidinous joys only,
Give me the drench of my passions, give me life
    coarse and rank,
To-day I go consort with Nature's darlings, to-
    night too,
I am for those who believe in loose delights, I
    share the midnight orgies of young men,

I dance with the dancers and drink with the
    drinkers,
The echoes ring with our indecent calls, I pick
    out some low person for my dearest friend,
He shall be lawless, rude, illiterate, he shall be
    one condemn'd by others for deeds done,
I will play a part no longer, why should I exile
    myself from my companions?
O you shunn'd persons, I at least do not shun
    you,
I come forthwith in your midst, I will be your
    poet,
I will be more to you than to any of the rest.

Once I Pass'd Through a Populous City

ONCE I pass'd through a populous city
    imprinting my brain for future use with its
    shows, architecture, customs, traditions,
Yet now of all that city I remember only a
    woman I casually met there who detain'd me
    for love of me,
Day by day and night by night we were
    together-all else has long been forgotten
    by me,
I remember I say only that woman who
    passionately clung to me,
Again we wander, we love, we separate again,
Again she holds me by the hand, I must not go,

I see her close beside me with silent lips sad and
    tremulous.

I HEARD YOU SOLEMN-SWEET PIPES
OF THE ORGAN

I HEARD you solemn-sweet pipes of the organ
    as last Sunday morn I pass'd the church,
Winds of autumn, as I walk'd the woods at dusk
    I heard your long-stretch'd sighs up above so
    mournful,
I heard the perfect Italian tenor singing at the
    opera, I heard the soprano in the midst of the
    quartet singing;
Heart of my love! you too I heard murmuring
    low through one of the wrists around my
    head,
Heard the pulse of you when all was still ringing
    little bells last night under my ear.

FACING WEST FROM CALIFORNIA'S SHORES

FACING west from California's shores,
Inquiring, tireless, seeking what is yet
    unfound,
I, a child, very old, over waves, towards the
    house of maternity, the land of migrations,
    look afar,

Look off the shores of my Western sea, the circle
    almost circled;
For starting westward from Hindustan, from the
    vales of Kashmere,
From Asia, from the north, from the God, the
    sage, and the hero,
From the south, from the flowery peninsulas
    and the spice islands,
Long having wander'd since, round the earth
    having wander'd,
Now I face home again, very pleas'd and joyous,
(But where is what I started for so long ago?
And why is it yet unfound?)

As Adam Early in the Morning

AS Adam early in the morning,
Walking forth from the bower refresh'd with
    sleep,
Behold me where I pass, hear my voice,
 approach,
Touch me, touch the palm of your hand to my
    body as I pass,
Be not afraid of my body.

IN PATHS UNTRODDEN

IN paths untrodden,
In the growth by margins of pond-waters,
Escaped from the lite that exhibits itself,
From all the standards hitherto publish'd, from
    the pleasures, profits, conformities,
Which too long I was offering to feed my soul,
Clear to me now standards not yet publish'd,
    clear to me that my soul,
That the soul of the man I speak for rejoices in
    comrades,
Here by myself away from the clank of the
    world,
Tallying and talk'd to here by tongues aromatic,
No longer abash'd, (for in this secluded spot I
    can respond as I would not dare elsewhere,)
Strong upon me the life that does not exhibit
    itself, yet contains all the rest,
Resolv'd to sing no songs to-day but those of
    manly attachment,
Projecting them along that substantial life,
Bequeathing hence types of athletic love,
Afternoon this delicious Ninth-month in my
    forty-first year,
I proceed for all who are or have been young
    men,
To tell the secret my nights and days,
To celebrate the need of comrades.

Calamus

SCENTED HERBAGE OF MY BREAST

SCENTED herbage of my breast,
Leaves from you I glean, I write, to be perused
    best afterwards,
Tomb-leaves, body-leaves growing up above me
    above death,
Perennial roots, tall leaves, O the winter shall
    not freeze you delicate leaves,
Every year shall you bloom again, out from
    where you retired you shall emerge again;
O I do not know whether many passing by will
    discover you or inhale your faint odor, but I
    believe a few will;
O slender leaves! O blossoms of my blood! I
    permit you to tell in your own way of the
    heart that is under you,
O I do not know what you mean there
    underneath yourselves, you are not happiness,
You are often more bitter than I can bear, you
    burn and sting me,
Yet you are beautiful to me you faint tinged
    roots, you make me think of death,
Death is beautiful from you, (what indeed is
    finally beautiful except death and love?)

O I think it is not for life I am chanting here my
    chant of lovers, I think it must be for death,
For how calm, how solemn it grows to ascend
    to the atmosphere of lovers,
Death or life I am then indifferent, my soul
    declines to prefer,
(I am not sure but the high soul of lovers
    welcomes death most,)
Indeed O death, I think now these leaves mean
    precisely the same as you mean,
Grow up taller sweet leaves that I may see! grow
    up out of my breast!
Spring away from the conceal'd heart there!
Do not fold yourself so in your pink-tinged
    roots timid leaves!
Do not remain down there so ashamed, herbage
    of my breast!
Come I am determin'd to unbare this broad
    breast of mine, I have long enough stifled and
    choked;
Emblematic and capricious blades I leave you,
    now you serve me not,
I will say what I have to say by itself,
I will sound myself and comrades only, I will
    never again utter a call only their call,
I will raise with it immortal reverberations
    through the States,
I will give an example to lovers to take
    permanent shape and will through the States,

Through me shall the words be said to make
  death exhilarating,
Give me your tone therefore O death, that I
  may accord with it,
Give me yourself, for I see that you belong to
  me now above all, and are folded inseparably
  together, you love and death are,
Nor will I allow you to balk me any more with
  what I was calling life,
For now it is convey'd to me that you are the
  purports essential,
That you hide in these shifting forms of life, for
  reasons, and that they are mainly for you,
That you beyond them come forth to remain,
  the real reality,
That behind the mask of materials you patiently
  wait, no matter how long,
That you will one day perhaps take control of
  all,
That you will perhaps dissipate this entire show
  of appearance,
That may-be you are what it is all for, but it
  does not last so very long,
But you will last very long.

WHOEVER YOU ARE HOLDING ME NOW IN HAND

WHOEVER you are holding me now in hand,
Without one thing all will be useless,
I give you fair warning before you attempt me
    further,
I am not what you supposed, but far different.

Who is he that would become my follower?
Who would sign himself a candidate for my
    affections?

The way is suspicious, the result uncertain,
    perhaps destructive,
You would have to give up all else, I alone
    would expect to be your sole and exclusive
    standard,
Your novitiate would even then be long and
    exhausting,
The whole past theory of your life and all
    conformity to the lives around you would
    have to be abandon'd,
Therefore release me now before troubling
    yourself any further, let go your hand from
    my shoulders,
Put me down and depart on your way.

Or else by stealth in some wood for trial,
Or back of a rock in the open air,

(For in any roof'd room of a house I emerge
not, nor in company,
And in libraries I lie as one dumb, a gawk, or
unborn, or dead,)
But just possibly with you on a high hill, first
watching lest any person for miles around
approach unawares,
Or possibly with you sailing at sea, or on the
beach of the sea or some quiet island,
Here to put your lips upon mine I permit
you,
With the comrade's long-dwelling kiss or the
new husband's kiss,
For I am the new husband and I am the
comrade.

Or if you will, thrusting me beneath your
clothing,
Where I may feel the throbs of your heart or
rest upon your hip,
Carry me when you go forth over land or sea;
For thus merely touching you is enough,
is best,
And thus touching you would I silently sleep
and be carried eternally.

But these leaves conning you con at peril,
For these leaves and me you will not
understand,

They will elude you at first and still more
  afterward, I will certainly elude you.
Even while you should think you had
  unquestionably caught me, behold!
Already you see I have escaped from you.

For it is not for what I have put into it that I
  have written this book,
Nor is it by reading it you will acquire it,
Nor do those know me best who admire me and
  vauntingly praise me,
Nor will the candidates for my love (unless at
  most a very few) prove victorious,
Nor will my poems do good only, they will do
  just as much evil, perhaps more,
For all is useless without that which you may
  guess at many times and not hit, that which I
  hinted at;
Therefore release me and depart on your way.

FOR YOU O DEMOCRACY

COME, I Will make the continent indissoluble,
I will make the most splendid race the sun
  ever shone upon,
I will make divine magnetic lands,
With the love of comrades,
With the life-long love of comrades.

I will plant companionship thick as trees along
    all the rivers of America, and along the shores
    of the great lakes, and all over the prairies,
I will make inseparable cities with their arms
    about each other's necks,
By the love of comrades,
By the manly love of comrades.

For you these from me, O Democracy, to serve
    you ma femme!
For you, for you I am trilling these songs.

THESE I SINGING IN SPRING

THESE I singing in spring collect for lovers,
(For who but I should understand lovers and all
    their sorrow and joy?
And who but I should be the poet of
    comrades?)
Collecting I traverse the garden the world, but
    soon I pass the gates,
Now along the pond-side, now wading in a
    little, fearing not the wet,
Now by the post-and-rail fences where the old
    stones thrown there, pick'd from the fields,
    have accumulated,
(Wild-flowers and vines and weeds come up
    through the stones and partly cover them,
    beyond these I pass,)

Far, far in the forest, or sauntering later in
    summer, before I think where I go,
Solitary, smelling the earthy smell, stopping now
    and then in the silence,
Alone I had thought, yet soon a troop gathers
    around me,
Some walk by my side and some behind, and
    some embrace my arms or neck,
They the spirits of dear friends dead or alive,
    thicker they come, a great crowd, and I in the
    middle,
Collecting, dispensing, singing, there I wander
    with them,
Plucking something for tokens, tossing toward
    whoever is near me,
Here, lilac, with a branch of pine,
Here, out of my pocket, some moss which I
    pull'd off a live-oak in Florida as it hung
    trailing down,
Here, some pinks and laurel leaves, and a
    handful of sage,
And here what I now draw from the water,
    wading in the pondside,
(O here I last saw him that tenderly loves
    me, and returns again never to separate
    from me,
And this, O this shall henceforth be the token
    of comrades, this calamus-root shall,
Interchange it youths with each other! let none
    render it back!)

And twigs of maple and a bunch of wild orange
    and chestnut,
And stems of currants and plum-blows, and the
    aromatic cedar,
These I compass'd around by a thick cloud of
    spirits,
Wandering, point to or touch as I pass, or throw
    them loosely from me,
Indicating to each one what he shall have, giving
    something to each;
But what I drew from the water by the pond-
    side, that I reserve,
I will give of it, but only to them that love as I
    myself am capable of loving.

NOT HEAVING FROM MY RIBB'D BREAST ONLY

NOT heaving from my ribb'd breast only,
Not in sighs at night in rage dissatisfied with
    myself,
Not in those long-drawn, ill-supprest sighs,
Not in many an oath and promise broken,
Not in my willful and savage soul's volition,
Not in the subtle nourishment of the air,
Not in this beating and pounding at my temples
    and wrists,
Not in the curious systole and diastole within
    which will one day cease,

Not in many a hungry wish told to the skies
    only,
Not in cries, laughter, defiancies, thrown from
    me when alone far in the wilds,
Not in husky pantings through clinch'd teeth,
Not in sounded and resounded words,
    chattering words, echoes, dead words,
Not in the murmurs of my dreams while I sleep,
Nor the other murmurs of these incredible
    dreams of every day,
Nor in the limbs and senses of my body that
    take you and dismiss you continually- not
    there,
Not in any or all of them O adhesiveness! O
    pulse of my life!
Need I that you exist and show yourself any
    more than in these songs.

OF THE TERRIBLE DOUBT OF APPEARANCES

OF the terrible doubt of appearances,
Of the uncertainty after all, that we may be
    deluded,
That may-be reliance and hope are but
    speculations after all,
That may-be identity beyond the grave is a
    beautiful fable only,
May-be the things I perceive, the animals,
    plants, men, hills, shining and flowing waters,

The skies of day and night, colors, densities,
    forms, may-be these are (as doubtless they
    are) only apparitions, and the real something
    has yet to be known,
(How often they dart out of themselves as if to
    confound me and mock me!
How often I think neither I know, nor any man
    knows, aught of them,)
May-be seeming to me what they are (as
    doubtless they indeed but seem) as from my
    present point of view, and might prove (as of
    course they would) nought of what they
    appear, or nought anyhow, from entirely
    changed points of view;
To me these and the like of these are curiously
    answer'd by my lovers, my dear friends,
When he whom I love travels with me or sits a
    long while holding me by the hand,
When the subtle air, the impalpable, the sense
    that words and reason hold not, surround us
    and pervade us,
Then I am charged with untold and untellable
    wisdom, I am silent, I require nothing
    further,
I cannot answer the question of appearances or
    that of identity beyond the grave,
But I walk or sit indifferent, I am satisfied,
He ahold of my hand has completely satisfied
    me.

THE BASE OF ALL METAPHYSICS

AND now gentlemen,
A word I give to remain in your memories and
    minds,
As base and finale too for all metaphysics.

(So to the students the old professor,
At the close of his crowded course.)

Having studied the new and antique, the Greek
    and Germanic systems,
Kant having studied and stated, Fichte and
    Schelling and Hegel,
Stated the lore of Plato, and Socrates greater
    than Plato,
And greater than Socrates sought and stated,
    Christ divine having studied long,
I see reminiscent to-day those Greek and
    Germanic systems,
See the philosophies all, Christian churches and
    tenets see,
Yet underneath Socrates clearly see, and
    underneath Christ the divine I see,
The dear love of man for his comrade, the
    attraction of friend to friend,
Of the well-married husband and wife, of
    children and parents,
Of city for city and land for land.

RECORDERS AGES HENCE

RECORDERS ages hence,
Come, I will take you down underneath this
impassive exterior, I will tell you what to say
of me,
Publish my name and hang up my picture as
that of the tenderest lover,
The friend the lover's portrait, of whom his
friend his lover was fondest,
Who was not proud of his songs, but of the
measureless ocean of love within him, and
freely pour'd it forth,
Who often walk'd lonesome walks thinking of
his dear friends, his lovers,
Who pensive away from one he lov'd often lay
sleepless and dissatisfied at night,
Who knew too well the sick, sick dread lest the
one he lov'd might secretly be indifferent to
him,
Whose happiest days were far away through
fields, in woods, on hills, he and another
wandering hand in hand, they twain apart
from other men,
Who oft as he saunter'd the streets curv'd with
his arm the shoulder of his friend, while the
arm of his friend rested upon him also.

WHEN I HEARD AT THE CLOSE OF THE DAY

WHEN I heard at the close of the day how my
name had been receiv'd with plaudits in the
capitol, still it was not a happy night for me
that follow'd,
And else when I carous'd, or when my plans
were accomplish'd, still I was not happy,
But the day when I rose at dawn from the bed
of perfect health, refresh'd, singing, inhaling
the ripe breath of autumn,
When I saw the full moon in the west grow pale
and disappear in the morning light,
When I wander'd alone over the beach, and
undressing bathed, laughing with the cool
waters, and saw the sun rise,
And when I thought how my dear friend my
lover was on his way coming, O then I was
happy,
O then each breath tasted sweeter, and all that
day my food nourish'd me more, and the
beautiful day pass'd well,
And the next came with equal joy, and with the
next at evening came my friend,
And that night while all was still I heard the
waters roll slowly continually up the shores,
I heard the hissing rustle of the liquid and sands
as directed to me whispering to congratulate
me,

For the one I love most lay sleeping by me
    under the same cover in the cool night,
In the stillness in the autumn moonbeams his
    face was inclined toward me,
And his arm lay lightly around my breast—and
    that night I was happy.

ARE YOU THE NEW PERSON DRAWN TOWARD ME?

ARE you the new person drawn toward me?
To begin with take warning, I am surely far
    different from what you suppose;
Do you suppose you will find in me your ideal?
Do you think it so easy to have me become your
    lover?
Do you think the friendship me would be
    unalloy'd satisfaction?
Do you think I am trusty and faithful?
Do you see no further than this facade, this
    smooth and tolerant manner of me?
Do you suppose yourself advancing on real
    ground toward a real heroic man?
Have you no thought O dreamer that it may be
    all maya, illusion?

ROOTS AND LEAVES THEMSELVES ALONE

ROOTS and leaves themselves alone are
    these,
Scents brought to men and women from the
    wild woods and pond-side,
Breast-sorrel and pinks of love, fingers that wind
    around tighter than vines,
Gushes from the throats of birds hid in the
    foliage of trees as the sun is risen,
Breezes of land and love set from living shores
    to you on the living sea, to you O sailors!
Frost-mellow'd berries and Third-month twigs
    offer'd fresh to young persons wandering out
    in the fields when the winter breaks up,
Love-buds put before you and within you
    whoever you are,
Buds to be unfolded on the old terms,
If you bring the warmth of the sun to them
    they will open and bring form, color,
    perfume, to you,
If you become the aliment and the wet they will
    become flowers, fruits, tall branches and trees.

NOT HEAT FLAMES UP AND CONSUMES

NOT heat flames up and consumes,
Not sea-waves hurry in and out,

Not the air delicious and dry, the air of ripe
    summer, bears lightly along white down-balls
    of myriads of seeds,
Waited, sailing gracefully, to drop where they may;
Not these, O none of these more than the
    flames of me, consuming, burning for his love
    whom I love,
O none more than I hurrying in and out;
Does the tide hurry, seeking something, and
    never give up? O I the same,
O nor down-balls nor perfumes, nor the high
    rain-emitting clouds, are borne through the
    open air,
Any more than my soul is borne through the
    open air,
Waited in all directions O love, for friendship,
    for you.

TRICKLE DROPS

TRICKLE drops! my blue veins leaving!
O drops of me! trickle, slow drops,
Candid from me falling, drip, bleeding drops,
From wounds made to free you whence you
    were prison'd,
From my face, from my forehead and lips,
From my breast, from within where I was
    conceal'd, press forth red drops, confession
    drops,

Stain every page, stain every song I sing, every
    word I say, bloody drops,
Let them know your scarlet heat, let them
    glisten,
Saturate them with yourself all ashamed and wet,
Glow upon all I have written or shall write,
    bleeding drops,
Let it all be seen in your light, blushing drops.

City of Orgies

CITY of orgies, walks, and joys,
City whom that I have lived and sung in your
    midst will one day make
Not the pageants of you, not your shifting
    tableaus, your spectacles, repay me,
Not the interminable rows of your houses, nor
    the ships at the wharves,
Nor the processions in the streets, nor the bright
    windows with goods in them,
Nor to converse with learn'd persons, or bear
    my share in the soiree or feast;
Not those, but as I pass O Manhattan, your
    frequent and swift flash of eyes offering me
    love,
Offering response to my own—these repay me,
Lovers, continual lovers, only repay me.

BEHOLD THIS SWARTHY FACE

BEHOLD this swarthy face, these gray eyes,
This beard, the white wool unclipt upon my
　　neck,
My brown hands and the silent manner of me
　　without charm;
Yet comes one a Manhattanese and ever at
　　parting kisses me lightly on the lips with
　　robust love,
And I on the crossing of the street or on the
　　ship's deck give a kiss in return,
We observe that salute of American comrades
　　land and sea,
We are those two natural and nonchalant
　　persons.

I SAW IN LOUISIANA A LIVE-OAK GROWING

I SAW in Louisiana a live-oak growing,
All alone stood it and the moss hung down from
　　the branches,
Without any companion it grew there uttering
　　joyous of dark green,
And its look, rude, unbending, lusty, made me
　　think of myself,
But I wonder'd how it could utter joyous leaves
　　standing alone there without its friend near,
　　for I knew I could not,

And I broke off a twig with a certain number of
leaves upon it and twined around it a little
moss,
And brought it away, and I have placed it in
sight in my room,
It is not needed to remind me as of my own
dear friends,
(For I believe lately I think of little else than of
them,)
Yet it remains to me a curious token, it makes
me think of manly love;
For all that, and though the live-oak glistens
there in Louisiana solitary in a wide in a wide
flat space,
Uttering joyous leaves all its life without a friend
a lover near,
I know very well I could not.

TO A STRANGER

PASSING stranger! you do not know how
longingly I look upon you,
You must be he I was seeking, or she I was
seeking, (it comes to me as of a dream,)
I have somewhere surely lived a life of joy with you,
All is recall'd as we flit by each other, fluid,
affectionate, chaste, matured,
You grew up with me, were a boy with me or a
girl with me,

I ate with you and slept with you, your body has
    become not yours only nor left my body mine
    only,
You give me the pleasure of your eyes, face,
    flesh, as we pass, you take of my beard,
    breast, hands, in return,
I am not to speak to you, I am to think of you
    when I sit alone or wake at night alone,
I am to wait, I do not doubt I am to meet you
    again,
I am to see to it that I do not lose you.

THIS MOMENT YEARNING AND THOUGHTFUL

THIS moment yearning and thoughtful sitting
    alone,
It seems to me there are other men in other
    lands yearning and thoughtful,
It seems to me I can look over and behold them
    in Germany, Italy, France, Spain,
Or far, far away, in China, or in Russia or talking
    other dialects,
And it seems to me if I could know those men I
    should become attached to them as I do to
    men in my own lands,
O I know we should be brethren and lovers,
I know I should be happy with them.

I HEAR IT WAS CHARGED AGAINST ME

I HEAR it was charged against me that I sought
　　to destroy institutions,
But really I am neither for nor against
　　institutions,
(What indeed have I in common with them? or
　　what with the destruction of them?)
Only I will establish in the Mannahatta and in
　　every city of these States inland and seaboard,
And in the fields and woods, and above every
　　keel little or large that dents the water,
Without edifices or rules or trustees or any
　　argument,
The institution of the dear love of comrades.

THE PRAIRIE-GRASS DIVIDING

THE prairie-grass dividing, its special odor
　　breathing,
I demand of it the spiritual corresponding,
Demand the most copious and close
　　companionship of men,
Demand the blades to rise of words, acts,
　　beings,
Those of the open atmosphere, coarse, sunlit,
　　fresh, nutritious,
Those that go their own gait, erect, stepping with
　　freedom and command, leading not following,

Those with a never-quell'd audacity, those with
    sweet and lusty flesh clear of taint,
Those that look carelessly in the faces of
    Presidents and governors, as to say Who are
    you?
Those of earth-born passion, simple, never
    constrain'd, never obedient,
Those of inland America.

WHEN I PERSUE THE CONQUER'D FAME

WHEN I peruse the conquer'd fame of heroes
    and the victories of mighty generals, I do not
    envy the generals,
Nor the President in his Presidency, nor the rich
    in his great house,
But when I hear of the brotherhood of lovers,
    how it was with them,
How together through life, through dangers,
    odium, unchanging, long and long,
youth and through middle and old age, how
    unfaltering, how affectionate and faithful they
    were,
Then I am pensive—I hastily walk away fill'd
    with the bitterest envy.

WE TWO BOYS TOGETHER CLINGING

WE two boys together clinging,
One the other never leaving,
Up and down the roads going, North and South
  excursions making,
Power enjoying, elbows stretching, fingers
  clutching,
Arm'd and fearless, eating, drinking, sleeping,
  loving.
No law less than ourselves owning, sailing,
  soldiering, thieving, threatening,
Misers, menials, priests alarming, air breathing,
  water drinking, on the turf or the sea-beach
  dancing,
Cities wrenching, ease scorning, statutes
  mocking, feebleness chasing, our foray.

A PROMISE TO CALIFORNIA

A PROMISE to California,
Or inland to the great pastoral Plains, and on to
  Puget sound and Oregon;
Sojourning east a while longer, soon I travel
  toward you, to remain, to teach robust
  American love,
For I know very well that I and robust love
  belong among you, inland, and along the
  Western sea;

For these States tend inland and toward the
Western sea, and I will also.

Here the Frailest Leaves of Me

HERE the frailest leaves of me and yet my
strongest lasting,
Here I shade and hide my thoughts, I myself do
not expose them,
And yet they expose me more than all my other
poems.

No Labor-Saving Machine

NO labor-saving machine,
Nor discovery have I made,
Nor will I be able to leave behind me any
wealthy bequest to found hospital or library,
Nor reminiscence of any deed of courage for
America,
Nor literary success nor intellect; nor book for
the book-shelf,
But a few carols vibrating through the air I
leave,
For comrades and lovers.

A Glimpse

A GLIMPSE through an interstice caught,
Of a crowd of workmen and drivers in a bar-
    room around the stove late of a winter night,
    and I unremark'd seated in a corner,
Of a youth who loves me and whom I love,
    silently approaching and seating himself near,
    that he may hold me by the hand,
A long while amid the noises of coming and
    going, of drinking and oath and smutty jest,
There we two, content, happy in being together,
    speaking little, perhaps not a word.

A Leaf for Hand in Hand

A LEAF for hand in hand;
You natural persons old and young!
You on the Mississippi and on all the branches
    and bayous of the Mississippi!
You friendly boatmen and mechanics! you
    roughs!
You twain! and all processions moving along the
    streets!
I wish to infuse myself among you till I see it
    common for you to walk hand in hand.

Earth, My Likeness

EARTH, my likeness,
Though you look so impassive, ample and
    spheric there,
I now suspect that is not all;
I now suspect there is something fierce in you
    eligible to burst forth,
For an athlete is enamour'd of me, and I of him,
But toward him there is something fierce and
    terrible in me eligible to burst forth,
I dare not tell it in words, not even in these
    songs.

I Dream'd in a Dream

I DREAM'D in a dream I saw a city invincible
    to the attacks of the whole of the rest of the
    earth,
I dream'd that was the new city of Friends,
Nothing was greater there than the quality of
    robust love, it led the rest,
It was seen every hour in the actions of the men
    of that city,
And in all their looks and words.

What Think You I Take My Pen in Hand?

WHAT think you I take my pen in hand to
   record?
The battle-ship, perfect-model'd, majestic,
   that I saw pass the offing to-day under full
   sail?
The splendors of the past day? or the splendor
   of the night that envelops me?
Or the vaunted glory and growth of the great
   city spread around me?—no;
But merely of two simple men I saw to-day on
   the pier in the midst of the crowd, parting the
   parting of dear friends,
The one to remain hung on the other's neck
   and passionately kiss'd him,
While the one to depart tightly prest the one to
   remain in his arms.

To the East and to the West

TO the East and to the West,
To the man of the Seaside State and of
   Pennsylvania,
To the Kanadian of the north, to the Southerner
   I love,
These with perfect trust to depict you as myself,
   the germs are in all men,

I believe the main purport of these States is to
 found a superb friendship, exalte, previously
 unknown,
Because I perceive it waits, and has been always
 waiting, latent in all men.

SOMETIMES WITH ONE I LOVE

SOMETIMES with one I love I fill myself with
 rage for fear I effuse unreturn'd love,
But now I think there is no unreturn'd love, the
 pay is certain one way or another,
(I loved a certain person ardently and my love
 was not return'd,
Yet out of that I have written these songs.)

TO A WESTERN BOY

MANY things to absorb I teach to help you
 become eleve of mine;
Yet if blood like mine circle not in your veins,
If you be not silently selected by lovers and do
 not silently select lovers,
Of what use is it that you seek to become eleve
 of mine?

FAST ANCHOR'D ETERNAL O LOVE!

FAST-ANCHOR'D eternal O love! O woman I
    love!
O bride! O wife! more resistless than I can tell,
    the thought of you!
Then separate, as disembodied or another born,
Ethereal, the last athletic reality, my consolation,
I ascend, I float in the regions of your love O
    man,
O sharer of my roving life.

AMONG THE MULTITUDE

AMONG the men and women the multitude,
I perceive one picking me out by secret and
    divine signs,
Acknowledging none else, not parent, wife,
    husband, brother, child, any nearer than I am,
Some are baffled, but that one is not—that one
    knows me.

Ah lover and perfect equal,
I meant that you should discover me so by faint
    indirections,
And I when I meet you mean to discover you by
    the like in you.

O You Whom I Often and Silently Come

O YOU whom I often and silently come where
    you are that I may be with you,
As I walk by your side or sit near, or remain in
    the same room with you,
Little you know the subtle electric fire that for
    your sake is playing within me.

That Shadow My Likeness

THAT shadow my likeness that goes to and fro
    seeking a livelihood, chattering, chaffering,
How often I find myself standing and looking at
    it where it flits,
How often I question and doubt whether that is
    really me;
But among my lovers and caroling these songs,
O I never doubt whether that is really me.

Full of Life Now

FULL of life now, compact, visible,
I, forty years old the eighty-third year of the
    States,
To one a century hence or any number of
    centuries hence,
To you yet unborn these, seeking you.

When you read these I that was visible am
  become invisible,
Now it is you, compact, visible, realizing my
  poems, seeking me,
Fancying how happy you were if I could be with
  you and become your comrade;
Be it as if I were with you. (Be not too certain
  but I am now with you.)

Salut au Monde!

1

O TAKE my hand Walt Whitman!
Such gliding wonders! such sights and sounds!
Such join'd unended links, each hook'd to the
    next,
Each answering all, each sharing the earth with all.

What widens within you Walt Whitman?
What waves and soils exuding?
What climes? what persons and cities are here?
Who are the infants, some playing, some
    slumbering?
Who are the girls? who are the married women?
Who are the groups of old men going slowly
    with their arms about each other's necks?
What rivers are these? what forests and fruits are
    these?
What are the mountains call'd that rise so high
    in the mists?
What myriads of dwellings are they fill'd with
    dwellers?

2

Within me latitude widens, longitude lengthens,
Asia, Africa, Europe, are to the east—America is
    provided for in the west,

Banding the bulge of the earth winds the hot
    equator,
Curiously north and south turn the axis-ends,
Within me is the longest day, the sun wheels in
    slanting rings, it does not set for months,
Stretch'd in due time within me the midnight sun
    just rises above the horizon and sinks again,
Within me zones, seas, cataracts, forests,
    volcanoes, groups,
Malaysia, Polynesia, and the great West Indian
    islands.

3

What do you hear Walt Whitman?

I hear the workman singing and the farmer's
    wife singing,
I hear in the distance the sounds of children and
    of animals early in the day,
I hear emulous shouts of Australians pursuing
    the wild horse,
I hear the Spanish dance with castanets in the
    chestnut shade, to the rebeck and guitar,
I hear continual echoes from the Thames,
I hear fierce French liberty songs,
I hear of the Italian boat-sculler the musical
    recitative of old poems,
I hear the locusts in Syria as they strike the grain
    and grass with the showers of their terrible
    clouds,

I hear the Coptic refrain toward sundown,
   pensively falling on the breast of the black
   venerable vast mother the Nile,
I hear the chirp of the Mexican muleteer, and
   the bells of the mule,
I hear the Arab muezzin calling from the top of
   the mosque,
I hear the Christian priests at the altars of their
   churches, I hear the responsive base and
   soprano,
I hear the cry of the Cossack, and the sailor's
   voice putting to sea at Okotsk,
I hear the wheeze of the slave-coffle as the slaves
   march on, as the husky gangs pass on by twos
   and threes, fasten'd together with wrist-chains
   and ankle-chains,
I hear the Hebrew reading his records and psalms,
I hear the rhythmic myths of the Greeks, and
   the strong legends of the Romans,
I hear the tale of the divine life and bloody
   death of the beautiful God the Christ,
I hear the Hindoo teaching his favorite pupil the
   loves, wars, adages, transmitted safely to this
   day from poets who wrote three thousand
   years ago.

4

What do you see Walt Whitman?
Who are they you salute, and that one after
   another salute you?

I see a great round wonder rolling through
    space,
I see diminute farms, hamlets, ruins, graveyards,
    jails, factories, palaces, hovels, huts of
    barbarians, tents of nomads upon the surface,
I see the shaded part on one side where the
    sleepers are sleeping, and the sunlit part on
    the other side,
I see the curious rapid change of the light and
    shade,
I see distant lands, as real and near to the
    inhabitants of them as my land is to me.

I see plenteous waters,
I see mountain peaks, I see the sierras of Andes
    where they range,
I see plainly the Himalayas, Chian Shahs, Altays,
    Ghauts,
I see the giant pinnacles of Elbruz, Kazbek,
    Bazardjusi,
I see the Styrian Alps, and the Karnac Alps,
I see the Pyrenees, Balks, Carpathians, and to
    the north the Dofrafields, and off at sea
    mount Hecla,
I see Vesuvius and Etna, the mountains of the
    Moon, and the Red mountains of
    Madagascar,
I see the Lybian, Arabian, and Asiatic deserts,
I see huge dreadful Arctic and Antarctic
    icebergs,

I see the superior oceans and the inferior
    ones, the Atlantic and Pacific, the sea of
    Mexico, the Brazilian sea, and the sea
    of Peru,
The waters of Hindustan, the China sea, and the
    gulf of Guinea,
The Japan waters, the beautiful bay of Nagasaki
    land-lock'd in its mountains,
The spread of the Baltic, Caspian, Bothnia, the
    British shores, and the bay of Biscay,
The clear-sunn'd Mediterranean, and from one
    to another of its islands,
The White sea, and the sea around Greenland.

I behold the mariners of the world,
Some are in storms, some in the night with the
    watch on the lookout,
Some drifting helplessly, some with contagious
    diseases.

I behold the sail and steamships of the world,
    some in clusters in port, some on their
    voyages,
Some double the cape of Storms, some cape
    Verde, others capes Guardafui, Bon, or
    Bajadore,
Others Dondra head, others pass the straits of
    Sunda, others cape Lopatka, others Behring's
    straits,

Others cape Horn, others sail the gulf of Mexico
    or along Cuba or Hayti, others Hudson's bay
    or Baffin's bay,
Others pass the straits of Dover, others enter the
    Wash, others the firth of Solway, others round
    cape Clear, others the Land's End,
Others traverse the Zuyder Zee or the
    Scheld,
Others as comers and goers at Gibraltar or
    the Dardanelles,
Others sternly push their way through the
    northern winter-packs,
Others descend or ascend the Obi or the
    Lena,
Others the Niger or the Congo, others the
    Indus, the Burampooter and Cambodia,
Others wait steam'd up ready to start in the
    ports of Australia,
Wait at Liverpool, Glasgow, Dublin, Marseilles,
    Lisbon, Naples,
Hamburg, Bremen, Bordeaux, the Hague,
    Copenhagen,
Wait at Valparaiso, Rio Janeiro, Panama.

5

I see the tracks of the railroads of the earth,
I see them in Great Britain, I see them in
    Europe,
I see them in Asia and in Africa.

I see the electric telegraphs of the earth,
I see the filaments of the news of the wars,
   deaths, losses, gains, passions, of my race.

I see the long river-stripes of the earth,
I see the Amazon and the Paraguay,
I see the four great rivers of China, the Amour,
   the Yellow River, the Yiang-tse, and the Pearl,
I see where the Seine flows, and where the
   Danube, the Loire, the Rhone, and the
   Guadalquiver flow,
I see the windings of the Volga, the Dnieper, the
   Oder,
I see the Tuscan going down the Arno, and the
   Venetian along the Po,
I see the Greek seaman sailing out of Egina bay.

6

I see the site of the old empire of Assyria, and
   that of Persia, and that of India,
I see the falling of the Ganges over the high rim
   of Saukara.

I see the place of the idea of the Deity
   incarnated by avatars in human forms,
I see the spots of the successions of priests on
   the earth, oracles, sacrificers, brahmins,
   sabians, llamas, monks, muftis, exhorters,
I see where druids walk'd the groves of Mona, I
   see the mistletoe and vervain,

I see the temples of the deaths of the bodies of
    Gods, I see the old signifiers.

I see Christ eating the bread of his last supper in
    the midst of youths and old persons,
I see where the strong divine young man the
    Hercules toil'd faithfully and long and then
    died,
I see the place of the innocent rich life and
    hapless fate of the beautiful nocturnal son, the
    full-limb'd Bacchus,
I see Kneph, blooming, drest in blue, with the
    crown of feathers on his head,
I see Hermes, unsuspected, dying, well-belov'd,
    saying to the people, Do not weep for me,
This is not my true country, I have lived
    banish'd from my true country, I now go
    back there,
I return to the celestial sphere where every one
    goes in his turn.

7

I see the battle-fields of the earth, grass grows
    upon them and blossoms and corn,
I see the tracks of ancient and modern
    expeditions.

I see the nameless masonries, venerable messages
    of the unknown events, heroes, records of the
    earth.

I see the places of the sagas,
I see pine-trees and fir-trees torn by northern
    blasts,
I see granite bowlders and cliffs, I see green
    meadows and lakes,
I see the burial-cairns of Scandinavian warriors,
I see them raised high with stones by the marge
    of restless oceans, that the dead men's spirits
    when they wearied of their quiet graves might
    rise up through the mounds and gaze on the
    tossing billows, and be refresh'd by storms,
    immensity, liberty, action.

I see the steppes of Asia,
I see the tumuli of Mongolia, I see the tents of
    Kalmucks and Baskirs,
I see the nomadic tribes with herds of oxen and
    cows,
I see the table-lands notch'd with ravines, I see
    the jungles and deserts,
I see the camel, the wild steed, the bustard, the
    fat-tail'd sheep, the antelope, and the
    burrowing wolf

I see the highlands of Abyssinia,
I see flocks of goats feeding, and see the fig-tree,
    tamarind, date,
And see fields of teff-wheat and places of
    verdure and gold.

I see the Brazilian vaquero,
I see the Bolivian ascending mount Sorata,
I see the Wacho crossing the plains, I see the
    incomparable rider of horses with his lasso on
    his arm,
I see over the pampas the pursuit of wild cattle
    for their hides.

8

I see the regions of snow and ice,
I see the sharp-eyed Samoiede and the Finn,
I see the seal-seeker in his boat poising his lance,
I see the Siberian on his slight-built sledge
    drawn by dogs,
I see the porpoise-hunters, I see the whale-
    crews of the south Pacific and the north
    Atlantic,
I see the cliffs, glaciers, torrents, valleys, of
    Switzerland- I mark the long winters and the
    isolation.

I see the cities of the earth and make myself at
    random a part of them,
I am a real Parisian,
I am a habitan of Vienna, St. Petersburg, Berlin,
    Constantinople,
I am of Adelaide, Sidney, Melbourne,
I am of London, Manchester, Bristol,
    Edinburgh, Limerick,

I am of Madrid, Cadiz, Barcelona, Oporto,
Lyons, Brussels, Berne, Frankfort, Stuttgart,
Turin, Florence,
I belong in Moscow, Cracow, Warsaw, or
northward in Christiania or Stockholm, or
in Siberian Irkutsk, or in some street in
Iceland,
I descend upon all those cities, and rise from
them again.

10

I see vapors exhaling from unexplored
countries,
I see the savage types, the bow and arrow,
the poison'd splint, the fetich, and the obi.
I see African and Asiatic towns,
I see Algiers, Tripoli, Derne, Mogadore,
Timbuctoo, Monrovia,
I see the swarms of Pekin, Canton, Benares,
Delhi, Calcutta, Tokio,
I see the Kruman in his hut, and the Dahoman
and Ashantee-man in their huts,
I see the Turk smoking opium in Aleppo,
I see the picturesque crowds at the fairs of Khiva
and those of Herat,
I see Teheran, I see Muscat and Medina and the
intervening sands, see the caravans toiling
onward,
I see Egypt and the Egyptians, I see the
pyramids and obelisks.

I look on chisell'd histories, records of
    conquering kings, dynasties, cut in slabs of
    sand-stone, or on granite-blocks,
I see at Memphis mummy-pits containing
    mummies embalm'd, swathed in linen cloth,
    lying there many centuries,
I look on the fall'n Theban, the large-ball'd
    eyes, the side-drooping neck, the hands
    folded across the breast.

I see all the menials of the earth, laboring,
I see all the prisoners in the prisons,
I see the defective human bodies of the earth,
The blind, the deaf and dumb, idiots,
    hunchbacks, lunatics,
The pirates, thieves, betrayers, murderers,
    slave-makers of the earth,
The helpless infants, and the helpless old men
    and women.

I see male and female everywhere,
I see the serene brotherhood of philosophs,
I see the constructiveness of my race,
I see the results of the perseverance and industry
    of my race,
I see ranks, colors, barbarisms, civilizations, I go
    among them, I mix indiscriminately,
And I salute all the inhabitants of the earth.

11

You whoever you are!

You daughter or son of England!

You of the mighty Slavic tribes and empires! you
Russ in Russia!

You dim-descended, black, divine-soul'd African,
large, fine-headed, nobly-form'd, superbly
destin'd, on equal terms with me!

You Norwegian! Swede! Dane! Icelander! you
Prussian!

You Spaniard of Spain! you Portuguese!

You Frenchwoman and Frenchman of France!

You Belge! you liberty-lover of the Netherlands!
(you stock whence I myself have descended;)

You sturdy Austrian! you Lombard! Hun!
Bohemian! farmer of Styria!

You neighbor of the Danube!

You working-man of the Rhine, the Elbe, or the
Weser! you working-woman too!

You Sardinian! you Bavarian! Swabian! Saxon!
Wallachian! Bulgarian!

You Roman! Neapolitan! you Greek!

You lithe matador in the arena at Seville!

You mountaineer living lawlessly on the Taurus
or Caucasus!

You Bokh horse-herd watching your mares and
stallions feeding!

You beautiful-bodied Persian at full speed in the
saddle shooting arrows to the mark!

You Chinaman and Chinawoman of China! you
    Tartar of Tartary!
You women of the earth subordinated at your
    tasks!
You Jew journeying in your old age through
    every risk to stand once on Syrian ground!
You other Jews waiting in all lands for your
    Messiah!
You thoughtful Armenian pondering by some
    stream of the Euphrates! you peering amid
    the ruins of Nineveh! you ascending mount
    Ararat!
You foot-worn pilgrim welcoming the far-away
    sparkle of the minarets of Mecca!
You sheiks along the stretch from Suez to
    Bab-el-mandeb ruling your families and
    tribes!
You olive-grower tending your fruit on fields of
    Nazareth, Damascus, or lake Tiberias!
You Thibet trader on the wide inland or
    bargaining in the shops of Lassa!
You Japanese man or woman! you liver in
    Madagascar, Ceylon, Sumatra, Borneo!
All you continentals of Asia, Africa, Europe,
    Australia, indifferent of place!
All you on the numberless islands of the
    archipelagoes of the sea!
And you of centuries hence when you listen
    to me!

And you each and everywhere whom I specify
    not, but include just the same!
Health to you! good will to you all, from me
    and America sent!

Each of us inevitable,
Each of us limitless—each of us with his or her
    right upon the earth,
Each of us allow'd the eternal purports of the
    earth,
Each of us here as divinely as any is here.

12

You Hottentot with clicking palate! you woolly-
    hair'd hordes!
You own'd persons dropping sweat-drops or
    blood-drops!
You human forms with the fathomless ever-
    impressive countenances of brutes!
You poor koboo whom the meanest of the rest
    look down upon for all your glimmering
    language and spirituality!
You dwarf'd Kamtschatkan, Greenlander,
    Lapp!
You Austral negro, naked, red, sooty, with
    protrusive lip, groveling, seeking your food!
You Caffre, Berber, Soudanese!
You haggard, uncouth, untutor'd Bedowee!
You plague-swarms in Madras, Nankin, Kaubul,
    Cairo!

You benighted roamer of Amazonia! you
    Patagonian! you Feejeeman!
I do not prefer others so very much before you
    either,
I do not say one word against you, away back
    there where you stand,
(You will come forward in due time to my side.)

13

My spirit has pass'd in compassion and
    determination around the whole earth,
I have look'd for equals and lovers and found
    them ready for me in all lands,
I think some divine rapport has equalized me
    with them.

You vapors, I think I have risen with you, moved
    away to distant continents, and fallen down
    there, for reasons,
I think I have blown with you you winds;
You waters I have finger'd every shore with
    you,
I have run through what any river or strait of
    the globe has run through,
I have taken my stand on the bases of peninsulas
    and on the high embedded rocks, to cry
    thence:

What cities the light or warmth penetrates I
    penetrate those cities myself,

All islands to which birds wing their way I wing
   my way myself.

Toward you all, in America's name,
I raise high the perpendicular hand, I make the
   signal,
To remain after me in sight forever,
For all the haunts and homes of men.

Song of the Open Road

1

AFOOT and light-hearted I take to the open
   road,
Healthy, free, the world before me,
The long brown path before me leading
   wherever I choose.

Henceforth I ask not good-fortune, I myself am
   good-fortune,
Henceforth I whimper no more, postpone no
   more, need nothing,
Done with indoor complaints, libraries,
   querulous criticisms,
Strong and content I travel the open road.

The earth, that is sufficient,
I do not want the constellations any nearer,
I know they are very well where they are,
I know they suffice for those who belong to
   them.

(Still here I carry my old delicious burdens,
I carry them, men and women, I carry them
   with me wherever I go,
I swear it is impossible for me to get rid of
   them,

I am fill'd with them, and I will fill them in
    return.)

2

You road I enter upon and look around, I
    believe you are not all that is here,
I believe that much unseen is also here.

Here the profound lesson of reception, nor
    preference nor denial,
The black with his woolly head, the felon,
    the diseas'd, the illiterate person, are not
    denied;
The birth, the hasting after the physician, the
    beggar's tramp, the drunkard's stagger, the
    laughing party of mechanics,
The escaped youth, the rich person's carriage,
    the fop, the eloping couple,
The early market-man, the hearse, the moving of
    furniture into the town, the return back from
    the town,
They pass, I also pass, any thing passes, none
    can be interdicted,
None but are accepted, none but shall be dear
    to me.

3

You air that serves me with breath to speak!
You objects that call from diffusion my
    meanings and give them shape!

You light that wraps me and all things in delicate
 equable showers!
You paths worn in the irregular hollows by the
 roadsides!
I believe you are latent with unseen existences,
 you are so dear to me.

You flagg'd walks of the cities! you strong curbs
 at the edges!
You ferries! you planks and posts of wharves!
 you timber-lined side! you distant ships!
You rows of houses! you window-pierc'd
 facades! you roofs!
You porches and entrances! you copings and
 iron guards!
You windows whose transparent shells might
 expose so much!
You doors and ascending steps! you arches!
You gray stones of interminable pavements! you
 trodden crossings!
From all that has touch'd you I believe you have
 imparted to yourselves, and now would
 impart the same secretly to me,
From the living and the dead you have peopled
 your impassive surfaces, and the spirits thereof
 would be evident and amicable with me.

4
The earth expanding right hand and left hand,
The picture alive, every part in its best light,

The music falling in where it is wanted, and
    stopping where it is not wanted,
The cheerful voice of the public road, the gay
    fresh sentiment of the road.

O highway I travel, do you say to me Do not
    leave me?
Do you say Venture not—if you leave me you
    are lost?
Do you say I am already prepared, I am well-
    beaten and undenied, adhere to me?

O public road, I say back I am not afraid to
    leave you, yet I love you,
You express me better than I can express myself,
You shall be more to me than my poem.

I think heroic deeds were all conceiv'd in the
    open air, and all free poems also,
I think I could stop here myself and do miracles,
I think whatever I shall meet on the road I
    shall like, and whoever beholds me shall
    like me,
I think whoever I see must be happy.

5

From this hour I ordain myself loos'd of limits
    and imaginary lines,
Going where I list, my own master total and
    absolute,

Listening to others, considering well what they say,
Pausing, searching, receiving, contemplating,
Gently, but with undeniable will, divesting
    myself of the holds that would hold me.

I inhale great draughts of space,
The east and the west are mine, and the north
    and the south are mine.

I am larger, better than I thought,
I did not know I held so much goodness.

All seems beautiful to me,
can repeat over to men and women You have
    done such good to me I would do the same
    to you,
I will recruit for myself and you as I go,
I will scatter myself among men and women as
    I go,
I will toss a new gladness and roughness among
    them,
Whoever denies me it shall not trouble me,
Whoever accepts me he or she shall be blessed
    and shall bless me.

6

Now if a thousand perfect men were to appear it
    would not amaze me,
Now if a thousand beautiful forms of women
    appear'd it would not astonish me.

Now I see the secret of the making of the best
    persons,
It is to grow in the open air and to eat and sleep
    with the earth.

Here a great personal deed has room,
(Such a deed seizes upon the hearts of the whole
    race of men,
Its effusion of strength and will overwhelms law
    and mocks all authority and all argument
    against it.)

Here is the test of wisdom,
Wisdom is not finally tested in schools,
Wisdom cannot be pass'd from one having it to
    another not having it,
Wisdom is of the soul, is not susceptible of
    proof, is its own proof,
Applies to all stages and objects and qualities
    and is content,
Is the certainty of the reality and immortality of
    things, and the excellence of things;
Something there is in the float of the sight of
    things that provokes it out of the soul.

Now I re-examine philosophies and religions,
They may prove well in lecture-rooms, yet not
    prove at all under the spacious clouds and
    along the landscape and flowing currents.

Here is realization,
Here is a man tallied—he realizes here what he
    has in him,
The past, the future, majesty, love—if they are
    vacant of you, you are vacant of them.

Only the kernel of every object nourishes;
Where is he who tears off the husks for you and
    me?
Where is he that undoes stratagems and
    envelopes for you and me?

Here is adhesiveness, it is not previously
    fashion'd, it is apropos;
Do you know what it is as you pass to be loved
    by strangers?
Do you know the talk of those turning eye-balls?

7

Here is the efflux of the soul,
The efflux of the soul comes from within
    through embower'd gates, ever provoking
    questions,
These yearnings why are they? these thoughts in
    the darkness why are they?
Why are there men and women that while they
    are nigh me the sunlight expands my blood?
Why when they leave me do my pennants of joy
    sink flat and lank?

Why are there trees I never walk under but
    large and melodious thoughts descend upon
    me?
(I think they hang there winter and summer on
    those trees and always drop fruit as I pass;)
What is it I interchange so suddenly with
    strangers?
What with some driver as I ride on the seat by
    his side?
What with some fisherman drawing his seine by
    the shore as I walk by and pause?
What gives me to be free to a woman's and
    man's good-will? what gives them to be free
    to mine?

8

The efflux of the soul is happiness, here is
    happiness,
I think it pervades the open air, waiting at all
    times,
Now it flows unto us, we are rightly charged.

Here rises the fluid and attaching character,
The fluid and attaching character is the freshness
    and sweetness of man and woman,
(The herbs of the morning sprout no fresher
    and sweeter every day out of the roots of
    themselves, than it sprouts fresh and sweet
    continually out of itself.)

Toward the fluid and attaching character exudes
the sweat of the love of young and old,
From it falls distill'd the charm that mocks
beauty and attainments,
Toward it heaves the shuddering longing ache of
contact.

9

Allons! whoever you are come travel with me!
Traveling with me you find what never tires.

The earth never tires,
The earth is rude, silent, incomprehensible at
first, Nature is rude and incomprehensible at
first,
Be not discouraged, keep on, there are divine
things well envelop'd,
I swear to you there are divine things more
beautiful than words can tell.

Allons! we must not stop here,
However sweet these laid-up stores, however
convenient this dwelling we cannot remain
here,
However shelter'd this port and however calm
these waters we must not anchor here,
However welcome the hospitality that surrounds
us we are permitted to receive it but a little
while.

10

Allons! the inducements shall be greater,
We will sail pathless and wild seas,
We will go where winds blow, waves dash,
    and the Yankee clipper speeds by under full
    sail.

Allons! with power, liberty, the earth, the
    elements,
Health, defiance, gayety, self-esteem,
    curiosity;
Allons! from all formules!
From your formules, O bat-eyed and
    materialistic priests.

The stale cadaver blocks up the passage-the
    burial waits no longer.

Allons! yet take warning!
He traveling with me needs the best blood,
    thews, endurance,
None may come to the trial till he or she bring
    courage and health,
Come not here if you have already spent the
    best of yourself,
Only those may come who come in sweet and
    determin'd bodies,
No diseas'd person, no rum-drinker or venereal
    taint is permitted here.

(I and mine do not convince by arguments,
    similes, rhymes,
We convince by our presence.)

11

Listen! I will be honest with you,
I do not offer the old smooth prizes, but offer
    rough new prizes,
These are the days that must happen to you:
You shall not heap up what is call'd riches,
You shall scatter with lavish hand all that you
    earn or achieve,
You but arrive at the city to which you were
    destin'd, you hardly settle yourself to
    satisfaction before you are call'd by an
    irresistible call to depart,
You shall be treated to the ironical smiles and
    mockings of those who remain behind you,
What beckonings of love you receive you shall
    only answer with passionate kisses of parting,
You shall not allow the hold of those who
    spread their reach'd hands toward you.

12

Allons! after the great Companions, and to
    belong to them!
They too are on the road—they are the swift and
    majestic men—they are the greatest women,
Enjoyers of calms of seas and storms of seas,

Sailors of many a ship, walkers of many a mile of
land,
Habitues of many distant countries, habitues of
far-distant dwellings,
Trusters of men and women, observers of cities,
solitary toilers,
Pausers and contemplators of tufts, blossoms,
shells of the shore,
Dancers at wedding-dances, kissers of brides,
tender helpers of children, bearers of children,
Soldiers of revolts, standers by gaping graves,
lowerers-down of coffins,
Journeyers over consecutive seasons, over the
years, the curious years each emerging from
that which preceded it,
Journeyers as with companions, namely their
own diverse phases,
Forth-steppers from the latent unrealized baby-
days,
Journeyers gayly with their own youth,
journeyers with their bearded and well-grain'd
manhood,
Journeyers with their womanhood, ample,
unsurpass'd, content,
Journeyers with their own sublime old age of
manhood or womanhood,
Old age, calm, expanded, broad with the
haughty breadth of the universe,
Old age, flowing free with the delicious near-by
freedom of death.

13

Allons! to that which is endless as it was
   beginningless,
To undergo much, tramps of days, rests of
   nights,
To merge all in the travel they tend to, and the
   days and nights they tend to,
Again to merge them in the start of superior
   journeys,
To see nothing anywhere but what you may
   reach it and pass it,
To conceive no time, however distant, but what
   you may reach it and pass it,
To look up or down no road but it stretches and
   waits for you, however long but it stretches
   and waits for you,
To see no being, not God's or any, but you also
   go thither,
To see no possession but you may possess it,
   enjoying all without labor or purchase,
   abstracting the feast yet not abstracting one
   particle of it,
To take the best of the farmer's farm and the
   rich man's elegant villa, and the chaste
   blessings of the well-married couple, and the
   fruits of orchards and flowers of gardens,
To take to your use out of the compact cities as
   you pass through,
To carry buildings and streets with you
   afterward wherever you go,

To gather the minds of men out of their brains
  as you encounter them, to gather the love out
  of their hearts,
To take your lovers on the road with
  you, for all that you leave them behind
  you,
To know the universe itself as a road, as many
  roads, as roads for traveling souls.

All parts away for the progress of souls,
All religion, all solid things, arts, governments—
  all that was or is apparent upon this globe or
  any globe, falls into niches and corners before
  the procession of souls along the grand roads
  of the universe.

Of the progress of the souls of men and women
  along the grand roads of the universe, all
  other progress is the needed emblem and
  sustenance.

Forever alive, forever forward,
Stately, solemn, sad, withdrawn, baffled, mad,
  turbulent, feeble, dissatisfied,
Desperate, proud, fond, sick, accepted by men,
  rejected by men,
They go! they go! I know that they go, but I
  know not where they go,
But I know that they go toward the best—
  toward something great.

Whoever you are, come forth! or man or woman
    come forth!
You must not stay sleeping and dallying there in
    the house, though you built it, or though it
    has been built for you.

Out of the dark confinement! out from behind
    the screen!
It is useless to protest, I know all and expose it.

Behold through you as bad as the rest,
Through the laughter, dancing, dining, supping,
    of people,
Inside of dresses and ornaments, inside of those
    wash'd and trimm'd faces,
Behold a secret silent loathing and despair.

No husband, no wife, no friend, trusted to hear
    the confession,
Another self, a duplicate of every one, skulking
    and hiding it goes,
Formless and wordless through the streets of the
    cities, polite and bland in the parlors,
In the cars of railroads, in steamboats, in the
    public assembly,
Home to the houses of men and women, at the
    table, in the bedroom, everywhere,
Smartly attired, countenance smiling, form
    upright, death under the breast-bones, hell
    under the skull-bones,

Under the broadcloth and gloves, under the
    ribbons and artificial flowers,
Keeping fair with the customs, speaking not a
    syllable of itself,
Speaking of any thing else but never of itself.

14

Allons! through struggles and wars!
The goal that was named cannot be
    countermanded.

Have the past struggles succeeded?
What has succeeded? yourself? your nation?
    Nature?
Now understand me well—it is provided in the
    essence of things that from any fruition of
    success, no matter what, shall come forth
    something to make a greater struggle
    necessary.

My call is the call of battle, I nourish active
    rebellion,
He going with me must go well arm'd,
He going with me goes often with spare diet,
    poverty, angry enemies, desertions.

15

Allons! the road is before us!
It is safe—I have tried it—my own feet have
    tried it well—be not detain'd!

Let the paper remain on the desk unwritten, and
the book on the shelf unopen'd!
Let the tools remain in the workshop! let the
money remain unearn'd!
Let the school stand! mind not the cry of the
teacher!
Let the preacher preach in his pulpit! let the
lawyer plead in the court, and the judge
expound the law.

Camerado, I give you my hand!
I give you my love more precious than money,
I give you myself before preaching or law;
Will you give me yourselp. will you come travel
with me?
Shall we stick by each other as long as we live?

Crossing Brooklyn Ferry

1

FLOOD-TIDE below me! I see you face to
   face!
Clouds of the west-sun there half an hour
   high—I see you also face to face.

Crowds of men and women attired in the usual
   costumes, how curious you are to me!
On the ferry-boats the hundreds and hundreds
   that cross, returning home, are more curious
   to me than you suppose,
And you that shall cross from shore to shore
   years hence are more to me, and more in my
   meditations, than you might suppose.

2

The impalpable sustenance of me from all things
   at all hours of the day,
The simple, compact, well-join'd scheme, myself
   disintegrated, every one disintegrated yet part
   of the scheme,
The similitudes of the past and those of the
   future,
The glories strung like beads on my smallest
   sights and hearings, on the walk in the street
   and the passage over the river,

The current rushing so swiftly and swimming
   with me far away,
The others that are to follow me, the ties
   between me and them,
The certainty of others, the life, love, sight,
   hearing of others.

Others will enter the gates of the ferry and cross
   from shore to shore,
Others will watch the run of the flood-tide,
Others will see the shipping of Manhattan north
   and west, and the heights of Brooklyn to the
   south and east,
Others will see the islands large and small;
Fifty years hence, others will see them as they
   cross, the sun half an hour high,
A hundred years hence, or ever so many
   hundred years hence, others will see them,
Will enjoy the sunset, the pouring-in of the
   flood-tide, the falling-back to the sea of the
   ebb-tide.

3

It avails not, time nor place—distance avails
   not,
I am with you, you men and women of a
   generation, or ever so many generations
   hence,
Just as you feel when you look on the river and
   sky, so I felt,

Just as any of you is one of a living crowd, I was
    one of a crowd,
Just as you are refresh'd by the gladness of the
    river and the bright flow, I was refresh'd,
Just as you stand and lean on the rail, yet hurry
    with the swift current, I stood yet was
    hurried,
Just as you look on the numberless masts of
    ships and the thick-stemm'd pipes of
    steamboats, I look'd.

I too many and many a time cross'd the river of
    old,
Watched the Twelfth-month sea-gulls, saw them
    high in the air floating with motionless wings,
    oscillating their bodies,
Saw how the glistening yellow lit up parts of
    their bodies and left the rest in strong
    shadow,
Saw the slow-wheeling circles and the gradual
    edging toward the south,
Saw the reflection of the summer sky in the
    water,
Had my eyes dazzled by the shimmering track of
    beams,
Look'd at the fine centrifugal spokes of light
    round the shape of my head in the sunlit
    water,
Look'd on the haze on the hills southward and
    south-westward,

Look'd on the vapor as it flew in fleeces tinged
    with violet,
Look'd toward the lower bay to notice the
    vessels arriving,
Saw their approach, saw aboard those that were
    near me,
Saw the white sails of schooners and sloops, saw
    the ships at anchor,
The sailors at work in the rigging or out astride
    the spars,
The round masts, the swinging motion of the
    hulls, the slender serpentine pennants,
The large and small steamers in motion, the
    pilots in their pilothouses,
The white wake left by the passage, the quick
    tremulous whirl of the wheels,
The flags of all nations, the falling of them at
    sunset, The scallop-edged waves in the
    twilight, the ladled cups, the frolicsome crests
    and glistening,
The stretch afar growing dimmer and dimmer,
    the gray walls of the granite storehouses by
    the docks,
On the river the shadowy group, the big
    steam-tug closely flank'd on each side
    by the barges, the hay-boat, the belated
    lighter,
On the neighboring shore the fires from the
    foundry chimneys burning high and glaringly
    into the night,

Casting their flicker of black contrasted with
    wild red and yellow light over the tops of
    houses, and down into the clefts of streets.

4

These and all else were to me the same as they
    are to you,
I loved well those cities, loved well the stately
    and rapid river,
The men and women I saw were all near to me,
Others the same—others who look back on me
    because I look'd forward to them,
(The time will come, though I stop here to-day
    and to-night.)

5

What is it then between us?
What is the count of the scores or hundreds of
    years between us?

Whatever it is, it avails not—distance avails not,
    and place avails not,
I too lived, Brooklyn of ample hills was mine,
I too walk'd the streets of Manhattan island, and
    bathed in the waters around it,
I too felt the curious abrupt questionings stir
    within me,
In the day among crowds of people sometimes
    they came upon me,

In my walks home late at night or as I lay in my
    bed they came upon me,
I too had been struck from the float forever held
    in solution,
I too had receiv'd identity by my body,
That I was I knew was of my body, and what I
    should be I knew I should be of my body.

6

It is not upon you alone the dark patches fall,
The dark threw its patches down upon me
    also,
The best I had done seem'd to me blank and
    suspicious,
My great thoughts as I supposed them, were
    they not in reality meagre?
Nor is it you alone who know what it is to be
    evil,
I am he who knew what it was to be evil,
I too knitted the old knot of contrariety,
Blabb'd, blush'd, resented, lied, stole, grudg'd,
Had guile, anger, lust, hot wishes I dared not
    speak,
Was wayward, vain, greedy, shallow, sly,
    cowardly, malignant,
The wolf, the snake, the hog, not wanting in
    me.
The cheating look, the frivolous word, the
    adulterous wish, not wanting,

Refusals, hates, postponements, meanness,
    laziness, none of these wanting,
Was one with the rest, the days and haps of the
    rest,
Was call'd by my nighest name by clear loud
    voices of young men as they saw me
    approaching or passing,
Felt their arms on my neck as I stood, or the
    negligent leaning of their flesh against me as I
    sat,
Saw many I loved in the street or ferry-boat or
    public assembly, yet never told them a word,
Lived the same life with the rest, the same old
    laughing, gnawing, sleeping,
Play'd the part that still looks back on the actor
    or actress,
The same old role, the role that is what we make
    it, as great as we like,
Or as small as we like, or both great and small.

7

Closer yet I approach you,
What thought you have of me now, I had as
    much of you- I laid in my stores in advance,
I consider'd long and seriously of you before
    you were born.

Who was to know what should come home to
    me?
Who knows but I am enjoying this?

Who knows, for all the distance, but I am as
    good as looking at you now, for all you
    cannot see me?

8

Ah, what can ever be more stately and admirable
    to me than mast-hemm'd Manhattan?
River and sunset and scallop-edg'd waves of
    flood-tide?
The sea-gulls oscillating their bodies, the hay-
    boat in the twilight, and the belated lighter?
What gods can exceed these that clasp me by the
    hand, and with voices I love call me promptly
    and loudly by my nighest name as approach?
What is more subtle than this which ties me to
    the woman or man that looks in my face?
Which fuses me into you now, and pours my
    meaning into you?

We understand then do we not?
What I promis'd without mentioning it, have
    you not accepted?
What the study could not teach—what the
    preaching could not accomplish is
    accomplish'd, is it not?

9

Flow on, river! flow with the flood-tide, and ebb
    with the ebb-tide!
Frolic on, crested and scallop-edg'd waves!

Gorgeous clouds of the sunset! drench with
    your splendor me, or the men and women
    generations after me!
Cross from shore to shore, countless crowds of
    passengers!
Stand up, tall masts of Mannahatta! stand up,
    beautiful hills of Brooklyn!
Throb, baffled and curious brain! throw out
    questions and answers!
Suspend here and everywhere, eternal float of
    solution!
Gaze, loving and thirsting eyes, in the house or
    street or public assembly!
Sound out, voices of young men! loudly and
    musically call me by my nighest name!
Live, old life! play the part that looks back on
    the actor or actress!
Play the old role, the role that is great or small
    according as one makes it!
Consider, you who peruse me, whether I may
    not in unknown ways be looking upon you;
Be firm, rail over the river, to support those
    who lean idly, yet haste with the hasting
    current;
Fly on, sea-birds! fly sideways, or wheel in large
    circles high in the air;
Receive the summer sky, you water, and
    faithfully hold it till all downcast eyes have
    time to take it from you!

Diverge, fine spokes of light, from the shape of
my head, or any one's head, in the sunlit
water!
Come on, ships from the lower bay! pass up or
down, white-sail'd schooners, sloops, lighters!
Flaunt away, flags of all nations! be duly lower'd
at sunset!
Burn high your fires, foundry chimneys! cast
black shadows at nightfall! cast red and yellow
light over the tops of the houses!
Appearances, now or henceforth, indicate what
you are,
You necessary film, continue to envelop the
soul,
About my body for me, and your body for you,
be hung our divinest aromas,
Thrive, cities—bring your freight, bring your
shows, ample and sufficient rivers,
Expand, being than which none else is perhaps
more spiritual,
Keep your places, objects than which none else
is more lasting.

You have waited, you always wait, you dumb,
beautiful ministers,
We receive you with free sense at last, and are
insatiate henceforward,
Not you any more shall be able to foil us, or
withhold yourselves from us,

We use you, and do not cast you aside-we plant
you permanently within us,
We fathom you not—we love you—there is
perfection in you also,
You furnish your parts toward eternity,
Great or small, you furnish your parts toward
the soul.

Song of the Answerer

1

NOW list to my morning's romanza, I tell the
  signs of the Answerer,
To the cities and farms I sing as they spread in
  the sunshine before me.

A young man comes to me bearing a message
  from his brother,
How shall the young man know the whether
  and when of his brother?
Tell him to send me the signs. And I stand
  before the young man face to face, and take
  his right hand in my left hand and his left
  hand in my right hand,
And I answer for his brother and for men, and I
  answer for him that answers for all, and send
  these signs.

Him all wait for, him all yield up to, his word is
  decisive and final,
Him they accept, in him lave, in him perceive
  themselves as amid light,
Him they immerse and he immerses them.

Beautiful women, the haughtiest nations, laws,
  the landscape, people, animals,

The profound earth and its attributes and the
    unquiet ocean, (so tell I my morning's
    romanza,)
All enjoyments and properties and money, and
    whatever money will buy,
The best farms, others toiling and planting and
    he unavoidably reaps,
The noblest and costliest cities, others
    grading and building and he domiciles
    there,
Nothing for any one but what is for him,
    near and far are for him, the ships in the
    offing,
The perpetual shows and marches on land are
    for him if they are for anybody.

He puts things in their attitudes,
He puts to-day out of himself with plasticity
    and love,
He places his own times, reminiscences, parents,
    brothers and sisters, associations,
    employment, politics, so that the rest never
    shame them afterward, nor assume to
    command them.

He is the Answerer,
What can be answer'd he answers, and what
    cannot be answer'd he shows how it cannot
    be answer'd.

A man is a summons and challenge,
(It is vain to skulk- do you hear that mocking
   and laughter? do you hear the ironical
   echoes?)

Books, friendships, philosophers, priests, action,
   pleasure, pride, beat up and down seeking to
   give satisfaction,
He indicates the satisfaction, and indicates them
   that beat up and down also.

Whichever the sex, whatever the season or place,
   he may go freshly and gently and safely by
   day or by night,
He has the pass-key of hearts, to him the
   response of the prying of hands on the knobs.

His welcome is universal, the flow of beauty is
   not more welcome or universal than he is,
The person he favors by day or sleeps with at
   night is blessed.

Every existence has its idiom, every thing has an
   idiom and tongue,
He resolves all tongues into his own and
   bestows it upon men, and any man translates,
   and any man translates himself also,
One part does not counteract another part, he is
   the joiner, he sees how they join.

He says indifferently and alike How are you
    friend? to the President at his levee,
And he says Good-day my brother, to Cudge
    that hoes in the sugar-field,
And both understand him and know that his
    speech is right.

He walks with perfect ease in the capitol,
He walks among the Congress, and one
    Representative says to another, Here is our
    equal appearing and new.

Then the mechanics take him for a mechanic,
And the soldiers suppose him to be a
    soldier, and the sailors that he has follow'd
    the sea,
And the authors take him for an author, and the
    artists for an artist,
And the laborers perceive he could labor with
    them and love them,
No matter what the work is, that he is the one
    to follow it or has follow'd it,
No matter what the nation, that he might find
    his brothers and sisters there.

The English believe he comes of their English
    stock,
A Jew to the Jew he seems, a Russ to the Russ,
    usual and near, removed from none.

Whoever he looks at in the traveler's coffee-
house claims him,
The Italian or Frenchman is sure, the German is
sure, the Spaniard is sure, and the island
Cuban is sure,
The engineer, the deck-hand on the great lakes,
or on the Mississippi or St. Lawrence or
Sacramento, or Hudson or Paumanok sound,
claims him.

The gentleman of perfect blood acknowledges
his perfect blood,
The insulter, the prostitute, the angry person,
the beggar, see themselves in the ways of him,
he strangely transmutes them,
They are not vile any more, they hardly know
themselves they are so grown.

2

The indications and tally of time,
Perfect sanity shows the master among philosophs,
Time, always without break, indicates itself in
parts,
What always indicates the poet is the crowd of the
pleasant company of singers, and their words,
The words of the singers are the hours or
minutes of the light or dark, but the words of
the maker of poems are the general light and
dark,

The maker of poems settles justice, reality,
  immortality,
His insight and power encircle things and the
  human race,
He is the glory and extract thus far of things
  and of the human race.

The singers do not beget, only the Poet begets,
The singers are welcom'd, understood, appear
  often enough, but rare has the day been,
  likewise the spot, of the birth of the maker of
  poems, the Answerer,
(Not every century nor every five centuries has
  contain'd such a day, for all its names.)

The singers of successive hours of centuries may
  have ostensible names, but the name of each
  of them is one of the singers,
The name of each is, eye-singer, ear-singer, head-
  singer, sweet-singer, night-singer, parlor-singer,
  love-singer, weird-singer, or something else.

All this time and at all times wait the words of
  true poems,
The words of true poems do not merely
  please,
The true poets are not followers of beauty but
  the august masters of beauty;
The greatness of sons is the exuding of the
  greatness of mothers and fathers,

The words of true poems are the tuft and final
    applause of science.

Divine instinct, breadth of vision, the law of
    reason, health, rudeness of body,
    withdrawnness,
Gayety, sun-tan, air-sweetness, such are some of
    the words of poems.

The sailor and traveler underlie the maker of
    poems, the Answerer,
The builder, geometer, chemist, anatomist,
    phrenologist, artist, all these underlie the
    maker of poems, the Answerer.

The words of the true poems give you more
    than poems,
They give you to form for yourself poems,
    religions, politics, war, peace, behavior,
    histories, essays, daily life, and every thing else,
They balance ranks, colors, races, creeds, and
    the sexes,
They do not seek beauty, they are sought,
Forever touching them or close upon them
    follows beauty, longing, fain, love-sick.

They prepare for death, yet are they not the
    finish, but rather the outset,
They bring none to his or her terminus or to be
    content and full,

Whom they take they take into space to behold
    the birth of stars, to learn one of the
    meanings,
To launch off with absolute faith, to sweep
    through the ceaseless rings and never be quiet
    again.

Our Old Feuillage

ALWAYS our old feuillage!
Always Florida's green peninsula—always the
    priceless delta of Louisiana—always the
    cotton-fields of Alabama and Texas,
Always California's golden hills and hollows, and
    the silver mountains of New Mexico—always
    soft-breath'd Cuba,
Always the vast slope drain'd by the Southern
    sea, inseparable with the slopes drain'd by the
    Eastern and Western seas,
The area the eighty-third year of these States,
    the three and a half millions of square miles,
The eighteen thousand miles of sea-coast and
    bay-coast on the main, the thirty thousand
    miles of river navigation,
The seven millions of distinct families and the
    same number of dwellings—always these, and
    more, branching forth into numberless
    branches,
Always the free range and diversity—always the
    continent of Democracy;
Always the prairies, pastures, forests, vast cities,
    travelers, Kanada, the snows;
Always these compact lands tied at the hips with
    the belt stringing the huge oval lakes;

Always the West with strong native persons, the
    increasing density there, the habitans, friendly,
    threatening, ironical, scorning invaders;
All sights, South, North, East-all deeds,
    promiscuously done at all times,
All characters, movements, growths, a few
    noticed, myriads unnoticed,
Through Mannahatta's streets I walking, these
    things gathering,
On interior rivers by night in the glare of pine
    knots, steamboats wooding up,
Sunlight by day on the valley of the
    Susquehanna, and on the valleys of the
    Potomac and Rappahannock, and the valleys
    of the Roanoke and Delaware,
In their northerly wilds beasts of prey haunting
    the Adirondacks the hills, or lapping the
    Saginaw waters to drink,
In a lonesome inlet a sheldrake lost from the
    flock, sitting on the water rocking silently,
In farmers' barns oxen in the stable, their
    harvest labor done, they rest standing, they
    are too tired,
Afar on arctic ice the she-walrus lying drowsily
    while her cubs play around,
The hawk sailing where men have not yet sail'd,
    the farthest polar sea, ripply, crystalline, open,
    beyond the floes,
White drift spooning ahead where the ship in
    the tempest dashes,

On solid land what is done in cities as the bells
strike midnight together,
In primitive woods the sounds there also
sounding, the howl of the wolf, the scream of
the panther, and the hoarse bellow of the elk,
In winter beneath the hard blue ice of
Moosehead lake, in summer visible through
the clear waters, the great trout swimming,
In lower latitudes in warmer air in the Carolinas
the large black buzzard floating slowly high
beyond the tree tops,
Below, the red cedar festoon'd with tylandria,
the pines and cypresses growing out of the
white sand that spreads far and flat,
Rude boats descending the big Pedee, climbing
plants, parasites with color'd flowers and
berries enveloping huge trees,
The waving drapery on the live-oak trailing long
and low, noiselessly waved by the wind,
The camp of Georgia wagoners just after dark,
the supper-fires and the cooking and eating
by whites and negroes,
Thirty or forty great wagons, the mules, cattle,
horses, feeding from troughs,
The shadows, gleams, up under the leaves of the
old sycamore-trees, the flames with the black
smoke from the pitch-pine curling and rising;
Southern fishermen fishing, the sounds and
inlets of North Carolina's coast, the shad-
fishery and the herring-fishery, the large

sweep-seines, the windlasses on shore work'd
    by horses, the clearing, curing, and packing-
    houses;
Deep in the forest in piney woods turpentine
    dropping from the incisions in the trees, there
    are the turpentine works,
There are the negroes at work in good health,
    the ground in all directions is cover'd with
    pine straw;
In Tennessee and Kentucky slaves busy in the
    coalings, at the forge, by the furnace-blaze, or
    at the corn-shucking,
In Virginia, the planter's son returning after a
    long absence, joyfully welcom'd and kiss'd by
    the aged mulatto nurse,
On rivers boatmen safely moor'd at nightfall in
    their boats under shelter of high banks,
Some of the younger men dance to the sound of
    the banjo or fiddle, others sit on the gunwale
    smoking and talking;
Late in the afternoon the mocking-bird, the
    American mimic, singing in the Great Dismal
    Swamp,
There are the greenish waters, the resinous odor,
    the plenteous moss, the cypress-tree, and the
    juniper-tree;
Northward, young men of Mannahatta, the
    target company from an excursion returning
    home at evening, the musket-muzzles all bear
    bunches of flowers presented by women;

Children at play, or on his father's lap a young
  boy fallen asleep, (how his lips move! how he
  smiles in his sleep!)
The scout riding on horseback over the plains
  west of the Mississippi, he ascends a knoll and
  sweeps his eyes around;
California life, the miner, bearded, dress'd in his
  rude costume, the stanch California friendship,
  the sweet air, the graves one in passing meets
  solitary just aside the horse-path;
Down in Texas the cotton-field, the negro-
  cabins, drivers driving mules or oxen before
  rude carts, cotton bales piled on banks and
  wharves;
Encircling all, vast-darting up and wide, the
  American Soul, with equal hemispheres, one
  Love, one Dilation or Pride;
In arriere the peace-talk with the Iroquois the
  aborigines, the calumet, the pipe of good-will,
  arbitration, and indorsement,
The sachem blowing the smoke first toward the
  sun and then toward the earth,
The drama of the scalp-dance enacted with
  painted faces and guttural exclamations,
The setting out of the war-party, the long and
  stealthy march,
The single file, the swinging hatchets, the
  surprise and slaughter of enemies;
All the acts, scenes, ways, persons, attitudes of
  these States, reminiscences, institutions,

All these States compact, every square mile of
    these States without excepting a particle;
Me pleas'd, rambling in lanes and country fields,
    Paumanok's fields,
Observing the spiral flight of two little yellow
    butterflies shuffling between each other,
    ascending high in the air,
The darting swallow, the destroyer of insects,
    the fall traveler southward but returning
    northward early in the spring,
The country boy at the close of the day driving
    the herd of cows and shouting to them as
    they loiter to browse by the roadside,
The city wharf, Boston, Philadelphia, Baltimore,
    Charleston, New Orleans, San Francisco,
The departing ships when the sailors heave at
    the capstan;
Evening-me in my room—the setting sun,
The setting summer sun shining in my open
    window, showing the swarm of flies,
    suspended, balancing in the air in the centre
    of the room, darting athwart, up and down,
    casting swift shadows in specks on the
    opposite wall where the shine is;
The athletic American matron speaking in public
    to crowds of listeners,
Males, females, immigrants, combinations, the
    copiousness, the individuality of the States,
    each for itself—the moneymakers,

Factories, machinery, the mechanical forces, the
windlass, lever, pulley, all certainties,
The certainty of space, increase, freedom,
futurity,
In space the sporades, the scatter'd islands, the
stars- on the firm earth, the lands, my lands,
O lands! all so dear to me—what you are,
(whatever it is,) I putting it at random in
these songs, become a part of that, whatever
it is,
Southward there, I screaming, with wings slow
flapping, with the myriads of gulls wintering
along the coasts of Florida,
Otherways there atwixt the banks of the
Arkansaw, the Rio Grande, the Nueces, the
Brazos, the Tombigbee, the Red River, the
Saskatchawan or the Osage, I with the spring
waters laughing and skipping and running,
Northward, on the sands, on some shallow bay
of Paumanok, I with parties of snowy herons
wading in the wet to seek worms and aquatic
plants,
Retreating, triumphantly twittering, the king-
bird, from piercing the crow with its bill, for
amusement-and I triumphantly twittering,
The migrating flock of wild geese alighting in
autumn to refresh themselves, the body of the
flock feed, the sentinels outsidemove around
with erect heads watching, and are from time

to time reliev'd by other sentinels—and
I feeding and taking turns with the
rest,
In Kanadian forests the moose, large as an
ox, corner'd by hunters, rising desperately
on his hind-feet, and plunging with his
fore-feet, the hoofs as sharp as knives—and I,
plunging at the hunters, corner'd and
desperate,
In the Mannahatta, streets, piers, shipping,
store-houses, and the countless workmen
working in the shops,
And I too of the Mannahatta, singing thereof-
and no less in myself than the whole of the
Mannahatta in itself,
Singing the song of These, my ever-united
lands-my body no more inevitably united,
part to part, and made out of a thousand
diverse contributions one identity, any more
than my lands are inevitably united and made
ONE IDENTITY;
Nativities, climates, the grass of the great
pastoral Plains,
Cities, labors, death, animals, products, war,
good and evil—these me,
These affording, in all their particulars, the old
feuillage to me and to America, how can I do
less than pass the clew of the union of them,
to afford the like to you?

Whoever you are! how can I but offer you
   divine leaves, that you also be eligible as I am?
How can I but as here chanting, invite you for
   yourself to collect bouquets of the
   incomparable feuillage of these States?

A Song of Joys

O TO make the most jubilant song!
Full of music-full of manhood, womanhood,
    infancy!
Full of common employments—full of grain and
    trees.

O for the voices of animals—O for the swiftness
    and balance of fishes!
O for the dropping of raindrops in a song!
O for the sunshine and motion of waves in a song!

O the joy of my spirit—it is uncaged—it darts
    like lightning!
It is not enough to have this globe or a certain
    time,
I will have thousands of globes and all time.

O the engineer's joys! to go with a locomotive!
To hear the hiss of steam, the merry shriek, the
    steam-whistle, the laughing locomotive!
To push with resistless way and speed off in the
    distance.

O the gleesome saunter over fields and hillsides!
The leaves and flowers of the commonest weeds,
    the moist fresh stillness of the woods,

The exquisite smell of the earth at daybreak, and
    all through the forenoon.

O the horseman's and horsewoman's joys!
The saddle, the gallop, the pressure upon the
    seat, the cool gurgling by the ears and hair.

O the fireman's joys!
I hear the alarm at dead of night,
I hear bells, shouts! I pass the crowd, I run!
The sight of the flames maddens me with
    pleasure.

O the joy of the strong-brawn'd fighter,
    towering in the arena in perfect condition,
    conscious of power, thirsting to meet his
    opponent.

O the joy of that vast elemental sympathy
    which only the human soul is capable of
    generating and emitting in steady and
    limitless floods.

O the mother's joys!
The watching, the endurance, the precious love,
    the anguish, the patiently yielded life.

O the of increase, growth, recuperation,
The joy of soothing and pacifying, the joy of
    concord and harmony.

O to go back to the place where I was born,
To hear the birds sing once more,
To ramble about the house and barn and over
the fields once more,
And through the orchard and along the old
lanes once more.

O to have been brought up on bays, lagoons,
creeks, or along the coast,
To continue and be employ'd there all my life,
The briny and damp smell, the shore, the salt
weeds exposed at low water,
The work of fishermen, the work of the
eel-fisher and clam-fisher;
I come with my clam-rake and spade, I come
with my eel-spear,
Is the tide out? I Join the group of clam-diggers
on the flats,
I laugh and work with them, I joke at my work
like a mettlesome young man;
In winter I take my eel-basket and eel-spear and
travel out on foot on the ice—I have a small
axe to cut holes in the ice,
Behold me well-clothed going gayly or
returning in the afternoon, my brood of
tough boys accompanying me,
My brood of grown and part-grown boys, who
love to be with no one else so well as they
love to be with me,

By day to work with me, and by night to sleep
with me.

Another time in warm weather out in a boat, to
lift the lobster-pots where they are sunk with
heavy stones, (I know the buoys,)
O the sweetness of the Fifth-month morning
upon the water as I row just before sunrise
toward the buoys,
I pull the wicker pots up slantingly, the dark
green lobsters are desperate with their claws
as I take them out, I insert wooden pegs in
the 'oints of their pincers,

I go to all the places one after another, and then
row back to the shore,
There in a huge kettle of boiling water the
lobsters shall be boil'd till their color becomes
scarlet.

Another time mackerel-taking,
Voracious, mad for the hook, near the surface,
they seem to fill the water for miles;
Another time fishing for rock-fish in Chesapeake
bay, I one of the brown-faced crew;
Another time trailing for blue-fish off
Paumanok, I stand with braced body,
My left foot is on the gunwale, my right arm
throws far out the coils of slender rope,

In sight around me the quick veering and
　　darting of fifty skiffs, my companions.

O boating on the rivers,
The voyage down the St. Lawrence, the superb
　　scenery, the steamers,
The ships sailing, the Thousand Islands, the
　　occasional timber-raft and the raftsmen with
　　long-reaching sweep-oars,
The little huts on the rafts, and the stream of
　　smoke when they cook supper at evening.

(O something pernicious and dread!
Something far away from a puny and pious
　　life!
Something unproved! something in a trance!
Something escaped from the anchorage and
　　driving free.)

O to work in mines, or forging iron,
Foundry casting, the foundry itself, the rude
　　high roof, the ample and shadow'd space,
The furnace, the hot liquid pour'd out and
　　running.

O to resume the joys of the soldier!
To feel the presence of a brave commanding
　　officer—to feel his sympathy!
To behold his calmness—to be warm'd in the
　　rays of his smile!

To go to battle—to hear the bugles play and the
    drums beat!
To hear the crash of artillery—to see the
    glittering of the bayonets and musket-barrels
    in the sun!

To see men fall and die and not complain!
To taste the savage taste of blood—to be so
    devilish!
To gloat so over the wounds and deaths of the
    enemy.

O the whaleman's joys! O I cruise my old cruise
    again!
I feel the ship's motion under me, I feel the
    Atlantic breezes fanning me,
I hear the cry again sent down from the mast-
    head, There—she blows!
Again I spring up the rigging to look with
    the rest—we descend, wild with excitement,
I leap in the lower'd boat, we row toward our
    prey where he lies,
We approach stealthy and silent, I see the
    mountainous mass, lethargic, basking,
I see the harpooneer standing up, I see the
    weapon dart from his vigorous arm;
O swift again far out in the ocean the wounded
    whale, settling, running to windward, tows me,
Again I see him rise to breathe, we row close
    again,

I see a lance driven through his side, press'd
    deep, turn'd in the wound,
Again we back off, I see him settle again, the life
    is leaving him fast,
As he rises he spouts blood, I see him swim in
    circles narrower and narrower, swiftly cutting
    the water—I see him die,
He gives one convulsive leap in the center of the
    circle, and then falls flat and still in the bloody
    foam.

O the old manhood of me, my noblest joy of all!
My children and grand-children, my white hair
    and beard,
My largeness, calmness, majesty, out of the long
    stretch of my life.

O ripen'd joy of womanhood! O happiness at last!
I am more than eighty years of age, I am the
    most venerable mother,
How clear is my mind—how all people draw
    nigh to me!
What attractions are these beyond any before?
    what bloom more than the bloom of youth?
What beauty is this that descends upon me and
    rises out of me?

O the orator's joys!
To inflate the chest, to roll the thunder of the
    voice out from the ribs and throat,

To make the people rage, weep, hate, desire,
with yourself,
To lead America-to quell America with a great
tongue.

O the joy of my soul leaning pois'd on itself,
receiving identity through materials and
loving them, observing characters and
absorbing them,
My soul vibrated back to me from them, from
sight, hearing, touch, reason, articulation,
comparison, memory, and the like,
The real life of my senses and flesh transcending
my senses and flesh,
My body done with materials, my sight done
with my material eyes,
Proved to me this day beyond cavil that it is not
my material eyes which finally see,
Nor my material body which finally loves, walks,
laughs, shouts, embraces, procreates.

O the farmer's joys!
Ohioan's, Illinoisian's, Wisconsinese',
Kanadian's, Iowan's, Kansian's, Missourian's,
Oregonese' joys!
To rise at peep of day and pass forth nimbly to
work,
To plough land in the fall for winter-sown
crops,
To plough land in the spring for maize,

To train orchards, to graft the trees, to gather
    apples in the fall.

O to bathe in the swimming-bath, or in a good
    place along shore,
To splash the water! to walk ankle-deep, or race
    naked along the shore.

O to realize space!
The plenteousness of all, that there are no
    bounds,
To emerge and be of the sky, of the sun and
    moon and flying clouds, as one with them.

O the joy a manly self-hood!
To be servile to none, to defer to none, not to
    any tyrant known or unknown,
To walk with erect carriage, a step springy and
    elastic,
To look with calm gaze or with a flashing eye,
To speak with a full and sonorous voice out of a
    broad chest,
To confront with your personality all the other
    personalities of the earth.

Knowist thou the excellent joys of youth?
Joys of the dear companions and of the merry
    word and laughing face?
Joy of the glad light-beaming day, joy of the
    wide-breath'd games?

Joy of sweet music, joy of the lighted ball-room
and the dancers?
Joy of the plenteous dinner, strong carouse and
drinking?

Yet O my soul supreme!
Knowist thou the joys of pensive thought?
Joys of the free and lonesome heart, the tender,
gloomy heart?
Joys of the solitary walk, the spirit bow'd yet
proud, the suffering and the struggle?
The agonistic throes, the ecstasies, joys of the
solemn musings day or night?
Joys of the thought of Death, the great spheres
Time and Space?
Prophetic joys of better, loftier love's ideals, the
divine wife, the sweet, eternal, perfect
comrade?
Joys all thine own undying one, joys worthy
thee O soul.

O while I live to be the ruler of life, not a slave,
To meet life as a powerful conqueror,
No fumes, no ennui, no more complaints or
scornful criticisms,
To these proud laws of the air, the water and the
ground, proving my interior soul
impregnable,
And nothing exterior shall ever take command
of me.

For not life's joys alone I sing, repeating—the
joy of death!
The beautiful touch of Death, soothing and
benumbing a few moments, for reasons,
Myself discharging my excrementitious body to
be burn'd, or render'd to powder, or buried,
My real body doubtless left to me for other
spheres,
My voided body nothing more to me, returning
to the purifications, further offices, eternal
uses of the earth.

O to attract by more than attraction!
How it is I know not—yet behold! the
something which obeys none of the rest,
It is offensive, never defensive—yet how
magnetic it draws.

O to struggle against great odds, to meet
enemies undaunted!
To be entirely alone with them, to find how
much one can stand!
To look strife, torture, prison, popular odium,
face to face!
To mount the scaffold, to advance to the
muzzles of guns with perfect nonchalance!
To be indeed a God!

O to sail to sea in a ship!
To leave this steady unendurable land,

To leave the tiresome sameness of the streets,
    the sidewalks and the houses,
To leave you O you solid motionless land, and
    entering a ship,
To sail and sail and sail!

O to have life henceforth a poem of new joys!
To dance, clap hands, exult, shout, skip, leap,
    roll on, float on!
To be a sailor of the world bound for all ports,
A ship itself, (see indeed these sails I spread to
    the sun and air,)
A swift and swelling ship full of rich words, full
    of joys.

Song of the Broad-Axe

1

WEAPON shapely, naked, wan,
Head from the mother's bowels drawn,
Wooded flesh and metal bone, limb only one
   and lip only one,
Gray-blue leaf by red-heat grown, helve
   produced from a little seed sown,
Resting the grass amid and upon,
To be lean'd and to lean on.

Strong shapes and attributes of strong shapes,
   masculine trades, sights and sounds.
Long varied train of an emblem, dabs of music,
Fingers of the organist skipping staccato over
   the keys of the great organ.

2

Welcome are all earth's lands, each for its kind,
Welcome are lands of pine and oak,
Welcome are lands of the lemon and fig,
Welcome are lands of gold,
Welcome are lands of wheat and maize, welcome
   those of the grape,
Welcome are lands of sugar and rice,
Welcome the cotton-lands, welcome those of the
   white potato and sweet potato,

Welcome are mountains, flats, sands, forests,
    prairies,
Welcome the rich borders of rivers, table-lands,
    openings,
Welcome the measureless grazing-lands,
    welcome the teeming soil of orchards, flax,
    honey, hemp;
Welcome just as much the other more
    hard-faced lands,
Lands rich as lands of gold or wheat and fruit
    lands,
Lands of mines, lands of the manly and rugged
    ores,
Lands of coal, copper, lead, tin, zinc,
Lands of iron-lands of the make of the axe.

3

The log at the wood-pile, the axe supported
    by it,
The sylvan hut, the vine over the doorway, the
    space clear'd for garden,
The irregular tapping of rain down on the leaves
    after the storm is lull'd,
The walling and moaning at intervals, the
    thought of the sea,
The thought of ships struck in the storm and
    put on their beam ends, and the cutting away
    of masts,
The sentiment of the huge timbers of
    old-fashion'd houses and barns,

The remember'd print or narrative, the voyage
   at a venture of men, families, goods,
The disembarkation, the founding of a new city,
The voyage of those who sought a New England
   and found it, the outset anywhere,
The settlements of the Arkansas, Colorado,
   Ottawa, Willamette,
The slow progress, the scant fare, the axe, rifle,
   saddle-bags;
The beauty of all adventurous and daring
   persons,
The beauty of wood-boys and wood-men with
   their clear untrimm'd faces,
The beauty of independence, departure, actions
   that rely on themselves,
The American contempt for statutes and
   ceremonies, the boundless impatience of
   restraint,
The loose drift of character, the inkling through
   random types, the solidification;
The butcher in the slaughter-house, the hands
   aboard schooners and sloops, the raftsman,
   the pioneer,
Lumbermen in their winter camp, daybreak in
   the woods, stripes of snow on the limbs of
   trees, the occasional snapping,
The glad clear sound of one's own voice, the
   merry song, the natural life of the woods, the
   strong day's work,

The blazing fire at night, the sweet taste of
    supper, the talk, the bed of hemlock-boughs
    and the bear-skin;
The house-builder at work in cities or anywhere,
The preparatory jointing, squaring, sawing,
    mortising,
The hoist-up of beams, the push of them in
    their places, laying them regular,
Setting the studs by their tenons in the mortises
    according as they were prepared,
The blows of mallets and hammers, the attitudes
    of the men, their curv'd limbs,
Bending, standing, astride the beams, driving in
    pins, holding on by posts and braces,
The hook'd arm over the plate, the other arm
    wielding the axe,
The floor-men forcing the planks close to be nail'd,
Their postures bringing their weapons
    downward on the bearers,
The echoes resounding through the vacant
    building:
The huge storehouse carried up in the city well
    under way,
The six framing-men, two in the middle and two
    at each end, carefully bearing on their
    shoulders a heavy stick for a cross-beam,
The crowded line of masons with trowels in their
    right hands rapidly laying the long side-wall,
    two hundred feet from front to rear,

The flexible rise and fall of backs, the continual
    click of the trowels striking the bricks,
The bricks one after another each laid so
    workmanlike in its place, and set with a knock
    of the trowel-handle,
The piles of materials, the mortar on the
    mortar-boards, and the steady replenishing by
    the hod-men;
Spar-makers in the spar-yard, the swarming row
    of well-grown apprentices,
The swing of their axes on the square-hew'd log
    shaping it toward the shape of a mast,
The brisk short crackle of the steel driven
    slantingly into the pine,
The butter-color'd chips flying off in great flakes
    and slivers,
The limber motion of brawny young arms and
    hips in easy costumes,
The constructor of wharves, bridges, piers,
    bulk-heads, floats, stays against the sea;
The city fireman, the fire that suddenly bursts
    forth in the close-pack'd square,
The arriving engines, the hoarse shouts, the
    nimble stepping and daring,
The strong command through the fire-trumpets,
    the falling in line, the rise and fall of the arms
    forcing the water,
The slender, spasmic, blue-white jets, the
    bringing to bear of the hooks and ladders and
    their execution,

The crash and cut away of connecting
  wood-work, or through floors if the fire
  smoulders under them,
The crowd with their lit faces watching, the
  glare and dense shadows;
The forger at his forge-furnace and the user of
  iron after him,
The maker of the axe large and small, and the
  welder and temperer,
The chooser breathing his breath on the cold
  steel and trying the edge with his thumb,
The one who clean-shapes the handle and sets it
  firmly in the socket;
The shadowy processions of the portraits of the
  past users also,
The primal patient mechanics, the architects and
  engineers,
The far-off Assyrian edifice and Mizra edifice,
The Roman lictors preceding the consuls,
The antique European warrior with his axe in
  combat,
The uplifted arm, the clatter of blows on the
  helmeted head,
The death-howl, the limpsy tumbling body, the
  rush of friend and foe thither,
The siege of revolted lieges determin'd for
  liberty,
The summons to surrender, the battering at
  castle gates, the truce and parley,
The sack of an old city in its time,

The bursting in of mercenaries and bigots
    tumultuously and disorderly,
Roar, flames, blood, drunkenness, madness,
Goods freely rifled from houses and temples,
    screams of women in the gripe of brigands,
Craft and thievery of camp-followers, men
    running, old persons despairing,
The hell of war, the cruelties of creeds,
The list of all executive deeds and words just or
    unjust,
The power of personality just or unjust.

4

Muscle and pluck forever!
What invigorates life invigorates death,
And the dead advance as much as the living
    advance,
And the future is no more uncertain than the
    present,
For the roughness of the earth and of man
    encloses as much as the delicatesse of the
    earth and of man,
And nothing endures but personal qualities.

What do you think endures?
Do you think a great city endures?
Or a teeming manufacturing state? or a prepared
    constitution? or the best built steamships?
Or hotels of granite and iron? or any chef-
    d'oeuvres of engineering, forts, armaments?

Away! these are not to be cherish'd for
    themselves,
They fill their hour, the dancers dance, the
    musicians play for them,
The show passes, all does well enough of course,
All does very well till one flash of defiance.

A great city is that which has the greatest men
    and women,
If it be a few ragged huts it is still the greatest
    city in the whole world.

5

The place where a great city stands is not the
    place of stretch'd wharves, docks,
    manufactures, deposits of produce merely,
Nor the place of ceaseless salutes of new-comers
    or the anchor-lifters of the departing,
Nor the place of the tallest and costliest
    buildings or shops selling goods from the rest
    of the earth,
Nor the place of the best libraries and schools,
    nor the place where money is plentiest,
Nor the place of the most numerous population.

Where the city stands with the brawniest breed
    of orators and bards,
Where the city stands that is belov'd by these,
    and loves them in return and understands
    them,

Where no monuments exist to heroes but in the
common words and deeds,
Where thrift is in its place, and prudence is in its
place,
Where the men and women think lightly of the
laws,
Where the slave ceases, and the master of slaves
ceases,
Where the populace rise at once against the
never-ending audacity of elected persons,
Where fierce men and women pour forth as the
sea to the whistle of death pours its sweeping
and unript waves,
Where outside authority enters always after the
precedence of inside authority,
Where the citizen is always the head and ideal,
and President, Mayor, Governor, and what
not, are agents for pay,
Where children are taught to be laws to
themselves, and to depend on themselves,
Where equanimity is illustrated in affairs,
Where speculations on the soul are encouraged,
Where women walk in public processions in the
streets the same as the men,
Where they enter the public assembly and take
places the same as the men;
Where the city of the faithfulest friends stands,
Where the city of the cleanliness of the sexes
stands,
Where the city of the healthiest fathers stands,

Where the city of the best-bodied mothers stands,
There the great city stands.

6

How beggarly appear arguments before a defiant
    deed!
How the floridness of the materials of cities
    shrivels before a man's or woman's look!

All waits or goes by default till a strong being
    appears;
A strong being is the proof of the race and of
    the ability of the universe,
When he or she appears materials are overaw'd,
The dispute on the soul stops,
The old customs and phrases are confronted,
    turn'd back, or laid away.

What is your money-making now? what can it
    do now?
What is your respectability now?
What are your theology, tuition, society,
    traditions, statute-books, now?
Where are your jibes of being now?
Where are your cavils about the soul now?

7

A sterile landscape covers the ore, there is as
    good as the best for all the forbidding
    appearance,

There is the mine, there are the miners,
The forge-furnace is there, the melt is
accomplish'd, the hammersmen are at hand
with their tongs and hammers,
What always served and always serves is at hand.

Than this nothing has better served, it has
served all,
Served the fluent-tongued and subtle-sensed
Greek, and long ere the Greek,
Served in building the buildings that last longer
than any,
Served the Hebrew, the Persian, the most
ancient Hindustanee,
Served the mound-raiser on the Mississippi,
served those whose relics remain in Central
America,
Served Albic temples in woods or on plains, with
unhewn pillars and the druids,
Served the artificial clefts, vast, high, silent, on
the snow-cover'd hills of Scandinavia,
Served those who time out of mind made on the
granite walls rough sketches of the sun,
moon, stars, ships, ocean waves,
Served the paths of the irruptions of the Goths,
served the pastoral tribes and nomads,
Served the long distant Kelt, served the hardy
pirates of the Baltic,
Served before any of those the venerable and
harmless men of Ethiopia,

Served the making of helms for the galleys of
pleasure and the making of those for war,
Served all great works on land and all great
works on the sea,
For the mediaeval ages and before the mediaeval
ages,
Served not the living only then as now, but
served the dead.

8

I see the European headsman,
He stands mask'd, clothed in red, with huge legs
and strong naked arms,
And leans on a ponderous axe.

(Whom have you slaughter'd lately European
headsman?
Whose is that blood upon you so wet and
sticky?)

I see the clear sunsets of the martyrs,
I see from the scaffolds the descending
ghosts,
Ghosts of dead lords, uncrown'd ladies,
impeach'd ministers, rejected kings,
Rivals, traitors, poisoners, disgraced chieftains
and the rest.

I see those who in any land have died for the
good cause,

The seed is spare, nevertheless the crop shall
    never run out,
(Mind you O foreign kings, O priests, the crop
    shall never run out.)

I see the blood wash'd entirely away from the
    axe,
Both blade and helve are clean,
They spirt no more the blood of European
    nobles, they clasp no more the necks of
    queens.

I see the headsman withdraw and become
    useless,
I see the scaffold untrodden and mouldy, I see
    no longer any axe upon it,

I see the mighty and friendly emblem of the
    power of my own race, the newest, largest
    race.

9

(America! I do not vaunt my love for you,
I have what I have.)

The axe leaps!
The solid forest gives fluid utterances,
They tumble forth, they rise and form,
Hut, tent, landing, survey,
Flail, plough, pick, crowbar, spade,

Shingle, rail, prop, wainscot, lamb, lath, panel,
	gable,
Citadel, ceiling, saloon, academy, organ,
	exhibition-house, library,
Cornice, trellis, pilaster, balcony, window, turret,
	porch,
Hoe, rake, pitchfork, pencil, wagon, staff, saw,
	jack-plane, mallet, wedge, rounce,
Chair, tub, hoop, table, wicket, vane, sash,
	floor,
Work-box, chest, string'd instrument, boat,
	frame, and what not,
Capitols of States, and capitol of the nation of
	States,
Long stately rows in avenues, hospitals for
	orphans or for the poor or sick,
Manhattan steamboats and clippers taking the
	measure of all seas.

The shapes arise!
Shapes of the using of axes anyhow, and the
	users and all that neighbors them,
Cutters down of wood and haulers of it to the
	Penobscot or Kenebec,
Dwellers in cabins among the Californian
	mountains or by the little lakes, or on the
	Columbia,
Dwellers south on the banks of the Gila or Rio
	Grande, friendly gatherings, the characters
	and fun,

Dwellers along the St. Lawrence, or north in
  Kanada, or down by the Yellowstone, dwellers
  on coasts and off coasts,
Seal-fishers, whalers, arctic seamen breaking
  passages through the ice.

The shapes arise!
Shapes of factories, arsenals, foundries, markets,
Shapes of the two-threaded tracks of railroads,
Shapes of the sleepers of bridges, vast
  frameworks, girders, arches,
Shapes of the fleets of barges, tows, lake and
  canal craft, river craft,
Ship-yards and dry-docks along the Eastern and
  Western seas, and in many a bay and by-place,
The live-oak kelsons, the pine planks, the spars,
  the hackmatack-roots for knees,
The ships themselves on their ways, the tiers of
  scaffolds, the workmen busy outside and
  inside,
The tools lying around, the great auger and little
  auger, the adze, bolt, line, square, gouge, and
  bead-plane.

10

The shapes arise!
The shape measur'd, saw'd, jack'd, join'd,
  stain'd,
The coffin-shape for the dead to lie within in his
  shroud,

The shape got out in posts, in the bedstead
  posts, in the posts of the bride's bed,
The shape of the little trough, the shape of the
  rockers beneath, the shape of the babe's
  cradle,
The shape of the floor-planks, the floor-planks
  for dancers' feet,
The shape of the planks of the family home, the
  home of the friendly parents and children,
The shape of the roof of the home of the happy
  young man and woman, the roof over the
  well-married young man and woman,
The roof over the supper joyously cook'd by the
  chaste wife, and joyously eaten by the chaste
  husband, content after his day's work.

The shapes arise!
The shape of the prisoner's place in the court-
  room, and of him or her seated in the place,
The shape of the liquor-bar lean'd against by the
  young rum-drinker and the old rum-drinker,
The shape of the shamed and angry stairs trod
  by sneaking foot-steps,
The shape of the sly settee, and the adulterous
  unwholesome couple,
The shape of the gambling-board with its
  devilish winnings and losings,
The shape of the step-ladder for the convicted
  and sentenced murderer, the murderer with
  haggard face and pinion'd arms,

The sheriff at hand with his deputies, the silent
    and white-lipp'd crowd, the dangling of the
    rope.

The shapes arise!
Shapes of doors giving many exits and entrances,
The door passing the dissever'd friend flush'd
    and in haste,
The door that admits good news and bad news,
The door whence the son left home confident
    and puff'd up,
The door he enter'd again from a long and
    scandalous absence, diseas'd, broken down,
    without innocence, without means.

11

Her shape arises,
She less guarded than ever, yet more guarded
    than ever,
The gross and soil'd she moves among do not
    make her gross and soil'd,
She knows the thoughts as she passes, nothing is
    conceal'd from her,
She is none the less considerate or friendly
    therefor,
She is the best belov'd, it is without exception,
    she has no reason to fear and she does not
    fear,
Oaths, quarrels, hiccupp'd songs, smutty
    expressions, are idle to her as she passes,

She is silent, she is possess'd of herself, they do
　　not offend her,
She receives them as the laws of Nature receive
　　them, she is strong,
She too is a law of Nature—there is no law
　　stronger than she is.

12

The main shapes arise!
Shapes of Democracy total, result of centuries,
Shapes ever projecting other shapes,
Shapes of turbulent manly cities,
Shapes of the friends and home-givers of the
　　whole earth,
Shapes bracing the earth and braced with the
　　whole earth.

Song of the Exposition

1

(AH little recks the laborer,
How near his work is holding him to God,
The loving Laborer through space and time.)

After all not to create only, or found only,
But to bring perhaps from afar what is already
    founded,
To give it our own identity, average, limitless,
    free,
To fill the gross the torpid bulk with vital
    religious fire,
Not to repel or destroy so much as accept, fuse,
    rehabilitate,
To obey as well as command, to follow more
    than to lead,
These also are the lessons of our New World;
While how little the New after all, how much
    the Old, Old World!

Long and long has the grass been growing,
Long and long has the rain been falling,
Long has the globe been rolling round.

2

Come Muse migrate from Greece and Ionia,
Cross out please those immensely overpaid
    accounts,
That matter of Troy and Achilles' wrath, and
    AEneas', Odysseus' wanderings,
Placard "Removed" and "To Let" on the rocks
    of your snowy Parnassus,
Repeat at Jerusalem, place the notice high on
    Jaffa's gate and on Mount Moriah,
The same on the walls of your German, French
    and Spanish castles, and Italian collections,
For know a better, fresher, busier sphere, a wide,
    untried domain awaits, demands you.

3

Responsive to our summons,
Or rather to her long-nurs'd inclination,
Join'd with an irresistible, natural gravitation,
She comes! I hear the rustling of her gown,
I scent the odor of her breath's delicious
    fragrance,
I mark her step divine, her curious eyes
    a-turning, rolling,
Upon this very scene.

The dame of dames! can I believe then,
Those ancient temples, sculptures classic, could
    none of them retain her?

Nor shades of Virgil and Dante, nor myriad
    memories, poems, old associations,
    magnetize, and hold on to her?
But that she's left them all—and here?

Yes, if you will allow me to say so,
I, my friends, if you do not, can plainly see her,
The same undying soul of earth's, activity's,
    beauty's, heroism's expression,
Out from her evolutions hither come, ended the
    strata of her former themes,
Hidden and cover'd by to-day's, foundation of
    to-day's,
Ended, deceas'd through time, her voice by
    Castaly's fountain,
Silent the broken-lipp'd Sphynx in Egypt, silent
    all those century-baffling tombs,
Ended for aye the epics of Asia's, Europe's
    helmeted warriors, ended the primitive call of
    the muses,
Calliope's call forever closed, Clio, Melpomene,
    Thalia dead,
Ended the stately rhythmus of Una and Oriana,
    ended the quest of the holy Graal,
Jerusalem a handful of ashes blown by the wind,
    extinct,
The Crusaders' streams of shadowy midnight
    troops sped with the sunrise,
Amadis, Tancred, utterly gone, Charlemagne,
    Roland, Oliver gone,

Palmerin, ogre, departed, vanish'd the turrets
    that Usk from its waters reflected,
Arthur vanish'd with all his knights, Merlin and
    Lancelot and Galahad, all gone, dissolv'd
    utterly like an exhalation;
Pass'd! pass'd! for us, forever pass'd, that once
    so mighty world, now void, inanimate,
    phantom world,
Embroider'd, dazzling, foreign world, with all
    its gorgeous legends, myths,
Its kings and castles proud, its priests and
    warlike lords and courtly dames,
Pass'd to its charnel vault, coffin'd with crown
    and armor on,
Blazon'd with Shakspere's purple page,
And dirged by Tennyson's sweet sad rhyme.

I say I see, my friends, if you do not, the
    illustrious emigre, (having it is true in her day,
    although the same, changed, journey'd
    considerable,)
Making directly for this rendezvous, vigorously
    clearing a path for herself, striding through
    the confusion,
By thud of machinery and shrill steam-whistle
    undismay'd,
Bluff'd not a bit by drain-pipe, gasometers,
    artificial fertilizers,
Smiling and pleas'd with palpable intent to stay,
She's here, install'd amid the kitchen ware!

4

But hold—don't I forget my manners?
To introduce the stranger, (what else indeed do
    I live to chant for?) to thee Columbia;
In liberty's name welcome immortal! clasp
    hands,
And ever henceforth sisters dear be both.

Fear not O Muse! truly new ways and days
    receive, surround you,
I candidly confess a queer, queer race, of novel
    fashion,
And yet the same old human race, the same
    within, without,
Faces and hearts the same, feelings the same,
    yearnings the same,
The same old love, beauty and use the same.

5

We do not blame thee elder World, nor really
    separate ourselves from thee,
(Would the son separate himself from the
    father?)
Looking back on thee, seeing thee to thy duties,
    grandeurs, through past ages bending,
    building,
We build to ours to-day.

Mightier than Egypt's tombs,
Fairer than Grecia's, Roma's temples,

Prouder than Milan's statued, spired cathedral,
More picturesque than Rhenish castle-keeps,
We plan even now to raise, beyond them all,
Thy great cathedral sacred industry, no tomb,
A keep for life for practical invention.

As in a waking vision,
E'en while I chant I see it rise, I scan and
    prophesy outside and in,
Its manifold ensemble.

Around a palace, loftier, fairer, ampler than any
    yet,
Earth's modern wonder, history's seven
    outstripping,
High rising tier on tier with glass and iron
    facades,
Gladdening the sun and sky, enhued in
    cheerfulest hues,
Bronze, lilac, robin's-egg, marine and crimson,
Over whose golden roof shall flaunt, beneath thy
    banner Freedom,
The banners of the States and flags of every
    land,
A brood of lofty, fair, but lesser palaces shall
    cluster.

Somewhere within their walls shall all that
    forwards perfect human life be started,
Tried, taught, advanced, visibly exhibited.

Not only all the world of works, trade, products,
But all the workmen of the world here to be
    represented.

Here shall you trace in flowing operation,
In every state of practical, busy movement, the
    rills of civilization,
Materials here under your eye shall change their
    shape as if by magic,
The cotton shall be pick'd almost in the very
    field,
Shall be dried, clean'd, ginn'd, baled, spun into
    thread and cloth before you,
You shall see hands at work at all the old
    processes and all the new ones,
You shall see the various grains and how flour is
    made and then bread baked by the bakers,
You shall see the crude ores of California and
    Nevada passing on and on till they become
    bullion,
You shall watch how the printer sets type, and
    learn what a composing-stick is,
You shall mark in amazement the Hoe press
    whirling its cylinders, shedding the printed
    leaves steady and fast,
The photograph, model, watch, pin, nail, shall
    be created before you.

In large calm halls, a stately museum shall teach
    you the infinite lessons of minerals,

In another, woods, plants, vegetation shall be
    illustrated—in another animals, animal life
    and development.

One stately house shall be the music house,
Others for other arts-learning, the sciences, shall
    all be here,
None shall be slighted, none but shall here be
    honor'd, help'd, exampled.

6

(This, this and these, America, shall be your
    pyramids and obelisks,
Your Alexandrian Pharos, gardens of Babylon,
Your temple at Olympia.)

The male and female many laboring not,
Shall ever here confront the laboring many,
With precious benefits to both, glory to all,
To thee America, and thee eternal Muse.

And here shall ye inhabit powerful Matrons!
In your vast state vaster than all the old,
Echoed through long, long centuries to come,
To sound of different, prouder songs, with
    stronger themes,
Practical, peaceful life, the people's life, the
    People themselves,
Lifted, illumin'd, bathed in peace-elate, secure in
    peace.

7

Away with themes of war! away with war
   itself!
Hence from my shuddering sight to never
   more return that show of blacken'd,
   mutilated corpses!
That hell unpent and raid of blood, fit for wild
   tigers or for lop-tongued wolves, not
   reasoning men,
And in its stead speed industry's campaigns,
With thy undaunted armies, engineering,
Thy pennants labor, loosen'd to the breeze,
Thy bugles sounding loud and clear.

Away with old romance!
Away with novels, plots and plays of foreign
   courts,
Away with love-verses sugar'd in rhyme, the
   intrigues, amours of idlers,
Fitted for only banquets of the night where
   dancers to late music slide,
The unhealthy pleasures, extravagant dissipations
   of the few,
With perfumes, heat and wine, beneath the
   dazzling chandeliers.

To you ye reverent sane sisters,
I raise a voice for far superber themes for poets
   and for art,

To exalt the present and the real,

To teach the average man the glory of his daily
walk and trade,

To sing in songs how exercise and chemical life
are never to be baffled,

To manual work for each and all, to plough,
hoe, dig,

To plant and tend the tree, the berry, vegetables,
flowers,

For every man to see to it that he really do
something, for every woman too;

To use the hammer and the saw, (rip, or cross-
cut,)

To cultivate a turn for carpentering, plastering,
painting,

To work as tailor, tailoress, nurse, hostler,
porter,

To invent a little, something ingenious, to aid
the washing, cooking, cleaning,

And hold it no disgrace to take a hand at them
themselves.

I say I bring thee Muse to-day and here,

All occupations, duties broad and close,

Toil, healthy toil and sweat, endless, without
cessation,

The old, old practical burdens, interests, joys,

The family, parentage, childhood, husband and
wife,

The house-comforts, the house itself and all its
     belongings,
Food and its preservation, chemistry applied to it,
Whatever forms the average, strong, complete,
     sweet-blooded man or woman, the perfect
     longeve personality,
And helps its present life to health and
     happiness, and shapes its soul,
For the eternal real life to come.

With latest connections, works, the inter-
     transportation of the world,
Steam-power, the great express lines, gas,
     petroleum,
These triumphs of our time, the Atlantic's
     delicate cable,
The Pacific railroad, the Suez canal, the Mont
     Cenis and Gothard and Hoosac tunnels, the
     Brooklyn bridge,
This earth all spann'd with iron rails, with lines
     of steamships threading in every sea,
Our own rondure, the current globe I bring.

8

And thou America,
Thy offspring towering e'er so high, yet higher
     Thee above all towering,
With Victory on thy left, and at thy right hand
     Law;

Thou Union holding all, fusing, absorbing,
  tolerating all,
Thee, ever thee, I sing.

Thou, also thou, a World,
With all thy wide geographies, manifold,
  different, distant,
Rounded by thee in one-one common orbic
  language,
One common indivisible destiny for All.

And by the spells which ye vouchsafe to those
  your ministers in earnest,
I here personify and call my themes, to make
  them pass before ye.

Behold, America! (and thou, ineffable guest and
  sister!)
For thee come trooping up thy waters and thy
  lands;
Behold! thy fields and farms, thy far-off woods
  and mountains,
As in procession coming.

Behold, the sea itself,
And on its limitless, heaving breast, the
  ships;
See, where their white sails, bellying in the
  wind, speckle the green and blue,

See, the steamers coming and going, steaming
   in or out of port,
See, dusky and undulating, the long pennants
   of smoke.

Behold, in Oregon, far in the north and
   west,
Or in Maine, far in the north and east, thy
   cheerful axemen,
Wielding all day their axes.

Behold, on the lakes, thy pilots at their wheels,
   thy oarsmen,
How the ash writhes under those muscular
   arms!

There by the furnace, and there by the
   anvil,
Behold thy sturdy blacksmiths swinging their
   sledges,
Overhand so steady, overhand they turn and fall
   with joyous clank,
Like a tumult of laughter.

Mark the spirit of invention everywhere, thy
   rapid patents,
Thy continual workshops, foundries, risen or
   rising,
See, from their chimneys how the tall flame-fires
   stream.

Mark, thy interminable farms, North, South,
Thy wealthy daughter-states, Eastern and
  Western,
The varied products of Ohio, Pennsylvania,
  Missouri, Georgia, Texas, and the rest,
Thy limitless crops, grass, wheat, sugar, oil,
  corn, rice, hemp, hops,
Thy barns all fill'd, the endless freight-train and
  the bulging store-house,
The grapes that ripen on thy vines, the apples in
  thy orchards,
Thy incalculable lumber, beef, pork, potatoes,
  thy coal, thy gold and silver,
The inexhaustible iron in thy mines.

All thine O sacred Union!
Ships, farms, shops, barns, factories, mines,
City and State, North, South, item and
  aggregate,
We dedicate, dread Mother, all to thee!

Protectress absolute, thou! bulwark of all!
For well we know that while thou givest each
  and all, (generous as God,)
Without thee neither all nor each, nor land,
  home,
Nor ship, nor mine, nor any here this day
  secure,
Nor aught, nor any day secure.

9

And thou, the Emblem waving over all!

Delicate beauty, a word to thee, (it may be
    salutary,)

Remember thou hast not always been as
    here to-day so comfortably ensovereign'd,

In other scenes than these have I observ'd thee
    flag,

Not quite so trim and whole and freshly
    blooming in folds of stainless silk,

But I have seen thee bunting, to tatters torn
    upon thy splinter'd staff,

Or clutch'd to some young color-bearer's breast
    with desperate hands,

Savagely struggled for, for life or death, fought
    over long,

'Mid cannons' thunder-crash and many a curse
    and groan and yell, and rifle-volleys cracking
    sharp,

And moving masses as wild demons surging,
    and lives as nothing risk'd,

For thy mere remnant grimed with dirt and
    smoke and sopp'd in blood,

For sake of that, my beauty, and that thou
    might'st dally as now secure up there,

Many a good man have I seen go under.

Now here and these and hence in peace, all
    thine O Flag!

And here and hence for thee, O universal Muse!
    and thou for them!
And here and hence O Union, all the work and
    workmen thine!
None separate from thee—henceforth One only,
    we and thou,
(For the blood of the children, what is it, only
    the blood maternal?
And lives and works, what are they all at last,
    except the roads to faith and death?)

While we rehearse our measureless wealth, it is
    for thee, dear Mother,
We own it all and several to-day indissoluble in
    thee;
Think not our chant, our show, merely for
    products gross or lucre—it is for thee, the
    soul in thee, electric, spiritual!
Our farms, inventions, crops, we own in thee!
    cities and States in thee!
Our freedom all in thee! our very lives in thee!

Song of the Redwood-Tree

1

A CALIFORNIA song,
A prophecy and indirection, a thought
    impalpable to breathe as air,
A chorus of dryads, fading, departing, or
    hamadryads departing,
A murmuring, fateful, giant voice, out of the
    earth and sky,
Voice of a mighty dying tree in the redwood
    forest dense.

Farewell my brethren,
Farewell O earth and sky, farewell ye
    neighboring waters,
My time has ended, my term has come.

Along the northern coast,
Just back from the rock-bound shore and the
    caves,
In the saline air from the sea in the Mendocino
    country,
With the surge for base and accompaniment low
    and hoarse,
With crackling blows of axes sounding musically
    driven by strong arms,

Riven deep by the sharp tongues of the axes,
    there in the redwood forest dense,
I heard the might tree its death-chant
    chanting.

The choppers heard not, the camp shanties
    echoed not,
The quick-ear'd teamsters and chain and jack-
    screw men heard not,
As the wood-spirits came from their haunts of a
    thousand years to join the refrain,
But in my soul I plainly heard.

Murmuring out of its myriad leaves,
Down from its lofty top rising two hundred feet
    high,
Out of its stalwart trunk and limbs, out of its
    foot-thick bark,
That chant of the seasons and time, chant not of
    the past only but the future.

You untold life of me,
And all you venerable and innocent joys,
Perennial hardy life of me with joys 'mid rain
    and many a summer sun,
And the white snows and night and the wild
    winds;
O the great patient rugged joys, my soul's
    strong joys unreck'd by man,

(For know I bear the soul befitting me, I too
    have consciousness, identity,
And all the rocks and mountains have, and all
    the earth,)
Joys of the life befitting me and brothers mine,
Our time, our term has come.

Nor yield we mournfully majestic brothers,
We who have grandly fill'd our time,
With Nature's calm content, with tacit huge
    delight,
We welcome what we wrought for through the
    past,
And leave the field for them.

For them predicted long,
For a superber race, they too to grandly fill their
    time,
For them we abdicate, in them ourselves ye
    forest kings.'
In them these skies and airs, these mountain
    peaks, Shasta, Nevadas,
These huge precipitous cliffs, this amplitude,
    these valleys, far Yosemite,
To be in them absorb'd, assimilated.

Then to a loftier strain,
Still prouder, more ecstatic rose the chant,
As if the heirs, the deities of the West,
Joining with master-tongue bore part.

Not wan from Asia's fetiches,
Nor red from Europe's old dynastic
   slaughter-house,
(Area of murder-plots of thrones, with scent left
   yet of wars and scaffolds everywhere,
But come from Nature's long and harmless
   throes, peacefully builded thence,
These virgin lands, lands of the Western shore,
To the new culminating man, to-you, the
   empire new,
You promis'd long, we pledge, we dedicate.

You occult deep volitions,
You average spiritual manhood, purpose of all,
   pois'd on yourself, giving not taking law,
You womanhood divine, mistress and source of
   all, whence life and love and aught that comes
   from life and love,
You unseen moral essence of all the vast
   materials of America, age upon age working
   in death the same as life,)
You that, sometimes known, oftener unknown,
   really shape and mould the New World,
   adjusting it to Time and Space,
You hidden national will lying in your abysms,
   conceal'd but ever alert,
You past and present purposes tenaciously
   pursued, may-be unconscious of yourselves,
Unswerv'd by all the passing errors,
   perturbations of the surface;

You vital, universal, deathless germs, beneath all
    creeds, arts, statutes, literatures,
Here build your homes for good, establish here,
    these areas entire, lands of the Western shore,
We pledge, we dedicate to you.

For man of you, your characteristic race,
Here may he hardy, sweet, gigantic grow, here
    tower proportionate to Nature,
Here climb the vast pure spaces unconfined,
    uncheck'd by wall or roof,
Here laugh with storm or sun, here joy, here
    patiently inure,
Here heed himself, unfold himself, (not others'
    formulas heed,)
here fill his time,
To duly fall, to aid, unreck'd at last,
To disappear, to serve.

Thus on the northern coast,
In the echo of teamsters' calls and the clinking
    chains, and the music of choppers' axes,
The falling trunk and limbs, the crash, the
    muffled shriek, the groan,
Such words combined from the redwood-tree,
    as of voices ecstatic, ancient and rustling,
The century-lasting, unseen dryads, singing,
    withdrawing,
All their recesses of forests and mountains
    leaving,

From the Cascade range to the Wahsatch, or
    Idaho far, or Utah,
To the deities of the modern henceforth
    yielding,
The chorus and indications, the vistas of coming
    humanity, the settlements, features all,
In the Mendocino woods I caught.

2

The flashing and golden pageant of
    California,
The sudden and gorgeous drama, the sunny
    and ample lands,
The long and varied stretch from Puget sound
    to Colorado south,
Lands bathed in sweeter, rarer, healthier air,
    valleys and mountain cliffs,
The fields of Nature long prepared and fallow,
    the silent, cyclic chemistry,
The slow and steady ages plodding, the
    unoccupied surface ripening, the rich ores
    forming beneath;
At last the New arriving, assuming, taking
    possession,
A swarming and busy race settling and
    organizing everywhere,
Ships coming in from the whole round world,
    and going out to the whole world,
To India and China and Australia and the
    thousand island paradises of the Pacific,

Populous cities, the latest inventions, the
    steamers on the rivers, the railroads, with
    many a thrifty farm, with machinery,
And wool and wheat and the grape, and
    diggings of yellow gold.

3

But more in you than these, lands of the
    Western shore,
(These but the means, the implements, the
    standing-ground,)
I see in you, certain to come, the promise of
    thousands of years, till now deferr'd,
Promis'd to be fulfill'd, our common kind, the
    race.

The new society at last, proportionate to
    Nature,
In man of you, more than your mountain peaks
    or stalwart trees imperial,
In woman more, far more, than all your gold or
    vines, or even vital air.

Fresh come, to a new world indeed, yet long
    prepared,
I see the genius of the modern, child of the real
    and ideal,
Clearing the ground for broad humanity, the
    true America, heir of the past so grand,
To build a grander future.

A Song for Occupations

A SONG for occupations!
In the labor of engines and trades and the labor
    of fields I find the developments,
And find the eternal meanings.

Workmen and Workwomen!
Were all educations practical and ornamental
    well display'd out of me, what would it
    amount to?
Were I as the head teacher, charitable
    proprietor, wise statesman, what would it
    amount to?
Were I to you as the boss employing and paying
    you, would that satisfy you?

The learn'd, virtuous, benevolent, and the usual
    terms,
A man like me and never the usual terms.

Neither a servant nor a master I,
I take no sooner a large price than a small
    price, I will have my own whoever enjoys
    me,
I will be even with you and you shall be even
    with me.

If you stand at work in a shop I stand as nigh as
    the nighest in the same shop,
If you bestow gifts on your brother or dearest
    friend I demand as good as your brother or
    dearest friend,
If your lover, husband, wife, is welcome by day
    or night, I must be personally as welcome,
If you become degraded, criminal, ill, then I
    become so for your sake,
If you remember your foolish and outlaw'd
    deeds, do you think I cannot remember my
    own foolish and outlaw'd deeds?
If you carouse at the table I carouse at the
    opposite side of the table,
If you meet some stranger in the streets and love
    him or her, why I often meet strangers in the
    street and love them.

Why what have you thought of yourself?
Is it you then that thought yourself less?
Is it you that thought the President greater than
    you?
Or the rich better off than you? or the educated
    wiser than you?

(Because you are greasy or pimpled, or were
    once drunk, or a thief,
Or that you are diseas'd, or rheumatic, or a
    prostitute,

Or from frivolity or impotence, or that you
    are no scholar and never saw your name in
    print,
Do you give in that you are any less immortal?)

2

Souls of men and women! it is not you I call
    unseen, unheard, untouchable and
    untouching,
It is not you I go argue pro and con about, and
    to settle whether you are alive or no,
I own publicly who you are, if nobody else
    owns.

Grown, half-grown and babe, of this country
    and every country, in-doors and out-doors,
    one just as much as the other, I see,
And all else behind or through them.

The wife, and she is not one jot less than the
    husband,
The daughter, and she is just as good as the son,
The mother, and she is every bit as much as the
    father.

Offspring of ignorant and poor, boys
    apprenticed to trades,
Young fellows working on farms and old fellows
    working on farms,

Sailor-men, merchant-men, coasters, immigrants,
All these I see, but nigher and farther the same I
    see,
None shall escape me and none shall wish to
    escape me.

I bring what you much need yet always have,
Not money, amours, dress, eating, erudition, but
    as good,
I send no agent or medium, offer no
    representative of value, but offer the value
    itself.

There is something that comes to one now and
    perpetually,
It is not what is printed, preach'd, discussed, it
    eludes discussion and print,
It is not to be put in a book, it is not in this
    book,
It is for you whoever you are, it is no farther
    from you than your hearing and sight are
    from you,
It is hinted by nearest, commonest, readiest, it is
    ever provoked by them.

You may read in many languages, yet read
    nothing about it,
You may read the President's message and read
    nothing about it there,

Nothing in the reports from the State
department or Treasury department, or in the
daily papers or weekly papers,
Or in the census or revenue returns, prices
current, or any accounts of stock.

3

The sun and stars that float in the open air,
The apple-shaped earth and we upon it, surely
the drift of them is something grand,
I do not know what it is except that it is grand,
and that it is happiness,
And that the enclosing purport of us here is not
a speculation or bon-mot or reconnoissance,
And that it is not something which by luck may
turn out well for us, and without luck must
be a failure for us,
And not something which may yet be retracted
in a certain contingency.

The light and shade, the curious sense of body
and identity, the greed that with perfect
complaisance devours all things,
The endless pride and outstretching of man,
unspeakable joys and sorrows,
The wonder every one sees in every one else he
sees, and the wonders that fill each minute of
time forever,
What have you reckon'd them for, camerado?

Have you reckon'd them for your trade or farm-
  work? or for the profits of your store?
Or to achieve yourself a position? or to fill a
  gentleman's leisure, or a lady's leisure?

Have you reckon'd that the landscape took
  substance and form that it might be painted
  in a picture?
Or men and women that they might be written
  of, and songs sung?
Or the attraction of gravity, and the great laws
  and harmonious combinations and the fluids
  of the air, as subjects for the savans?
Or the brown land and the blue sea for maps
  and charts?
Or the stars to be put in constellations and
  named fancy names?
Or that the growth of seeds is for agricultural
  tables, or agriculture itself?

Old institutions, these arts, libraries, legends,
  collections, and the practice handed along
  in manufactures, will we rate them so
  high?
Will we rate our cash and business high? I have
  no objection,
I rate them as high as the highest—then a child
  born of a woman and man I rate beyond all
  rate.

We thought our Union grand, and our
 Constitution grand,
I do not say they are not grand and good, for
 they are,
I am this day just as much in love with them as
 you,
Then I am in love with You, and with all my
 fellows upon the earth.

We consider bibles and religions divine—I do
 not say they are not divine,
I say they have all grown out of you, and may
 grow out of you still,
It is not they who give the life, it is you who
 give the life,
Leaves are not more shed from the trees, or
 trees from the earth, than they are shed out
 of you.

4

The sum of all known reverence I add up in you
 whoever you are,
The President is there in the White House
 for you, it is not you who are here for
 him,
The Secretaries act in their bureaus for you, not
 you here for them,
The Congress convenes every Twelfth-month
 for you,

Laws, courts, the forming of States, the charters
  of cities, the going and coming of commerce
  and malls, are all for you.

List close my scholars dear,
Doctrines, politics and civilization exurge from
  you,
Sculpture and monuments and any thing
  inscribed anywhere are tallied in you,
The gist of histories and statistics as far back as
  the records reach is in you this hour, and
  myths and tales the same,
If you were not breathing and walking here,
  where would they all be?
The most renown'd poems would be ashes,
  orations and plays would be vacuums.

All architecture is what you do to it when you
  look upon it,
(Did you think it was in the white or gray stone?
  or the lines of the arches and cornices?)

All music is what awakes from you when you are
  reminded by the instruments,
It is not the violins and the cornets, it is not the
  oboe nor the beating drums, nor the score of
  the baritone singer singing his sweet romanza,
  nor that of the men's chorus, nor that of the
  women's chorus,
It is nearer and farther than they.

5

Will the whole come back then?
Can each see signs of the best by a look in the
    looking-glass? is there nothing greater or
    more?
Does all sit there with you, with the mystic
    unseen soul?

Strange and hard that paradox true I give,
Objects gross and the unseen soul are one.

House-building, measuring, sawing the boards,
Blacksmithing, glass-blowing, nail-making,
    coopering, tin-roofing, shingle-dressing,
Ship-joining, dock-building, fish-curing, flagging
    of sidewalks by flaggers,
The pump, the pile-driver, the great derrick, the
    coal-kiln and brickkiln,
Coal-mines and all that is down there, the lamps
    in the darkness, echoes, songs, what
    meditations, what vast native thoughts
    looking through smutch'd faces,
Iron-works, forge-fires in the mountains or by
    river-banks, men around feeling the melt with
    huge crowbars, lumps of ore, the due
    combining of ore, limestone, coal,
The blast-furnace and the puddling-furnace, the
    loup-lump at the bottom of the melt at last,
    the rolling-mill, the stumpy bars of pig-iron,
    the strong clean-shaped Trail for railroads,

Oil-works, silk-works, white-lead-works, the
sugar-house, steam-saws, the great mills and
factories,
Stone-cutting, shapely trimmings for facades or
window or door-lintels, the mallet, the tooth-
chisel, the jib to protect the thumb,
The calking-iron, the kettle of boiling vault-
cement, and the fire under the kettle,
The cotton-bale, the stevedore's hook, the saw
and buck of the sawyer, the mould of the
moulder, the working-knife of the butcher,
the ice-saw, and all the work with ice,
The work and tools of the rigger, grappler, sail-
maker, block-maker,
Goods of gutta-percha, papier-mache, colors,
brushes, brush-making, glazier's implements,
The veneer and glue-pot, the confectioner's
ornaments, the decanter and glasses, the
shears and flat-iron,
The awl and knee-strap, the pint measure and
quart measure, the counter and stool, the
writing-pen of quill or metal, the making of
all sorts of edged tools,
The brewery, brewing, the malt, the vats, every
thing that is done by brewers, wine-makers,
vinegar-makers,
Leather-dressing, coach-making, boiler-making,
rope-twisting, distilling, sign-painting, lime-
burning, cotton-picking, electroplating,
electrotyping, stereotyping,

Stave-machines, planing-machines, reaping-
machines, ploughing-machines, thrashing-
machines, steam wagons,
The cart of the carman, the omnibus, the
ponderous dray,
Pyrotechny, letting off color'd fireworks at
night, fancy figures and jets;
Beef on the butcher's stall, the slaughter-house
of the butcher, the butcher in his killing-
clothes,
The pens of live pork, the killing-hammer, the
hog-hook, the scalder's tub, gutting, the
cutter's cleaver, the packer's maul, and the
plenteous winterwork of pork-packing,
Flour-works, grinding of wheat, rye, maize, rice,
the barrels and the half and quarter barrels,
the loaded barges, the high piles on wharves
and levees,
The men and the work of the men on ferries,
railroads, coasters, fish-boats, canals;
The hourly routine of your own or any man's
life, the shop, yard, store, or factory,
These shows all near you by day and night—
workman! whoever you are, your daily life!

In that and them the heft of the heaviest—in
that and them far more than you estimated,
(and far less also,)
In them realities for you and me, in them poems
for you and me,

In them, not yourself—you and your soul
     enclose all things, regardless of estimation,
In them the development good—in them all
     themes, hints, possibilities.

I do not affirm that what you see beyond is
     futile, I do not advise you to stop,
I do not say leadings you thought great are not
     great,
But I say that none lead to greater than these
     lead to.

6

Will you seek afar off—? you surely come back
     at last,
In things best known to you finding the best, or
     as good as the best,
In folks nearest to you finding the sweetest,
     strongest, lovingest,
Happiness, knowledge, not in another place
     but this place, not for another hour but this
     hour,
Man in the first you see or touch, always in
     friend, brother, nighest neighbor-woman in
     mother, sister, wife,
The popular tastes and employments taking
     precedence in poems or anywhere,
You workwomen and workmen of these States
     having your own divine and strong life,

And all else giving place to men and women like
you.
When the psalm sings instead of the singer,

When the script preaches instead of the
preacher,
When the pulpit descends and goes instead of
the carver that carved the supporting desk,
When I can touch the body of books by night or
by day, and when they touch my body back
again,
When a university course convinces like a
slumbering woman and child convince,
When the minted gold in the vault smiles like
the night-watchman's daughter,
When warrantee deeds loafe in chairs opposite
and are my friendly companions,
I intend to reach them my hand, and make as
much of them as I do of men and women like
you.

A Song of the Rolling Earth

1

A SONG of the rolling earth, and of words
    according,
Were you thinking that those were the words,
    those upright lines? those curves, angles,
    dots?
No, those are not the words, the substantial
    words are in the ground and sea,
They are in the air, they are in you.

Were you thinking that those were the words,
    those delicious sounds out of your friends'
    mouths?
No, the real words are more delicious than
    they.

Human bodies are words, myriads of words,
(In the best poems re-appears the body, man's
    or woman's, well-shaped, natural, gay,
Every part able, active, receptive, without shame
    or the need of shame.)

Air, soil, water, fire-those are words,
I myself am a word with them—my qualities
    interpenetrate with theirs—my name is
    nothing to them,

Though it were told in the three thousand
languages, what would air, soil, water, fire,
know of my name?

A healthy presence, a friendly or commanding
gesture, are words, sayings, meanings,
The charms that go with the mere looks of some
men and women, are sayings and meanings
also.

The workmanship of souls is by those inaudible
words of the earth,
The masters know the earth's words and use
them more than audible words.

Amelioration is one of the earth's words,
The earth neither lags nor hastens,
It has all attributes, growths, effects, latent in
itself from the jump,
It is not half beautiful only, defects and
excrescences show just as much as perfections
show.

The earth does not withhold, it is generous
enough,
The truths of the earth continually wait, they are
not so conceal'd either,
They are calm, subtle, untransmissible by print,
They are imbued through all things conveying
themselves willingly,

Conveying a sentiment and invitation, I utter
    and utter,
I speak not, yet if you hear me not of what avail
    am I to you?
To bear, to better, lacking these of what avail
    am I?

(Accouche! accouchez!
Will you rot your own fruit in yourself there?
Will you squat and stifle there?)

The earth does not argue,
Is not pathetic, has no arrangements,
Does not scream, haste, persuade, threaten,
    promise,
Makes no discriminations, has no conceivable
    failures,
Closes nothing, refuses nothing, shuts none out,
Of all the powers, objects, states, it notifies,
    shuts none out.

The earth does not exhibit itself nor refuse to
    exhibit itself, possesses still underneath,
Underneath the ostensible sounds, the august
    chorus of heroes, the wail of slaves,
Persuasions of lovers, curses, gasps of the dying,
    laughter of young people, accents of
    bargainers,
Underneath these possessing words that never
    fall.

To her children the words of the eloquent dumb
    great mother never fail,
The true words do not fail, for motion does not
    fail and reflection does not fall,
Also the day and night do not fall, and the
    voyage we pursue does not fall.

Of the interminable sisters,
Of the ceaseless cotillons of sisters,
Of the centripetal and centrifugal sisters, the
    elder and younger sisters,
The beautiful sister we know dances on with the
    rest.

With her ample back towards every beholder,
With the fascinations of youth and the equal
    fascinations of age,
Sits she whom I too love like the rest, sits
    undisturb'd,
Holding up in her hand what has the character
    of a mirror, while her eyes glance back
    from it,
Glance as she sits, inviting none, denying none,
Holding a mirror day and night tirelessly before
    her own face.

Seen at hand or seen at a distance,
Duly the twenty-four appear in public every day,
Duly approach and pass with their companions
    or a companion,

Looking from no countenances of their own,
 but from the countenances of those who are
 with them,
From the countenances of children or women or
 the manly countenance,
From the open countenances of animals or from
 inanimate things,
From the landscape or waters or from the
 exquisite apparition of the sky,
From our countenances, mine and yours,
 faithfully returning them,
Every day in public appearing without fall, but
 never twice with the same companions.

Embracing man, embracing all, proceed the
 three hundred and sixty-five resistlessly round
 the sun;
Embracing all, soothing, supporting, follow
 close three hundred and sixty-five offsets of
 the first, sure and necessary as they.

Tumbling on steadily, nothing dreading,
Sunshine, storm, cold, heat, forever
 withstanding, passing, carrying,
The soul's realization and determination still
 inheriting,
The fluid vacuum around and ahead still
 entering and dividing,
No balk retarding, no anchor anchoring, on no
 rock striking,

Swift, glad, content, unbereav'd, nothing losing,
Of all able and ready at any time to give strict
    account,
The divine ship sails the divine sea.

2

Whoever you are! motion and reflection are
    especially for you,
The divine ship sails the divine sea for you.

Whoever you are! you are he or she for whom
    the earth is solid and liquid,
You are he or she for whom the sun and moon
    hang in the sky,
For none more than you are the present and the
    past,
For none more than you is immortality.

Each man to himself and each woman to herself,
    is the word of the past and present, and the
    true word of immortality;
No one can acquire for another—not one,
Not one can grow for another—not one.

The song is to the singer, and comes back most
    to him,
The teaching is to the teacher, and comes back
    most to him,
The murder is to the murderer, and comes back
    most to him,

The theft is to the thief, and comes back most
  to him,
The love is to the lover, and comes back most to
  him,
The gift is to the giver, and comes back most to
  him-it cannot fail,
The oration is to the orator, the acting is to the
  actor and actress not to the audience,
And no man understands any greatness or
  goodness but his own, or the indication of his
  own.

3
I swear the earth shall surely be complete to him
  or her who shall be complete,
The earth remains jagged and broken only to
  him or her who remains jagged and broken.

I swear there is no greatness or power that does
  not emulate those of the earth,
There can be no theory of any account unless it
  corroborate the theory of the earth,
No politics, song, religion, behavior, or what
  not, is of account, unless it compare with the
  amplitude of the earth,
Unless it face the exactness, vitality, impartiality,
  rectitude of the earth.

I swear I begin to see love with sweeter spasms
  than that which responds love,

It is that which contains itself, which never
    invites and never refuses.

I swear I begin to see little or nothing in audible
    words,
All merges toward the presentation of the
    unspoken meanings of the earth,
Toward him who sings the songs of the body
    and of the truths of the earth,
Toward him who makes the dictionaries of
    words that print cannot touch.

I swear I see what is better than to tell the
    best,
It is always to leave the best untold.

When I undertake to tell the best I find I
    cannot,
My tongue is ineffectual on its pivots,
My breath will not be obedient to its organs,
I become a dumb man.

The best of the earth cannot be told anyhow, all
    or any is best,
It is not what you anticipated, it is cheaper,
    easier, nearer,
Things are not dismiss'd from the places they
    held before,
The earth is just as positive and direct as it was
    before,

Facts, religions, improvements, politics, trades,
    are as real as before,
But the soul is also real, it too is positive and
    direct,
No reasoning, no proof has establish'd it,
Undeniable growth has establish'd it.

4

These to echo the tones of souls and the phrases
    of souls,
(If they did not echo the phrases of souls what
    were they then?
If they had not reference to you in especial what
    were they then?)

I swear I will never henceforth have to do with
    the faith that tells the best,
I will have to do only with that faith that leaves
    the best untold.

Say on, sayers! sing on, singers!
Delve! mould! pile the words of the earth!
Work on, age after age, nothing is to be lost,
It may have to wait long, but it will certainly
    come in use,
When the materials are all prepared and ready,
    the architects shall appear.

I swear to you the architects shall appear
    without fall,

I swear to you they will understand you and
    justify you,
The greatest among them shall be he who
    best knows you, and encloses all and is
    faithful to all,
He and the rest shall not forget you, they shall
    perceive that you are not an iota less than
    they,
You shall be fully glorified in them.

Youth, Day, Old Age and Night

YOUTH, large, lusty, loving—youth full of
 grace, force, fascination,
Do you know that Old Age may come after you
 with equal grace, force, fascination?

Day full-blown and splendid—day of the
 immense sun, action, ambition, laughter,
The Night follows close with millions of suns,
 and sleep and restoring darkness.

Birds of Passage

SONG OF THE UNIVERSAL

1

COME said the Muse,
Sing me a song no poet yet has chanted,
Sing me the universal.

In this broad earth of ours,
Amid the measureless grossness and the slag,
Enclosed and safe within its central heart,
Nestles the seed perfection.

By every life a share or more or less,
None born but it is born, conceal'd or
    unconceal'd the seed is waiting.

2

Lo! keen-eyed towering science,
As from tall peaks the modern overlooking,
Successive absolute fiats issuing.

Yet again, lo! the soul, above all science,
For it has history gather'd like husks around the
    globe,
For it the entire star-myriads roll through the
    sky.

In spiral routes by long detours,
(As a much-tacking ship upon the sea,)
For it the partial to the permanent flowing,
For it the real to the ideal tends.

For it the mystic evolution,
Not the right only justified, what we call evil
    also justified.

Forth from their masks, no matter what,
From the huge festering trunk, from craft and
    guile and tears,
Health to emerge and joy, joy universal.

Out of the bulk, the morbid and the shallow,
Out of the bad majority, the varied countless
    frauds of men and states,
Electric, antiseptic yet, cleaving, suffusing all,
Only the good is universal.

3

Over the mountain-growths disease and
    sorrow,
An uncaught bird is ever hovering, hovering,
High in the purer, happier air.

From imperfection's murkiest cloud,
Darts always forth one ray of perfect light,
One flash of heaven's glory.

To fashion's, custom's discord,
To the mad Babel-din, the deafening orgies,
Soothing each lull a strain is heard, just
    heard,
From some far shore the final chorus
    sounding.

O the blest eyes, the happy hearts,
That see, that know the guiding thread so
    fine,
Along the mighty labyrinth.

4

And thou America,
For the scheme's culmination, its thought and
    its reality,
For these (not for thyself) thou hast arrived.

Thou too surroundest all,
Embracing carrying welcoming all, thou too by
    pathways broad and new,
To the ideal tendest.

The measure'd faiths of other lands, the
    grandeurs of the past,
Are not for thee, but grandeurs of thine own,
Deific faiths and amplitudes, absorbing,
    comprehending all,
All eligible to all.

All, all for immortality,
Love like the light silently wrapping all,
Nature's amelioration blessing all,
The blossoms, fruits of ages, orchards divine and
    certain,
Forms, objects, growths, humanities, to spiritual
    images ripening.

Give me O God to sing that thought,
Give me, give him or her I love this quenchless
    faith,
In Thy ensemble, whatever else withheld
    withhold not from us,
Belief in plan of Thee enclosed in Time and
    Space,
Health, peace, salvation universal.

Is it a dream?
Nay but the lack of it the dream,
And failing it life's lore and wealth a
    dream,
And all the world a dream.

Pioneers! O Pioneers!

COME my tan-faced children,
Follow well in order, get your weapons
      ready,
Have you your pistols? have you your sharp-
      edged axes?
Pioneers! O pioneers!

For we cannot tarry here,
We must march my darlings, we must bear the
      brunt of danger,
We the youthful sinewy races, all the rest on us
      depend,
Pioneers! O pioneers!

O you youths, Western youths,
So impatient, full of action, full of manly pride
      and friendship,
Plain I see you Western youths, see you
      tramping with the foremost,
Pioneers! O pioneers!

Have the elder races halted?
Do they droop and end their lesson, wearied
      over there beyond the seas?
We take up the task eternal, and the burden
      and the lesson,
Pioneers! O pioneers!

All the past we leave behind,
We debouch upon a newer mightier world,
    varied world,
Fresh and strong the world we seize, world of
    labor and the march,
Pioneers! O pioneers!

We detachments steady throwing,
Down the edges, through the passes, up the
    mountains steep,
Conquering, holding, daring, venturing as we
    go the unknown ways,
Pioneers! O pioneers!

We primeval forests felling,
We the rivers stemming, vexing we and piercing
    deep the mines within,
We the surface broad surveying, we the virgin
    soil upheaving,
Pioneers! O pioneers!

Colorado men are we,
From the peaks gigantic, from the great sierras
    and the high plateaus,
From the mine and from the gully, from the
    hunting trail we come,
Pioneers! O pioneers!

From Nebraska, from Arkansas,
Central inland race are we, from Missouri,
   with the continental blood
   intervein'd,
All the hands of comrades clasping, all the
   Southern, all the Northern,
Pioneers! O pioneers!

O resistless restless race!
O beloved race in all! O my breast aches with
   tender love for all!
O I mourn and yet exult, I am rapt with love for
   all,
Pioneers! O pioneers!

Raise the mighty mother mistress,
Waving high the delicate mistress, over all
   the starry mistress, (bend your heads all,)
Raise the fang'd and warlike mistress, stern,
   impassive, weapon'd mistress,
Pioneers! O pioneers!

See my children, resolute children,
By those swarms upon our rear we must never
   yield or falter,
Ages back in ghostly millions frowning there
   behind us urging,
Pioneers! O pioneers!

On and on the compact ranks,
With accessions ever waiting, with the places of
    the dead quickly fill'd,
Through the battle, through defeat, moving yet
    and never stopping,
Pioneers! O pioneers!

O to die advancing on!
Are there some of us to droop and die? has the
    hour come?
Then upon the march we fittest die, soon and
    sure the gap is fill'd.
Pioneers! O pioneers!

All the pulses of the world,
Falling in they beat for us, with the Western
    movement beat,
Holding single or together, steady moving to
    the front, all for us,
Pioneers! O pioneers!

Life's involv'd and varied pageants,
All the forms and shows, all the workmen at
    their work,
All the seamen and the landsmen, all the masters
    with their slaves,
Pioneers! O pioneers!

All the hapless silent lovers,
All the prisoners in the prisons, all the righteous
    and the wicked,
All the joyous, all the sorrowing, all the living,
    all the dying,
Pioneers! O pioneers!

I too with my soul and body,
We, a curious trio, picking, wandering on our
    way,
Through these shores amid the shadows, with
    the apparitions pressing,
Pioneers! O pioneers!

Lo, the darting bowling orb!
Lo, the brother orbs around, all the clustering
    suns and planets,
All the dazzling days, all the mystic nights with
    dreams,
Pioneers! O pioneers!

These are of us, they are with us,
All for primal needed work, while the follow-
    ers there in embryo wait behind,
We to-day's procession heading, we the route
    for travel clearing,
Pioneers! O pioneers!

O you daughters of the West!
O you young and elder daughters! O you
    mothers and you wives!
Never must you be divided, in our ranks you
    move united,
Pioneers! O pioneers!

Minstrels latent on the prairies!
(Shrouded bards of other lands, you may rest,
    you have done your work,)
Soon I hear you coming warbling, soon you rise
    and tramp amid us,
Pioneers! O pioneers!

Not for delectations sweet,
Not the cushion and the slipper, not the
    peaceful and the studious,
Not the riches safe and palling, not for us the
    tame enjoyment,
Pioneers! O pioneers!

Do the feasters gluttonous feast?
Do the corpulent sleepers sleep? have they
    lock'd and bolted doors?
Still be ours the diet hard, and the blanket on
    the ground,
Pioneers! O pioneers!

Has the night descended?
Was the road of late so toilsome? did we stop
    discouraged nodding on our way?
Yet a passing hour I yield you in your tracks to
    pause oblivious,
Pioneers! O pioneers!

Till with sound of trumpet,
Far, far off the daybreak call—hark! how loud
    and clear I hear it wind,
Swift! to the head of the army!—swift! spring to
    your places,
Pioneers! O pioneers!

TO YOU

WHOEVER you are, I fear you are walking the
    walks of dreams,
I fear these supposed realities are to melt from
    under your feet and hands,
Even now your features, joys, speech, house,
    trade, manners, troubles, follies, costume,
    crimes, dissipate away from you,
Your true soul and body appear before me.
They stand forth out of affairs, out of commerce,
    shops, work, farms, clothes, the house, buying,
    selling, eating, drinking, suffering, dying.

Whoever you are, now I place my hand upon
   you, that you be my poem,
I whisper with my lips close to your ear.
I have loved many women and men, but I love
   none better than you.

O I have been dilatory and dumb,
I should have made my way straight to you long
   ago,
I should have blabb'd nothing but you, I should
   have chanted nothing but you.

I will leave all and come and make the hymns of
   you,
None has understood you, but I understand
   you,
None has done justice to you, you have not
   done justice to yourself,
None but has found you imperfect, I only find
   no imperfection in you,
None but would subordinate you, I only am he
   who will never consent to subordinate you,
I only am he who places over you no master,
   owner, better, God, beyond what waits
   intrinsically in yourself.

Painters have painted their swarming groups and
   the centre-figure of all,
From the head of the centre-figure spreading a
   nimbus of gold-color'd light,

But I paint myriads of heads, but paint no
head without its nimbus of gold-color'd
light,
From my hand from the brain of every man and
woman it streams, effulgently flowing forever.

O I could sing such grandeurs and glories about
you!
You have not known what you are, you have
slumber'd upon yourself all your life,
Your eyelids have been the same as closed most
of the time,
What you have done returns already in mockeries,
(Your thrift, knowledge, prayers, if they do not
return in mockeries, what is their return?)

The mockeries are not you,
Underneath them and within them I see you
lurk, I pursue you where none else has
pursued you,
Silence, the desk, the flippant expression, the
night, the accustom'd routine, if these conceal
you from others or from yourself, they do not
conceal you from me,
The shaved face, the unsteady eye, the impure
complexion, if these balk others they do not
balk me,
The pert apparel, the deform'd attitude,
drunkenness, greed, premature death, all
these I part aside.

There is no endowment in man or woman that
    is not tallied in you,
There is no virtue, no beauty in man or woman,
    but as good is in you,
No pluck, no endurance in others, but as good
    is in you,
No pleasure waiting for others, but an equal
    pleasure waits for you.

As for me, I give nothing to any one except I
    give the like carefully to you,
I sing the songs of the glory of none, not God,
    sooner than I sing the songs of the glory of
    you.

Whoever you are! claim your own at any hazard!
These shows of the East and West are tame
    compared to you,
These immense meadows, these interminable
    rivers, you are immense and interminable as
    they,
These furies, elements, storms, motions of
    Nature, throes of apparent dissolution, you
    are he or she who is master or mistress over
    them,
Master or mistress in your own right over
    Nature, elements, pain, passion, dissolution.

The hopples fall from your ankles, you find an
    unfailing sufficiency,

Old or young, male or female, rude, low,
    rejected by the rest, whatever you are
    promulges itself,
Through birth, life, death, burial, the means are
    provided, nothing is scanted,
Through angers, losses, ambition, ignorance,
    ennui, what you are picks its way.

FRANCE

FRANCE,
THE 18TH YEAR OF THESE STATES.

A GREAT year and place
A harsh discordant natal scream out-sounding, to
    touch the mother's heart closer than any yet.

I walk'd the shores of my Eastern sea,
Heard over the waves the little voice,
Saw the divine infant where she woke
    mournfully wailing, amid the roar of cannon,
    curses, shouts, crash of falling buildings,
Was not so sick from the blood in the gutters
    running, nor from the single corpses, nor those
    in heaps, nor those borne away in the tumbrils,
Was not so desperate at the battues of death-was
    not so shock'd at the repeated fusillades of
    the guns.

Pale, silent, stern, what could I say to that long-
    accrued retribution?
Could I wish humanity different?
Could I wish the people made of wood and
    stone?
Or that there be no justice in destiny or time?

O Liberty! O mate for me!
Here too the blaze, the grape-shot and the
    axe, in reserve, to fetch them out in case of
    need,
Here too, though long represt, can never be
    destroy'd,
Here too could rise at last murdering and
    ecstatic,
Here too demanding full arrears of vengeance.

Hence I sign this salute over the sea,
And I do not deny that terrible red birth and
    baptism,
But remember the little voice that I heard
    wailing, and wait with perfect trust, no matter
    how long,
And from to-day sad and cogent I maintain the
    bequeath'd cause, as for all lands,
And I send these words to Paris with my love,
And I guess some chansonniers there will
    understand them,

For I guess there is latent music yet in France,
    floods of it,
O I hear already the bustle of instruments, they
    will soon be drowning all that would
    interrupt them,
O I think the east wind brings a triumphal
    and free march,
It reaches hither, it swells me to Joyful
    madness,
I will run transpose it in words, to justify
I will yet sing a song for you ma femme.

Myself and Mine

MYSELF and mine gymnastic ever,
To stand the cold or heat, to take good aim with
    a gun, to sail a boat, to manage horses, to
    beget superb children,
To speak readily and clearly, to feel at home
    among common people,
And to hold our own in terrible positions on
    land and sea.

Not for an embroiderer,
(There will always be plenty of embroiderers, I
    welcome them also,)
But for the fiber of things and for inherent men
    and women.

Not to chisel ornaments,
But to chisel with free stroke the heads and
    limbs of plenteous supreme Gods, that
    the States may realize them walking and
    talking.

Let me have my own way,
Let others promulge the laws, I will make no
    account of the laws,
Let others praise eminent men and hold up
    peace, I hold up agitation and conflict,
I praise no eminent man, I rebuke to his face
    the one that was thought most worthy.

(Who are you? and what are you secretly guilty
    of all your life?
Will you turn aside all your life? will you grub
    and chatter all your life?
And who are you, blabbing by rote, years, pages,
    languages, reminiscences,
Unwitting to-day that you do not know how to
    speak properly a single word?)

Let others finish specimens, I never finish
    specimens,
I start them by exhaustless laws as Nature does,
    fresh and modern continually.
I give nothing as duties,

What others give as duties I give as living
    impulses,
(Shall I give the heart's action as a duty?)

Let others dispose of questions, I dispose of
    nothing, I arouse unanswerable questions,
Who are they I see and touch, and what about
    them?
What about these likes of myself that draw me
    so close by tender directions and indirections?

I call to the world to distrust the accounts of
    my friends, but listen to my enemies, as I
    myself do,
I charge you forever reject those who would
    expound me, for I cannot expound myself,
I charge that there be no theory or school
    founded out of me,
I charge you to leave all free, as I have left all free.

After me, vista!
O I see life is not short, but immeasurably long,
I henceforth tread the world chaste, temperate,
    an early riser, a steady grower,
Every hour the semen of centuries, and still of
    centuries.

I must follow up these continual lessons of the
    air, water, earth,
I perceive I have no time to lose.

YEAR OF METEORS
(1859–60)

YEAR of meteors! brooding year!
I would bind in words retrospective some of
    your deeds and signs,
I would sing your contest for the 19th
    Presidentiad,
I would sing how an old man, tall, with white
    hair, mounted the scaffold in Virginia,
(I was at hand, silent I stood with teeth shut
    close, I watch'd,
I stood very near you old man when cool and
    indifferent, but trembling with age and your
    unheal'd wounds you mounted the scaffold;)
I would sing in my copious song your census
    returns of the States,
The tables of population and products, I would
    sing of your ships and their cargoes,
The proud black ships of Manhattan arriving,
    some fill'd with immigrants, some from the
    isthmus with cargoes of gold,
Songs thereof would I sing, to all that
    hitherward comes would welcome give,
And you would I sing, fair stripling! welcome to
    you from me, young prince of England!
(Remember you surging Manhattan's crowds as
    you pass'd with your cortege of nobles?
There in the crowds stood I, and singled you
    out with attachment;)

Nor forget I to sing of the wonder, the ship as
    she swam up my bay,
Well-shaped and stately the *Great Eastern* swam
    up my bay, she was 600 feet long,
Her moving swiftly surrounded by myriads of
    small craft I forget not to sing;
Nor the comet that came unannounced out of
    the north flaring in heaven,
Nor the strange huge meteor-procession
    dazzling and clear shooting over our heads,
(A moment, a moment long it sail'd its balls of
    unearthly light over our heads,
Then departed, dropt in the night, and was
    gone;)
Of such, and fitful as they, I sing—with gleams
    from them would gleam and patch these
    chants,
Your chants, O year all mottled with evil and
    good-year of forebodings!
Year of comets and meteors transient and
    strange-lo! even here one equally transient
    and strange!
As I flit through you hastily, soon to fall and be
    gone, what is this chant,
What am I myself but one of your meteors?

WITH ANTECEDENTS

1

WITH antecedents,
With my fathers and mothers and the
　accumulations of past ages,
With all which, had it not been, I would not
　now be here, as I am,
With Egypt, India, Phenicia, Greece and Rome,
With the Kelt, the Scandinavian, the Alb and the
　Saxon,
With antique maritime ventures, laws,
　artisanship, wars and journeys,
With the poet, the skald, the saga, the myth, and
　the oracle,
With the sale of slaves, with enthusiasts, with the
　troubadour, the crusader, and the monk,
With those old continents whence we have come
　to this new continent,
With the fading kingdoms and kings over there,
With the fading religions and priests,
With the small shores we look back to from our
　own large and present shores,
With countless years drawing themselves onward
　and arrived at these years,
You and me arrived—America arrived and
　making this year,
This year! sending itself ahead countless years to
　come.

2

O but it is not the years—it is I, it is You,
We touch all laws and tally all antecedents,
We are the skald, the oracle, the monk and the
  knight, we easily include them and more,
We stand amid time beginningless and endless,
  we stand amid evil and good,
All swings around us, there is as much darkness
  as light,
The very sun swings itself and its system of
  planets around us,
Its sun, and its again, all swing around us.

As for me, (torn, stormy, amid these vehement
  days,)
I have the idea of all, and am all and believe in
  all,
I believe materialism is true and spiritualism is
  true, I reject no part.

(Have I forgotten any part? any thing in the
  past?
Come to me whoever and whatever, till I give
  you recognition.)

I respect Assyria, China, Teutonia, and the
  Hebrews,
I adopt each theory, myth, god, and demigod,
I see that the old accounts, bibles, genealogies,
  are true, without exception,

I assert that all past days were what they must
    have been,
And that they could no-how have been better
    than they were,
And that to-day is what it must be, and that
    America is,
And that to-day and America could no-how be
    better than they are.

3

In the name of these States and in your and my
    name, the Past,
And in the name of these States and in your and
    my name, the Present time.

I know that the past was great and the future
    will be great,
And I know that both curiously conjoint in the
    present time,
(For the sake of him I typify, for the common
    average man's sake, your sake if you are he,)
And that where I am or you are this present day,
    there is the center of all days, all races,
And there is the meaning to us of all that has
    ever come of races and days, or ever will
    come.

A Broadway Pageant

1

OVER the Western sea hither from Niphon
    come,
Courteous, the swart-cheek'd two-sworded
    envoys,
Leaning back in their open barouches, bare-
    headed, impassive,
Ride to-day through Manhattan.

Libertad! I do not know whether others behold
    what I behold,
In the procession along with the nobles of
    Niphon, the errand-bearers,
Bringing up the rear, hovering above, around, or
    in the ranks marching,
But I will sing you a song of what I behold
    Libertad.

When million-footed Manhattan unpent
    descends to her pavements,
When the thunder-cracking guns arouse me with
    the proud roar love,
When the round-mouth'd guns out of the
    smoke and smell I love spit their salutes,

When the fire-flashing guns have fully alerted
    me, and heaven-clouds canopy my city with a
    delicate thin haze,
When gorgeous the countless straight stems,
    the forests at the wharves, thicken with
    colors,
When every ship richly drest carries her flag at
    the peak,
When pennants trail and street-festoons hang
    from the windows,
When Broadway is entirely given up to foot-
    passengers and foot-standers, when the mass
    is densest,
When the facades of the houses are alive with
    people, when eyes gaze riveted tens of
    thousands at a time,
When the guests from the islands advance, when
    the pageant moves forward visible,
When the summons is made, when the
    answer that waited thousands of years
    answers,
I too arising, answering, descend to the
    pavements, merge with the crowd, and gaze
    with them.

2

Superb-faced Manhattan!
Comrade Americanos! to us, then at last the
    Orient comes.
To us, my city,

Where our tall-topt marble and iron beauties
   range on opposite sides, to walk in the space
   between,
To-day our Antipodes comes.

The Originatress comes,
The nest of languages, the bequeather of poems,
   the race of eld,
Florid with blood, pensive, rapt with musings,
   hot with passion,
Sultry with perfume, with ample and flowing
   garments,
With sunburnt visage, with intense soul and
   glittering eyes,
The race of Brahma comes.

See my cantabile! these and more are flashing to
   us from the procession,
As it moves changing, a kaleidoscope divine it
   moves changing before us.

For not the envoys nor the tann'd Japanee from
   his island only,
Lithe and silent the Hindoo appears, the Asiatic
   continent itself appears, the past, the dead,
The murky night-morning of wonder and fable
   inscrutable,
The envelop'd mysteries, the old and unknown
   hive-bees,

The north, the sweltering south, eastern Assyria,
   the Hebrews, the ancient of ancients,
Vast desolated cities, the gliding present, all of
   these and more are in the pageant-procession.

Geography, the world, is in it,
The Great Sea, the brood of islands, Polynesia,
   the coast beyond,
The coast you henceforth are facing—you
   Libertad! from your Western golden shores,
The countries there with their populations, the
   millions en-masse are curiously here,
The swarming market-places, the temples with
   idols ranged along the sides or at the end,
   bonze, brahmin, and llama,
Mandarin, farmer, merchant, mechanic, and
   fisherman,
The singing-girl and the dancing-girl, the
   ecstatic persons, the secluded emperors,
Confucius himself, the great poets and heroes,
   the warriors, the castes, all,
Trooping up, crowding from all directions, from
   the Altay mountains,
From Thibet, from the four winding and far-
   flowing rivers of China,
From the southern peninsulas and the demi-
   continental islands, from Malaysia,
These and whatever belongs to them palpable
   show forth to me, and are seiz'd by me,

And I am seiz'd by them, and friendlily held by
    them,
Till as here them all I chant, Libertad! for
    themselves and for you.

For I too raising my voice join the ranks of this
    pageant,
I am the chanter, I chant aloud over the
    pageant,
I chant the world on my Western sea,
I chant copious the islands beyond, thick as stars
    in the sky,
I chant the new empire grander than any before,
    as in a vision it comes to me,
I chant America the mistress, I chant a greater
    supremacy,
I chant projected a thousand blooming cities yet
    in time on those groups of sea-islands,
My sail-ships and steam-ships threading the
    archipelagoes,
My stars and stripes fluttering in the wind,
Commerce opening, the sleep of ages having
    done its work, races reborn, refresh'd,
Lives, works resumed—the object I know not—
    but the old, the Asiatic renew'd as it must be,
Commencing from this day surrounded by the
    world.

3

And you Libertad of the world!
You shall sit in the middle well-pois'd thousands
    and thousands of years,
As to-day from one side the nobles of Asia come
    to you,
As to-morrow from the other side the queen of
    England sends her eldest son to you.

The sign is reversing, the orb is enclosed,
The ring is circled, the journey is done,
The box-lid is but perceptibly open'd,
    nevertheless the perfume pours copiously out
    of the whole box.

Young Libertad! with the venerable Asia, the all-
    mother,
Be considerate with her now and ever hot
    Libertad, for you are all,
Bend your proud neck to the long-off mother
    now sending messages over the archipelagoes
    to you,
Bend your proud neck low for once, young
    Libertad.

Here the children straying westward so long? so
    wide the tramping?
Were the precedent dim ages debouching
    westward from Paradise so long?

Were the centuries steadily footing it that way,
    all the while unknown, for you, for reasons?

They are justified, they are accomplish'd, they
    shall now be turn'd the other way also, to
    travel toward you thence,
They shall now also march obediently eastward
    for your sake
Libertad.

Sea-Drift

OUT OF THE CRADLE ENDLESSLY ROCKING

OUT of the cradle endlessly rocking,
Out of the mocking-bird's throat, the musical
  shuttle,
Out of the Ninth-month midnight,
Over the sterile sands and the fields beyond,
  where the child leaving his bed wander'd
  alone, bareheaded, barefoot,
Down from the shower'd halo,
Up from the mystic play of shadows twining
  and twisting as if they were alive,
Out from the patches of briers and
  blackberries,
From the memories of the bird that chanted
  to me,
From your memories sad brother, from the fitful
  risings and fallings I heard,
From under that yellow half-moon late-risen and
  swollen as if with tears,
From those beginning notes of yearning and
  love there in the mist,
From the thousand responses of my heart never
  to cease,
From the myriad thence-arous'd words,

From the word stronger and more delicious
    than any,
From such as now they start the scene revisiting,
As a flock, twittering, rising, or overhead passing,
Borne hither, ere all eludes me, hurriedly,
A man, yet by these tears a little boy again,
Throwing myself on the sand, confronting the
    waves,
I, chanter of pains and joys, uniter of here and
    hereafter,
Taking all hints to use them, but swiftly leaping
    beyond them,
A reminiscence sing.

Once Paumanok,
When the lilac-scent was in the air and Fifth-
    month grass was growing,
Up this seashore in some briers,
Two feather'd guests from Alabama, two
    together,
And their nest, and four light-green eggs
    spotted with brown,
And every day the he-bird to and fro near at
    hand,
And every day the she-bird crouch'd on her
    nest, silent, with bright eyes,
And every day I, a curious boy, never too close,
    never disturbing them,
Cautiously peering, absorbing, translating.

Shine! shine! shine!
Pour down your warmth, great sun.
While we bask, we two together.

Two together!
Winds blow south, or winds blow north,
Day come white, or night come black,
Home, or rivers and mountains from home,
Singing all time, minding no time,
While we two keep together.

Till of a sudden,
May-be kill'd, unknown to her mate,
One forenoon the she-bird crouch'd not on
    the nest,
Nor return'd that afternoon, nor the next,
Nor ever appear'd again.

And thenceforward all summer in the sound of
    the sea,
And at night under the full of the moon in
    calmer weather,
Over the hoarse surging of the sea,
Or flitting from brier to brier by day,
I saw, I heard at intervals the remaining one, the
    he-bird,
The solitary guest from Alabama.

Blow! blow! blow!
Blow up sea-winds along Paumanok's shore,—

I wait and I wait till you blow my mate to
    me.

Yes, when the stars glisten'd,
All night long on the prong of a moss-scallop'd
    stake,
Down almost amid the slapping waves,
Sat the lone singer wonderful causing tears.

He call'd on his mate,
He pour'd forth the meanings which I of all
    men know.

Yes my brother I know,
The rest might not, but I have treasur'd every
    note,
For more than once dimly down to the beach
    gliding,
Silent, avoiding the moonbeams, blending
    myself with the shadows,
Recalling now the obscure shapes, the echoes,
    the sounds and sights after their sorts,
The white arms out in the breakers tirelessly
    tossing,
I, with bare feet, a child, the wind waiting my hair,
Listen'd long and long.

Listen'd to keep, to sing, now translating the
    notes,
Following you my brother.

Soothe! soothe! soothe!
Close on its wave soothes the wave behind,
And again another behind embracing and
   lapping, every one close,
But my love soothes not me, not me.

Low hangs the moon, it rose late,
It is lagging—O I think it is heavy with love,
   with love.

O madly the sea pushes upon the land,
With love, with love.

O night! do I not see my love fluttering out
   among the breakers?
What is that little black thing I see there in the
   white?

Loud! loud! loud!
Loud I call to you, my love!
High and clear I shoot my voice over the
   waves,
Surely you must know who is here, is here,
You must know who I am, my love.

Low-hanging moon!
What is that dusky spot in your brown yellow?
O it is the shape, the shape of my mate.
O moon do not keep her from me any longer.

Land! land! O land!
Whichever way I turn, O I think you could give
     me my mate back again if you only would,
For I am almost sure I see her dimly whichever
     way I look.

O rising stars!
Perhaps the one I want so much will rise, will
     rise with some of you.

O throat! O trembling throat!
Sound clearer through the atmosphere!
Pierce the woods, the earth,
Somewhere listening to catch you must be the
     one I want.

Shake out carols!
Solitary here, the night's carols!
Carols of lonesome love! death's carols!
Carols under that lagging, yellow, waning
     moon!
O under that moon where she droops almost
     down into the sea!
O reckless despairing carols.

But soft! sink low!
Soft! let me just murmur,
And do you wait a moment you husky-nois'd
     sea,

For somewhere I believe I heard my mate
    responding to me,
So faint, I must be still, be still to listen,
But not altogether still, for then she might not
    come immediately to me.

Hither my love!
Here I am! here!
With this just-sustain'd note I announce myself
    to you,
This gentle call is for you my love, for you.

Do not be decoy'd elsewhere,
That is the whistle of the wind, it is not my
    voice,
That is the fluttering, the fluttering of the spray,
Those are the shadows of leaves.

O darkness! O in vain!
O I am very sick and sorrowful

O brown halo in the sky near the moon,
    drooping upon the sea!
O troubled reflection in the sea!
O throat! O throbbing heart!
And I singing uselessly, uselessly all the night.

O past! O happy life! O songs of joy!
In the air, in the woods, over fields,
Loved! loved! loved! loved! loved!

But my mate no more, no more with me!
We two together no more.

The aria sinking,
All else continuing, the stars shining,
The winds blowing, the notes of the bird
    continuous echoing,
With angry moans the fierce old mother
    incessantly moaning,
On the sands of Paumanok's shore gray and
    rustling,
The yellow half-moon enlarged, sagging down,
    drooping, the face of the sea almost touching,
The boy ecstatic, with his bare feet the waves,
    with his hair the atmosphere dallying,
The love in the heart long pent, now loose, now
    at last tumultuously bursting,
The aria's meaning, the ears, the soul, swiftly
    depositing,
The strange tears down the cheeks coursing,
The colloquy there, the trio, each uttering,
The undertone, the savage old mother
    incessantly crying,
To the boy's soul's questions sullenly timing,
    some drown'd secret hissing,
To the outsetting bard.

Demon or bird! (said the boy's soul,)
Is it indeed toward your mate you sing? or is it
    really to me?

For I, that was a child, my tongue's use
  sleeping, now I have heard you,
Now in a moment I know what I am for, I
  awake,
And already a thousand singers, a thousand
  songs, clearer, louder and more sorrowful
  than yours,
A thousand warbling echoes have started to life
  within me, never to die.

O you singer solitary, singing by yourself,
  projecting me,
O solitary me listening, never more shall I cease
  perpetuating you,
Never more shall I escape, never more the
  reverberations,
Never more the cries of unsatisfied love be
  absent from me,
Never again leave me to be the peaceful child I
  was before what there in the night,
By the sea under the yellow and sagging moon,
The messenger there arous'd, the fire, the sweet
  hell within,
The unknown want, the destiny of me.

O give me the clew! (it lurks in the night here
  somewhere,)
O if I am to have so much, let me have more!
A word then, (for I will conquer it,)
The word final, superior to all,

Subtle, sent up—what is it?—I listen;
Are you whispering it, and have been all the
    time, you sea-waves?
Is that it from your liquid rims and wet sands?

Whereto answering, the sea,
Delaying not, hurrying not,
Whisper'd me through the night, and very
    plainly before daybreak,
Lisp'd to me the low and delicious word
    death,
And again death, death, death, death
Hissing melodious, neither like the bird nor like
    my arous'd child's heart,
But edging near as privately for me rustling at
    my feet,
Creeping thence steadily up to my ears and
    laving me softly all over,
Death, death, death, death, death.

Which I do not forget.
But fuse the song of my dusky demon and
    brother,
That he sang to me in the moonlight on
    Paumanok's gray beach,
With the thousand responsive songs at random,
My own songs awaked from that hour,
And with them the key, the word up from the
    waves,
The word of the sweetest song and all songs,

That strong and delicious word which, creeping
    to my feet,
(Or like some old crone rocking the cradle,
    swathed in sweet garments, bending aside,)
The sea whisper'd me.

As I Ebb'd with the Ocean of Life

1

As I ebb'd with the ocean of life,
As I wended the shores I know,
As I walk'd where the ripples continually wash
    you Paumanok,
Where they rustle up hoarse and sibilant,
Where the fierce old mother endlessly cries for
    her castaways,
I musing late in the autumn day, gazing off
    southward,
Held by this electric self out of the pride of
    which I utter poems,
Was seiz'd by the spirit that trails in the lines
    underfoot,
The rim, the sediment that stands for all the
    water and all the land of the globe.

Fascinated, my eyes reverting from the south,
    dropt, to follow those slender windrows,
Chaff, straw, splinters of wood, weeds, and the
    sea-gluten,

Scum, scales from shining rocks, leaves of salt-
    lettuce, left by the tide,
Miles walking, the sound of breaking waves the
    other side of me,
Paumanok there and then as I thought the old
    thought of likenesses,
These you presented to me you fish-shaped island,
As I wended the shores I know,
As I walk'd with that electric self seeking types.

2

As I wend to the shores I know not,
As I list to the dirge, the voices of men and
    women wreck'd,
As I inhale the impalpable breezes that set in
    upon me,
As the ocean so mysterious rolls toward me
    closer and closer,
I too but signify at the utmost a little wash'd-up
    drift,
A few sands and dead leaves to gather,
Gather, and merge myself as part of the sands
    and drift.

O baffled, balk'd, bent to the very earth,
Oppress'd with myself that I have dared to open
    my mouth,
Aware now that amid all that blab whose echoes
    recoil upon me I have not once had the least
    idea who or what I am,

But that before all my arrogant poems the real
  Me stands yet untouch'd, untold, altogether
  unreach'd,
Withdrawn far, mocking me with mock-
  congratulatory signs and bows,
With peals of distant ironical laughter at every
  word I have written,
Pointing in silence to these songs, and then to
  the sand beneath.

I perceive I have not really understood any
  thing, not a single object, and that no man
  ever can,
Nature here in sight of the sea taking advantage
  of me to dart upon me and sting me,
Because I have dared to open my mouth to sing
  at all.

3

You oceans both, I close with you,
We murmur alike reproachfully rolling sands and
  drift, knowing not why,
These little shreds indeed standing for you and
  me and all.

You friable shore with trails of debris,
You fish-shaped island, I take what is
  underfoot,
What is yours is mine my father.

I too Paumanok,
I too have bubbled up, floated the measureless
    float, and been wash'd on your shores,
I too am but a trail of drift and debris,
I too leave little wrecks upon you, you fish-
    shaped island.

I throw myself upon your breast my father,
I cling to you so that you cannot unloose me,
I hold you so firm till you answer me
    something.

Kiss me my father,
Touch me with your lips as I touch those I love,
Breathe to me while I hold you close the secret
    of the murmuring I envy.

4

Ebb, ocean of life, (the flow will return,)
Cease not your moaning you fierce old mother,
Endlessly cry for your castaways, but fear not,
    deny not me,
Rustle not up so hoarse and angry against my
    feet as I touch you or gather from you.

I mean tenderly by you and all,
I gather for myself and for this phantom looking
    down where we lead, and following me and
    mine.

Me and mine, loose windrows, little corpses,
Froth, snowy white, and bubbles,
(See, from my dead lips the ooze exuding at last,
See, the prismatic colors glistening and rolling,)
Tufts of straw, sands, fragments,
Buoy'd hither from many moods, one
    contradicting another,
From the storm, the long calm, the darkness,
    the swell,
Musing, pondering, a breath, a briny tear, a dab
    of liquid or soil,
Up just as much out of fathomless workings
    fermented and thrown,
A limp blossom or two, torn, just as much over
    waves floating, drifted at random,
Just as much for us that sobbing dirge of
    Nature,
Just as much whence we come that blare of the
    cloud-trumpets,
We, capricious, brought hither we know not
    whence, spread out before you,
You up there walking or sitting,
Whoever you are, we too lie in drifts at your
    feet.

TEARS

TEARS! tears! tears!
In the night, in solitude, tears,
On the white shore dripping, dripping, suck'd in
    by the sand,
Tears, not a star shining, all dark and desolate,
Moist tears from the eyes of a muffled head;
O who is that ghost? that form in the dark, with
    tears?
What shapeless lump is that, bent, crouch'd
    there on the sand?
Streaming tears, sobbing tears, throes, choked
    with wild cries;
O storm, embodied, rising, careering with swift
    steps along the beach!
O wild and dismal night storm, with wind—O
    belching and desperate!
O shade so sedate and decorous by day, with
    calm countenance and regulated pace,
But away at night as you fly, none looking—O
    then the unloosen'd ocean,
Of tears! tears! tears!

To the Man-of-War-Bird

THOU who hast slept all night upon the storm,
Waking renew'd on thy prodigious pinions,
(Burst the wild storm? above it thou
    ascended'st,
And rested on the sky, thy slave that cradled
    thee,)
Now a blue point, far, far in heaven floating,
As to the light emerging here on deck I watch
    thee,
(Myself a speck, a point on the world's floating
    vast.)

Far, far at sea,
After the night's fierce drifts have strewn the
    shore with wrecks,
With re-appearing day as now so happy and
    serene,
The rosy and elastic dawn, the flashing sun,
The limpid spread of air cerulean,
Thou also re-appearest.

Thou born to match the gale, (thou art all
    wings,)
To cope with heaven and earth and sea and
    hurricane,
Thou ship of air that never furl'st thy sails,
Days, even weeks untired and onward, through
    spaces, realms gyrating,

At dusk that lookist on Senegal, at morn
   America,
That sport'st amid the lightning-flash and
   thunder-cloud,
In them, in thy experiences, had'st thou my
   soul,
What joys! what joys were thine!

ABOARD AT A SHIP'S HELM

ABOARD at a ship's helm,
A young steersman steering with care.

Through fog on a sea-coast dolefully ringing,
An ocean-bell—O a warning bell, rock'd by the
   waves.

O you give good notice indeed, you bell by the
   sea-reefs ringing,
Ringing, ringing, to warn the ship from its
   wreck-place.

For as on the alert O steersman, you mind the
   loud admonition,
The bows turn, the freighted ship tacking speeds
   away under her gray sails,
The beautiful and noble ship with all her
   precious wealth speeds away gayly and
   safe.

But O the ship, the immortal ship! O ship
 aboard the ship!
Ship of the body, ship of the soul, voyaging,
 voyaging, voyaging.

ON THE BEACH AT NIGHT

ON the beach at night,
Stands a child with her father,
Watching the east, the autumn sky.

Up through the darkness,
While ravening clouds, the burial clouds, in
 black masses spreading,
Lower sullen and fast athwart and down the sky,
Amid a transparent clear belt of ether yet left in
 the east,
Ascends large and calm the lord-star Jupiter,
And nigh at hand, only a very little above,
Swim the delicate sisters the Pleiades.

From the beach the child holding the hand of
 her father,
Those burial-clouds that lower victorious soon
 to devour all,
Watching, silently weeps.

Weep not, child,
Weep not, my darling,

With these kisses let me remove your tears,
The ravening clouds shall not long be
    victorious,
They shall not long possess the sky, they devour
    the stars only in apparition,
Jupiter shall emerge, be patient, watch again
    another night, the Pleiades shall emerge,
They are immortal, all those stars both silvery
    and golden shall shine out again,
The great stars and the little ones shall shine out
    again, they endure,
The vast immortal suns and the long-enduring
    pensive moons shall again shine.

Then dearest child mournest thou only for
    jupiter?
Considerest thou alone the burial of the stars?

Something there is,
(With my lips soothing thee, adding I whisper,
I give thee the first suggestion, the problem and
    indirection,)
Something there is more immortal even than the
    stars,
(Many the burials, many the days and nights,
    passing away,)
Something that shall endure longer even than
    lustrous Jupiter
Longer than sun or any revolving satellite,
Or the radiant sisters the Pleiades.

The World below the Brine

THE world below the brine,
Forests at the bottom of the sea, the branches
and leaves,
Sea-lettuce, vast lichens, strange flowers and
seeds, the thick tangle openings, and pink
turf,
Different colors, pale gray and green, purple,
white, and gold, the play of light through the
water,
Dumb swimmers there among the rocks, coral,
gluten, grass, rushes, and the aliment of the
swimmers,
Sluggish existences grazing there suspended, or
slowly crawling close to the bottom,
The sperm-whale at the surface blowing air and
spray, or disporting with his flukes,
The leaden-eyed shark, the walrus, the turtle,
the hairy sea-leopard, and the sting-ray,
Passions there, wars, pursuits, tribes, sight in
those ocean-depths, breathing that thick-
breathing air, as so many do,
The change thence to the sight here, and to the
subtle air breathed by beings like us who walk
this sphere,
The change onward from ours to that of beings
who walk other spheres.

On the Beach at Night Alone

ON the beach at night alone,
As the old mother sways her to and fro singing
 her husky song,
As I watch the bright stars shining, I think a
 thought of the clef of the universes and of the
 future.

A vast similitude interlocks all,
All spheres, grown, ungrown, small, large, suns,
 moons, planets,
All distances of place however wide,
All distances of time, all inanimate forms,
All souls, all living bodies though they be ever
 so different, or in different worlds,
All gaseous, watery, vegetable, mineral processes,
 the fishes, the brutes,
All nations, colors, barbarisms, civilizations,
 languages,
All identities that have existed or may exist on
 this globe, or any globe,
All lives and deaths, all of the past, present,
 future,
This vast similitude spans them, and always has
 spann'd,
And shall forever span them and compactly hold
 and enclose them.

SONG FOR ALL SEAS, ALL SHIPS

1

TO-DAY a rude brief recitative,
Of ships sailing the seas, each with its special flag
    or ship-signal,
Of unnamed heroes in the ships-of waves
    spreading and spreading far as the eye can
    reach,
Of dashing spray, and the winds piping and
    blowing,
And out of these a chant for the sailors of all
    nations,
Fitful, like a surge.

Of sea-captains young or old, and the mates,
    and of all intrepid sailors,
Of the few, very choice, taciturn, whom fate can
    never surprise nor death dismay.
Pick'd sparingly without noise by thee old
    ocean, chosen by thee,
Thou sea that pickest and cullest the race in
    time, and unitest nations,
Suckled by thee, old husky nurse, embodying thee,
Indomitable, untamed as thee.

(Ever the heroes on water or on land, by ones or
    twos appearing,
Ever the stock preserv'd and never lost, though
    rare, enough for seed preserv'd.)

2

Flaunt out O sea your separate flags of nations!
Flaunt out visible as ever the various ship-
 signals!
But do you reserve especially for yourself and for
 the soul of man one flag above all the rest,
A spiritual woven signal for all nations, emblem
 of man elate above death,
Token of all brave captains and all intrepid
 sailors and mates,
And all that went down doing their duty,
Reminiscent of them, twined from all intrepid
 captains young or old,
A pennant universal, subtly waving all time, o'er
 all brave sailors,
All seas, all ships.

PATROLING BARNEGAT

WILD, wild the storm, and the sea high
 running,
Steady the roar of the gale, with incessant
 undertone muttering,
Shouts of demoniac laughter fitfully piercing and
 pealing,
Waves, air, midnight, their savagest trinity
 lashing,
Out in the shadows there milk-white combs
 careering,

On beachy slush and sand spirts of snow fierce
    slanting,
Where through the murk the easterly death-
    wind breasting,
Through cutting swirl and spray watchful and
    firm advancing,
(That in the distance! is that a wreck? is the red
    signal flaring?)
Slush and sand of the beach tireless till daylight
    wending,
Steadily, slowly, through hoarse roar never remitting,
Along the midnight edge by those milk-white
    combs careering,
A group of dim, weird forms, struggling, the
    night confronting,
That savage trinity warily watching.

AFTER THE SEA-SHIP

AFTER the sea-ship, after the whistling winds,
After the white-gray sails taut to their spars and
    ropes,
Below, a myriad myriad waves hastening, lifting
    up their necks,
Tending in ceaseless flow toward the track of the
    ship,
Waves of the ocean bubbling and gurgling,
    blithely prying,

Waves, undulating waves, liquid, uneven,
    emulous waves,
Toward that whirling current, laughing and
    buoyant, with curves,
Where the great vessel sailing and tacking
    displaced the surface,
Larger and smaller waves in the spread of the
    ocean yearnfully flowing,
The wake of the sea-ship after she passes,
    flashing and frolicsome under the sun,
A motley procession with many a fleck of foam
    and many fragments,
Following the stately and rapid ship, in the wake
    following.

A BOSTON BALLAD
(1854)

TO get betimes in Boston town I rose this
    morning early,
Here's a good place at the corner, I must stand
    and see the show.

Clear the way there Jonathan!
Way for the President's marshal—way for the
    government cannon!
Way for the Federal foot and dragoons, (and the
    apparitions copiously tumbling.)

I love to look on the Stars and Stripes, I hope
   the fifes will play Yankee Doodle.
How bright shine the cutlasses of the foremost
   troops!
Every man holds his revolver, marching stiff
   through Boston town.

A fog follows, antiques of the same come
   limping,
Some appear wooden-legged, and some appear
   bandaged and bloodless.

Why this is indeed a show—it has called the
   dead out of the earth!
The old graveyards of the hills have hurried to
   see!
Phantoms! phantoms countless by flank and rear!
Cock'd hats of mothy mould—crutches made of
   mist!
Arms in slings-old men leaning on young men's
   shoulders.

What troubles you Yankee phantoms? what is all
   this chattering of bare gums?
Does the ague convulse your limbs? do you
   mistake your crutches for firelocks and level
   them?

If you blind your eyes with tears you will not see
   the President's marshal,

If you groan such groans you might balk the
    government cannon.

For shame old maniacs—bring down those
    toss'd arms, and let your white hair be,
Here gape your great grandsons, their wives
    gaze at them from the windows,
See how well dress'd, see how orderly they
    conduct themselves.

Worse and worse—can't you stand it? are you
    retreating?
Is this hour with the living too dead for you?

Retreat then—pell-mell!
To your graves—back—back to the hills old
    limpers!
I do not think you belong here anyhow.

But there is one thing that belongs here—shall
    I tell you what it is, gentlemen of
    Boston?

I will whisper it to the Mayor, he shall send a
    committee to England,
They shall get a grant from the Parliament, go
    with a cart to the royal vault,
Dig out King George's coffin, unwrap him quick
    from the graveclothes, box up his bones for a
    journey,

Find a swift Yankee clipper—here is freight for
    you, black-bellied clipper,
Up with your anchor—shake out your sails—
    steer straight toward Boston bay.

Now call for the President's marshal again, bring
    out the government cannon,
Fetch home the roarers from Congress, make
    another procession, guard it with foot and
    dragoons.

This centre-piece for them;
Look, all orderly citizens—look from the
    windows, women!

The committee open the box, set up the regal
    ribs, glue those that will not stay,
Clap the skull on top of the ribs, and clap a
    crown on top of the skull.
You have got your revenge, old buster—the
    crown is come to its own, and more than its
    own.

Stick your hands in your pockets, Jonathan—
    you are a made man from this day,
You are mighty cute—and here is one of your
    bargains.

Europe,
The 72d and 73d Years of These States

SUDDENLY Out of its stale and drowsy lair,
the lair of slaves,
Like lightning it le'pt forth half startled at
itself,
Its feet upon the ashes and the rags, its hands
tight to the throats of kings.

O hope and faith!
O aching close of exiled patriots' lives!
O many a sicken'd heart!
Turn back unto this day and make yourselves
afresh.

And you, paid to defile the People—you liars,
mark!
Not for numberless agonies, murders, lusts,
For court thieving in its manifold mean forms,
worming from his simplicity the poor man's
wages,
For many a promise sworn by royal lips and
broken and laugh'd at in the breaking,

Then in their power not for all these did the
blows strike revenge, or the heads of the
nobles fall;
The People scorn'd the ferocity of kings.

But the sweetness of mercy brew'd bitter
    destruction, and the frighten'd monarchs
    come back,
Each comes in state with his train, hangman,
    priest, tax-gatherer,
Soldier, lawyer, lord, jailer, and sycophant.

Yet behind all lowering stealing, lo, a shape,
Vague as the night, draped interminably, head,
    front and form, in scarlet folds,
Whose face and eyes none may see,
Out of its robes only this, the red robes lifted by
    the arm,
One finger crook'd pointed high over the top,
    like the head of a snake appears.

Meanwhile corpses lie in new-made graves,
    bloody corpses of young men,
The rope of the gibbet hangs heavily, the bullets
    of princes are flying, the creatures of power
    laugh aloud,
And all these things bear fruits, and they are
    good.

Those corpses of young men,
Those martyrs that hang from the gibbets, those
    hearts pierc'd by the gray lead,
Cold and motionless as they seem live elsewhere
    with unslaughter'd vitality.

They live in other young men O kings!
They live in brothers again ready to defy you,
They were purified by death, they were taught
    and exalted.

Not a grave of the murder'd for freedom but
    grows seed for freedom, in its turn to bear
    seed,
Which the winds carry afar and re-sow, and the
    rains and the snows nourish.

Not a disembodied spirit can the weapons of
    tyrants let loose,
But it stalks invisibly over the earth, whispering,
    counseling, cautioning.
Liberty, let others despair of you—I never
    despair of you.

Is the house shut? is the master away?
Nevertheless, be ready, be not weary of
    watching,
He will soon return, his messengers come anon.

By the Roadside

A Hand-Mirror

HOLD it up sternly—see this it sends back,
    (who is it? is it you?)
Outside fair costume, within ashes and filth,
No more a flashing eye, no more a sonorous
    voice or springy step,
Now some slave's eye, voice, hands, step,
A drunkard's breath, unwholesome eater's face,
    venerealee's flesh,
Lungs rotting away piecemeal, stomach sour and
    cankerous,
Joints rheumatic, bowels clogged with
    abomination,
Blood circulating dark and poisonous streams,
Words babble, hearing and touch callous,
No brain, no heart left, no magnetism of sex;
Such from one look in this looking-glass ere you
    go hence,
Such a result so soon—and from such a
    beginning!

GODS

LOVER divine and perfect Comrade,
Waiting content, invisible yet, but certain,
Be thou my God.

Thou, thou, the Ideal Man,
Fair, able, beautiful, content, and loving,
Complete in body and dilate in spirit,
Be thou my God.

O Death, (for Life has served its turn,)
Opener and usher to the heavenly mansion,
Be thou my God.

Aught, aught of mightiest, best I see, conceive,
    or know,
(To break the stagnant tie-thee, thee to free, O
    soul,)
Be thou my God.

All great ideas, the races' aspirations,
All heroisms, deeds of rapt enthusiasts,
Be ye my Gods.

Or Time and Space,
Or shape of Earth divine and wondrous,
Or some fair shape I viewing, worship,
Or lustrous orb of sun or star by night,
Be ye my Gods.

GERMS

FORMS, qualities, lives, humanity, language,
  thoughts,
The ones known, and the ones unknown, the
  ones on the stars,
The stars themselves, some shaped, others
  unshaped,
Wonders as of those countries, the soil, trees,
  cities, inhabitants, whatever they may be,
Splendid suns, the moons and rings, the
  countless combinations and effects,
Such-like, and as good as such-like, visible here
  or anywhere, stand provided for a handful of
  space, which I extend my arm and half
  enclose with my hand,
That containing the start of each and all, the
  virtue, the germs of all.

THOUGHTS

OF ownership—as if one fit to own things could
  not at pleasure enter upon all, and
  incorporate them into himself or herself;
Of vista—suppose some sight in arriere through
  the formative chaos, presuming the
  growth, fulness, life, now attain'd on the
  journey,

(But I see the road continued, and the journey
    ever continued;)
Of what was once lacking on earth, and in due
    time has become supplied—and of what will
    yet be supplied,
Because all I see and know I believe to have its
    main purport in what will yet be supplied.

WHEN I HEARD THE LEARN'D ASTRONOMER

WHEN I heard the learn'd astronomer,
When the proofs, the figures, were ranged in
    columns before me,
When I was shown the charts and diagrams, to
    add, divide, and measure them,
When I sitting heard the astronomer where he
    lectured with much applause in the lecture-
    room,
How soon unaccountable I became tired and
    sick,
Till rising and gliding out I wander'd off by
    myself,
In the mystical moist night-air, and from time to
    time,
Look'd up in perfect silence at the stars.

PERFECTIONS

ONLY themselves understand themselves and
   the like of themselves,
As souls only understand souls.

O ME! O LIFE!

O ME! O life! of the questions of these
   recurring,
Of the endless trains of the faithless, of cities
   fill'd with the foolish,
Of myself forever reproaching myself, (for
   who more foolish than I, and who more
   faithless?)
Of eyes that vainly crave the light, of the objects
   mean, of the struggle ever renew'd,
Of the poor results of all, of the plodding and
   sordid crowds I see around me,
Of the empty and useless years of the rest, with
   the rest me intertwined,
The question, O me! so sad, recurring-What
   good amid these, O me,
O life?

Answer.
That you are here—that life exists and identity,
That the powerful play goes on, and you may
   contribute a verse.

To a President

ALL you are doing and saying is to America dangled mirages,
You have not learn'd of Nature—of the politics of Nature you have not learn'd the great amplitude, rectitude, impartiality,
You have not seen that only such as they are for these States,
And that what is less than they must sooner or later lift off from these States.

I Sit and Look Out

I SIT and look out upon all the sorrows of the world, and upon all oppression and shame,
I hear secret convulsive sobs from young men at anguish with themselves, remorseful after deeds done,
I see in low life the mother misused by her children, dying, neglected, gaunt, desperate,
I see the wife misused by her husband, I see the treacherous seducer of young women,
I mark the ranklings of jealousy and unrequited love attempted to be hid, I see these sights on the earth,
I see the workings of battle, pestilence, tyranny, I see martyrs and prisoners,

I observe a famine at sea, I observe the sailors
    casting lots who shall be kill'd to preserve the
    lives of the rest,
I observe the slights and degradations cast by
    arrogant persons upon laborers, the poor, and
    upon negroes, and the like;
All these—all the meanness and agony without
    end I sitting look out upon,
See, hear, and am silent.

To Rich Givers

WHAT YOU give me I cheerfully accept,
A little sustenance, a hut and garden, a little
    money, as I rendezvous with my poems,
A traveler's lodging and breakfast as journey
    through the States,—why should I be
    ashamed to own such gifts? why to advertise
    for them?
For I myself am not one who bestows nothing
    upon man and woman,
For I bestow upon any man or woman the
    entrance to all the gifts of the universe.

THE DALLIANCE OF THE EAGLES

SKIRTING the river road, (my forenoon walk,
    my rest,)
Skyward in air a sudden muffled sound, the
    dalliance of the eagles,
The rushing amorous contact high in space
    together,
The clinching interlocking claws, a living, fierce,
    gyrating wheel,
Four beating wings, two beaks, a swirling mass
    tight grappling,
In tumbling turning clustering loops, straight
    downward falling,
Till o'er the river pois'd, the twain yet one, a
    moment's lull,
A motionless still balance in the air, then
    parting, talons loosing,
Upward again on slow-firm pinions slanting,
    their separate diverse flight,
She hers, he his, pursuing.

ROAMING IN THOUGHT
(AFTER READING HEGEL)

ROAMING in thought over the Universe, I saw
    the little that is Good steadily hastening
    towards immortality,

And the vast all that is call'd Evil I saw hastening
    to merge itself and become lost and dead.

A FARM PICTURE

THROUGH the ample open door of the
    peaceful country barn,
A sunlit pasture field with cattle and horses
    feeding,
And haze and vista, and the far horizon fading
    away.

A CHILD'S AMAZE

SILENT and amazed even when a little boy,
I remember I heard the preacher every Sunday
    put God in his statements,
As contending against some being or influence.

THE RUNNER

ON a flat road runs the well-train'd runner,
He is lean and sinewy with muscular legs,
He is thinly clothed, he leans forward as he
    runs,
With lightly closed fists and arms partially rais'd.

Beautiful Women

WOMEN sit or move to and fro, some old,
   some young,
The young are beautiful—but the old are more
   beautiful than the young.

Mother and Babe

I SEE the sleeping babe nestling the breast of its
   mother,
The sleeping mother and babe—hush'd, I study
   them long and long.

Thought

OF obedience, faith, adhesiveness;
As I stand aloof and look there is to me
   something profoundly affecting in large
   masses of men following the lead of those
   who do not believe in men.

VISOR'D

A MASK, a perpetual natural disguiser of
    herself,
Concealing her face, concealing her form,
Changes and transformations every hour, every
    moment,
Falling upon her even when she sleeps.

THOUGHT

OF JUSTICE—as If could be any thing but the
    same ample law, expounded by natural judges
    and saviors,
As if it might be this thing or that thing,
    according to decisions.

GLIDING O'ER ALL

GLIDING O'er all, through all,
Through Nature, Time, and Space,
As a ship on the waters advancing,
The voyage of the soul—not life alone,
Death, many deaths I'll sing.

Hast Never Come to Thee an Hour

HAST never come to thee an hour,
A sudden gleam divine, precipitating, bursting
    all these bubbles, fashions, wealth?
These eager business aims—books, politics, art,
    amours,
To utter nothingness?

Thought

OF Equality-as if it harm'd me, giving others
    the same chances and rights as myself-as if it
    were not indispensable to my own rights that
    others possess the same.

To Old Age

I SEE in you the estuary that enlarges and
    spreads itself grandly as it pours in the
    great sea.

Locations and Times

LOCATIONS and times—what is it in me that
    meets them all, whenever and wherever, and
    makes me at home?

Forms, colors, densities, odors—what is it in me
that corresponds with them?

OFFERINGS

A THOUSAND perfect men and women
appear,
Around each gathers a cluster of friends, and gay
children and youths, with offerings.
To The States,

TO IDENTIFY THE 16TH, 17TH, OR 18TH PRESIDENTIAD.

WHY reclining, interrogating? why myself and
all drowsing?
What deepening twilight—scum floating atop of
the waters,
Who are they as bats and night-dogs askant in
the capitol?
What a filthy Presidentiad! (O South, your
torrid suns! O North, your arctic freezings!)
Are those really Congressmen? are those the
great Judges? is that the President?
Then I will sleep awhile yet, for I see that these
States sleep, for reasons;
(With gathering murk, with muttering thunder
and lambent shoots we all duly awake,

South, North, East, West, inland and seaboard,
   we will surely awake.)

First O Songs for a Prelude

FIRST O songs for a prelude,
Lightly strike on the stretch'd tympanum pride
   and joy in my city,
How she led the rest to arms, how she gave the
   cue,
How at once with lithe limbs unwaiting a
   moment she sprang,
(O superb! O Manhattan, my own, my peerless!
O strongest you in the hour of danger, in crisis!
   O truer than steel!)
How you sprang—how you threw off the
   costumes of peace with indifferent hand,
How your soft opera-music changed, and the
   drum and fife were heard in their stead,
How you led to the war, (that shall serve for our
   prelude, songs of soldiers,)
How Manhattan drum-taps led.

Forty years had I in my city seen soldiers
   parading,
Forty years as a pageant, till unawares the lady of
   this teeming and turbulent city,
Sleepless amid her ships, her houses, her
   incalculable wealth,

With her million children around her,
    suddenly,
At dead of night, at news from the south,
Incens'd struck with clinch'd hand the
    pavement.

A shock electric, the night sustain'd it,
Till with ominous hum our hive at daybreak
    pour'd out its myriads.

From the houses then and the workshops, and
    through all the doorways,
Leapt they tumultuous, and lo! Manhattan
    arming.

To the drum-taps prompt,
The young men falling in and arming,
The mechanics arming, (the trowel, the jack-
    plane, the blacksmith's hammer, tost aside
    with precipitation,)
The lawyer leaving his office and arming, the
    judge leaving the court,
The driver deserting his wagon in the street,
    jumping down, throwing the reins abruptly
    down on the horses' backs,
The salesman leaving the store, the boss, book-
    keeper, porter, all leaving;
Squads gather everywhere by common consent
    and arm,

The new recruits, even boys, the old men show
    them how to wear their accoutrements, they
    buckle the straps carefully,
Outdoors arming, indoors arming, the flash of
    the musket-barrels,
The white tents cluster in camps, the arm'd
    sentries around, the sunrise cannon and again
    at sunset,
Arm'd regiments arrive every day, pass through
    the city, and embark from the wharves,
(How good they look as they tramp down to
    the river, sweaty, with their guns on their
    shoulders!
How I love them! how I could hug them, with
    their brown faces and their clothes and
    knapsacks cover'd with dust!)
The blood of the city up-arm'd! arm'd! the cry
    everywhere,
The flags flung out from the steeples of
    churches and from all the public buildings
    and stores,
The tearful parting, the mother kisses her son,
    the son kisses his mother,
(Loth is the mother to part, yet not a word does
    she speak to detain him,)
The tumultuous escort, the ranks of policemen
    preceding, clearing the way,
The unpent enthusiasm, the wild cheers of the
    crowd for their favorites,

The artillery, the silent cannons bright as gold,
    drawn along, rumble lightly over the stones,
(Silent cannons, soon to cease your silence,
Soon unlimber'd to begin the red business;)
All the mutter of preparation, all the determin'd
    arming,
The hospital service, the lint, bandages and
    medicines,
The women volunteering for nurses, the work
    begun for in earnest, no mere parade now;
War! an arm'd race is advancing! the welcome
    for battle, no turning away!
War! be it weeks, months, or years, an arm'd
    race is advancing to welcome it.

Mannahatta a-march—and it's O to sing it well!
It's O for a manly life in the camp.

And the sturdy artillery,
The guns bright as gold, the work for giants, to
    serve well the guns,
Unlimber them! (no more as the past forty years
    for salutes for courtesies merely,
Put in something now besides powder and
    wadding.)

And you lady of ships, you Mannahatta,
Old matron of this proud, friendly, turbulent
    city,

Often in peace and wealth you were pensive or
    covertly frown'd amid all your children,
But now you smile with joy exulting old
    Mannahatta.

EIGHTEEN SIXTY-ONE

ARM'D year—year of the struggle,
No dainty rhymes or sentimental love verses for
    you terrible year,
Not you as some pale poetling seated at a desk
    lisping cadenzas piano,
But as a strong man erect, clothed in blue
    clothes, advancing, carrying rifle on your
    shoulder,
With well-gristled body and sunburnt face
    and hands, with a knife in the belt at your
    side,
As I heard you shouting loud, your sonorous
    voice ringing across the continent,
Your masculine voice O year, as rising amid the
    great cities,
Amid the men of Manhattan I saw you as one of
    the workmen, the dwellers in Manhattan,
Or with large steps crossing the prairies out of
    Illinois and Indiana,
Rapidly crossing the West with springy gait and
    descending the Allghanies,

Or down from the great lakes or in
    Pennsylvania, or on deck along the Ohio
    river,
Or southward along the Tennessee or
    Cumberland rivers, or at Chattanooga on the
    mountain top,
Saw I your gait and saw I your sinewy limbs
    clothed in blue, bearing weapons, robust year,
Heard your determin'd voice launch'd forth
    again and again,
Year that suddenly sang by the mouths of the
    round-lipp'd cannon,
I repeat you, hurrying, crashing, sad, distracted
    year.

Drum-Taps

BEAT! BEAT! DRUMS!

BEAT! beat! drums!—blow! bugles! blow!
Through the windows—through doors—burst
  like a ruthless force,
Into the solemn church, and scatter the
  congregation,
Into the school where the scholar is studying;
Leave not the bridegroom quiet-no happiness
  must he have now with his bride,
Nor the peaceful farmer any peace, ploughing
  his field or gathering his grain,
So fierce you whirr and pound you drums—so
  shrill you bugles blow.

Beat! beat! drums!—blow! bugles! blow!
Over the traffic of cities—over the rumble of
  wheels in the streets;
Are beds prepared for sleepers at night in the
  houses? no sleepers must sleep in those beds,
No bargainers' bargains by day—no brokers or
  speculators—would they continue?
Would the talkers be talking? would the singer
  attempt to sing?
Would the lawyer rise in the court to state his
  case before the judge?

Then rattle quicker, heavier drums-you bugles
    wilder blow.

Beat! beat! drums!—blow! bugles! blow!
Make no parley—stop for no expostulation,
Mind not the timid—mind not the weeper or
    prayer,
Mind not the old man beseeching the young
    man,
Let not the child's voice be heard, nor the
    mother's entreaties,
Make even the trestles to shake the dead where
    they lie awaiting the hearses,
So strong you thump O terrible drums-so loud
    you bugles blow.

FROM PAUMANOK STARTING
I FLY LIKE A BIRD

FROM Paumanok starting I fly like a bird,
Around and around to soar to sing the idea of
    all,
To the north betaking myself to sing there arctic
    songs,
To Kanada till I absorb Kanada in myself, to
    Michigan then,
To Wisconsin, Iowa, Minnesota, to sing their
    songs, (they are inimitable;)

Then to Ohio and Indiana to sing theirs, to
    Missouri and Kansas and Arkansas to sing
    theirs,
To Tennessee and Kentucky, to the Carolinas
    and Georgia to sing theirs,
To Texas and so along up toward California, to
    roam accepted everywhere;
To sing first, (to the tap of the war-drum if need
    be,)
The idea of all, of the Western world one and
    inseparable,
And then the song of each member of these
    States.
Song of the Banner at Daybreak

Poet.
O A new song, a free song,
Flapping, flapping, flapping, flapping, by sounds,
    by voices clearer,
By the wind's voice and that of the drum,
By the banner's voice and child's voice and sea's
    voice and father's voice,
Low on the ground and high in the air,
On the ground where father and child stand,
In the upward air where their eyes turn,
Where the banner at daybreak is flapping.

Words! book-words! what are you?
Words no more, for hearken and see,

My song is there in the open air, and I must
    sing,
With the banner and pennant a-flapping.

I'll weave the chord and twine in,
Man's desire and babe's desire, I'll twine them
    in, I'll put in life,
I'll put the bayonet's flashing point, I'll let
    bullets and slugs whizz,
(As one carrying a symbol and menace far into
    the future,
Crying with trumpet voice, Arouse and beware!
    Beware and arouse!)
I'll pour the verse with streams of blood, full of
    volition, full of joy,
Then loosen, launch forth, to go and
    compete,
With the banner and pennant a-flapping.

Pennant.
Come up here, bard, bard,
Come up here, soul, soul,
Come up here, dear little child,
To fly in the clouds and winds with me, and play
    with the measureless light.

Child.
Father what is that in the sky beckoning to me
    with long finger?
And what does it say to me all the while?

Father.
Nothing my babe you see in the sky,
And nothing at all to you it says—but look you
  my babe,
Look at these dazzling things in the houses, and
  see you the money—shops opening,
And see you the vehicles preparing to crawl
  along the streets with goods;
These, ah these, how valued and toil'd for these!
How envied by all the earth.

Poet.
Fresh and rosy red the sun is mounting high,
On floats the sea in distant blue careering
  through its channels,
On floats the wind over the breast of the sea
  setting in toward land,
The great steady wind from west or west-by-
  south,
Floating so buoyant with milk-white foam on
  the waters.

But I am not the sea nor the red sun,
I am not the wind with girlish laughter,
Not the immense wind which strengthens, not
  the wind which lashes,
Not the spirit that ever lashes its own body to
  terror and death,
But I am that which unseen comes and sings,
  sings, sings,

Which babbles in brooks and scoots in showers
   on the land,
Which the birds know in the woods mornings
   and evenings,
And the shore-sands know and the hissing wave,
   and that banner and pennant,
Aloft there flapping and flapping.

Child.
O father it is alive—it is full of people—it has
   children,
O now it seems to me it is talking to its
   children,
I hear it—it talks to me-O it is wonderful!
O it stretches—it spreads and runs so fast—O
   my father,
It is so broad it covers the whole sky.

Father.
Cease, cease, my foolish babe,
What you are saying is sorrowful to me, much 't
   displeases me;
Behold with the rest again I say, behold not
   banners and pennants aloft,
But the well-prepared pavements behold, and
   mark the solid-wall'd houses.

Banner and Pennant.
Speak to the child O bard out of Manhattan,

To our children all, or north or south of
Manhattan,
Point this day, leaving all the rest, to us over
all—and yet we know not why,
For what are we, mere strips of cloth profiting
nothing,
Only flapping in the wind?

Poet.
I hear and see not strips of cloth alone,
I hear the tramp of armies, I hear the
challenging sentry,
I hear the jubilant shouts of millions of men, I
hear Liberty!
I hear the drums beat and the trumpets
blowing,
I myself move abroad swift-rising flying then,
I use the wings of the land-bird and use the
wings of the sea-bird, and look down as from
a height,
I do not deny the precious results of peace, I see
populous cities with wealth incalculable,
I see numberless farms, I see the farmers
working in their fields or barns,
I see mechanics working, I see buildings
everywhere founded, going up, or finish'd,
I see trains of cars swiftly speeding along railroad
tracks drawn by the locomotives,

I see the stores, depots, of Boston, Baltimore,
    Charleston, New Orleans,
I see far in the West the immense area of grain, I
    dwell awhile hovering,
I pass to the lumber forests of the North, and
    again to the Southern plantation, and again to
    California;
Sweeping the whole I see the countless profit,
    the busy gatherings, earn'd wages,
See the Identity formed out of thirty-eight
    spacious and haughty States, (and many more
    to come,)
See forts on the shores of harbors, see ships
    sailing in and out;
Then over all, (aye! aye!) my little and
    lengthen'd pennant shaped like a sword,
Runs swiftly up indicating war and defiance-and
    now the halyards have rais'd it,
Side of my banner broad and blue, side of my
    starry banner,
Discarding peace over all the sea and land.

Banner and Pennant.
Yet louder, higher, stronger, bard! yet farther,
    wider cleave!
No longer let our children deem us riches and
    peace alone,
We may be terror and carnage, and are so now,
Not now are we any one of these spacious and
    haughty States, (nor any five, nor ten,)

Nor market nor depot we, nor money-bank in
the city,
But these and all, and the brown and spreading
land, and the mines below, are ours,
And the shores of the sea are ours, and the rivers
great and small,
And the fields they moisten, and the crops and
the fruits are ours,
Bays and channels and ships sailing in and out
are ours-while we over all,
Over the area spread below, the three or four
millions of square miles, the capitals,
The forty millions of people,—O bard! in life
and death supreme,
We, even we, henceforth flaunt out masterful,
high up above,
Not for the present alone, for a thousand years
chanting through you,
This song to the soul of one poor little child.

Child.
O my father I like not the houses,
They will never to me be any thing, nor do I
like money,
But to mount up there I would like, O father
dear, that banner I like,
That pennant I would be and must be.

Father.
Child of mine you fill me with anguish,

To be that pennant would be too fearful,

Little you know what it is this day, and after this
day, forever,

It is to gain nothing, but risk and defy every
thing,

Forward to stand in front of wars-and O, such
wars!-what have you to do with them?

With passions of demons, slaughter, premature
death?

Banner.

Demons and death then I sing,

Put in all, aye all will I, sword-shaped pennant
for war,

And a pleasure new and ecstatic, and the
prattled yearning of children,

Blent with the sounds of the peaceful land and
the liquid wash of the sea,

And the black ships fighting on the sea
envelop'd in smoke,

And the icy cool of the far, far north, with
rustling cedars and pines,

And the whirr of drums and the sound of
soldiers marching, and the hot sun shining
south,

And the beach-waves combing over the beach
on my Eastern shore, and my Western shore
the same,

And all between those shores, and my ever
running Mississippi with bends and chutes,

And my Illinois fields, and my Kansas fields, and
  my fields of Missouri,
The Continent, devoting the whole identity
  without reserving an atom,
Pour in! whelm that which asks, which sings,
  with all and the yield of all,
Fusing and holding, claiming, devouring the
  whole,
No more with tender lip, nor musical labial sound,
But out of the night emerging for good, our
  voice persuasive no more,
Croaking like crows here in the wind.

Poet.
My limbs, my veins dilate, my theme is clear at
  last,
Banner so broad advancing out of the night, I
  sing you haughty and resolute,
I burst through where I waited long, too long,
  deafen'd and blinded,
My hearing and tongue are come to me, (a little
  child taught me,)
I hear from above O pennant of war your
  ironical call and demand,
Insensate! insensate! (yet I at any rate chant
  you,) O banner!
Not houses of peace indeed are you, nor any nor
  all their prosperity, (if need be, you shall again
  have every one of those houses to destroy
  them,

You thought not to destroy those valuable
    houses, standing fast, full of comfort, built
    with money,
May they stand fast, then? not an hour except
    you above them and all stand fast;)
O banner, not money so precious are you, not
    farm produce you, nor the material good
    nutriment,
Nor excellent stores, nor landed on wharves
    from the ships,
Not the superb ships with sail-power or steam-
    power, fetching and carrying cargoes,
Nor machinery, vehicles, trade, nor revenues-but
    you as henceforth I see you,
Running up out of the night, bringing your
    cluster of stars, (ever-enlarging stars,)
Divider of daybreak you, cutting the air, touch'd
    by the sun, measuring the sky,
(Passionately seen and yearn'd for by one poor
    little child,
While others remain busy or smartly talking,
    forever teaching thrift, thrift;)
O you up there! O pennant! where you undulate
    like a snake hissing so curious,
Out of reach, an idea only, yet furiously
    fought for, risking bloody death, loved
    by me,
So loved—O you banner leading the day with
    stars brought from the night!

Valueless, object of eyes, over all and demanding
   all-(absolute owner of all)—O banner and
   pennant!
I too leave the rest-great as it is, it is nothing—
   houses, machines are nothing-I see them
   not,
I see but you, O warlike pennant! O banner so
   broad, with stripes, sing you only,
Flapping up there in the wind.

RISE O DAYS FROM YOUR FATHOMLESS DEEPS

1

RISE O days from your fathomless deeps, till
   you loftier, fiercer sweep,
Long for my soul hungering gymnastic I
   devour'd what the earth gave me,
Long I roam'd amid the woods of the north,
   long I watch'd Niagara pouring,
I travel'd the prairies over and slept on their
   breast, I cross'd the Nevadas, I cross'd the
   plateaus,
I ascended the towering rocks along the Pacific,
   I sail'd out to sea,
I sail'd through the storm, I was refresh'd by the
   storm,
I watch'd with joy the threatening maws of the
   waves,

I mark'd the white combs where they career'd
so high, curling over,
I heard the wind piping, I saw the black clouds,
Saw from below what arose and mounted, (O
superb! O wild as my heart, and powerful!)
Heard the continuous thunder as it bellow'd
after the lightning,
Noted the slender and jagged threads of
lightning as sudden and fast amid the din they
chased each other across the sky;
These, and such as these, I, elate, saw—saw with
wonder, yet pensive and masterful,
All the menacing might of the globe uprisen
around me,
Yet there with my soul I fed, I fed content,
supercilious.

2

'Twas well, O soul—'twas a good preparation
you gave me,
Now we advance our latent and ampler hunger
to fill,
Now we go forth to receive what the earth and
the sea never gave us,
Not through the mighty woods we go, but
through the mightier cities,
Something for us is pouring now more than
Niagara pouring,
Torrents of men, (sources and rills of the
Northwest are you indeed inexhaustible?)

What, to pavements and homesteads here, what
    were those storms of the mountains and sea?
What, to passions I witness around me to-day?
    was the sea risen?
Was the wind piping the pipe of death under the
    black clouds?
Lo! from deeps more unfathomable, something
    more deadly and savage,
Manhattan rising, advancing with menacing
    front—Cincinnati, Chicago, unchain'd;
What was that swell I saw on the ocean? behold
    what comes here,
How it climbs with daring feet and hands—how
    it dashes!
How the true thunder bellows after the
    lightning—how bright the flashes of lightning!
How Democracy with desperate vengeful port
    strides on, shown through the dark by those
    flashes of lightning!
(Yet a mournful wall and low sob I fancied I
    heard through the dark,
In a lull of the deafening confusion.)

3

Thunder on! stride on, Democracy! strike with
    vengeful stroke!
And do you rise higher than ever yet O days, O
    cities!
Crash heavier, heavier yet O storms! you have
    done me good,

My soul prepared in the mountains absorbs your
    immortal strong nutriment,
Long had I walk'd my cities, my country roads
    through farms, only half satisfied,
One doubt nauseous undulating like a snake,
    crawl'd on the ground before me,
Continually preceding my steps, turning upon
    me oft, ironically hissing low;
The cities I loved so well I abandon'd and left, I
    sped to the certainties suitable to me,
Hungering, hungering, hungering, for primal
    energies and Nature's dauntlessness,
I refresh'd myself with it only, I could relish it
    only,
I waited the bursting forth of the pent fire—on
    the water and air waited long;
But now I no longer wait, I am fully satisfied, I
    am glutted,
I have witness'd the true lightning, I have
    witness'd my cities electric,
I have lived to behold man burst forth and
    warlike America rise,
Hence I will seek no more the food of the
    northern solitary wilds,
No more the mountains roam or sail the stormy
    sea.

VIRGINIA—THE WEST

THE noble sire fallen on evil days,
I saw with hand uplifted, menacing,
   brandishing,
(Memories of old in abeyance, love and faith in
   abeyance,)
The insane knife toward the Mother of All.

The noble son on sinewy feet advancing,
I saw, out of the land of prairies, land of Ohio's
   waters and of Indiana,
To the rescue the stalwart giant hurry his
   plenteous offspring,
Drest in blue, bearing their trusty rifles on their
   shoulders.

Then the Mother of All with calm voice
   speaking,
As to you Rebellious, (I seemed to hear her
   say,) why strive against me, and why seek
   my life?
When you yourself forever provide to defend
   me?
For you provided me Washington—and now
   these also.

CITY OF SHIPS

CITY of ships!
(O the black ships! O the fierce ships!
O the beautiful sharp-bow'd steam-ships and
    sail-ships!)
City of the world! (for all races are here,
All the lands of the earth make contributions
    here;)
City of the sea! city of hurried and glittering
    tides!
City whose gleeful tides continually rush or
    recede, whirling in and out with eddies and
    foam!
City of wharves and stores—city of tall facades
    of marble and iron!
Proud and passionate city—mettlesome, mad,
    extravagant city!
Spring up O city—not for peace alone, but be
    indeed yourself, warlike!
Fear not—submit to no models but your own O
    city!
Behold me- incarnate me as I have incarnated
    you!
I have rejected nothing you offer'd me—whom
    you adopted I have adopted,
Good or bad I never question you—I love all—
    I do not condemn any thing,
I chant and celebrate all that is yours—yet peace
    no more,

In peace I chanted peace, but now the drum of
    war is mine,
War, red war is my song through your streets,
    O city!

THE CENTENARIAN'S STORY
VOLUNTEER OF 1861–2,
(AT WASHINGTON PARK, BROOKLYN,
ASSISTING THE CENTENARIAN.)

GIVE me your hand old Revolutionary,
The hill-top is nigh, but a few steps, (make
    room gentlemen,)
Up the path you have follow'd me well, spite of
    your hundred and extra years,
You can walk old man, though your eyes are
    almost done,
Your faculties serve you, and presently I must
    have them serve me.

Rest, while I tell what the crowd around us
    means,
On the plain below recruits are drilling and
    exercising,
There is the camp, one regiment departs to-
    morrow,
Do you hear the officers giving their orders?
Do you hear the clank of the muskets?
Why what comes over you now old man?

Why do you tremble and clutch my hand so
    convulsively?
The troops are but drilling, they are yet
    surrounded with smiles,
Around them at hand the well-drest friends and
    the women,
While splendid and warm the afternoon sun
    shines down,
Green the midsummer verdure and fresh blows
    the dallying breeze,
O'er proud and peaceful cities and arm of the
    sea between.

But drill and parade are over, they march back
    to quarters,
Only hear that approval of hands! hear what a
    clapping!

As wending the crowds now part and disperse—
    but we old man,
Not for nothing have I brought you hither—
    we must remain,
You to speak in your turn, and I to listen and
    tell.

The Centenarian
When I clutch'd your hand it was not with
    terror,
But suddenly pouring about me here on every
    side,

And below there where the boys were drilling,
   and up the slopes they ran,
And where tents are pitch'd, and wherever you
   see south and south-east and south-west,
Over hills, across lowlands, and in the skirts of
   woods,
And along the shores, in mire (now fill'd over)
   came again and suddenly raged,
As eighty-five years agone no mere parade
   receiv'd with applause of friends,
But a battle which I took part in myself—aye,
   long ago as it is, I took part in it,
Walking then this hilltop, this same ground.

Aye, this is the ground,
My blind eyes even as I speak behold it
   repeopled from graves,
The years recede, pavements and stately houses
   disappear,
Rude forts appear again, the old hoop'd guns
   are mounted,
I see the lines of rais'd earth stretching from
   river to bay,
I mark the vista of waters, I mark the uplands
   and slopes;
Here we lay encamp'd, it was this time in
   summer also.

As I talk I remember all, I remember the
   Declaration,

It was read here, the whole army paraded, it was
    read to us here,
By his staff surrounded the General stood in the
    middle, he held up his unsheath'd sword,
It glitter'd in the sun in full sight of the army.

Twas a bold act then—the English war-ships had
    just arrived,
We could watch down the lower bay where they
    lay at anchor,
And the transports swarming with soldiers.

A few days more and they landed, and then the
    battle.

Twenty thousand were brought against us,
A veteran force furnish'd with good artillery.

I tell not now the whole of the battle,
But one brigade early in the forenoon order'd
    forward to engage the red-coats,
Of that brigade I tell, and how steadily it march'd,
And how long and well it stood confronting
    death.

Who do you think that was marching steadily
    sternly confronting death?
It was the brigade of the youngest men, two
    thousand strong,

Rais'd in Virginia and Maryland, and most of
    them known personally to the General.

Jauntily forward they went with quick step
    toward Gowanus' waters,
Till of a sudden unlook'd for by defiles through
    the woods, gain'd at night,
The British advancing, rounding in from the
    east, fiercely playing their guns,
That brigade of the youngest was cut off and at
    the enemy's mercy.

The General watch'd them from this hill,
They made repeated desperate attempts to burst
    their environment,
Then drew close together, very compact, their
    flag flying in the middle,
But O from the hills how the cannon were
    thinning and thinning them!

It sickens me yet, that slaughter!
I saw the moisture gather in drops on the face of
    the General.
I saw how he wrung his hands in anguish.

Meanwhile the British manoeuvr'd to draw us
    out for a pitch'd battle,
But we dared not trust the chances of a pitch'd
    battle.

We fought the fight in detachments,
Sallying forth we fought at several points, but in
    each the luck was against us,
Our foe advancing, steadily getting the best of
    it, push'd us back to the works on this hill,
Till we turn'd menacing here, and then he left
    us.

That was the going out of the brigade of the
    youngest men, two thousand strong,
Few return'd, nearly all remain in Brooklyn.

That and here my General's first battle,
No women looking on nor sunshine to bask in,
    it did not conclude with applause,
Nobody clapp'd hands here then.

But in darkness in mist on the ground under a
    chill rain,
Wearied that night we lay foil'd and sullen,
While scornfully laugh'd many an arrogant lord
    off against us encamp'd,
Quite within hearing, feasting, clinking
    wineglasses together over their victory.

So dull and damp and another day,
But the night of that, mist lifting, rain ceasing,
Silent as a ghost while they thought they were
    sure of him, my
General retreated.

I saw him at the river-side,
Down by the ferry lit by torches, hastening the
    embarcation;
My General waited till the soldiers and wounded
    were all pass'd over,
And then, (it was just ere sunrise,) these eyes
    rested on him for the last time.

Every one else seem'd fill'd with gloom,
Many no doubt thought of capitulation.

But when my General pass'd me,
As he stood in his boat and look'd toward the
    coming sun,
I saw something different from capitulation.

Terminus
Enough, the Centenarian's story ends,
The two, the past and present, have interchanged,
I myself as connecter, as chansonnier of a great
    future, am now speaking.

And is this the ground Washington trod?
And these waters I listlessly daily cross, are these
    the waters he cross'd,
As resolute in defeat as other generals in their
    proudest triumphs?

I must copy the story, and send it eastward and
    westward,

I must preserve that look as it beam'd on you
    rivers of Brooklyn.

See—as the annual round returns the phantoms
    return,
It is the 27th of August and the British have
    landed,
The battle begins and goes against us, behold
    through the smoke Washington's face,
The brigade of Virginia and Maryland have
    march'd forth to intercept the enemy,
They are cut off, murderous artillery from the
    hills plays upon them,
Rank after rank falls, while over them silently
    droops the flag,
Baptized that day in many a young man's
    bloody wounds.
In death, defeat, and sisters', mothers' tears.

Ah, hills and slopes of Brooklyn! I perceive you
    are more valuable than your owners supposed;
In the midst of you stands an encampment very
    old,
Stands forever the camp of that dead brigade.

CAVALRY CROSSING A FORD

A LINE in long array where they wind betwixt
    green islands,
They take a serpentine course, their arms flash in
    the sun-hark to the musical clank,
Behold the silvery river, in it the splashing
    horses loitering stop to drink,
Behold the brown-faced men, each group, each
    person a picture, the negligent rest on the
    saddles,
Some emerge on the opposite bank, others are
    just entering the ford—while,
Scarlet and blue and snowy white,
The guidon flags flutter gayly in the wind.

BIVOUAC ON A MOUNTAIN SIDE

I SEE before me now a traveling army
    halting,
Below a fertile valley spread, with barns and the
    orchards of summer,
Behind, the terraced sides of a mountain,
    abrupt, in places rising high,
Broken, with rocks, with clinging cedars, with
    tall shapes dingily seen,
The numerous camp-fires scatter'd near and far,
    some away up on the mountain,

The shadowy forms of men and horses,
    looming, large-sized, flickering,
And over all the sky-the sky! far, far out of
    reach, studded, breaking out, the eternal
    stars.

An Army Corps on the March

WITH its cloud of skirmishers in advance,
With now the sound of a single shot snapping
    like a whip, and now an irregular volley,
The swarming ranks press on and on, the dense
    brigades press on,
Glittering dimly, toiling under the sun—the
    dust-cover'd men,
In columns rise and fall to the undulations of
    the ground,
With artillery interspers'd—the wheels rumble,
    the horses sweat,
As the army corps advances.

By the Bivouac's Fitful Flame

BY the bivouac's fitful flame,
A procession winding around me, solemn and
    sweet and slow—but first I note,
The tents of the sleeping army, the fields' and
    woods' dim outline,

The darkness lit by spots of kindled fire, the
    silence,
Like a phantom far or near an occasional figure
    moving,
The shrubs and trees, (as I lift my eyes they
    seem to be stealthily watching me,)
While wind in procession thoughts, O tender
    and wondrous thoughts,
Of life and death, of home and the past and
    loved, and of those that are far away;
A solemn and slow procession there as I sit on
    the ground,
By the bivouac's fitful flame.

COME UP FROM THE FIELDS FATHER

COME up from the fields father, here's a letter
    from our Pete,
And come to the front door mother, here's a
    letter from thy dear son.

Lo, 'tis autumn,
Lo, where the trees, deeper green, yellower and
    redder,
Cool and sweeten Ohio's villages with leaves
    fluttering in the moderate wind,
Where apples ripe in the orchards hang and
    grapes on the trellis'd vines,
(Smell you the smell of the grapes on the vines?

Smell you the buckwheat where the bees were
 lately buzzing?)

Above all, lo, the sky so calm, so transparent
 after the rain, and with wondrous clouds,
Below too, all calm, all vital and beautiful, and
 the farm prospers well.

Down in the fields all prospers well,
But now from the fields come father, come at
 the daughter's call.
And come to the entry mother, to the front
 door come right away.

Fast as she can she hurries, something ominous,
 her steps trembling,
She does not tarry to smooth her hair nor adjust
 her cap.

Open the envelope quickly,
O this is not our son's writing, yet his name is
 sign'd,
O a strange hand writes for our dear son, O
 stricken mother's soul!
All swims before her eyes, flashes with black, she
 catches the main words only,
Sentences broken, gunshot wound in the
 breast, cavalry skirmish, taken to
 hospital,
At present low, but will soon be better.

Ah now the single figure to me,
Amid all teeming and wealthy Ohio with all its
 cities and farms,
Sickly white in the face and dull in the head,
 very faint,
By the jamb of a door leans.

Grieve not so, dear mother, (the just-grown
 daughter speaks through her sobs,
The little sisters huddle around speechless and
 dismay'd,)
See, dearest mother, the letter says Pete will
 soon be better.

Alas poor boy, he will never be better, (nor may-
 be needs to be better, that brave and simple
 soul,)
While they stand at home at the door he is dead
 already,
The only son is dead.

But the mother needs to be better,
She with thin form presently drest in black,
By day her meals untouch'd, then at night
 fitfully sleeping, often waking,
In the midnight waking, weeping, longing with
 one deep longing,
O that she might withdraw unnoticed, silent
 from life escape and withdraw,
To follow, to seek, to be with her dear dead son.

VIGIL STRANGE I KEPT ON THE FIELD ONE NIGHT

VIGIL strange I kept on the field one night;
When you my son and my comrade dropt at my
    side that day,
One look I but gave which your dear eyes
    return'd with a look I shall never forget,
One touch of your hand to mine O boy, reach'd
    up as you lay on the ground,
Then onward I sped in the battle, the even-
    contested battle,
Till late in the night reliev'd to the place at last
    again I made my way,
Found you in death so cold dear comrade,
    found your body son of responding kisses,
    (never again on earth responding,)
Bared your face in the starlight, curious the
    scene, cool blew the moderate night-wind,
Long there and then in vigil I stood, dimly
    around me the battlefield spreading,
Vigil wondrous and vigil sweet there in the
    fragrant silent night,
But not a tear fell, not even a long-drawn sigh,
    long, long I gazed,
Then on the earth partially reclining sat by your
    side leaning my chin in my hands,
Passing sweet hours, immortal and mystic hours
    with you dearest comrade—not a tear, not a
    word,

Vigil of silence, love and death, vigil for you my
son and my soldier,

As onward silently stars aloft, eastward new ones
upward stole,

Vigil final for you brave boy, (I could not save
you, swift was your death,

I faithfully loved you and cared for you living, I
think we shall surely meet again,) Till at latest
lingering of the night, indeed just as the dawn
appear'd,

My comrade I wrapt in his blanket, envelop'd
well his form,

Folded the blanket well, tucking it carefully over
head and carefully under feet,

And there and then and bathed by the rising
sun, my son in his grave, in his rude-dug
grave I deposited,

Ending my vigil strange with that, vigil of night
and battle-field dim,

Vigil for boy of responding kisses, (never again
on earth responding,)

Vigil for comrade swiftly slain, vigil I never
forget, how as day brighten'd,

I rose from the chill ground and folded my
soldier well in his blanket,

And buried him where he fell.

A March in the Ranks Hard-Prest, and the Road Unknown

A MARCH in the ranks hard-prest, and the road
    unknown,
A route through a heavy wood with muffled
    steps in the darkness,
Our army foil'd with loss severe, and the sullen
    remnant retreating,
Till after midnight glimmer upon us the lights of
    a dim-lighted building,
We come to an open space in the woods, and
    halt by the dim-lighted building,
'Tis a large old church at the crossing roads,
    now an impromptu hospital,
Entering but for a minute I see a sight beyond
    all the pictures and poems ever made,
Shadows of deepest, deepest black, just lit by
    moving candles and lamps,
And by one great pitchy torch stationary with
    wild red flame and clouds of smoke,
By these, crowds, groups of forms vaguely
    I see on the floor, some in the pews laid
    down,
At my feet more distinctly a soldier, a mere lad,
    in danger of bleeding to death, (he is shot in
    the abdomen,)
I stanch the blood temporarily, (the youngster's
    face is white as a lily,)

Then before I depart I sweep my eyes o'er the
    scene fain to absorb it all,
Faces, varieties, postures beyond description,
    most in obscurity, some of them dead,
Surgeons operating, attendants holding lights,
    the smell of ether, odor of blood,
The crowd, O the crowd of the bloody forms,
    the yard outside also fill'd,
Some on the bare ground, some on planks or
    stretchers, some in the death-spasm sweating,
An occasional scream or cry, the doctor's
    shouted orders or calls,
The glisten of the little steel instruments
    catching the glint of the torches,
These I resume as I chant, I see again the forms,
    I smell the odor,
Then hear outside the orders given, Fall in, my
    men, fall in;
But first I bend to the dying lad, his eyes open,
    a half-smile gives he me,
Then the eyes close, calmly close, and I speed
    forth to the darkness,
Resuming, marching, ever in darkness marching,
    on in the ranks,
The unknown road still marching.

A Sight in Camp in the Daybreak Gray and Dim

A SIGHT in camp in the daybreak gray and dim,
As from my tent I emerge so early sleepless,
As slow I walk in the cool fresh air the path near
    by the hospital tent,
Three forms I see on stretchers lying, brought
    out there untended lying,
Over each the blanket spread, ample brownish
    woolen blanket,
Gray and heavy blanket, folding, covering all.

Curious I halt and silent stand,
Then with light fingers I from the face of the
    nearest the first just lift the blanket;
Who are you elderly man so gaunt and grim,
    with well-gray'd hair, and flesh all sunken
    about the eyes?
Who are you my dear comrade?
Then to the second I step—and who are you my
    child and darling?
Who are you sweet boy with cheeks yet
    blooming?
Then to the third—a face nor child nor old, very
    calm, as of beautiful yellow-white ivory;
Young man I think I know you—I think this
    face is the face of the Christ himself,
Dead and divine and brother of all, and here
    again he lies.

As Toilsome I Wander'd Virginia's Woods

To the music of rustling leaves kick'd by my
   feet, (for 'twas autumn,)
I mark'd at the foot of a tree the grave of a
   soldier;
Mortally wounded he and buried on the retreat,
   (easily all could understand,)
The halt of a mid-day hour, when up! no time
   to lose—yet this sign left,
On a tablet scrawl'd and nail'd on the tree by
   the grave,
Bold, cautious, true, and my loving comrade.

Long, long I muse, then on my way go
   wandering,
Many a changeful season to follow, and many a
   scene of life,
Yet at times through changeful season and
   scene, abrupt, alone, or in the crowded street,
Comes before me the unknown soldier's grave,
   comes the inscription rude in Virginia's
   woods,
Bold, cautious, true, and my loving comrade.

Not the Pilot

NOT the pilot has charged himself to bring his
   ship into port, though beaten back and many
   times baffled;

Not the pathfinder penetrating inland weary and
    long,
By deserts parch'd, snows chill'd, rivers wet,
    perseveres till he reaches his destination,
More than I have charged myself, heeded or
    unheeded, to compose march for these States,
For a battle-call, rousing to arms if need be,
    years, centuries hence.

YEAR THAT TREMBLED AND REEL'D BENEATH ME

YEAR that trembled and reel'd beneath me!
Your summer wind was warm enough, yet the
    air I breathed froze me,
A thick gloom fell through the sunshine and
    darken'd me,
Must I change my triumphant songs? said I to
    myself,
Must I indeed learn to chant the cold dirges of
    the baffled?
And sullen hymns of defeat?

THE WOUND-DRESSER

1

AN old man bending I come among new faces,
Years looking backward resuming in answer to
    children,

Come tell us old man, as from young men and
  maidens that love me,
(Arous'd and angry, I'd thought to beat the
  alarum, and urge relentless war,
But soon my fingers fail'd me, my face droop'd
  and I resign'd myself,
To sit by the wounded and soothe them, or
  silently watch the dead;)
Years hence of these scenes, of these furious
  passions, these chances,
Of unsurpass'd heroes, (was one side so brave?
  the other was equally brave;)
Now be witness again, paint the mightiest
  armies of earth,
Of those armies so rapid so wondrous what saw
  you to tell us?
What stays with you latest and deepest? of
  curious panics,
Of hard-fought engagements or sieges
  tremendous what deepest remains?

2

O maidens and young men I love and that
  love me,
What you ask of my days those the strangest and
  sudden your talking recalls,
Soldier alert I arrive after a long march cover'd
  with sweat and dust,
In the nick of time I come, plunge in the fight,
  loudly shout in the rush of successful charge,

Enter the captur'd works—yet lo, like a swift-
    running river they fade,
Pass and are gone they fade—I dwell not on
    soldiers' perils or soldiers' joys,
(Both I remember well-many the hardships, few
    the joys, yet I was content.)

But in silence, in dreams' projections,
While the world of gain and appearance and
    mirth goes on,
So soon what is over forgotten, and waves wash
    the imprints off the sand,
With hinged knees returning I enter the doors,
    (while for you up there,
Whoever you are, follow without noise and be
    of strong heart.)

Bearing the bandages, water and sponge,
Straight and swift to my wounded I go,
Where they lie on the ground after the battle
    brought in,
Where their priceless blood reddens the grass
    the ground,
Or to the rows of the hospital tent, or under
    the roof'd hospital,
To the long rows of cots up and down each side
    I return,
To each and all one after another I draw near,
    not one do I miss,

An attendant follows holding a tray, he carries a
    refuse pail,
Soon to be fill'd with clotted rags and blood,
    emptied, and fill'd again.

I onward go, I stop,
With hinged knees and steady hand to dress
    wounds,
I am firm with each, the pangs are sharp yet
    unavoidable,
One turns to me his appealing eyes—poor boy!
    I never knew you,
Yet I think I could not refuse this
    moment to die for you, if that would
    save you.

3

On, on I go, (open doors of time! open
    hospital doors!)
The crush'd head I dress, (poor crazed hand
    tear not the bandage away,)
The neck of the cavalry-man with the
    bullet through and through examine,
Hard the breathing rattles, quite glazed
    already the eye, yet life struggles
    hard,
(Come sweet death! be persuaded O beautiful
    death!
In mercy come quickly.)

From the stump of the arm, the amputated
     hand,
I undo the clotted lint, remove the slough, wash
     off the matter and blood,
Back on his pillow the soldier bends with curv'd
     neck and side falling head,
His eyes are closed, his face is pale, he dares not
     look on the bloody stump,
And has not yet look'd on it.

I dress a wound in the side, deep, deep,
But a day or two more, for see the frame all
     wasted and sinking,
And the yellow-blue countenance see.

I dress the perforated shoulder, the foot with
     the bullet-wound,
Cleanse the one with a gnawing and putrid
     gangrene, so sickening, so offensive,
While the attendant stands behind aside me
     holding the tray and pail.

I am faithful, I do not give out,
The fractur'd thigh, the knee, the wound in the
     abdomen,
These and more I dress with impassive hand,
     (yet deep in my breast a fire, a burning
     flame.)

4

Thus in silence in dreams' projections,
Returning, resuming, I thread my way through
the hospitals,
The hurt and wounded I pacify with soothing
hand,
I sit by the restless all the dark night, some are
so young,
Some suffer so much, I recall the experience
sweet and sad,
(Many a soldier's loving arms about this neck
have cross'd and rested,
Many a soldier's kiss dwells on these bearded
lips.)

LONG, TOO LONG AMERICA

LONG, too long America,
Traveling roads all even and peaceful you learn'd
from joys and prosperity only,
But now, ah now, to learn from crises of
anguish, advancing, grappling with direst fate
and recoiling not,
And now to conceive and show to the
world what your children en-masse really
are,
(For who except myself has yet conceiv'd what
your children en-masse really are?)

GIVE ME THE SPLENDID SILENT SUN

1

GIVE me the splendid silent sun with all his
   beams full-dazzling,
Give me autumnal fruit ripe and red from the
   orchard,
Give me a field where the unmow'd grass grows,
Give me an arbor, give me the trellis'd grape,
Give me fresh corn and wheat, give me serene-
   moving animals teaching content,
Give me nights perfectly quiet as on high
   plateaus west of the Mississippi, and I looking
   up at the stars,
Give me odorous at sunrise a garden of beautiful
   flowers where I can walk undisturb'd,
Give me for marriage a sweet-breath'd woman
   of whom I should never tire,
Give me a perfect child, give me away aside from
   the noise of the world a rural domestic life,
Give me to warble spontaneous songs recluse by
   myself, for my own ears only,
Give me solitude, give me Nature, give me again
   O Nature your primal sanities!

These demanding to have them, (tired with
   ceaseless excitement, and rack'd by the war-
   strife,)
These to procure incessantly asking, rising in
   cries from my heart,

While yet incessantly asking still I adhere to my
city,
Day upon day and year upon year O city,
walking your streets,
Where you hold me enchain'd a certain time
refusing to give me up,
Yet giving to make me glutted, enrich'd of soul,
you give me forever faces;
(O I see what I sought to escape, confronting,
reversing my cries,
see my own soul trampling down what it ask'd
for.)

2

Keep your splendid silent sun,
Keep your woods O Nature, and the quiet
places by the woods,
Keep your fields of clover and timothy, and your
corn-fields and orchards,
Keep the blossoming buckwheat fields where the
Ninth-month bees hum;
Give me faces and streets—give me these
phantoms incessant and endless along the
trottoirs!
Give me interminable eyes—give me women—
give me comrades and lovers by the thousand!
Let me see new ones every day—let me hold
new ones by the hand every day!
Give me such shows—give me the streets of
Manhattan!

Give me Broadway, with the soldiers marching-
  give me the sound of the trumpets and
  drums!
(The soldiers in companies or regiments—some
  starting away, flush'd and reckless,
Some, their time up, returning with thinn'd
  ranks, young, yet very old, worn, marching,
  noticing nothing;)
Give me the shores and wharves heavy-fringed
  with black ships!
O such for me! O an intense life, full to
  repletion and varied!
The life of the theatre, bar-room, huge hotel,
  for me!
The saloon of the steamer! the crowded
  excursion for me! the torchlight procession!
The dense brigade bound for the war, with high
  piled military wagons following;
People, endless, streaming, with strong voices,
  passions, pageants,
Manhattan streets with their powerful throbs,
  with beating drums as now,
The endless and noisy chorus, the rustle and
  clank of muskets, (even the sight of the
  wounded,)
Manhattan crowds, with their turbulent musical
  chorus!
Manhattan faces and eyes forever for me.

DIRGE FOR TWO VETERANS

THE last sunbeam
Lightly falls from the finish'd Sabbath,
On the pavement here, and there beyond it is
    looking,
Down a new-made double grave.

Lo, the moon ascending,
Up from the east the silvery round moon,
Beautiful over the house-tops, ghastly, phantom
    moon,
Immense and silent moon.

I see a sad procession,
And I hear the sound of coming full-key'd
    bugles,
All the channels of the city streets they're
    flooding,
As with voices and with tears.

I hear the great drums pounding,
And the small drums steady whirring,
And every blow of the great convulsive drums,
Strikes me through and through.

For the son is brought with the father,
(In the foremost ranks of the fierce assault
    they fell,

Two veterans son and father dropt together,
And the double grave awaits them.)

Now nearer blow the bugles,
And the drums strike more convulsive,
And the daylight o'er the pavement quite has
    faded,
And the strong dead-march enwraps me.

In the eastern sky up-buoying,
The sorrowful vast phantom moves illumin'd,
('Tis some mother's large transparent face,
In heaven brighter growing.)

O strong dead-march you please me!
O moon immense with your silvery face you
    soothe me!
O my soldiers twain! O my veterans passing to
    burial!
What I have I also give you.

The moon gives you light,
And the bugles and the drums give you music,
And my heart, O my soldiers, my veterans,
My heart gives you love.

OVER THE CARNAGE ROSE PROPHETIC A VOICE

OVER the carnage rose prophetic a voice,
Be not dishearten'd, affection shall solve the
    problems of freedom yet,
Those who love each other shall become
    invincible,
They shall yet make Columbia victorious.

Sons of the Mother of All, you shall yet be
    victorious,
You shall yet laugh to scorn the attacks of all the
    remainder of the earth.

No danger shall balk Columbia's lovers,
If need be a thousand shall sternly immolate
    themselves for one.

One from Massachusetts shall be a Missourian's
    comrade,
From Maine and from hot Carolina, and
    another an Oregonese, shall be friends triune,
More precious to each other than all the riches
    of the earth.

To Michigan, Florida perfumes shall tenderly
    come,
Not the perfumes of flowers, but sweeter, and
    waited beyond death.

It shall be customary in the houses and streets
 to see manly affection,
The most dauntless and rude shall touch face to
 face lightly,
The dependence of Liberty shall be lovers,
The continuance of Equality shall be comrades.

These shall tie you and band you stronger than
 hoops of iron,
I, ecstatic, O partners! O lands! with the love of
 lovers tie you.

(Were you looking to be held together by
 lawyers?
Or by an agreement on a paper? or by arms?
Nay, nor the world, nor any living thing, will so
 cohere.)

I SAW OLD GENERAL AT BAY

I SAW old General at bay,
(Old as he was, his gray eyes yet shone out in
 battle like stars,)
His small force was now completely hemm'd in,
 in his works,
He call'd for volunteers to run the enemy's
 lines, a desperate emergency,
I saw a hundred and more step forth from the
 ranks, but two or three were selected,

I saw them receive their orders aside, they
  listen'd with care, the adjutant was very grave,
I saw them depart with cheerfulness, freely
  risking their lives.

THE ARTILLERYMAN'S VISION

WHILE my wife at my side lies slumbering, and
  the wars are over long,
And my head on the pillow rests at home, and
  the vacant midnight passes,
And through the stillness, through the dark, I
  hear, just hear, the breath of my infant,
There in the room as I wake from sleep this
  vision presses upon me;
The engagement opens there and then in fantasy
  unreal,
The skirmishers begin, they crawl cautiously
  ahead, I hear the irregular snap! snap!
I hear the sounds of the different missiles, the
  short t-h-t! t-h-t! of the rifle-balls,
I see the shells exploding leaving small white
  clouds, I hear the great shells shrieking as
  they pass,
The grape like the hum and whirr of wind
  through the trees, (tumultuous now the
  contest rages,)
All the scenes at the batteries rise in detail before
  me again,

The crashing and smoking, the pride of the men
in their pieces,
The chief-gunner ranges and sights his piece and
selects a fuse of the right time,
After firing I see him lean aside and look eagerly
off to note the effect;
Elsewhere I hear the cry of a regiment charging,
(the young colonel leads himself this time
with brandish'd sword,)
I see the gaps cut by the enemy's volleys,
(quickly fill'd up, no delay,)
I breathe the suffocating smoke, then the flat
clouds hover low concealing all;
Now a strange lull for a few seconds, not a shot
fired on either side,
Then resumed the chaos louder than ever, with
eager calls and orders of officers,
While from some distant part of the field the
wind waits to my ears a shout of applause,
(some special success,)
And ever the sound of the cannon far or near,
(rousing even in dreams a devilish exultation
and all the old mad joy in the depths of my
soul,)
And ever the hastening of infantry shifting
positions, batteries, cavalry, moving hither
and thither,
(The falling, dying, I heed not, the wounded
dripping and red heed not, some to the rear
are hobbling,)

Grime, heat, rush, aide-de-camps galloping by
  or on a full run,
With the patter of small arms, the warning s-s-t
  of the rifles, (these in my vision I hear or see,)
And bombs bursting in air, and at night the vari-
  color'd rockets.

ETHIOPIA SALUTING THE COLORS

WHO are you dusky woman, so ancient hardly
  human,
With your woolly-white and turban'd head, and
  bare bony feet?
Why rising by the roadside here, do you
  the colors greet?

('Tis while our army lines Carolina's sands and
  pines,
Forth from thy hovel door thou Ethiopia comist
  to me,
As under doughty Sherman I march toward
  the sea.)

Me master years a hundred since from my
  parents sunder'd,
A little child, they caught me as the savage beast
  is caught,
Then hither me across the sea the cruel slaver
  brought.

No further does she say, but lingering all the
    day,
Her high-borne turban'd head she wags, and
    rolls her darkling eye,
And courtesies to the regiments, the guidons
    moving by.

What is it fateful woman, so blear, hardly
    human?
Why wag your head with turban bound, yellow,
    red and green?
Are the things so strange and marvelous you see
    or have seen?

NOT YOUTH PERTAINS TO ME

NOT youth pertains to me,
Nor delicatesse, I cannot beguile the time with
    talk,
Awkward in the parlor, neither a dancer nor
    elegant,
In the learn'd coterie sitting constrain'd and
    still, for learning inures not to me,
Beauty, knowledge, inure not to me—yet there
    are two or three things inure to me,
I have nourish'd the wounded and sooth'd many
    a dying soldier,
And at intervals waiting or in the midst of camp,
Composed these songs.

RACE OF VETERANS

RACE of veterans—race of victors!
Race of the soil, ready for conflict—race of the
    conquering march!
(No more credulity's race, abiding-temper'd
    race,)
Race henceforth owning no law but the law of
    itself,
Race of passion and the storm.

WORLD TAKE GOOD NOTICE

WORLD take good notice, silver stars fading,
Milky hue ript, wet of white detaching,
Coals thirty-eight, baleful and burning,
Scarlet, significant, hands off warning,
Now and henceforth flaunt from these shores.

O TAN-FACED PRAIRIE-BOY

O TAN-FACED prairie-boy,
Before you came to camp came many a welcome
    gift,
Praises and presents came and nourishing food,
    till at last among the recruits,
You came, taciturn, with nothing to give—we
    but look'd on each other,

When lo! more than all the gifts of the world
you gave me.

LOOK DOWN FAIR MOON

Look down fair moon and bathe this scene,
Pour softly down night's nimbus floods on faces
ghastly, swollen, purple,
On the dead on their backs with arms toss'd
wide,
Pour down your unstinted nimbus sacred moon.

RECONCILIATION

WORD over all, beautiful as the sky,
Beautiful that war and all its deeds of carnage
must in time be utterly lost,
That the hands of the sisters Death and Night
incessantly softly wash again, and ever again,
this solid world;
For my enemy is dead, a man divine as myself is
dead,
I look where he lies white-faced and still in the
coffin—I draw near,
Bend down and touch lightly with my lips the
white face in the coffin.

How Solemn As One by One
(Washington City, 1865)

HOW solemn as one by one,
As the ranks returning worn and sweaty, as the
    men file by where stand,
As the faces the masks appear, as I glance at the
    faces studying the masks,
(As I glance upward out of this page studying
    you, dear friend, whoever you are,)
How solemn the thought of my whispering soul
    to each in the ranks, and to you,
I see behind each mask that wonder a kindred
    soul,
O the bullet could never kill what you really are,
    dear friend,
Nor the bayonet stab what you really are;
The soul! yourself I see, great as any, good as
    the best,
Waiting secure and content, which the bullet
    could never kill,
Nor the bayonet stab O friend.

As I Lay with My Head
In Your Lap Camerado

As I lay with my head in your lap camerado,
The confession I made I resume, what I said to
    you and the open air I resume,

I know I am restless and make others so,
I know my words are weapons full of danger,
    full of death,
For I confront peace, security, and all the settled
    laws, to unsettle them,
I am more resolute because all have denied me
    than I could ever have been had all accepted me,
I heed not and have never heeded either
    experience, cautions, majorities, nor ridicule,
And the threat of what is call'd hell is little or
    nothing to me,
And the lure of what is call'd heaven is little or
    nothing to me;
Dear camerado! I confess I have urged you
    onward with me, and still urge you, without
    the least idea what is our destination,
Or whether we shall be victorious, or utterly
    quell'd and defeated.

DELICATE CLUSTER

DELICATE cluster! flag of teeming life!
Covering all my lands—all my seashores lining!
Flag of death! (how I watch'd you through the
    smoke of battle pressing!
How I heard you flap and rustle, cloth defiant!)
Flag cerulean—sunny flag, with the orbs of
    night dappled!

Ah my silvery beauty—ah my woolly white and
crimson!
Ah to sing the song of you, my matron mighty!
My sacred one, my mother.

To a Certain Civilian

DID you ask dulcet rhymes from me?
Did you seek the civilian's peaceful and
languishing rhymes?
Did you find what I sang erewhile so hard to
follow?
Why I was not singing erewhile for you to
follow, to understand—nor am I now;
(I have been born of the same as the war was
born,
The drum-corps' rattle is ever to me sweet
music, I love well the martial dirge,
With slow wail and convulsive throb leading the
officer's funeral;)
What to such as you anyhow such a poet as I?
therefore leave my works,
And go lull yourself with what you can
understand, and with piano-tunes,
For I lull nobody, and you will never understand
me.

LO, VICTRESS ON THE PEAKS

LO, Victress on the peaks,
Where thou with mighty brow regarding the
   world,
(The world O Libertad, that vainly conspired
   against thee,)
Out of its countless beleaguering toils, after
   thwarting them all,
Dominant, with the dazzling sun around thee,
Flauntest now unharm'd in immortal soundness
   and bloom—lo, in these hours supreme,
No poem proud, I chanting bring to thee, nor
   mastery's rapturous verse,
But a cluster containing night's darkness and
   blood-dripping wounds,
And psalms of the dead.

SPIRIT WHOSE WORK IS DONE
(WASHINGTON CITY, 1865)

SPIRIT whose work is done—spirit of dreadful
   hours!
Ere departing fade from my eyes your forests of
   bayonets;
Spirit of gloomiest fears and doubts, (yet
   onward ever unfaltering pressing,)
Spirit of many a solemn day and many a savage
   scene—electric spirit,

That with muttering voice through the war now
closed, like a tireless phantom flitted,
Rousing the land with breath of flame, while
you beat and beat the drum,
Now as the sound of the drum, hollow and
harsh to the last, reverberates round me,
As your ranks, your immortal ranks, return,
return from the battles,
As the muskets of the young men yet lean over
their shoulders,
As I look on the bayonets bristling over their
shoulders,
As those slanted bayonets, whole forests of them
appearing in the distance, approach and pass
on, returning homeward,
Moving with steady motion, swaying to and fro
to the right and left,
Evenly lightly rising and falling while the steps
keep time;
Spirit of hours I knew, all hectic red one day, but
pale as death next day,
Touch my mouth ere you depart, press my lips
close,
Leave me your pulses of rage—bequeath them
to me—fill me with currents convulsive,
Let them scorch and blister out of my chants
when you are gone,
Let them identify you to the future in these
song.

ADIEU TO A SOLDIER

ADIEU O soldier,
You of the rude campaigning, (which we
    shared,)
The rapid march, the life of the camp,
The hot contention of opposing fronts, the long
    manoeuvre,
Red battles with their slaughter, the stimulus,
    the strong terrific game,
Spell of all brave and manly hearts, the trains
    of time through you and like of you all
    fill'd,
With war and war's expression.

Adieu dear comrade,
Your mission is fulfill'd—but I, more warlike,
Myself and this contentious soul of mine,
Still on our own campaigning bound,
Through untried roads with ambushes
    opponents lined,
Through many a sharp defeat and many a crisis,
    often baffled,
Here marching, ever marching on, a war fight
    out—aye here,
To fiercer, weightier battles give expression.

TURN O LIBERTAD

TURN O Libertad, for the war is over,
From it and all henceforth expanding,
    doubting no more, resolute, sweeping the
    world,
Turn from lands retrospective recording proofs
    of the past,
From the singers that sing the trailing glories of
    the past,
From the chants of the feudal world, the
    triumphs of kings, slavery, caste,
Turn to the world, the triumphs reserv'd and to
    come—give up that backward world,
Leave to the singers of hitherto, give them the
    trailing past,
But what remains remains for singers for you-
    wars to come are for you,
(Lo, how the wars of the past have duly inured
    to you, and the wars of the present also
    inure;)
Then turn, and be not alarm'd O Libertad—
    turn your undying face,
To where the future, greater than all the past,
Is swiftly, surely preparing for you.
To the Leaven'd Soil They Trod

To the leaven'd soil they trod calling I sing for
    the last,

(Forth from my tent emerging for good,
    loosing, untying the tent-ropes,)
In the freshness the forenoon air, in the far-
    stretching circuits and vistas again to peace
    restored,
To the fiery fields emanative and the endless
    vistas beyond, to the South and the North,
To the leaven'd soil of the general Western
    world to attest my songs,
To the Alleghanian hills and the tireless
    Mississippi,
To the rocks I calling sing, and all the trees in
    the woods,
To the plains of the poems of heroes, to the
    prairies spreading wide,
To the far-off sea and the unseen winds, and the
    sane impalpable air;
And responding they answer all, (but not in
    words,)
The average earth, the witness of war and peace,
    acknowledges mutely,
The prairie draws me close, as the father to
    bosom broad the son,
The Northern ice and rain that began me
    nourish me to the end,
But the hot sun of the South is to fully ripen my
    songs.

Memories of President lincoln

WHEN LILACS LAST IN THE DOORYARD BLOOM'D

1

WHEN lilacs last in the dooryard bloom'd,
And the great star early droop'd in the western
  sky in the night,
I mourn'd, and yet shall mourn with ever-
  returning spring.

Ever-returning spring, trinity sure to me you
  bring,
Lilac blooming perennial and drooping star in
  the west,
And thought of him I love.

2

O powerful western fallen star!
O shades of night—O moody, tearful night!
O great star disappear'd—O the black murk that
  hides the star!
O cruel hands that hold me powerless-
  O helpless soul of me!
O harsh surrounding cloud that will not free my
  soul.

3

In the dooryard fronting an old farm-house near
    the white-wash'd palings,
Stands the lilac-bush tall-growing with heart-
    shaped leaves of rich green,
With many a pointed blossom rising delicate,
    with the perfume strong I love,
With every leaf a miracle—and from this bush in
    the dooryard,
With delicate-color'd blossoms and heart-shaped
    leaves of rich green,
A sprig with its flower I break.

4

In the swamp in secluded recesses,
A shy and hidden bird is warbling a song.

Solitary the thrush,
The hermit withdrawn to himself, avoiding the
    settlements,
Sings by himself a song.

Song of the bleeding throat,
Death's outlet song of life, (for well dear
    brother I know,
If thou wast not granted to sing thou wouldist
    surely die.)

5

Over the breast of the spring, the land, amid
    cities,
Amid lanes and through old woods, where lately
    the violets peep'd from the ground, spotting
    the gray debris,
Amid the grass in the fields each side of the
    lanes, passing the endless grass,
Passing the yellow-spear'd wheat, every grain
    from its shroud in the dark-brown fields
    uprisen,
Passing the apple-tree blows of white and pink
    in the orchards,
Carrying a corpse to where it shall rest in the
    grave,
Night and day journeys a coffin.

6

Coffin that passes through lanes and streets,
Through day and night with the great cloud
    darkening the land,
With the pomp of the inloop'd flags with the
    cities draped in black,
With the show of the States themselves as of
    crape-veil'd women standing,
With processions long and winding and the
    flambeaus of the night,
With the countless torches lit, with the silent sea
    of faces and the unbared heads,

With the waiting depot, the arriving coffin, and
  the sombre faces,
With dirges through the night, with the
  thousand voices rising strong and solemn,
With all the mournful voices of the dirges
  pour'd around the coffin,
The dim-lit churches and the shuddering
  organs-where amid these you journey,
With the tolling tolling bells' perpetual clang,
Here, coffin that slowly passes,
I give you my sprig of lilac.

7

(Nor for you, for one alone,
Blossoms and branches green to coffins all I
  bring,
For fresh as the morning, thus would I chant a
  song for you O sane and sacred death.

All over bouquets of roses,
O death, I cover you over with roses and early
  lilies,
But mostly and now the lilac that blooms the
  first,
Copious I break, I break the sprigs from the
  bushes,
With loaded arms I come, pouring for you,
For you and the coffins all of you O death.)

8

O western orb sailing the heaven,
Now I know what you must have meant as a
    month since I walk'd,
As I walk'd in silence the transparent shadowy
    night,
As I saw you had something to tell as you bent
    to me night after night,
As you droop'd from the sky low down as if to
    my side, (while the other stars all look'd on,)
As we wander'd together the solemn night, (for
    something I know not what kept me from
    sleep,)
As the night advanced, and I saw on the rim of
    the west how full you were of woe,
As I stood on the rising ground in the breeze in
    the cool transparent night,
As I watch'd where you pass'd and was lost in
    the netherward black of the night,
As my soul in its trouble dissatisfied sank, as
    where you sad orb,
Concluded, dropt in the night, and was gone.

9

Sing on there in the swamp,
O singer bashful and tender, I hear your notes, I
    hear your call,
I hear, I come presently, I understand you,
But a moment I linger, for the lustrous star has
    detain'd me,

The star my departing comrade holds and
   detains me.

10

O how shall I warble myself for the dead one
   there I loved?
And how shall I deck my song for the large
   sweet soul that has gone?
And what shall my perfume be for the grave of
   him I love?

Sea-winds blown from east and west,
Blown from the Eastern sea and blown from the
   Western sea, till there on the prairies meeting,
These and with these and the breath of my
   chant,
I'll perfume the grave of him I love.

11

O what shall I hang on the chamber walls?
And what shall the pictures be that I hang on
   the walls,
To adorn the burial-house of him I love?
Pictures of growing spring and farms and
   homes,
With the Fourth-month eve at sundown, and
   the gray smoke lucid and bright,
With floods of the yellow gold of the gorgeous,
   indolent, sinking sun, burning, expanding the
   air,

With the fresh sweet herbage under foot, and
   the pale green leaves of the trees prolific,
In the distance the flowing glaze, the breast
   of the river, with a wind-dapple here and
   there,
With ranging hills on the banks, with many a
   line against the sky, and shadows,
And the city at hand with dwellings so dense,
   and stacks of chimneys,
And all the scenes of life and the workshops, and
   the workmen homeward returning.

12

Lo, body and soul—this land,
My own Manhattan with spires, and the
   sparkling and hurrying tides, and the ships,
The varied and ample land, the South and the
   North in the light, Ohio's shores and flashing
   Missouri,
And ever the far-spreading prairies cover'd with
   grass and corn.

Lo, the most excellent sun so calm and haughty,
The violet and purple morn with just-felt
   breezes,
The gentle soft-born measureless light,
The miracle spreading bathing all, the fulfill'd
   noon,
The coming eve delicious, the welcome night
   and the stars,

Over my cities shining all, enveloping man and
    land.

13

Sing on, sing on you gray-brown bird,
Sing from the swamps, the recesses, pour your
    chant from the bushes,
Limitless out of the dusk, out of the cedars and
    pines.

Sing on dearest brother, warble your reedy
    song,
Loud human song, with voice of uttermost woe.

O liquid and free and tender!
O wild and loose to my soul—O wondrous
    singer!
You only I hear—yet the star holds me, (but will
    soon depart,)
Yet the lilac with mastering odor holds me.

14

Now while I sat in the day and look'd forth,
In the close of the day with its light and the
    fields of spring, and the farmers preparing
    their crops,
In the large unconscious scenery of my land
    with its lakes and forests,
In the heavenly aerial beauty, (after the
    perturb'd winds and the storms,)

Under the arching heavens of the afternoon
    swift passing, and the voices of children and
    women,
The many-moving sea-tides, and I saw the ships
    how they sail'd,
And the summer approaching with richness, and
    the fields all busy with labor,
And the infinite separate houses, how they all
    went on, each with its meals and minutia of
    daily usages,
And the streets how their throbbings throbb'd,
    and the cities pent—lo, then and there,
Falling upon them all and among them all,
    enveloping me with the rest,
Appear'd the cloud, appear'd the long black trail,
And I knew death, its thought, and the sacred
    knowledge of death.

Then with the knowledge of death as walking
    one side of me,
And the thought of death close-walking the
    other side of me,
And I in the middle as with companions, and as
    holding the hands of companions,
I fled forth to the hiding receiving night that
    talks not,
Down to the shores of the water, the path by
    the swamp in the dimness,
To the solemn shadowy cedars and ghostly pines
    so still.

And the singer so shy to the rest receiv'd me,
The gray-brown bird I know receiv'd us
    comrades three,
And he sang the carol of death, and a verse for
    him I love.

From deep secluded recesses,
From the fragrant cedars and the ghostly pines
    so still,
Came the carol of the bird.

And the charm of the carol rapt me,
As I held as if by their hands my comrades in
    the night,
And the voice of my spirit tallied the song of the
    bird.

Come lovely and soothing death,
Undulate round the world, serenely arriving,
    arriving,
In the day, in the night, to all, to each,
Sooner or later delicate death.

Prais'd be the fathomless universe,
For life and joy, and for objects and knowledge
    curious,
And for love, sweet love—but praise! praise! praise!
For the sure-enwinding arms of cool-enfolding
    death.

Dark mother always gliding near with soft feet,
Have none chanted for thee a chant of fullest
    welcome?
Then I chant it for thee, I glorify thee above
    all,
I bring thee a song that when thou must indeed
    come, come unfalteringly.

Approach strong deliveress,
When it is so, when thou hast taken them I
    joyously sing the dead,
Lost in the loving floating ocean of thee,
Laved in the flood of thy bliss O death.

From me to thee glad serenades,
Dances for thee I propose saluting thee,
    adornments and feastings for thee,
And the sights of the open landscape and the
    high-spread shy are fitting,
And life and the fields, and the huge and
    thoughtful night.

The night in silence under many a star,
The ocean shore and the husky whispering wave
    whose voice I know,
And the soul turning to thee O vast and well-
    veil'd death,
And the body gratefully nestling close to
    thee.

Over the tree-tops I float thee a song,
Over the rising and sinking waves, over the
    myriad fields and the prairies wide,
Over the dense-pack'd cities all and the teeming
    wharves and ways,
I float this carol with joy, with joy to thee O
    death.

15

To the tally of my soul,
Loud and strong kept up the gray-brown bird,
With pure deliberate notes spreading filling the
    night.

Loud in the pines and cedars dim,
Clear in the freshness moist and the swamp-
    perfume,
And I with my comrades there in the night.

While my sight that was bound in my eyes
    unclosed,
As to long panoramas of visions.

And I saw askant the armies,
I saw as in noiseless dreams hundreds of battle-
    flags,
Borne through the smoke of the battles and
    pierc'd with missiles I saw them,
And carried hither and yon through the smoke,
    and torn and bloody,

And at last but a few shreds left on the staffs,
  (and all in silence,)
And the staffs all splinter'd and broken.

I saw battle-corpses, myriads of them,
And the white skeletons of young men, I saw
  them,
I saw the debris and debris of all the slain
  soldiers of the war,
But I saw they were not as was thought,
They themselves were fully at rest, they suffer'd
  not,
The living remain'd and suffer'd, the mother
  suffer'd,
And the wife and the child and the musing
  comrade suffer'd,
And the armies that remain'd suffer'd.

16

Passing the visions, passing the night,
Passing, unloosing the hold of my comrades'
  hands,
Passing the song of the hermit bird and the
  tallying song of my soul,
Victorious song, death's outlet song, yet varying
  ever-altering song,
As low and wailing, yet clear the notes, rising
  and falling, flooding the night,
Sadly sinking and fainting, as warning and
  warning, and yet again bursting with joy,

Covering the earth and filling the spread of the
    heaven,
As that powerful psalm in the night I heard
    from recesses,
Passing, I leave thee lilac with heart-shaped
    leaves,
I leave thee there in the door-yard, blooming,
    returning with spring.

I cease from my song for thee,
From my gaze on thee in the west, fronting the
    west, communing with thee,
O comrade lustrous with silver face in the night.

Yet each to keep and all, retrievements out of
    the night,
The song, the wondrous chant of the gray-
    brown bird,
And the tallying chant, the echo arous'd in my
    soul,
With the lustrous and drooping star with the
    countenance full of woe,
With the holders holding my hand nearing the
    call of the bird,
Comrades mine and I in the midst, and their
    memory ever to keep, for the dead I loved so
    well,
For the sweetest, wisest soul of all my days and
    lands—and this for his dear sake,

Lilac and star and bird twined with the chant of
my soul,
There in the fragrant pines and the cedars dusk
and dim.

O CAPTAIN! MY CAPTAIN!

O CAPTAIN! my Captain! our fearful trip is
done,
The ship has weather'd every rack, the prize we
sought is won,
The port is near, the bells I hear, the people all
exulting,
While follow eyes the steady keel, the vessel grim
and daring;
But O heart! heart! heart!
O the bleeding drops of red,
Where on the deck my Captain lies,
Fallen cold and dead.

O Captain! my Captain! rise up and hear the
bells;
Rise up—for you the flag is flung—for you the
bugle trills,
For you bouquets and ribbon'd wreaths—for
you the shores a-crowding,
For you they call, the swaying mass, their eager
faces turning;

Here Captain! dear father!
This arm beneath your head!
It is some dream that on the deck,
You've fallen cold and dead.

My Captain does not answer, his lips are pale
    and still,
My father does not feel my arm, he has no pulse
    nor will,
The ship is anchor'd safe and sound, its voyage
    closed and done,
From fearful trip the victor ship comes in with
    object won;
Exult O shores, and ring O bells!
But I with mournful tread,
Walk the deck my Captain lies,
Fallen cold and dead.

HUSH'D BE THE CAMPS TO-DAY
(MAY 4, 1865)

HUSH'D be the camps to-day,
And soldiers let us drape our war-worn weapons,
And each with musing soul retire to celebrate,
Our dear commander's death.

No more for him life's stormy conflicts,
Nor victory, nor defeat—no more time's dark
    events,

Charging like ceaseless clouds across the sky.
But sing poet in our name,

Sing of the love we bore him—because you,
  dweller in camps, know it truly.

As they invault the coffin there,
Sing—as they close the doors of earth upon
  him—one verse,
For the heavy hearts of soldiers.

THIS DUST WAS ONCE THE MAN

THIS dust was once the man,
Gentle, plain, just and resolute, under whose
  cautious hand,
Against the foulest crime in history known in
  any land or age,
Was saved the Union of these States.

By Blue Ontario's Shore

By blue Ontario's shore,
As I mused of these warlike days and of peace
    return'd, and the dead that return no more,
A Phantom gigantic superb, with stern visage
    accosted me,
Chant me the poem, it said, that comes from the
    soul of America, chant me the carol of victory,
And strike up the marches of Libertad, marches
    more powerful yet,
And sing me before you go the song of the
    throes of Democracy.

(Democracy, the destin'd conqueror, yet
    treacherous lip-smiles everywhere,
And death and infidelity at every step.)

2

A Nation announcing itself,
I myself make the only growth by which I can
    be appreciated,
I reject none, accept all, then reproduce all in
    my own forms.

A breed whose proof is in time and deeds,
What we are we are, nativity is answer enough
    to objections,

We wield ourselves as a weapon is wielded,
We are powerful and tremendous in ourselves,
We are executive in ourselves, we are sufficient
    in the variety of ourselves,
We are the most beautiful to ourselves and in
    ourselves,
We stand self-pois'd in the middle, branching
    thence over the world,
From Missouri, Nebraska, or Kansas, laughing
    attacks to scorn.

Nothing is sinful to us outside of ourselves,
Whatever appears, whatever does not appear, we
    are beautiful or sinful in ourselves only.

(O Mother—O Sisters dear!
If we are lost, no victor else has destroy'd us,
It is by ourselves we go down to eternal night.)

3

Have you thought there could be but a single
    supreme?
There can be any number of supremes-one does
    not countervail another any more than one
    eyesight countervails another, or one life
    countervails another.

All is eligible to all,
All is for individuals, all is for you,
No condition is prohibited, not God's or any.

All comes by the body, only health puts you
    rapport with the universe.

Produce great Persons, the rest follows.

4

Piety and conformity to them that like,
Peace, obesity, allegiance, to them that
    like,
I am he who tauntingly compels men, women,
    nations,
Crying, Leap from your seats and contend for
    your lives!

I am he who walks the States with a barb'd
    tongue, questioning every one I meet,
Who are you that wanted only to be told what
    you knew before?
Who are you that wanted only a book to join
    you in your nonsense?

(With pangs and cries as thine own O bearer of
    many children,
These clamors wild to a race of pride I give.)

O lands, would you be freer than all that has
    ever been before?
If you would be freer than all that has been
    before, come listen to me.

Fear grace, elegance, civilization, delicatesse,
Fear the mellow sweet, the sucking of
  honey-juice,
Beware the advancing mortal ripening of
  Nature,
Beware what precedes the decay of the
  ruggedness of states and men.

5

Ages, precedents, have long been accumulating
  undirected materials,
America brings builders, and brings its own
  styles.

The immortal poets of Asia and Europe have
  done their work and pass'd to other spheres,
A work remains, the work of surpassing all they
  have done.

America, curious toward foreign characters,
  stands by its own at all hazards,
Stands removed, spacious, composite, sound,
  initiates the true use of precedents,
Does not repel them or the past or what they
  have produced under their forms,
Takes the lesson with calmness, perceives the
  corpse slowly borne from the house,
Perceives that it waits a little while in the door,
  that it was fittest for its days,

That its life has descended to the stalwart and
    well-shaped heir who approaches,
And that he shall be fittest for his days.

Any period one nation must lead,
One land must be the promise and reliance of
    the future.

These States are the amplest poem,
Here is not merely a nation but a teeming
    Nation of nations,
Here the doings of men correspond with the
    broadcast doings of the day and night,
Here is what moves in magnificent masses
    careless of particulars,
Here are the roughs, beards, friendliness,
    combativeness, the soul loves,
Here the flowing trains, here the crowds,
    equality, diversity, the soul loves.

6

Land of lands and bards to corroborate!
Of them standing among them, one lifts to the
    light a west-bred face,
To him the hereditary countenance bequeath'd
    both mother's and father's,
His first parts substances, earth, water, animals,
    trees,
Built of the common stock, having room for far
    and near,

Used to dispense with other lands, incarnating
    this land,
Attracting it body and soul to himself,
    hanging on its neck with incomparable
    love,
Plunging his seminal muscle into its merits and
    demerits,
Making its cities, beginnings, events, diversities,
    wars, vocal in him,
Making its rivers, lakes, bays, embouchure in
    him,
Mississippi with yearly freshets and changing
    chutes, Columbia, Niagara, Hudson,
    spending themselves lovingly in him,
If the Atlantic coast stretch or the Pacific coast
    stretch, he stretching with them North or
    South,
Spanning between them East and West, and
    touching whatever is between them,
Growths growing from him to offset the
    growths of pine, cedar, hemlock, live-oak,
    locust, chestnut, hickory, cottonwood,
    orange, magnolia,
Tangles as tangled in him as any canebrake or
    swamp,
He likening sides and peaks of mountains,
    forests coated with northern transparent
    ice,
Off him pasturage sweet and natural as savanna,
    upland, prairie,

Through him flights, whirls, screams, answering
    those of the fish-hawk, mocking-bird, night-
    heron, and eagle,
His spirit surrounding his country's spirit,
    unclosed to good and evil,
Surrounding the essences of real things, old
    times and present times,
Surrounding just found shores, islands, tribes of
    red aborigines,
Weather-beaten vessels, landings, settlements,
    embryo stature and muscle,
The haughty defiance of the Year One, war,
    peace, the formation of the Constitution,
The separate States, the simple elastic scheme,
    the immigrants,
The Union always swarming with blatherers and
    always sure and impregnable,
The unsurvey'd interior, log-houses, clearings,
    wild animals, hunters, trappers,
Surrounding the multiform agriculture, mines,
    temperature, the gestation of new States,
Congress convening every Twelfth-month, the
    members duly coming up from the uttermost
    parts,
Surrounding the noble character of mechanics
    and farmers, especially the young men,
Responding their manners, speech, dress,
    friendships, the gait they have of persons who
    never knew how it felt to stand in the
    presence of superiors,

The freshness and candor of their physiognomy,
the copiousness and decision of their
phrenology,
The picturesque looseness of their carriage, their
fierceness when wrong'd,
The fluency of their speech, their delight in
music, their curiosity, good temper and open-
handedness, the whole composite make,
The prevailing ardor and enterprise, the large
amativeness,
The perfect equality of the female with the male,
the fluid movement of the population,
The superior marine, free commerce, fisheries,
whaling, gold-digging,
Wharf-hemm'd cities, railroad and steamboat
lines intersecting all points,
Factories, mercantile life, labor-saving
machinery, the Northeast, Northwest,
Southwest,
Manhattan firemen, the Yankee swap, southern
plantation life,
Slavery—the murderous, treacherous conspiracy
to raise it upon the ruins of all the rest,
On and on to the grapple with it—Assassin!
then your life or ours be the stake, and respite
no more.

7

(Lo, high toward heaven, this day,
Libertad, from the conqueress' field return'd,

I mark the new aureola around your head,
No more of soft astral, but dazzling and fierce,
With war's flames and the lambent lightnings
    playing,
And your port immovable where you stand,
With still the inextinguishable glance and the
    clinch'd and lifted fist,
And your foot on the neck of the menacing
    one, the scorner utterly crush'd beneath
    you,
The menacing arrogant one that strode and
    advanced with his senseless scorn, bearing the
    murderous knife,
The wide-swelling one, the braggart that would
    yesterday do so much,
To-day a carrion dead and damn'd, the despised
    of all the earth,
An offal rank, to the dunghill maggots spurn'd.)

8

Others take finish, but the Republic is ever
    constructive and ever keeps vista,
Others adorn the past, but you O days of the
    present, I adorn you,
O days of the future I believe in you—I isolate
    myself for your sake,
O America because you build for mankind I
    build for you,
O well-beloved stone-cutters, I lead them who
    plan with decision and science,

Lead the present with friendly hand toward the
    future.
(Bravas to all impulses sending sane children to
    the next age!
But damn that which spends itself with no
    thought of the stain, pains, dismay, feebleness,
    it is bequeathing.)

9

I listened to the Phantom by Ontario's shore,
I heard the voice arising demanding bards,
By them all native and grand, by them alone can
    these States be fused into the compact
    organism of a Nation.

To hold men together by paper and seal or by
    compulsion is no account,
That only holds men together which aggregates
    all in a living principle, as the hold of the
    limbs of the body or the fibres of plants.

Of all races and eras these States with veins full
    of poetical stuff most need poets, and are to
    have the greatest, and use them the greatest,
Their Presidents shall not be their common
    referee so much as their poets shall.

(Soul of love and tongue of fire!
Eye to pierce the deepest deeps and sweep the
    world!

Ah Mother, prolific and full in all besides, yet
    how long barren, barren?)

10

Of these States the poet is the equable man,
Not in him but off from him things are
    grotesque, eccentric, fail of their full returns,
Nothing out of its place is good, nothing in its
    place is bad,
He bestows on every object or quality its fit
    proportion, neither more nor less,
He is the arbiter of the diverse, he is the key,
He is the equalizer of his age and land,
He supplies what wants supplying, he checks
    what wants checking,
In peace out of him speaks the spirit of peace,
    large, rich, thrifty, building populous towns,
    encouraging agriculture, arts, commerce,
    lighting the study of man, the soul, health,
    immortality, government,
In war he is the best backer of the war, he
    fetches artillery as good as the engineer's, he
    can make every word he speaks draw blood,
The years straying toward infidelity he withholds
    by his steady faith,
He is no arguer, he is judgment, (Nature accepts
    him absolutely,)
He judges not as the judge judges but as the sun
    failing round helpless thing,
As he sees the farthest he has the most faith,

His thoughts are the hymns of the praise of
    things,
In the dispute on God and eternity he is silent,
He sees eternity less like a play with a prologue
    and dénouement,
He sees eternity in men and women, he does
    not see men and women as dreams or dots.

For the great Idea, the idea of perfect and free
    individuals,
For that, the bard walks in advance, leader of
    leaders,
The attitude of him cheers up slaves and
    horrifies foreign despots.

Without extinction is Liberty, without
    retrograde is Equality,
They live in the feelings of young men and the
    best women,
(Not for nothing have the indomitable heads of
    the earth been always ready to fall for
    Liberty.)

11

For the great Idea,
That, O my brethren, that is the mission of
    poets.

Songs of stern defiance ever ready,
Songs of the rapid arming and the march,

The flag of peace quick-folded, and instead the
    flag we know,
Warlike flag of the great Idea.

(Angry cloth I saw there leaping!
I stand again in leaden rain your flapping folds
    saluting,
I sing you over all, flying beckoning through the
    fight—O the hard-contested fight!
The cannons ope their rosy-flashing muzzles—
    the hurtled balls scream,
The battle-front forms amid the smoke-the
    volleys pour incessant from the line,
Hark, the ringing word Charge!—now the tussle
    and the furious maddening yells,
Now the corpses tumble curl'd upon the ground,
Cold, cold in death, for precious life of you,
Angry cloth I saw there leaping.)

12

Are you he who would assume a place to teach
    or be a poet here in the States?
The place is august, the terms obdurate.

Who would assume to teach here may well
    prepare himself body and mind,
He may well survey, ponder, arm, fortify,
    harden, make lithe himself,
He shall surely be question'd beforehand by me
    with many and stern questions.

Who are you indeed who would talk or sing to
    America?
Have you studied out the land, its idioms and
    men?
Have you learn'd the physiology, phrenology,
    politics, geography, pride, freedom, friendship
    of the land? its substratums and objects?
Have you consider'd the organic compact of the
    first day of the first year of Independence,
    sign'd by the Commissioners, ratified by the
    States, and read by Washington at the head of
    the army?
Have you possess'd yourself of the Federal
    Constitution?
Do you see who have left all feudal processes
    and poems behind them, and assumed the
    poems and processes of Democracy?
Are you faithful to things? do you teach what
    the land and sea, the bodies of men,
    womanhood, amativeness, heroic angers,
    teach?
Have you sped through fleeting customs,
    popularities?
Can you hold your hand against all seductions,
    follies, whirls, fierce contentions? are you very
    strong? are you really of the whole People?
Are you not of some coterie? some school or
    mere religion?
Are you done with reviews and criticisms of life?
    animating now to life itself?

Have you vivified yourself from the maternity of
these States?
Have you too the old ever-fresh forbearance and
impartiality?
Do you hold the like love for those hardening to
maturity? for the last-born? little and big? and
for the errant?

What is this you bring my America?
Is it uniform with my country?
Is it not something that has been better told or
done before?
Have you not imported this or the spirit of it in
some ship?
Is it not a mere tale? a rhyme? a prettiness?—Is
the good old cause in it?
Has it not dangled long at the heels of the
poets, politicians, literats, of enemies' lands?
Does it not assume that what is notoriously
gone is still here?
Does it answer universal needs? will it improve
manners?
Does it sound with trumpet-voice the proud
victory of the Union in that secession war?
Can your performance face the open fields and
the seaside?
Will it absorb into me as I absorb food, air, to
appear again in my strength, gait, face?
Have real employments contributed to it?
original makers, not mere amanuenses?

Does it meet modern discoveries, calibres, facts,
 face to face?
What does it mean to American persons,
 progresses, cities? Chicago, Kanada,
 Arkansas?
Does it see behind the apparent custodians
 the real custodians standing, menacing, silent,
 the mechanics, Manhattanese, Western men,
 Southerners, significant alike in their apathy,
 and in the promptness of their love?
Does it see what finally befalls, and has always
 finally befallen, each temporizer, patcher,
 outsider, partialist, alarmist, infidel, who has
 ever ask'd any thing of America?
What mocking and scornful negligence?
The track strew'd with the dust of skeletons,
By the roadside others disdainfully toss'd.

13

Rhymes and rhymers pass away, poems distill'd
 from poems pass away,
The swarms of reflectors and the polite pass, and
 leave ashes,
Admirers, importers, obedient persons, make
 but the soil of literature,
America justifies itself, give it time, no disguise
 can deceive it or conceal from it, it is
 impassive enough,
Only toward the likes of itself will it advance to
 meet them,

If its poets appear it will in due time advance to
    meet them, there is no fear of mistake,
(The proof of a poet shall be sternly deferr'd
    till his country absorbs him as affectionately
    as he has absorb'd it.)

He masters whose spirit masters, he tastes
    sweetest who results sweetest in the long
    run,
The blood of the brawn beloved of time is
    unconstraint;
In the need of songs, philosophy, an
    appropriate native grand-opera, shipcraft,
    any craft,
He or she is greatest who contributes the
    greatest original practical example.

Already a nonchalant breed, silently emerging,
    appears on the streets,
People's lips salute only doers, lovers, satisfiers,
    positive knowers,
There will shortly be no more priests, I say their
    work is done,
Death is without emergencies here, but life is
    perpetual emergencies here,
Are your body, days, manners, superb? after
    death you shall be superb,
Justice, health, self-esteem, clear the way with
    irresistible power;
How dare you place any thing before a man?

14

Fall behind me States!
A man before all—myself, typical, before all.

Give me the pay I have served for,
Give me to sing the songs of the great Idea,
    take all the rest,
I have loved the earth, sun, animals, I have
    despised riches,
I have given aims to every one that ask'd,
    stood up for the stupid and crazy, devoted
    my income and labor to others,
Hated tyrants, argued not concerning God, had
    patience and indulgence toward the people,
    taken off my hat to nothing known or
    unknown,
Gone freely with powerful uneducated persons
    and with the young, and with the mothers of
    families,
Read these leaves to myself in the open air, tried
    them by trees, stars, rivers,
Dismiss'd whatever insulted my own soul or
    defiled my body,
Claim'd nothing to myself which I have not
    carefully claim'd for others on the same
    terms,
Sped to the camps, and comrades found and
    accepted from every State,
(Upon this breast has many a dying soldier
    lean'd to breathe his last,

This arm, this hand, this voice, have nourish'd,
    rais'd, restored,
To life recalling many a prostrate form;)
I am willing to wait to be understood by the
    growth of the taste of myself,
Rejecting none, permitting all.

(Say O Mother, have I not to your thought
    been faithful?
Have I not through life kept you and yours
    before me?)

15

I swear I begin to see the meaning of these
    things,
It is not the earth, it is not America who is so
    great,
It is I who am great or to be great, it is You up
    there, or any one,
It is to walk rapidly through civilizations,
    governments, theories,
Through poems, pageants, shows, to form
    individuals.

Underneath all, individuals,
I swear nothing is good to me now that ignores
    individuals,
The American compact is altogether with
    individuals,

The only government is that which makes
  minute of individuals,
The whole theory of the universe is directed
  unerringly to one single individual—namely
  to You.

(Mother! with subtle sense severe, with the
  naked sword in your hand,
I saw you at last refuse to treat but directly with
  individuals.)

16

Underneath all, Nativity,
I swear I will stand by my own nativity, pious or
  impious so be it;
I swear I am charm'd with nothing except
  nativity,
Men, women, cities, nations, are only beautiful
  from nativity.

Underneath all is the Expression of love for men
  and women,
(I swear I have seen enough of mean and
  impotent modes of expressing love for men
  and women,
After this day I take my own modes of expressing
  love for men and women.) in myself,

I swear I will have each quality of my race in
  myself,

(Talk as you like, he only suits these States
    whose manners favor the audacity and
    sublime turbulence of the States.)

Underneath the lessons of things, spirits,
    Nature, governments, ownerships, I swear I
    perceive other lessons,
Underneath all to me is myself, to you yourself,
    (the same monotonous old song.)

17

O I see flashing that this America is only you
    and me,
Its power, weapons, testimony, are you and me,
Its crimes, lies, thefts, defections, are you and
    me,
Its Congress is you and me, the officers,
    capitols, armies, ships, are you and me,
Its endless gestations of new States are you and
    me,
The war, (that war so bloody and grim, the war
    I will henceforth forget), was you and me,
Natural and artificial are you and me,
Freedom, language, poems, employments, are
    you and me,
Past, present, future, are you and me.

I dare not shirk any part of myself,
Not any part of America good or bad,
Not to build for that which builds for mankind,

Not to balance ranks, complexions, creeds,
  and the sexes,
Not to justify science nor the march of
  equality,
Nor to feed the arrogant blood of the brawn
  belov'd of time.

I am for those that have never been master'd,
For men and women whose tempers have never
  been master'd,
For those whom laws, theories, conventions, can
  never master.

I am for those who walk abreast with the whole
  earth,
Who inaugurate one to inaugurate all.

I will not be outfaced by irrational things,
I will penetrate what it is in them that is sarcastic
  upon me,
I will make cities and civilizations defer to me,
This is what I have learnt from America—it is
  the amount, and it I teach again.

(Democracy, while weapons were everywhere
  aim'd at your breast,
I saw you serenely give birth to immortal
  children, saw in dreams your dilating form,
Saw you with spreading mantle covering the
  world.)

18

I will confront these shows of the day and night,
I will know if I am to be less than they,
I will see if I am not as majestic as they,
I will see if I am not as subtle and real as they,
I will see if I am to be less generous than they,
I will see if I have no meaning, while the houses
    and ships have meaning,
I will see if the fishes and birds are to be enough
    for themselves, and I am not to be enough
    for myself.

I match my spirit against yours you orbs,
    growths, mountains, brutes,
Copious as you are I absorb you all in myself,
    and become the master myself,
America isolated yet embodying all, what is it
    finally except myself?
These States, what are they except myself?

I know now why the earth is gross, tantalizing,
    wicked, it is for my sake,
I take you specially to be mine, you terrible,
    rude forms.

(Mother, bend down, bend close to me your
    face,
I know not what these plots and wars and
    deferments are for,

I know not fruition's success, but I know that
 through war and crime your work goes on,
 and must yet go on.)

19

Thus by blue Ontario's shore,
While the winds fann'd me and the waves came
 trooping toward me,
I thrill'd with the power's pulsations, and the
 charm of my theme was upon me,
Till the tissues that held me parted their ties
 upon me.

And I saw the free souls of poets,
The loftiest bards of past ages strode before
 me,
Strange large men, long unwaked, undisclosed,
 were disclosed to me.

20

O my rapt verse, my call, mock me not!
Not for the bards of the past, not to invoke
 them have I launch'd you forth,
Not to call even those lofty bards here by
 Ontario's shores,
Have I sung so capricious and loud my savage
 song.

Bards for my own land only I invoke,
(For the war the war is over, the field is clear'd,)

Till they strike up marches henceforth
    triumphant and onward,
To cheer O Mother your boundless expectant
    soul.

Bards of the great Idea! bards of the peaceful
    inventions! (for the war, the war is over!)
Yet bards of latent armies, a million soldiers
    waiting ever-ready,
Bards with songs as from burning coals or the
    lightning's fork'd stripes!
Ample Ohio's, Kanada's bards—bards of
    California! inland bards—bards of the war!
You by my charm I invoke.

Reversals

LET that which stood in front go behind,
Let that which was behind advance to the front,
Let bigots, fools, unclean persons, offer new
  propositions,
Let the old propositions be postponed,
Let a man seek pleasure everywhere except in
  himself,
Let a woman seek happiness everywhere except
  in herself

As Consequent, Etc.

AS consequent from store of summer rains,
Or wayward rivulets in autumn flowing,
Or many a herb-lined brook's reticulations,
Or subterranean sea-rills making for the sea,
Songs of continued years I sing.

Life's ever-modern rapids first, (soon, soon to
  blend,
With the old streams of death.)

Some threading Ohio's farm-fields or the
  woods,

Some down Colorado's canons from sources of
    perpetual snow,
Some half-hid in Oregon, or away southward in
    Texas,
Some in the north finding their way to Erie,
    Niagara, Ottawa,
Some to Atlantica's bays, and so to the great
    salt brine.

In you whoe'er you are my book perusing,
In I myself, in all the world, these currents
    flowing,
All, all toward the mystic ocean tending.

Currents for starting a continent new,
Overtures sent to the solid out of the
    liquid,
Fusion of ocean and land, tender and pensive
    waves,
(Not safe and peaceful only, waves rous'd and
    ominous too,
Out of the depths the storm's abysmic waves,
    who knows whence?
Raging over the vast, with many a broken spar
    and tatter'd sail.)

Or from the sea of Time, collecting vasting all, I
    bring,
A windrow-drift of weeds and shells.

O little shells, so curious-convolute, so limpid-
    cold and voiceless,
Will you not little shells to the tympans of
    temples held,
Murmurs and echoes still call up, eternity's
    music faint and far,
Waited inland, sent from Atlantica's rim, strains
    for the soul of the prairies,
Whisper'd reverberations, chords for the ear of
    the West joyously sounding,
Your tidings old, yet ever new and
    untranslatable,
Infinitesimals out of my life, and many a life,
(For not my life and years alone I give-all, all I
    give,)
These waifs from the deep, cast high and dry,
Wash'd on America's shores?

THE RETURN OF THE HEROES

1

FOR the lands and for these passionate days and
    for myself,
Now I awhile retire to thee O soil of autumn fields,
Reclining on thy breast, giving myself to thee,
Answering the pulses of thy sane and equable
    heart,
Turning a verse for thee.

O earth that hast no voice, confide to me a
    voice,
O harvest of my lands—O boundless summer
    growths,
O lavish brown parturient earth—O infinite
    teeming womb,
A song to narrate thee.

2

Ever upon this stage,
Is acted God's calm annual drama,
Gorgeous processions, songs of birds,
Sunrise that fullest feeds and freshens most the
    soul,
The heaving sea, the waves upon the shore, the
    musical, strong waves,
The woods, the stalwart trees, the slender,
    tapering trees,
The liliput countless armies of the grass,
The heat, the showers, the measureless
    pasturages,
The scenery of the snows, the winds' free
    orchestra,
The stretching light-hung roof of clouds, the
    clear cerulean and the silvery fringes,
The high-dilating stars, the placid beckoning
    stars,
The moving flocks and herds, the plains and
    emerald meadows,

The shows of all the varied lands and all the
 growths and products.

3

Fecund America—today,
Thou art all over set in births and joys!
Thou groan'st with riches, thy wealth clothes
 thee as a swathing-garment,
Thou laughest loud with ache of great
 possessions,
A myriad-twining life like interlacing vines binds
 all thy vast demesne,
As some huge ship freighted to water's edge
 thou ridest into port,
As rain falls from the heaven and vapors rise
 from earth, so have the precious values fallen
 upon thee and risen out of thee;
Thou envy of the globe! thou miracle!
Thou, bathed, choked, swimming in
 plenty,
Thou lucky Mistress of the tranquil barns,
Thou Prairie Dame that sittest in the middle
 and lookest out upon thy world, and lookest
 East and lookest West,
Dispensatress, that by a word givest a
 thousand miles, a million farms, and missest
 nothing,
Thou all-acceptress—thou hospitable, (thou
 only art hospitable as God is hospitable.)

4

When late I sang sad was my voice,
Sad were the shows around me with deafening
   noises of hatred and smoke of war;
In the midst of the conflict, the heroes, I stood,
Or pass'd with slow step through the wounded
   and dying.

But now I sing not war,
Nor the measur'd march of soldiers, nor the
   tents of camps,
Nor the regiments hastily coming up deploying
   in line of battle;
No more the sad, unnatural shows of war.

Ask'd room those flush'd immortal ranks, the
   first forth-stepping armies?
Ask room alas the ghastly ranks, the armies
   dread that follow'd.

(Pass, pass, ye proud brigades, with your
   tramping sinewy legs,
With your shoulders young and strong, with
   your knapsacks and your muskets;
How elate I stood and watch'd you, where
   starting off you march'd.

Pass—then rattle drums again,
For an army heaves in sight, O another
   gathering army,

Swarming, trailing on the rear, O you dread
    accruing army,
O you regiments so piteous, with your mortal
    diarrhoea, with your fever,
O my land's maim'd darlings, with the plenteous
    bloody bandage and the crutch,
Lo, your pallid army follows.)

5

But on these days of brightness,
On the far-stretching beauteous landscape, the
    roads and lanes the high-piled farm-wagons,
    and the fruits and barns,
Should the dead intrude?

Ah the dead to me mar not, they fit well in
    Nature,
They fit very well in the landscape under the
    trees and grass,
And along the edge of the sky in the horizon's
    far margin.

Nor do I forget you Departed,
Nor in winter or summer my lost ones,
But most in the open air as now when my
    soul is rapt and at peace, like pleasing
    phantoms,
Your memories rising glide silently by me.

6

I saw the day the return of the heroes,
(Yet the heroes never surpass'd shall never
    return,
Them that day I saw not.)

I saw the interminable corps, I saw the
    processions of armies,
I saw them approaching, defiling by with
    divisions,
Streaming northward, their work done, camping
    awhile in clusters of mighty camps.

No holiday soldiers—youthful, yet veterans,
Worn, swart, handsome, strong, of the stock of
    homestead and workshop,
Harden'd of many a long campaign and sweaty
    march,
Inured on many a hard-fought bloody field.

A pause—the armies wait,
A million flush'd embattled conquerors wait,
The world too waits, then soft as breaking night
    and sure as dawn,
They melt, they disappear.

Exult O lands! victorious lands!
Not there your victory on those red shuddering
    fields,
But here and hence your victory.

Melt, melt away ye armies—disperse ye blue-clad
    soldiers,
Resolve ye back again, give up for good your
    deadly arms,
Other the arms the fields henceforth for you, or
    South or North,
With saner wars, sweet wars, life-giving wars.

7

Loud O my throat, and clear O soul!
The season of thanks and the voice of full-
    yielding,
The chant of joy and power for boundless
    fertility.

All till'd and untill'd fields expand before me,
I see the true arenas of my race, or first or last,
Man's innocent and strong arenas.

I see the heroes at other toils,
I see well-wielded in their hands the better
    weapons.

I see where the Mother of All,
With full-spanning eye gazes forth, dwells
    long,
And counts the varied gathering of the products.

Busy the far, the sunlit panorama,
Prairie, orchard, and yellow grain of the North,

Cotton and rice of the South and Louisianian
　　cane,
Open unseeded fallows, rich fields of clover and
　　timothy,
Kine and horses feeding, and droves of sheep
　　and swine,
And many a stately river flowing and many a
　　jocund brook,
And healthy uplands with herby-perfumed
　　breezes,
And the good green grass, that delicate miracle
　　the ever-recurring grass.

8

Toil on heroes! harvest the products!
Not alone on those warlike fields the Mother of
　　All,
With dilated form and lambent eyes watch'd
　　you.

Toil on heroes! toil well! handle the weapons
　　well!
The Mother of All, yet here as ever she watches
　　you.

Well-pleased America thou beholdest,
Over the fields of the West those crawling
　　monsters,
The human-divine inventions, the labor-saving
　　implements;

Beholdest moving in every direction imbued as
   with life the revolving hay-rakes,
The steam-power reaping-machines and the
   horse-power machines
The engines, thrashers of grain and cleaners of
   grain, well separating the straw, the nimble
   work of the patent pitchfork,
Beholdest the newer saw-mill, the southern
   cotton-gin, and the rice-cleanser.

Beneath thy look O Maternal,
With these and else and with their own strong
   hands the heroes harvest.

All gather and all harvest,
Yet but for thee O Powerful, not a scythe might
   swing as now in security,
Not a maize-stalk dangle as now its silken tassels
   in peace.

Under thee only they harvest, even but a wisp of
   hay under thy great face only,
Harvest the wheat of Ohio, Illinois, Wisconsin,
   every barbed spear under thee,
Harvest the maize of Missouri, Kentucky,
   Tennessee, each ear in its light-green sheath,
Gather the hay to its myriad mows in the
   odorous tranquil barns,
Oats to their bins, the white potato, the
   buckwheat of Michigan, to theirs;

Gather the cotton in Mississippi or Alabama, dig
    and hoard the golden the sweet potato of
    Georgia and the Carolinas,
the wool of California or Pennsylvania,
Cut the flax in the Middle States, or hemp or
    tobacco in the Borders,
Pick the pea and the bean, or pull apples from
    the trees or bunches of grapes from the vines,
Or aught that ripens in all these States or North
    or South,
Under the beaming sun and under thee.

Autumn Rivulets

There Was a Child Went Forth

THERE was a child went forth every day,
And the first object he look'd upon, that object
    he became,
And that object became part of him for the day
    or a certain part of the day,
Or for many years or stretching cycles of years.

The early lilacs became part of this child,
And grass and white and red morning-glories,
    and white and red clover, and the song of the
    phoebe-bird,
And the Third-month lambs and the sow's pink-
    faint litter, and the mare's foal and the cow's
    calf,
And the noisy brood of the barnyard or by the
    mire of the pond-side,
And the fish suspending themselves so curiously
    below there, and the beautiful curious liquid,
And the water-plants with their graceful flat
    heads, all became part of him.

The field-sprouts of Fourth-month and Fifth-
    month became part of him,

Winter-grain sprouts and those of the light-
  yellow corn, and the esculent roots of the
  garden,
And the apple-trees cover'd with blossoms and
  the fruit afterward, and wood-berries, and the
  commonest weeds by the road,
And the old drunkard staggering home from the
  outhouse of the tavern whence he had lately
  risen,
And the schoolmistress that pass'd on her way to
  the school,
And the friendly boys that pass'd, and the
  quarrelsome boys,
And the tidy and fresh-cheek'd girls, and the
  barefoot negro boy and girl,
And all the changes of city and country
  wherever he went.

His own parents, he that had father'd him and
  she that had conceiv'd him in her womb and
  birth'd him,
They gave this child more of themselves than that,
They gave him afterward every day, they became
  part of him.

The mother at home quietly placing the dishes
  on the supper-table,
The mother with mild words, clean her cap and
  gown, a wholesome odor falling off her
  person and clothes as she walks by,

The father, strong, self-sufficient, manly, mean,
 anger'd, unjust,
The blow, the quick loud word, the tight
 bargain, the crafty lure,
The family usages, the language, the company,
 the furniture, the yearning and swelling heart,
Affection that will not be gainsay'd, the sense of
 what is real, the thought if after all it should
 prove unreal,
The doubts of day-time and the doubts of
 night-time, the curious whether and how,
Whether that which appears so is so, or is it all
 flashes and specks?
Men and women crowding fast in the streets,
 if they are not flashes and specks what are
 they?
The streets themselves and the facades of
 houses, and goods in the windows,
Vehicles, teams, the heavy-plank'd wharves, the
 huge crossing at the ferries,
The village on the highland seen from afar at
 sunset, the river between,
Shadows, aureola and mist, the light falling on
 roofs and gables of white or brown two miles
 off,
The schooner near by sleepily dropping
 down the tide, the little boat slack-tow'd
 astern,
The hurrying tumbling waves, quick-broken
 crests, slapping,

The strata of color'd clouds, the long bar of
 maroon-tint away solitary by itself, the spread
 of purity it lies motionless in,
The horizon's edge, the flying sea-crow, the
 fragrance of salt marsh and shore mud,
These became part of that child who went forth
 every day, and who now goes, and will always
 go forth every day.

OLD IRELAND

FAR hence amid an isle of wondrous beauty,
Crouching over a grave an ancient sorrowful
 mother,
Once a queen, now lean and tatter'd seated on
 the ground,
Her old white hair drooping dishevel'd round
 her shoulders,
At her feet fallen an unused royal harp,
Long silent, she too long silent, mourning her
 shrouded hope and heir,
Of all the earth her heart most full of sorrow
 because most full of love.

Yet a word ancient mother,
You need crouch there no longer on the cold
 ground with forehead between your knees,
O you need not sit there veil'd in your old white
 hair so dishevel'd,

For know you the one you mourn is not in that
grave,
It was an illusion, the son you love was not
really dead,
The Lord is not dead, he is risen again young
and strong in another country,
Even while you wept there by your fallen harp
by the grave,
What you wept for was translated, pass'd from
the grave,
The winds favor'd and the sea sail'd it,
And now with rosy and new blood,
Moves to-day in a new country.
The City Dead-House

By the city dead-house by the gate,
As idly sauntering wending my way from the
clangor,
I curious pause, for lo, an outcast form, a poor
dead prostitute brought,
Her corpse they deposit unclaim'd, it lies on the
damp brick pavement,
The divine woman, her body, I see the body, I
look on it alone,
That house once full of passion and beauty, all
else I notice not,
Nor stillness so cold, nor running water from
faucet, nor odors morbific impress me,
But the house alone—that wondrous house—
that delicate fair house—that ruin!

That immortal house more than all the rows of
　　dwellings ever built!
white-domed capitol with majestic figure
　　surmounted, or all the old high-spired
　　cathedrals,
That little house alone more than them all—
　　poor, desperate house!
Fair, fearful wreck—tenement of a soul—itself
　　a soul,
Unclaim'd, avoided house—take one breath
　　from my tremulous lips,
Take one tear dropt aside as I go for thought of
　　you,
Dead house of love—house of madness and sin,
　　crumbled, crush'd,
House of life, erewhile talking and laughing—
　　but ah, poor house, dead even then,
Months, years, an echoing, garnish'd house—
　　but dead, dead, dead.

THIS COMPOST

1
SOMETHING startles me where I thought I
　　was safest,
I withdraw from the still woods I loved,
I will not go now on the pastures to walk,
I will not strip the clothes from my body to
　　meet my lover the sea,

I will not touch my flesh to the earth as to other
    flesh to renew me.

O how can it be that the ground itself does not
    sicken?
How can you be alive you growths of spring?
How can you furnish health you blood of herbs,
    roots, orchards, grain?
Are they not continually putting distemper'd
    corpses within you?
Is not every continent work'd over and over
    with sour dead?

Where have you disposed of their carcasses?
Those drunkards and gluttons of so many
    generations?
Where have you drawn off all the foul liquid and
    meat?
I do not see any of it upon you to-day, or
    perhaps I am deceiv'd,
I will run a furrow with my plough, I will press
    my spade through the sod and turn it up
    underneath,
I am sure I shall expose some of the foul meat.

2

Behold this compost! behold it well!
Perhaps every mite has once form'd part of a
    sick person—yet behold!
The grass of spring covers the prairies,

The bean bursts noiselessly through the mould
    in the garden,
The delicate spear of the onion pierces upward,
The apple-buds cluster together on the apple-
    branches,
The resurrection of the wheat appears with pale
    visage out of its graves,
The tinge awakes over the willow-tree and the
    mulberry-tree,
The he-birds carol mornings and evenings while
    the she-birds sit on their nests,
The young of poultry break through the hatch'd
    eggs,
The new-born of animals appear, the calf is
    dropt from the cow, the colt from the mare,
Out of its little hill faithfully rise the potato's
    dark green leaves,
Out of its hill rises the yellow maize-stalk, the
    lilacs bloom in the dooryards,
The summer growth is innocent and disdainful
    above all those strata of sour dead.

What chemistry!
That the winds are really not infectious,
That this is no cheat, this transparent green-
    wash of the sea which is so amorous after me,
That it is safe to allow it to lick my naked body
    all over with its tongues,
That it will not endanger me with the fevers that
    have deposited themselves in it,

That all is clean forever and forever,
That the cool drink from the well tastes so good,
That blackberries are so flavorous and juicy,
That the fruits of the apple-orchard and the
    orange-orchard, that melons, grapes, peaches,
    plums, will none of them poison me,
That when I recline on the grass I do not catch
    any disease,
Though probably every spear of grass rises out
    of what was once catching disease.

Now I am terrified at the Earth, it is that calm
    and patient,
It grows such sweet things out of such
    corruptions,
It turns harmless and stainless on its axis, with
    such endless successions of diseas'd corpses,
It distills such exquisite winds out of such
    infused fetor,
It renews with such unwitting looks its prodigal,
    annual, sumptuous crops,
It gives such divine materials to men, and
    accepts such leavings from them at last.

To a Foil'd European Revolutionaire

COURAGE yet, my brother or my sister!
Keep on—Liberty is to be subserv'd whatever
    occurs;

That is nothing that is quell'd by one or two
    failures, or any number of failures,
Or by the indifference or ingratitude of the
    people, or by any unfaithfulness,
Or the show of the tushes of power, soldiers,
    cannon, penal statutes.

What we believe in waits latent forever through
    all the continents,
Invites no one, promises nothing, sits in
    calmness and light, is positive and composed,
    knows no discouragement,
Waiting patiently, waiting its time.

(Not songs of loyalty alone are these,
But songs of insurrection also,
For I am the sworn poet of every dauntless rebel
    the world over,
And he going with me leaves peace and routine
    behind him,
And stakes his life to be lost at any moment.)

The battle rages with many a loud alarm and
    frequent advance and retreat,
The infidel triumphs, or supposes he
    triumphs,
The prison, scaffold, garrote, handcuffs, iron
    necklace and leadballs do their work,
The named and unnamed heroes pass to other
    spheres,

The great speakers and writers are exiled, they
    lie sick in distant lands,
The cause is asleep, the strongest throats are
    choked with their own blood,
The young men droop their eyelashes toward
    the ground when they meet;
But for all this Liberty has not gone out of the
    place, nor the infidel enter'd into full
    possession.

When liberty goes out of a place it is not
    the first to go, nor the second or third
    to go,
It waits for all the rest to go, it is the last.

When there are no more memories of heroes
    and martyrs,
And when all life and all the souls of men and
    women are discharged from any part of the
    earth,
Then only shall liberty or the idea of liberty be
    discharged from that part of the earth,
And the infidel come into full possession.

Then courage European revolter, revoltress!
For till all ceases neither must you cease.

I do not know what you are for, (I do not know
    what I am for myself, nor what any thing is
    for,)

But I will search carefully for it even in being
  foil'd,
In defeat, poverty, misconception,
  imprisonment—for they too are great.

Did we think victory great?
So it is- but now it seems to me, when it cannot
  be help'd, that defeat is great,
And that death and dismay are great.

UNNAMED LAND

NATIONS ten thousand years before these
  States, and many times ten thousand years
  before these States,
Garner'd clusters of ages that men and women
  like us grew up and travel'd their course and
  pass'd on,
What vast-built cities, what orderly republics,
  what pastoral tribes and nomads,
What histories, rulers, heroes, perhaps
  transcending all others,
What laws, customs, wealth, arts, traditions,
What sort of marriage, what costumes, what
  physiology and phrenology,
What of liberty and slavery among them, what
  they thought of death and the soul,
Who were witty and wise, who beautiful and
  poetic, who brutish and undevelop'd,

Not a mark, not a record remains—and yet all
    remains.

O I know that those men and women were
    not for nothing, any more than we are for
    nothing,
I know that they belong to the scheme of the
    world every bit as much as we now belong
    to it.

Afar they stand, yet near to me they stand,
Some with oval countenances learn'd and
    calm,
Some naked and savage, some like huge
    collections of insects,
Some in tents, herdsmen, patriarchs, tribes,
    horsemen,
Some prowling through woods, some living
    peaceably on farms, laboring, reaping, filling
    barns,
Some traversing paved avenues, amid temples,
    palaces, factories, libraries, shows, courts,
    theatres, wonderful monuments.
Are those billions of men really gone?
Are those women of the old experience of the
    earth gone?
Do their lives, cities, arts, rest only with
    us?
Did they achieve nothing for good for
    themselves?

I believe of all those men and women that fill'd
    the unnamed lands, every one exists this hour
    here or elsewhere, invisible to us.
In exact proportion to what he or she grew
    from in life, and out of what he or she did,
    felt, became, loved, sinn'd, in life.

I believe that was not the end of those nations
    or any person of them, any more than this
    shall be the end of my nation, or of me;
Of their languages, governments, marriage,
    literature, products, games, wars, manners,
    crimes, prisons, slaves, heroes, poets,
I suspect their results curiously await in the yet
    unseen world, counterparts of what accrued
    to them in the seen world,
I suspect I shall meet them there,
I suspect I shall there find each old particular of
    those unnamed lands.

SONG OF PRUDENCE

MANHATTAN'S streets I saunter'd pondering,
On Time, Space, Reality—on such as these, and
    abreast with them
Prudence.

The last explanation always remains to be made
    about prudence,

Little and large alike drop quietly aside
    from the prudence that suits
    immortality.

The soul is of itself,
All verges to it, all has reference to what
    ensues,
All that a person does, says, thinks, is of
    consequence,
Not a move can a man or woman make,
    that affects him or her in a day, month, any
    part of the direct lifetime, or the hour of
    death,
But the same affects him or her onward
    afterward through the indirect lifetime.

The indirect is just as much as the direct,
The spirit receives from the body just as much
    as it gives to the body, if not more.

Not one word or deed, not venereal sore,
    discoloration, privacy of the onanist,
Putridity of gluttons or rum-drinkers, peculation,
    cunning, betrayal, murder, seduction,
    prostitution,
But has results beyond death as really as before
    death.

Charity and personal force are the only
    investments worth any thing.

No specification is necessary, all that a male or
    female does, that is vigorous, benevolent,
    clean, is so much profit to him or her,
In the unshakable order of the universe and
    through the whole scope of it forever.

Who has been wise receives interest,
Savage, felon, President, judge, farmer, sailor,
    mechanic, literat, young, old, it is the
    same,
The interest will come round—all will come
    round.

Singly, wholly, to affect now, affected their time,
    will forever affect, all of the past and all of the
    present and all of the future,
All the brave actions of war and peace,
All help given to relatives, strangers, the poor,
    old, sorrowful, young children, widows, the
    sick, and to shunn'd persons,
All self-denial that stood steady and aloof on
    wrecks, and saw others fill the seats of the
    boats,
All offering of substance or life for the good
    old cause, or for a friend's sake, or opinion's
    sake,
All pains of enthusiasts scoff'd at by their
    neighbors,
All the limitless sweet love and precious
    suffering of mothers,

All honest men baffled in strifes recorded or
    unrecorded,
All the grandeur and good of ancient nations
    whose fragments we inherit,
All the good of the dozens of ancient nations
    unknown to us by name, date, location,
All that was ever manfully begun, whether it
    succeeded or no,
All suggestions of the divine mind of man or the
    divinity of his mouth, or the shaping of his
    great hands,
All that is well thought or said this day on any
    part of the globe, or on any of the wandering
    stars, or on any of the fix'd stars, by those
    there as we are here,
All that is henceforth to be thought or done by
    you whoever you are, or by any one,
These inure, have inured, shall inure, to the
    identities from which they sprang, or shall
    spring.

Did you guess any thing lived only its
    moment?
The world does not so exist, no parts palpable
    or impalpable so exist,
No consummation exists without being from
    some long previous consummation, and that
    from some other,
Without the farthest conceivable one coming a
    bit nearer the beginning than any.

Whatever satisfies souls is true;
Prudence entirely satisfies the craving and glut
     of souls,
Itself only finally satisfies the soul,
The soul has that measureless pride which
     revolts from every lesson but its own.

Now I breathe the word of the prudence that
     walks abreast with time, space, reality,
That answers the pride which refuses every
     lesson but its own.

What is prudence is indivisible,
Declines to separate one part of life from every
     part,
Divides not the righteous from the unrighteous
     or the living from the dead,
Matches every thought or act by its correlative,
Knows no possible forgiveness or deputed
     atonement,
Knows that the young man who composedly
     peril'd his life and lost it has done exceedingly
     well for himself without doubt,
That he who never peril'd his life, but retains it
     to old age in riches and ease, has probably
     achiev'd nothing for himself worth
     mentioning,
Knows that only that person has really learn'd
     who has learn'd to prefer results,

Who favors body and soul the same,
Who perceives the indirect assuredly following
    the direct,
Who in his spirit in any emergency whatever
    neither hurries nor avoids death.

THE SINGER IN THE PRISON
1

O sight of pity, shame and dole!
O fearful thought—a convict soul

RANG the refrain along the hall, the prison,
Rose to the roof, the vaults of heaven above,
Pouring in floods of melody in tones so pensive
    sweet and strong the like whereof was never
    heard,
Reaching the far-off sentry and the armed
    guards, who ceas'd their pacing,
Making the hearer's pulses stop for ecstasy and awe.

2

The sun was low in the west one winter day,
When down a narrow aisle amid the thieves and
    outlaws of the land,
(There by the hundreds seated, sear-faced
    murderers, wily counterfeiters,
Gather'd to Sunday church in prison walls, the
    keepers round,

Plenteous, well-armed, watching with vigilant
    eyes,)
Calmly a lady walk'd holding a little innocent
    child by either hand,
Whom seating on their stools beside her on the
    platform,
She, first preluding with the instrument a low
    and musical prelude,
In voice surpassing all, sang forth a quaint old
    hymn.

A soul confined by bars and bands,
Cries, help! O help! and wrings her hands,
Blinded her eyes, bleeding her breast,
Nor pardon finds, nor balm of rest.

Ceaseless she paces to and fro,
O heart-sick days! O nights of woe!
Nor hand of friend, nor loving face,
Nor favor comes, nor word of grace.

It was not I that sinn'd the sin,
The ruthless body dragg'd me in;
Though long I strove courageously,
The body was too much for me.

Dear prison'd soul bear up a space,
For soon or late the certain grace;
To set thee free and bear thee home,

The heavenly pardoner death shall come.
Convict no more, nor shame, nor dole!
Depart—a God—enfranchis'd soul!

3

The singer ceas'd,
One glance swept from her clear calm eyes o'er
    all those upturn'd faces,
Strange sea of prison faces, a thousand
    varied, crafty, brutal, seam'd and beauteous
    faces,
Then rising, passing back along the narrow aisle
    between them,
While her gown touch'd them rustling in the
    silence,
She vanish'd with her children in the dusk.

While upon all, convicts and armed keepers ere
    they stirr'd,
(Convict forgetting prison, keeper his loaded
    pistol,)
A hush and pause fell down a wondrous minute,
With deep half-stifled sobs and sound of bad
    men bow'd and moved to weeping,
And youth's convulsive breathings, memories of
    home,
The mother's voice in lullaby, the sister's care,
    the happy childhood,
The long-pent spirit rous'd to reminiscence;

A wondrous minute then—but after in the
    solitary night, to many, many there,
Years after, even in the hour of death, the sad
    refrain, the tune, the voice, the words,
Resumed, the large calm lady walks the narrow
    aisle,
The wailing melody again, the singer in the
    prison sings,

O sight of pity, shame and dole!
O fearful thought—a convict soul.

WARBLE FOR LILAC-TIME

WARBLE me now for joy of lilac-time,
    (returning in reminiscence,)
Sort me O tongue and lips for Nature's sake,
    souvenirs of earliest summer,
Gather the welcome signs, (as children with
    pebbles or stringing shells,)
Put in April and May, the hylas croaking in the
    ponds, the elastic air,
Bees, butterflies, the sparrow with its simple notes,
Blue-bird and darting swallow, nor forget the
    high-hole flashing his golden wings,
The tranquil sunny haze, the clinging smoke,
    the vapor,
Shimmer of waters with fish in them, the
    cerulean above,

All that is jocund and sparkling, the brooks
running,
The maple woods, the crisp February days and
the sugar-making,
The robin where he hops, bright-eyed, brown-
breasted,
With musical clear call at sunrise, and again at
sunset,
Or flitting among the trees of the apple-orchard,
building the nest of his mate,
The melted snow of March, the willow sending
forth its yellow-green sprouts,
For spring-time is here! the summer is here! and
what is this in it and from it?
Thou, soul, unloosen'd—the restlessness after I
know not what;
Come, let us lag here no longer, let us be up
and away!
O if one could but fly like a bird!
O to escape, to sail forth as in a ship!
To glide with thee O soul, o'er all, in all, as a
ship o'er the waters;
Gathering these hints, the preludes, the blue sky,
the grass, the morning drops of dew,
The lilac-scent, the bushes with dark green
heart-shaped leaves,
Wood-violets, the little delicate pale blossoms
called innocence,
Samples and sorts not for themselves alone, but
for their atmosphere,

To grace the bush I love—to sing with the birds,
A warble for joy of returning in reminiscence.

OUTLINES FOR A TOMB
(G. P., BURIED 1870)

1

WHAT may we chant, O thou within this tomb?
What tablets, outlines, hang for thee, O
    millionnaire?
The life thou lived'st we know not,
But that thou walk'dst thy years in barter, 'mid
    the haunts of brokers,
Nor heroism thine, nor war, nor glory.

2

Silent, my soul,
With drooping lids, as waiting, ponder'd,
Turning from all the samples, monuments of
    heroes.

While through the interior vistas,
Noiseless uprose, phantasmic, (as by night
    Auroras of the north),
Lambent tableaus, prophetic, bodiless scenes,
Spiritual projections.

In one, among the city streets a laborer's home
    appear'd,

After his day's work done, cleanly, sweet-air'd,
  the gaslight burning,
The carpet swept and a fire in the cheerful stove.

In one, the sacred parturition scene,
A happy painless mother birth'd a perfect child.

In one, at a bounteous morning meal,
Sat peaceful parents with contented sons.

In one, by twos and threes, young people,
Hundreds concentring, walk'd the paths and
  streets and roads,
Toward a tall-domed school.

In one a trio beautiful,
Grandmother, loving daughter, loving
  daughter's daughter, sat,
Chatting and sewing.

In one, along a suite of noble rooms,
'Mid plenteous books and journals, paintings on
  the walls, fine statuettes,
Were groups of friendly journeymen, mechanics
  young and old,
Reading, conversing.

All, all the shows of laboring life,
City and country, women's, men's and
  children's,

Their wants provided for, hued in the sun and
    tinged for once with joy,
Marriage, the street, the factory, farm, the
    house-room, lodging-room,
Labor and toll, the bath, gymnasium,
    playground, library, college,
The student, boy or girl, led forward to be
    taught,
The sick cared for, the shoeless shod, the orphan
    father'd and mother'd,
The hungry fed, the houseless housed;
(The intentions perfect and divine,
The workings, details, haply human.)

3

O thou within this tomb,
From thee such scenes, thou stintless, lavish
    giver,
Tallying the gifts of earth, large as the earth,
Thy name an earth, with mountains, fields and
    tides.

Nor by your streams alone, you rivers,
By you, your banks Connecticut,
By you and all your teeming life old Thames,
By you Potomac laving the ground Washington
    trod, by you Patapsco,
You Hudson, you endless Mississippi—nor you
    alone,

But to the high seas launch, my thought, his
    memory.

OUT FROM BEHIND THIS MASH
(TO CONFRONT A PORTRAIT)

1

OUT from behind this bending rough-cut mask,
These lights and shades, this drama of the
    whole,
This common curtain of the face contain'd
    in me for me, in you for you, in each for
    each,
(Tragedies, sorrows, laughter, tears—O heaven!
The passionate teeming plays this curtain
    hid!)
This glaze of God's serenest purest sky,
This film of Satan's seething pit,
This heart's geography's map, this limitless small
    continent, this soundless sea;
Out from the convolutions of this globe,
This subtler astronomic orb than sun or moon,
    than Jupiter, Venus, Mars,
This condensation of the universe, (nay here the
    only universe,
Here the idea, all in this mystic handful wrapt;)
These burin'd eyes, flashing to you to pass to
    future time,

To launch and spin through space revolving
    sideling, from these to emanate,
To you whoe'er you—a look.

2
A traveler of thoughts and years, of peace and
    war,
Of youth long sped and middle age declining,
(As the first volume of a tale perused and laid
    away, and this the second,
Songs, ventures, speculations, presently to close,)
Lingering a moment here and now, to you I
    opposite turn,
As on the road or at some crevice door by
    chance, or open'd window,
Pausing, inclining, baring my head, you specially
    I greet,
To draw and clinch your soul for once
    inseparably with mine,
Then travel travel on.

VOCALISM

1
VOCALISM, measure, concentration,
    determination, and the divine power to speak
    words;
Are you full-lung'd and limber-lipp'd from long
    trial? from vigorous practice? from physique?

Do you move in these broad lands as broad as
    they?
Come duly to the divine power to speak words?
For only at last after many years, after chastity,
    friendship, procreation, prudence, and
    nakedness,
After treading ground and breasting river and
    lake,
After a loosen'd throat, after absorbing eras,
    temperaments, races, after knowledge,
    freedom, crimes,
After complete faith, after clarifyings, elevations,
    and removing obstructions,
After these and more, it is just possible there
    comes to a man, woman, the divine power to
    speak words;
Then toward that man or that woman swiftly
    hasten all—none refuse, all attend,
Armies, ships, antiquities, libraries, paintings,
    machines, cities, hate, despair, amity, pain,
    theft, murder, aspiration, form in close ranks,
They debouch as they are wanted to march
    obediently through the mouth of that man or
    that woman.

2

O what is it in me that makes me tremble so at
    voices?
Surely whoever speaks to me in the right voice,
    him or her I shall follow,

As the water follows the moon, silently, with
    fluid steps, anywhere around the globe.

All waits for the right voices;
Where is the practis'd and perfect organ? where
    is the develop'd soul?
For I see every word utter'd thence has deeper,
    sweeter, new sounds, impossible on less
    terms.

I see brains and lips closed, tympans and temples
    unstruck,
Until that comes which has the quality to strike
    and to unclose,
Until that comes which has the quality to bring
    forth what lies slumbering forever ready in all
    words.

To Him that was Crucified

My spirit to yours dear brother,
Do not mind because many sounding your name
    do not understand you,
I do not sound your name, but I understand you,
I specify you with joy O my comrade to salute
    you, and to salute those who are with you,
    before and since, and those to come also,
That we all labor together transmitting the same

charge and succession,

We few equals indifferent of lands, indifferent of times,

We, enclosers of all continents, all castes, allowers of all theologies,

Compassionaters, perceivers, rapport of men,

We walk silent among disputes and assertions, but reject not the disputers nor any thing that is asserted,

We hear the bawling and din, we are reach'd at by divisions, jealousies, recriminations on every side,

They close peremptorily upon us to surround us, my comrade,

Yet we walk unheld, free, the whole earth over, journeying up and down till we make our ineffaceable mark upon time and the diverse eras,

Till we saturate time and eras, that the men and women of races, ages to come, may prove brethren and lovers as we are.

You Felons on Trial in Courts

YOU felons on trial in courts,

You convicts in prison-cells, you sentenced assassins chain'd and handcuff'd with iron,

Who am I too that I am not on trial or in prison?

Me ruthless and devilish as any, that my wrists
    are not chain'd with iron, or my ankles with
    iron?

You prostitutes flaunting over the trottoirs or
    obscene in your rooms,
Who am I that I should call you more obscene
    than myself?

O culpable! I acknowledge—I expose!
(O admirers, praise not me—compliment not
    me—you make me wince,
I see what you do not—I know what you do
    not.)

Inside these breast-bones I lie smutch'd and
    choked,
Beneath this face that appears so impassive hell's
    tides continually run,
Lusts and wickedness are acceptable to me,
I walk with delinquents with passionate love,
I feel I am of them—I belong to those convicts
    and prostitutes myself,
And henceforth I will not deny them-for how
    can I deny myself?

LAWS FOR CREATIONS

LAWS for creations,
For strong artists and leaders, for fresh broods
    of teachers and perfect literats for America,
For noble savans and coming musicians.
All must have reference to the ensemble of
    the world, and the compact truth of the
    world,
There shall be no subject too pronounced-all
    works shall illustrate the divine law of
    indirections.

What do you suppose creation is?
What do you suppose will satisfy the soul, except
    to walk free and own no superior?
What do you suppose I would intimate to you in
    a hundred ways, but that man or woman is as
    good as God?
And that there is no God any more divine than
    Yourself?
And that that is what the oldest and newest
    myths finally mean?
And that you or any one must approach
    creations through such laws?

To a Common Prostitute

BE composed—be at ease with me—I am Walt
    Whitman, liberal and lusty as Nature,
Not till the sun excludes you do I exclude you,
Not till the waters refuse to glisten for you and
    the leaves to rustle for you, do my words
    refuse to glisten and rustle for you.

My girl I appoint with you an appointment, and
    I charge you that you make preparation to be
    worthy to meet me,
And I charge you that you be patient and
    perfect till I come.

Till then I salute you with a significant look that
    you do not forget me.

I was Looking a Long While

I WAS looking a long while for Intentions,
For a clew to the history of the past for myself,
    and for these chants—and now I have found it,
It is not in those paged fables in the libraries,
    (them I neither accept nor reject,)
It is no more in the legends than in all else,
It is in the present—it is this earth to-day,
It is in Democracy—(the purport and aim of all
    the past,)

It is the life of one man or one woman to-day—
the average man of to-day,
It is in languages, social customs, literatures,
arts,
It is in the broad show of artificial things, ships,
machinery, politics, creeds, modern
improvements, and the interchange of
nations,
All for the modern- all for the average man of
to-day.

THOUGHT

OF persons arrived at high positions,
ceremonies, wealth, scholarships, and
the like;
(To me all that those persons have arrived at
sinks away from them, except as it results
to their bodies and souls,
So that often to me they appear gaunt and
naked,
And often to me each one mocks the others,
and mocks himself or herself,
And of each one the core of life, namely
happiness, is full of the rotten excrement of
maggots,
And often to me those men and women pass
unwittingly the true realities of life, and go
toward false realities,

And often to me they are alive after what
    custom has served them, but nothing more,
And often to me they are sad, hasty, unwaked
    sonnambules walking the dusk.)

MIRACLES

WHY, who makes much of a miracle?
As to me I know of nothing else but miracles,
Whether I walk the streets of Manhattan,
Or dart my sight over the roofs of houses
    toward the sky,
Or wade with naked feet along the beach just in
    the edge of the water,
Or stand under trees in the woods,
Or talk by day with any one I love, or sleep in
    the bed at night with any one I love,
Or sit at table at dinner with the rest,
Or look at strangers opposite me riding in the
    car,
Or watch honey-bees busy around the hive of a
    summer forenoon,
Or animals feeding in the fields,
Or birds, or the wonderfulness of insects in the
    air,
Or the wonderfulness of the sundown, or of
    stars shining so quiet and bright,
Or the exquisite delicate thin curve of the new
    moon in spring;

These with the rest, one and all, are to me
    miracles,
The whole referring, yet each distinct and in its
    place.

To me every hour of the light and dark is a
    miracle,
Every cubic inch of space is a miracle,
Every square yard of the surface of the earth is
    spread with the same,
Every foot of the interior swarms with the
    same.
To me the sea is a continual miracle,
The fishes that swim—the rocks—the motion of
    the waves—the ships with men in them,
What stranger miracles are there?

SPARKLES FROM THE WHEEL

WHERE the city's ceaseless crowd moves on the
    livelong day,
Withdrawn I join a group of children watching,
    I pause aside with them.

By the curb toward the edge of the flagging,
A knife-grinder works at his wheel sharpening a
    great knife,
Bending over he carefully holds it to the stone,
    by foot and knee,

With measur'd tread he turns rapidly, as he
   presses with light but firm hand,
Forth issue then in copious golden jets,
Sparkles from the wheel.

The scene and all its belongings, how they seize
   and affect me,
The sad sharp-chinn'd old man with worn
   clothes and broad shoulder-band of leather,
Myself effusing and fluid, a phantom curiously
   floating, now here absorb'd and arrested,
The group, (an unminded point set in a vast
   surrounding,)
The attentive, quiet children, the loud, proud,
   restive base of the streets,
The low hoarse purr of the whirling stone, the
   light-press'd blade,
Diffusing, dropping, sideways-darting, in tiny
   showers of gold,
Sparkles from the wheel.

To a Pupil

IS reform needed? is it through you?
The greater the reform needed, the greater the
   Personality you need to accomplish it.

You! do you not see how it would serve to have
   eyes, blood, complexion, clean and sweet?

Do you not see how it would serve to have such
a body and soul that when you enter the
crowd an atmosphere of desire and command
enters with you, and every one is impress'd
with your Personality?

O the magnet! the flesh over and over!
Go, dear friend, if need be give up all else,
and commence to-day to inure yourself to
pluck, reality, self-esteem, definiteness,
elevatedness,
Rest not till you rivet and publish yourself of
your own Personality.

UNFOLDED OUT OF THE FOLDS

UNFOLDED out of the folds of the woman
man comes unfolded, and is always to come
unfolded,
Unfolded only out of the superbest woman of
the earth is to come the superbest man of the
earth,
Unfolded out of the friendliest woman is to
come the friendliest man,
Unfolded only out of the perfect body of a
woman can a man be form'd of perfect body,
Unfolded only out of the inimitable poems of
woman can come the poems of man, (only
thence have my poems come;)

Unfolded out of the strong and arrogant woman
    I love, only thence can appear the strong and
    arrogant man I love,
Unfolded by brawny embraces from the well-
    muscled woman love, only thence come the
    brawny embraces of the man,
Unfolded out of the folds of the woman's brain
    come all the folds of the man's brain, duly
    obedient,
Unfolded out of the justice of the woman all
    justice is unfolded,
Unfolded out of the sympathy of the woman is
    all sympathy;
A man is a great thing upon the earth and
    through eternity, but every of the greatness of
    man is unfolded out of woman;
First the man is shaped in the woman, he can
    then be shaped in himself.

WHAT AM I AFTER ALL

WHAT am I after all but a child, pleas'd with
    the sound of my own name? repeating it over
    and over;
I stand apart to hear—it never tires me.

To you your name also;
Did you think there was nothing but two or three
    pronunciations in the sound of your name?

KOSMOS

WHO includes diversity and is Nature,
Who is the amplitude of the earth, and the
    coarseness and sexuality of the earth, and the
    great charity of the earth, and the equilibrium
    also,
Who has not look'd forth from the windows the
    eyes for nothing, or whose brain held
    audience with messengers for nothing,
Who contains believers and disbelievers, who is
    the most majestic lover,
Who holds duly his or her triune proportion of
    realism, spiritualism, and of the aesthetic or
    intellectual,
Who having consider'd the body finds all its
    organs and parts good,
Who, out of the theory of the earth and of his
    or her body understands by subtle analogies
    all other theories,
The theory of a city, a poem, and of the large
    politics of these States;
Who believes not only in our globe with its sun
    and moon, but in other globes with their suns
    and moons,
Who, constructing the house of himself or
    herself, not for a day but for all time, sees
    races, eras, dates, generations,
The past, the future, dwelling there, like space,
    inseparable together.

OTHERS MAY PRAISE WHAT THEY LIKE

OTHERS may praise what they like;
But I, from the banks of the running Missouri,
   praise nothing in art or aught else,
Till it has well inhaled the atmosphere of this
   river, also the western prairie-scent,
And exudes it all again.

WHO LEARNS MY LESSON COMPLETE?

WHO learns my lesson complete?
Boss, journeyman, apprentice, churchman and
   atheist,
The stupid and the wise thinker, parents and
   offspring, merchant, clerk, porter and
   customer,
Editor, author, artist, and schoolboy—draw
   nigh and commence;
It is no lesson—it lets down the bars to a good
   lesson,
And that to another, and every one to another
   still.

The great laws take and effuse without
   argument,
I am of the same style, for I am their friend,
I love them quits and quits, I do not halt and
   make salaams.

I lie abstracted and hear beautiful tales of things
and the reasons of things,
They are so beautiful I nudge myself to listen.

I cannot say to any person what I hear—I
cannot say it to myself—it is very wonderful.

It is no small matter, this round and delicious
globe moving so exactly in its orbit for ever
and ever, without one jolt or the untruth of a
single second,
I do not think it was made in six days, nor
in ten thousand years, nor ten billions of
years,
Nor plann'd and built one thing after another as
an architect plans and builds a house.

I do not think seventy years is the time of a man
or woman,
Nor that seventy millions of years is the time of
a man or woman,
Nor that years will ever stop the existence of me,
or any one else.

Is it wonderful that I should be immortal? as
every one is immortal;
I know it is wonderful, but my eyesight is
equally wonderful, and how I was
conceived in my mother's womb is equally
wonderful,

And pass'd from a babe in the creeping trance
    of a couple of summers and winters to
    articulate and walk—all this is equally
    wonderful.

And that my soul embraces you this hour, and
    we affect each other without ever seeing each
    other, and never perhaps to see each other, is
    every bit as wonderful.

And that I can think such thoughts as these is
    just as wonderful,
And that I can remind you, and you think them
    and know them to be true, is just as
    wonderful.

And that the moon spins round the earth and
    on with the earth, is equally wonderful,
And that they balance themselves with the sun
    and stars is equally wonderful.

TESTS

ALL submit to them where they sit, inner,
    secure, unapproachable to analysis in the soul,
Not traditions, not the outer authorities are the
    judges,
They are the judges of outer authorities and of
    all traditions,

They corroborate as they go only whatever
　　corroborates themselves, and touches
　　themselves;
For all that, they have it forever in themselves to
　　corroborate far and near without one exception.

THE TORCH

ON my Northwest coast in the midst of the
　　night a fishermen's group stands watching,
Out on the lake that expands before them,
　　others are spearing salmon,
The canoe, a dim shadowy thing, moves across
　　the black water,
Bearing a torch ablaze at the prow.

O STAR OF FRANCE
1870–71

O STAR of France,
The brightness of thy hope and strength and
　　fame,
Like some proud ship that led the fleet so long,
Beseems to-day a wreck driven by the gale, a
　　mastless hulk,
And 'mid its teeming madden'd half-drown'd
　　crowds,
Nor helm nor helmsman.

Dim smitten star,
Orb not of France alone, pale symbol of my
    soul, its dearest hopes,
The struggle and the daring, rage divine for
    liberty,
Of aspirations toward the far ideal, enthusiast's
    dreams of brotherhood,
Of terror to the tyrant and the priest.

Star crucified—by traitors sold,
Star panting o'er a land of death, heroic land,
Strange, passionate, mocking, frivolous land.

Miserable! yet for thy errors, vanities, sins, I will
    not now rebuke thee,
Thy unexampled woes and pangs have quell'd
    them all,
And left thee sacred.

In that amid thy many faults thou ever aimedst
    highly,
In that thou wouldst not really sell thyself
    however great the price,
In that thou surely wakedst weeping from thy
    drugg'd sleep,
In that alone among thy sisters thou, giantess,
    didst rend the ones that shamed thee,
In that thou couldst not, wouldst not, wear the
    usual chains,

This cross, thy livid face, thy pierced hands and
    feet,
The spear thrust in thy side.

O star! O ship of France, beat back and baffled
    long!
Bear up O smitten orb! O ship continue on!

Sure as the ship of all, the Earth itself,
Product of deathly fire and turbulent chaos,
Forth from its spasms of fury and its poisons,
Issuing at last in perfect power and beauty,
Onward beneath the sun following its course,
So thee O ship of France!

Finish'd the days, the clouds dispel'd
The travail o'er, the long-sought extrication,
When lo! reborn, high o'er the European world,
(In gladness answering thence, as face afar to
    face, reflecting ours Columbia,)
Again thy star O France, fair lustrous star,
In heavenly peace, clearer, more bright than
    ever,
Shall beam immortal.

THE OX-TAMER

IN a far-away northern county in the placid
    pastoral region,
Lives my farmer friend, the theme of my
    recitative, a famous tamer of oxen,
There they bring him the three-year-olds and
    the four-year-olds to break them,
He will take the wildest steer in the world and
    break him and tame him,
He will go fearless without any whip where the
    young bullock chafes up and down the yard,
The bullock's head tosses restless high in the air
    with raging eyes,
Yet see you! how soon his rage subsides—how
    soon this tamer tames him;
See you! on the farms hereabout a hundred
    oxen young and old, and he is the man who
    has tamed them,
They all know him, all are affectionate to him;
See you! some are such beautiful animals, so
    lofty looking;
Some are buff-color'd, some mottled, one has a
    white line running along his back, some are
    brindled,
Some have wide flaring horns (a good sign)—
    see you! the bright hides,
See, the two with stars on their foreheads—
    see, the round bodies and broad backs,

How straight and square they stand on their
    legs—what fine sagacious eyes!
How straight they watch their tamer—they wish
    him near them- how they turn to look after
    him!
What yearning expression! how uneasy they are
    when he moves away from them;
Now I marvel what it can be he appears to
    them, (books, politics, poems, depart—all else
    departs,)
I confess I envy only his fascination—my silent,
    illiterate friend,
Whom a hundred oxen love there in his life on
    farms,
In the northern county far, in the placid pastoral
    region.

AN OLD MAN'S THOUGHT OF SCHOOL
For the Inauguration of a Public School,
Camden, New Jersey, 1874

AN old man's thought of school,
An old man gathering youthful memories and
    blooms that youth itself cannot.

Now only do I know you,
O fair auroral skies—O morning dew upon the
    grass!

And these I see, these sparkling eyes,
These stores of mystic meaning, these young
  lives,
Building, equipping like a fleet of ships,
  immortal ships,
Soon to sail out over the measureless seas,
On the soul's voyage.

Only a lot of boys and girls?
Only the tiresome spelling, writing, ciphering
  classes?
Only a public school?

Ah more, infinitely more;
(As George Fox rais'd his warning cry, "Is it this
  pile of brick and mortar, these dead floors,
  windows, rails, you call the church?
Why this is not the church at all-the church is
  living, ever living souls.")

And you America,
Cast you the real reckoning for your present?
The lights and shadows of your future, good
  or evil?
To girlhood, boyhood look, the teacher and
  the school.

Wandering at Morn

WANDERING at morn,
Emerging from the night from gloomy
  thoughts, thee in my thoughts,
Yearning for thee harmonious Union! thee,
  singing bird divine!
Thee coil'd in evil times my country, with craft
  and black dismay, with every meanness,
  treason thrust upon thee,
This common marvel I beheld—the parent
  thrush I watch'd feeding its young,
The singing thrush whose tones of joy and faith
  ecstatic,
Fail not to certify and cheer my soul.

There ponder'd, felt I,
If worms, snakes, loathsome grubs, may to sweet
  spiritual songs be turn'd,
If vermin so transposed, so used and bless'd may
  be,
Then may I trust in you, your fortunes, days, my
  country;
Who knows but these may be the lessons fit for
  you?
From these your future song may rise with
  joyous trills,
Destin'd to fill the world.

ITALIAN MUSIC IN DAKOTA
["The Seventeenth—the finest
Regimental Band I ever heard."]

THROUGH the soft evening air enwinding all,
Rocks, woods, fort, cannon, pacing sentries,
  endless wilds,
In dulcet streams, in flutes' and cornets' notes,
Electric, pensive, turbulent, artificial,
(Yet strangely fitting even here, meanings
  unknown before,
Subtler than ever, more harmony, as if born
  here, related here,
Not to the city's fresco'd rooms, not to the
  audience of the opera house,
Sounds, echoes, wandering strains, as really here
  at home,
Sonnambula's innocent love, trios with Norma's
  anguish,
And thy ecstatic chorus Poliuto);
Ray'd in the limpid yellow slanting sundown,
Music, Italian music in Dakota.

While Nature, sovereign of this gnarl'd realm,
Lurking in hidden barbaric grim recesses,
Acknowledging rapport however far remov'd,
(As some old root or soil of earth its last-born
  flower or fruit,)
Listens well pleas'd.

WITH ALL THY GIFTS

WITH all thy gifts America,
Standing secure, rapidly tending, overlooking
    the world,
Power, wealth, extent, vouchsafed to thee—with
    these and like of these vouchsafed to thee,
What if one gift thou lackest? (the ultimate
    human problem never solving,)
The gift of perfect women fit for thee—what if
    that gift of gifts thou lackest?
The towering feminine of thee? the beauty,
    health, completion, fit for thee?
The mothers fit for thee?

MY PICTURE-GALLERY

IN a little house keep I pictures suspended, it is
    not a fix'd house,
It is round, it is only a few inches from one side
    to the other;
Yet behold, it has room for all the shows of the
    world, all memories!
Here the tableaus of life, and here the groupings
    of death;
Here, do you know this? this is cicerone himself,
With finger rais'd he points to the prodigal
    pictures.

The Prairie States

A NEWER garden of creation, no—primal
  solitude,
Dense, joyous, modern, populous millions, cities
  and farms,
With iron interlaced, composite, tied, many in
  one,
By all the world contributed—freedom's and
  law's and thrift's society,
The crown and teeming paradise, so far, of
  time's accumulations,
To justify the past.

Proud Music of the Storm

1

PROUD music of the storm,
Blast that careers so free, whistling across the
   prairies,
Strong hum of forest tree-tops—wind of the
   mountains,
Personified dim shapes—you hidden orchestras,
You serenades of phantoms with instruments
   alert,
Blending with Nature's rhythmus all the tongues
   of nations;
You chords left as by vast composers—you
   choruses,
You formless, free, religious dances—you from
   the Orient,
You undertone of rivers, roar of pouring
   cataracts,
You sounds from distant guns with galloping
   cavalry,
Echoes of camps with all the different
   bugle-calls,
Trooping tumultuous, filling the midnight late,
   bending me powerless,
Entering my lonesome slumber-chamber, why
   have you seiz'd me?

2

Come forward O my soul, and let the rest
retire,
Listen, lose not, it is toward thee they tend,
Parting the midnight, entering my slumber-
chamber,
For thee they sing and dance O soul.

A festival song,
The duet of the bridegroom and the bride, a
marriage-march,
With lips of love, and hearts of lovers fill'd to
the brim with love,
The red-flush'd cheeks and perfumes, the
cortege swarming full of friendly faces young
and old,
To flutes' clear notes and sounding harps'
cantabile.

Now loud approaching drums,
Victoria! seest thou in powder-smoke the
banners torn but flying? the rout of the
baffled?
Hearest those shouts of a conquering army?

(Ah soul, the sobs of women, the wounded
groaning in agony,
The hiss and crackle of flames, the blacken'd
ruins, the embers of cities,
The dirge and desolation of mankind.)

Now airs antique and mediaeval fill me,
I see and hear old harpers with their harps at
    Welsh festivals,
I hear the minnesingers singing their lays of
    love,
I hear the minstrels, gleemen, troubadours, of
    the middle ages.

Now the great organ sounds,
Tremulous, while underneath, (as the hid
    footholds of the earth,
On which arising rest, and leaping forth depend,
All shapes of beauty, grace and strength, all hues
    we know,
Green blades of grass and warbling birds,
    children that gambol and play, the clouds of
    heaven above,)
The strong base stands, and its pulsations
    intermits not,
Bathing, supporting, merging all the rest,
    maternity of all the rest,
And with it every instrument in multitudes,
The players playing, all the world's musicians,
The solemn hymns and masses rousing
    adoration,
All passionate heart-chants, sorrowful appeals,
The measureless sweet vocalists of ages,
And for their solvent setting earth's own
    diapason,
Of winds and woods and mighty ocean waves,

A new composite orchestra, binder of years and
    climes, ten-fold renewer,
As of the far-back days the poets tell, the
    Paradiso,
The straying thence, the separation long, but
    now the wandering done,
The journey done, the journeyman come home,
And man and art with Nature fused again.

Tutti! for earth and heaven;
(The Almighty leader now for once has signal'd
    with his wand.)

The manly strophe of the husbands of the
    world,
And all the wives responding.

The tongues of violins,
(I think O tongues ye tell this heart, that cannot
    tell itself,
This brooding yearning heart, that cannot tell
    itself.)

3

Ah from a little child,
Thou knowest soul how to me all sounds
    became music,
My mother's voice in lullaby or hymn,
(The voice, O tender voices, memory's loving
    voices,

Last miracle of all, O dearest mother's, sister's,
  voices;)
The rain, the growing corn, the breeze among
  the long-leav'd corn,
The measur'd sea-surf beating on the sand,
The twittering bird, the hawk's sharp scream,
The wild-fowl's notes at night as flying low
  migrating north or south,
The psalm in the country church or mid the
  clustering trees, the open air camp-meeting,
The fiddler in the tavern, the glee, the long-
  strung sailor-song,
The lowing cattle, bleating sheep, the crowing
  cock at dawn.

All songs of current lands come sounding round
  me,
The German airs of friendship, wine and love,
Irish ballads, merry jigs and dances, English
  warbles,
Chansons of France, Scotch tunes, and o'er the rest,
Italia's peerless compositions.

Across the stage with pallor on her face, yet
  lurid passion,
Stalks Norma brandishing the dagger in her hand.

I see poor crazed Lucia's eyes' unnatural gleam,
Her hair down her back falls loose and
  dishevel'd.

I see where Ernani walking the bridal garden,
Amid the scent of night-roses, radiant, holding
his bride by the hand,
Hears the infernal call, the death-pledge of the
horn.

To crossing swords and gray hairs bared to
heaven,
The clear electric base and baritone of the
world,
The trombone duo, Libertad forever!
From Spanish chestnut trees' dense shade,
By old and heavy convent walls a wailing
song,
Song of lost love, the torch of youth and life
quench'd in despair,
Song of the dying swan, Fernando's heart is
breaking.

Awaking from her woes at last retriev'd Amina
sings,
Copious as stars and glad as morning light the
torrents of her joy.

(The teeming lady comes,
The lustrious orb, Venus contralto, the
blooming mother,
Sister of loftiest gods, Alboni's self I hear.)

4

I hear those odes, symphonies, operas,
I hear in the William Tell the music of an
   arous'd and angry people,
I hear Meyerbeer's Huguenots, the Prophet, or
   Robert,
Gounod's Faust, or Mozart's Don Juan.

I hear the dance-music of all nations,
The waltz, some delicious measure, lapsing,
   bathing me in bliss,
The bolero to tinkling guitars and clattering
   castanets.

I see religious dances old and new,
I hear the sound of the Hebrew lyre,
I see the crusaders marching bearing the
   cross on high, to the martial clang of
   cymbals,
I hear dervishes monotonously chanting,
   interspers'd with frantic shouts, as they spin
   around turning always towards Mecca,
I see the rapt religious dances of the Persians
   and the Arabs,
Again, at Eleusis, home of Ceres, I see the
   modern Greeks dancing,
I hear them clapping their hands as they bend
   their bodies,
I hear the metrical shuffling of their feet.

I see again the wild old Corybantian dance, the
  performers wounding each other,
I see the Roman youth to the shrill sound of
  flageolets throwing and catching their
  weapons,
As they fall on their knees and rise again.

I hear from the Mussulman mosque the
  muezzin calling,
I see the worshippers within, nor form nor
  sermon, argument nor word,
But silent, strange, devout, rais'd, glowing
  heads, ecstatic faces.

I hear the Egyptian harp of many strings,
The primitive chants of the Nile boatmen,
The sacred imperial hymns of China,
To the delicate sounds of the king, (the stricken
  wood and stone,)
Or to Hindu flutes and the fretting twang of
  the vina,
A band of bayaderes.

5

Now Asia, Africa leave me, Europe seizing
  inflates me,
To organs huge and bands I hear as from vast
  concourses of voices,
Luther's strong hymn Eine feste Burg ist unser
  Gott,

Rossini's Stabat Mater dolorosa,
Or floating in some high cathedral dim with
    gorgeous color'd windows,
The passionate Agnus Dei or Gloria in Excelsis.

Composers! mighty maestros!
And you, sweet singers of old lands, soprani,
    tenori, bassi!
To you a new bard caroling in the West,
Obeisant sends his love.

(Such led to thee O soul,
All senses, shows and objects, lead to thee,
But now it seems to me sound leads o'er all
    the rest.)

I hear the annual singing of the children in
    St. Paul's cathedral,
Or, under the high roof of some colossal hall,
    the symphonies, oratorios of Beethoven,
    Handel, or Haydn,
The Creation in billows of godhood laves me.

Give me to hold all sounds, (I madly struggling
    cry,)
Fill me with all the voices of the universe,
Endow me with their throbbings, Nature's also,
The tempests, waters, winds, operas and chants,
    marches and dances,
Utter, pour in, for I would take them all!

6

Then I woke softly,
And pausing, questioning awhile the music of
   my dream,
And questioning all those reminiscences, the
   tempest in its fury,
And all the songs of sopranos and tenors,
And those rapt oriental dances of religious
   fervor,
And the sweet varied instruments, and the
   diapason of organs,
And all the artless plaints of love and grief and
   death,
I said to my silent curious soul out of the bed of
   the slumber-chamber,
Come, for I have found the clew I sought so
   long,
Let us go forth refresh'd amid the day,
Cheerfully tallying life, walking the world, the
   real,
Nourish'd henceforth by our celestial dream.

And I said, moreover,
Haply what thou hast heard O soul was not the
   sound of winds,
Nor dream of raging storm, nor sea-hawk's
   flapping wings nor harsh scream,
Nor vocalism of sun-bright Italy,
Nor German organ majestic, nor vast concourse
   of voices, nor layers of harmonies,

Nor strophes of husbands and wives, nor sound
  of marching soldiers,
Nor flutes, nor harps, nor the bugle-calls of
  camps,
But to a new rhythmus fitted for thee,
Poems bridging the way from Life to Death,
  vaguely waited in night air, uncaught,
  unwritten,
Which let us go forth in the bold day and write.

Passage to India

1

SINGING my days,
Singing the great achievements of the present,
Singing the strong light works of engineers,
Our modern wonders, (the antique ponderous
    Seven outvied,)
In the Old World the east the Suez canal,
The New by its mighty railroad spann'd,
The seas inlaid with eloquent gentle wires;
Yet first to sound, and ever sound, the cry with
    thee O soul,
The Past! the Past! the Past!

The Past—the dark unfathom'd retrospect!
The teeming gulf—the sleepers and the shadows!
The past—the infinite greatness of the past!
For what is the present after all but a growth
    out of the past?
(As a projectile form'd, impell'd, passing a
    certain line, still keeps on,
So the present, utterly form'd, impell'd by the
    past.)

2

Passage O soul to India!
Eclaircise the myths Asiatic, the primitive fables.

Not you alone proud truths of the world,
Nor you alone ye facts of modern science,
But myths and fables of eld, Asia's, Africa's
 fables,
The far-darting beams of the spirit, the unloos'd
 dreams,
The deep diving bibles and legends,
The daring plots of the poets, the elder
 religions;
O you temples fairer than lilies pour'd over by
 the rising sun!
O you fables spurning the known, eluding the
 hold of the known, mounting to heaven!
You lofty and dazzling towers, pinnacled, red as
 roses, burnish'd with gold!
Towers of fables immortal fashion'd from mortal
 dreams!
You too I welcome and fully the same as the
 rest!
You too with joy I sing.

Passage to India!
Lo, soul, seest thou not God's purpose from the
 first?
The earth to be spann'd, connected by network,
The races, neighbors, to marry and be given in
 marriage,
The oceans to be cross'd, the distant brought
 near,
The lands to be welded together.

A worship new I sing,
You captains, voyagers, explorers, yours,
You engineers, you architects, machinists, yours,
You, not for trade or transportation only,
But in God's name, and for thy sake O soul.

3

Passage to India!
Lo soul for thee of tableaus twain,
I see in one the Suez canal initiated, open'd,
I see the procession of steamships, the Empress
    Engenie's leading the van,
I mark from on deck the strange landscape, the
    pure sky, the level sand in the distance,
I pass swiftly the picturesque groups, the
    workmen gather'd,
The gigantic dredging machines.

In one again, different, (yet thine, all thine, O
    soul, the same,)
I see over my own continent the Pacific railroad
    surmounting every barrier,
I see continual trains of cars winding along the
    Platte carrying freight and passengers,
I hear the locomotives rushing and roaring, and
    the shrill steam-whistle,
I hear the echoes reverberate through the
    grandest scenery in the world,
I cross the Laramie plains, I note the rocks in
    grotesque shapes, the buttes,

I see the plentiful larkspur and wild onions, the
    barren, colorless, sage-deserts,
I see in glimpses afar or towering immediately
    above me the great mountains, I see
    the Wind river and the Wahsatch
    mountains,
I see the Monument mountain and the Eagle's
    Nest, I pass the Promontory, I ascend the
    Nevadas,
I scan the noble Elk mountain and wind around
    its base,
I see the Humboldt range, I thread the valley
    and cross the river,
I see the clear waters of lake Tahoe, I see forests
    of majestic pines,
Or crossing the great desert, the alkaline plains,
    I behold enchanting mirages of waters and
    meadows,
Marking through these and after all, in duplicate
    slender lines,
Bridging the three or four thousand miles of
    land travel,
Tying the Eastern to the Western sea,
The road between Europe and Asia.

(Ah Genoese thy dream! thy dream!
Centuries after thou art laid in thy grave,
The shore thou foundest verifies thy dream.)

4

Passage to India!
Struggles of many a captain, tales of many a
     sailor dead,
Over my mood stealing and spreading they
     come,
Like clouds and cloudlets in the unreach'd sky.

Along all history, down the slopes,
As a rivulet running, sinking now, and now
     again to the surface rising,
A ceaseless thought, a varied train—lo, soul, to
     thee, thy sight, they rise,
The plans, the voyages again, the expeditions;
Again Vasco de Gama sails forth,
Again the knowledge gain'd, the mariner's
     compass,
Lands found and nations born, thou born
     America,
For purpose vast, man's long probation fill'd,
Thou rondure of the world at last accomplish'd.

5

O vast Rondure, swimming in space,
Cover'd all over with visible power and
     beauty,
Alternate light and day and the teeming
     spiritual darkness,
Unspeakable high processions of sun and moon
     and countless stars above,

Below, the manifold grass and waters, animals,
  mountains, trees,
With inscrutable purpose, some hidden
  prophetic intention,
Now first it seems my thought begins to span thee.

Down from the gardens of Asia descending
  radiating,
Adam and Eve appear, then their myriad
  progeny after them,
Wandering, yearning, curious, with restless
  explorations,
With questionings, baffled, formless, feverish,
  with never-happy hearts,
With that sad incessant refrain, Wherefore
  unsatisfied soul? and
Whither O mocking life?

Ah who shall soothe these feverish children?
Who Justify these restless explorations?
Who speak the secret of impassive earth?
Who bind it to us? what is this separate Nature
  so unnatural?
What is this earth to our affections? (unloving
  earth, without a throb to answer ours,
Cold earth, the place of graves.)

Yet soul be sure the first intent remains, and
  shall be carried out,
Perhaps even now the time has arrived.

After the seas are all cross'd, (as they seem
    already cross'd,)
After the great captains and engineers have
    accomplish'd their work,
After the noble inventors, after the scientists, the
    chemist, the geologist, ethnologist,
Finally shall come the poet worthy that name,
The true son of God shall come singing his
    songs.

Then not your deeds only O voyagers, O
    scientists and inventors, shall be justified,
All these hearts as of fretted children shall be
    sooth'd,
All affection shall be fully responded to, the
    secret shall be told,
All these separations and gaps shall be taken up
    and hook'd and link'd together,
The whole earth, this cold, impassive, voiceless
    earth, shall be completely Justified,
Trinitas divine shall be gloriously accomplish'd
    and compacted by the true son of God, the
    poet,
(He shall indeed pass the straits and conquer the
    mountains,
He shall double the cape of Good Hope to
    some purpose,)
Nature and Man shall be disjoin'd and diffused
    no more,
The true son of God shall absolutely fuse them.

6

Year at whose wide-flung door I sing!
Year of the purpose accomplish'd!
Year of the marriage of continents, climates and
    oceans!
(No mere doge of Venice now wedding the
    Adriatic,)
I see O year in you the vast terraqueous globe
    given and giving all,
Europe to Asia, Africa join'd, and they to the
    New World,
The lands, geographies, dancing before you,
    holding a festival garland,
As brides and bridegrooms hand in hand.

Passage to India!
Cooling airs from Caucasus far, soothing cradle
    of man,
The river Euphrates flowing, the past lit up
    again.

Lo soul, the retrospect brought forward,
The old, most populous, wealthiest of earth's
    lands,
The streams of the Indus and the Ganges and
    their many affluents,
(I my shores of America walking to-day behold,
    resuming all,)
The tale of Alexander on his warlike marches
    suddenly dying,

On one side China and on the other side Persia
   and Arabia,
To the south the great seas and the bay of
   Bengal,
The flowing literatures, tremendous epics,
   religions, castes,
Old occult Brahma interminably far back, the
   tender and junior Buddha,
Central and southern empires and all their
   belongings, possessors,
The wars of Tamerlane,the reign of Aurungzebe,
The traders, rulers, explorers, Moslems,
   Venetians, Byzantium, the Arabs, Portuguese,
The first travelers famous yet, Marco Polo,
   Batouta the Moor,
Doubts to be solv'd, the map incognita, blanks
   to be fill'd,
The foot of man unstay'd, the hands never at
   rest,
Thyself O soul that will not brook a challenge.

The mediaeval navigators rise before me,
The world of 1492, with its awaken'd enterprise,
Something swelling in humanity now like the
   sap of the earth in spring,
The sunset splendor of chivalry declining.

And who art thou sad shade?
Gigantic, visionary, thyself a visionary,
With majestic limbs and pious beaming eyes,

Spreading around with every look of thine a
 golden world,
Enhuing it with gorgeous hues.

As the chief histrion,
Down to the footlights walks in some great
 scena,
Dominating the rest I see the Admiral
 himself,
(History's type of courage, action, faith,)
Behold him sail from Palos leading his little
 fleet,
His voyage behold, his return, his great fame,
His misfortunes, calumniators, behold him a
 prisoner, chain'd,
Behold his dejection, poverty, death.

(Curious in time I stand, noting the efforts of
 heroes,
Is the deferment long? bitter the slander,
 poverty, death?
Lies the seed unreck'd for centuries in the
 ground? lo, to God's due occasion,
Uprising in the night, it sprouts, blooms,
And fills the earth with use and beauty.)

7

Passage indeed O soul to primal thought,
Not lands and seas alone, thy own clear
 freshness,

The young maturity of brood and bloom,
To realms of budding bibles.

O soul, repressless, I with thee and thou with me,
Thy circumnavigation of the world begin,
Of man, the voyage of his mind's return,
To reason's early paradise,
Back, back to wisdom's birth, to innocent
    intuitions,
Again with fair creation.

8

O we can wait no longer,
We too take ship O soul,
Joyous we too launch out on trackless seas,
Fearless for unknown shores on waves of ecstasy
    to sail,
Amid the wafting winds, (thou pressing me to
    thee, I thee to me, O soul,)
Caroling free, singing our song of God,
Chanting our chant of pleasant exploration.

With laugh and many a kiss,
(Let others deprecate, let others weep for sin,
    remorse, humiliation,)
O soul thou pleasest me, I thee.

Ah more than any priest O soul we too believe
    in God,
But with the mystery of God we dare not dally.

O soul thou pleasest me, I thee,
Sailing these seas or on the hills, or waking in
   the night,
Thoughts, silent thoughts, of Time and Space
   and Death, like waters flowing,
Bear me indeed as through the regions infinite,
Whose air I breathe, whose ripples hear, lave me
   all over,
Bathe me O God in thee, mounting to thee,
I and my soul to range in range of thee.

O Thou transcendent,
Nameless, the fibre and the breath,
Light of the light, shedding forth universes,
   thou centre of them,
Thou mightier center of the true, the good, the
   loving,
Thou moral, spiritual fountain—affection's
   source—thou reservoir,
(O pensive soul of me—O thirst unsatisfied—
   waitest not there?
Waitest not haply for us somewhere there the
   Comrade perfect?)
Thou pulse—thou motive of the stars, suns,
   systems,
That, circling, move in order, safe, harmonious,
Athwart the shapeless vastnesses of space,
How should I think, how breathe a single
   breath, how speak, if, out of myself,
I could not launch, to those, superior universes?

Swiftly I shrivel at the thought of God,
At Nature and its wonders, Time and Space and
    Death,
But that I, turning, call to thee O soul, thou
    actual Me,
And lo, thou gently masterest the orbs,
Thou matest Time, smilest content at Death,
And fillest, swellest full the vastnesses of Space.

Greater than stars or suns,
Bounding O soul thou journeyest forth;
What love than thine and ours could wider
    amplify?
What aspirations, wishes, outvie thine and ours
    O soul?
What dreams of the ideal? what plans of purity,
    perfection, strength?
What cheerful willingness for others' sake to
    give up all?
For others' sake to suffer all?

Reckoning ahead O soul, when thou, the time
    achiev'd,
The seas all cross'd, weather'd the capes, the
    voyage done,
Surrounded, copest, frontest God, yieldest, the
    aim attain'd,
As fill'd with friendship, love complete, the
    Elder Brother found,
The Younger melts in fondness in his arms.

9

Passage to more than India!
Are thy wings plumed indeed for such far
  flights?
O soul, voyagest thou indeed on voyages like
  those?
Disportest thou on waters such as those?
Soundest below the Sanscrit and the Vedas?
Then have thy bent unleash'd.

Passage to you, your shores, ye aged fierce
  enigmas!
Passage to you, to mastership of you, ye
  strangling problems!
You, strew'd with the wrecks of skeletons, that,
  living, never reach'd you.

Passage to more than India!
O secret of the earth and sky!
Of you O waters of the sea! O winding creeks
  and rivers!
Of you O woods and fields! of you strong
  mountains of my land!
Of you O prairies! of you gray rocks!
O morning red! O clouds! O rain and snows!
O day and night, passage to you!

O sun and moon and all you stars! Sirius and
  Jupiter!
Passage to you!

Passage, immediate passage! the blood burns in
my veins!
Away O soul! hoist instantly the anchor!

Cut the hawsers—haul out—shake out every
sail!
Have we not stood here like trees in the ground
long enough?
Have we not grovel'd here long enough, eating
and drinking like mere brutes?
Have we not darken'd and dazed ourselves with
books long enough?

Sail forth- steer for the deep waters only,
Reckless O soul, exploring, I with thee, and
thou with me,
For we are bound where mariner has not yet
dared to go,
And we will risk the ship, ourselves and all.

O my brave soul!
O farther farther sail!
O daring joy, but safe! are they not all the seas
of God?
O farther, farther, farther sail!

Prayer of Columbus

A BATTER'D, wreck'd old man,
Thrown on this savage shore, far, far from
    home,
Pent by the sea and dark rebellious brows,
    twelve dreary months,
Sore, stiff with many toils, sicken'd and nigh to
    death,
I take my way along the island's edge,
Venting a heavy heart.

I am too full of woe!
Haply I may not live another day;
I cannot rest O God, I cannot eat or drink or
    sleep,
Till I put forth myself, my prayer, once more to
    Thee,
Breathe, bathe myself once more in Thee,
    commune with Thee,
Report myself once more to Thee.

Thou knowest my years entire, my life,
My long and crowded life of active work, not
    adoration merely;
Thou knowest the prayers and vigils of my
    youth,

Thou knowest my manhood's solemn and
    visionary meditations,
Thou knowest how before I commenced I
    devoted all to come to Thee,
Thou knowest I have in age ratified all those
    vows and strictly kept them,
Thou knowest I have not once lost nor faith nor
    ecstasy in Thee,
In shackles, prison'd, in disgrace, repining not,
Accepting all from Thee, as duly come from
    Thee.

All my emprises have been fill'd with Thee,
My speculations, plans, begun and carried on in
    thoughts of Thee,
Sailing the deep or journeying the land for Thee;
Intentions, purports, aspirations mine, leaving
    results to Thee.

O I am sure they really came from Thee,
The urge, the ardor, the unconquerable will,
The potent, felt, interior command, stronger
    than words,
A message from the Heavens whispering to me
    even in sleep,
These sped me on.

By me and these the work so far accomplish'd,
By me earth's elder cloy'd and stifled lands
    uncloy'd, unloos'd,

By me the hemispheres rounded and tied, the
  unknown to the known.

The end I know not, it is all in Thee,
Or small or great I know not—haply what broad
  fields, what lands,
Haply the brutish measureless human
  undergrowth I know,
Transplanted there may rise to stature,
  knowledge worthy Thee,
Haply the swords I know may there indeed be
  turn'd to reaping-tools,
Haply the lifeless cross I know, Europe's dead
  cross, may bud and blossom there.

One effort more, my altar this bleak sand;
That Thou O God my life hast lighted,
With ray of light, steady, ineffable, vouch-safed
  of Thee,
Light rare untellable, lighting the very light,
Beyond all signs, descriptions, languages;
For that O God, be it my latest word, here on
  my knees,
Old, poor, and paralyzed, I thank Thee.

My terminus near,
The clouds already closing in upon me,
The voyage balk'd, the course disputed,
  lost,
I yield my ships to Thee.

My hands, my limbs grow nerveless,
My brain feels rack'd, bewilder'd,
Let the old timbers part, I will not part,
I will cling fast to Thee, O God, though the
    waves buffet me,
Thee, Thee at least I know.

Is it the prophet's thought I speak, or am I
    raving?
What do I know of life? what of myself—.
I know not even my own work past or present,
Dim ever-shifting guesses of it spread before me,
Of newer better worlds, their mighty
    parturition,
Mocking, perplexing me.

And these things I see suddenly, what mean
    they?
As if some miracle, some hand divine unseal'd
    my eyes,
Shadowy vast shapes smile through the air
    and sky,
And on the distant waves sail countless ships,
And anthems in new tongues I hear saluting me.

The Sleepers

1

I WANDER all night in my vision,
Stepping with light feet, swiftly and noiselessly
   stepping and stopping,
Bending with open eyes over the shut eyes of
   sleepers,
Wandering and confused, lost to myself, ill-
   assorted, contradictory,
Pausing, gazing, bending, and stopping.

How solemn they look there, stretch'd and still,
How quiet they breathe, the little children in
   their cradles.

The wretched features of ennuyes, the white
   features of corpses, the livid faces of
   drunkards, the sick-gray faces of onanists,
The gash'd bodies on battle-fields, the insane in
   their strong-door'd rooms, the sacred idiots,
   the new-born emerging from gates, and the
   dying emerging from gates,
The night pervades them and infolds them.

The married couple sleep calmly in their bed, he
   with his palm on the hip of the wife, and she
   with her palm on the hip of the husband,

The sisters sleep lovingly side by side in their
    bed,
The men sleep lovingly side by side in theirs,
And the mother sleeps with her little child
    carefully wrapt.

The blind sleep, and the deaf and dumb sleep,
The prisoner sleeps well in the prison, the
    runaway son sleeps,
The murderer that is to be hung next day, how
    does he sleep?
And the murder'd person, how does he sleep?

The female that loves unrequited sleeps,
And the male that loves unrequited sleeps,
The head of the money-maker that plotted all
    day sleeps,
And the enraged and treacherous dispositions,
    all, all sleep.

I stand in the dark with drooping eyes by the
    worst-suffering and the most restless,
I pass my hands soothingly to and fro a few
    inches from them,
The restless sink in their beds, they fitfully sleep.

Now I pierce the darkness, new beings appear,
The earth recedes from me into the night,
I saw that it was beautiful, and I see that what is
    not the earth is beautiful.

I go from bedside to bedside, I sleep close with
    the other sleepers each in turn,
I dream in my dream all the dreams of the other
    dreamers,
And I become the other dreamers.

I am a dance—play up there! the fit is whirling
    me fast!

I am the ever-laughing—it is new moon and
    twilight,
I see the hiding of douceurs, I see nimble ghosts
    whichever way look,
Cache and cache again deep in the ground
    and sea, and where it is neither ground nor
    sea.

Well do they do their jobs those journeymen
    divine,
Only from me can they hide nothing, and would
    not if they could,
I reckon I am their boss and they make me a pet
    besides,
And surround me and lead me and run ahead
    when I walk,
To lift their cunning covers to signify me with
    stretch'd arms, and resume the way;
Onward we move, a gay gang of blackguards!
    with mirth-shouting music and wild-flapping
    pennants of joy!

I am the actor, the actress, the voter, the
politician,
The emigrant and the exile, the criminal that
stood in the box,
He who has been famous and he who shall be
famous after to-day,
The stammerer, the well-form'd person, the
wasted or feeble person.

I am she who adorn'd herself and folded her
hair expectantly,
My truant lover has come, and it is dark.

Double yourself and receive me darkness,
Receive me and my lover too, he will not let me
go without him.

I roll myself upon you as upon a bed, I resign
myself to the dusk.

He whom I call answers me and takes the place
of my lover,
He rises with me silently from the bed.

Darkness, you are gentler than my lover, his
flesh was sweaty and panting,
I feel the hot moisture yet that he left me.

My hands are spread forth, I pass them in all
directions,

I would sound up the shadowy shore to which
    you are journeying.

Be careful darkness! already what was it touch'd
    me?
I thought my lover had gone, else darkness and
    he are one,
I hear the heart-beat, I follow, I fade away.

2

I descend my western course, my sinews are
    flaccid,
Perfume and youth course through me and I am
    their wake.

It is my face yellow and wrinkled instead of the
    old woman's,
I sit low in a straw-bottom chair and carefully
    darn my grandson's stockings.

It is I too, the sleepless widow looking out on
    the winter midnight,
I see the sparkles of starshine on the icy and
    pallid earth.

A shroud I see and I am the shroud, I wrap a
    body and lie in the coffin,
It is dark here under ground, it is not evil
    or pain here, it is blank here, for
    reasons.

(It seems to me that every thing in the light and
    air ought to be happy,
Whoever is not in his coffin and the dark grave
    let him know he has enough.)

3

I see a beautiful gigantic swimmer swimming
    naked through the eddies of the sea,
His brown hair lies close and even to his head,
    he strikes out with courageous arms, he urges
    himself with his legs,
I see his white body, I see his undaunted eyes,
I hate the swift-running eddies that would dash
    him head-foremost on the rocks.

What are you doing you ruffianly red-trickled
    waves?
Will you kill the courageous giant? will you kill
    him in the prime of his middle age?

Steady and long he struggles,
He is baffled, bang'd, bruis'd, he holds out
    while his strength holds out,
The slapping eddies are spotted with his blood,
    they bear him away, they roll him, swing him,
    turn him,
His beautiful body is borne in the circling
    eddies, it is continually bruis'd on rocks,
Swiftly and ought of sight is borne the brave
    corpse.

4

I turn but do not extricate myself,
Confused, a past-reading, another, but with
　darkness yet.

The beach is cut by the razory ice-wind, the
　wreck-guns sound,
The tempest lulls, the moon comes floundering
　through the drifts.

I look where the ship helplessly heads end on, I
　hear the burst as she strikes, I hear the howls
　of dismay, they grow fainter and fainter.

I cannot aid with my wringing fingers,
I can but rush to the surf and let it drench me
　and freeze upon me.

I search with the crowd, not one of the
　company is wash'd to us alive,
In the morning I help pick up the dead and lay
　them in rows in a barn.

5

Now of the older war-days, the defeat at
　Brooklyn,
Washington stands inside the lines, he stands on
　the intrench'd hills amid a crowd of officers.
His face is cold and damp, he cannot repress the
　weeping drops,

He lifts the glass perpetually to his eyes, the
    color is blanch'd from his cheeks,
He sees the slaughter of the southern braves
    confided to him by their parents.

The same at last and at last when peace is
    declared,
He stands in the room of the old tavern, the
    well-belov'd soldiers all pass through,
The officers speechless and slow draw near in
    their turns,
The chief encircles their necks with his arm and
    kisses them on the cheek,
He kisses lightly the wet cheeks one after
    another, he shakes hands and bids good-by to
    the army.

6

Now what my mother told me one day as we sat
    at dinner together,
Of when she was a nearly grown girl living
    home with her parents on the old homestead.

A red squaw came one breakfast-time to the old
    homestead,
On her back she carried a bundle of rushes for
    rush-bottoming chairs,
Her hair, straight, shiny, coarse, black, profuse,
    half-envelop'd her face,

Her step was free and elastic, and her voice
    sounded exquisitely as she spoke.

My mother look'd in delight and amazement at
    the stranger,
She look'd at the freshness of her tall-borne face
    and full and pliant limbs,
The more she look'd upon her she loved her,
Never before had she seen such wonderful
    beauty and purity,
She made her sit on a bench by the jamb of the
    fireplace, she cook'd food for her,
She had no work to give her, but she gave her
    remembrance and fondness.

The red squaw staid all the forenoon, and
    toward the middle of the afternoon she went
    away,
O my mother was loth to have her go away,
All the week she thought of her, she watch'd for
    her many a month,
She remember'd her many a winter and many a
    summer,
But the red squaw never came nor was heard of
    there again.

7

A show of the summer softness—a contact of
    something unseen-an amour of the light and air,

I am jealous and overwhelm'd with friendliness,
And will go gallivant with the light and air
    myself.

O love and summer, you are in the dreams and
    in me,
Autumn and winter are in the dreams, the
    farmer goes with his thrift,
The droves and crops increase, the barns are
    well-fill'd.

Elements merge in the night, ships make tacks in
    the dreams,
The sailor sails, the exile returns home,The
    fugitive returns unharm'd, the immigrant is
    back beyond months and years,
The poor Irishman lives in the simple house of
    his childhood with the well known neighbors
    and faces,
They warmly welcome him, he is barefoot again,
    he forgets he is well off,
The Dutchman voyages home, and the
    Scotchman and Welshman voyage home, and
    the native of the Mediterranean voyages
    home,
To every port of England, France, Spain, enter
    well-fill'd ships,
The Swiss foots it toward his hills, the Prussian
    goes his way, the Hungarian his way, and the
    Pole his way,

The Swede returns, and the Dane and
　Norwegian return.

The homeward bound and the outward
　bound,
The beautiful lost swimmer, the ennuye, the
　onanist, the female that loves unrequited, the
　money-maker,
The actor and actress, those through with their
　parts and those waiting to commence,
The affectionate boy, the husband and wife, the
　voter, the nominee that is chosen and the
　nominee that has fail'd,
The great already known and the great any time
　after to-day,
The stammerer, the sick, the perfect-form'd, the
　homely,
The criminal that stood in the box, the judge
　that sat and sentenced him, the fluent lawyers,
　the jury, the audience,
The laugher and weeper, the dancer, the
　midnight widow, the red squaw,
The consumptive, the erysipalite, the idiot, he
　that is wrong'd,
The antipodes, and every one between this and
　them in the dark,
I swear they are averaged now—one is no better
　than the other,
The night and sleep have liken'd them and
　restored them.

I swear they are all beautiful,
Every one that sleeps is beautiful, every thing in
  the dim light is beautiful,
The wildest and bloodiest is over, and all is
  peace.

Peace is always beautiful,
The myth of heaven indicates peace and night.

The myth of heaven indicates the soul,
The soul is always beautiful, it appears more
  or it appears less, it comes or it lags
  behind,
It comes from its embower'd garden and looks
  pleasantly on itself and encloses the world,
Perfect and clean the genitals previously
  jetting,and perfect and clean the womb
  cohering,
The head well-grown proportion'd and plumb,
  and the bowels and joints proportion'd and
  plumb.

The soul is always beautiful,
The universe is duly in order, every thing is in its
  place,
What has arrived is in its place and what waits
  shall be in its place,
The twisted skull waits, the watery or rotten
  blood waits,

The child of the glutton or venerealee waits
    long, and the child of the drunkard waits
    long, and the drunkard himself waits long,
The sleepers that lived and died wait, the far
    advanced are to go on in their turns, and the
    far behind are to come on in their turns,
The diverse shall be no less diverse, but they
    shall flow and unite—they unite now.

8

The sleepers are very beautiful as they lie
    unclothed,
They flow hand in hand over the whole earth
    from east to west as they lie unclothed,
The Asiatic and African are hand in hand, the
    European and American are hand in hand,
Learn'd and unlearn'd are hand in hand, and
    male and female are hand in hand,
The bare arm of the girl crosses the bare breast
    of her lover, they press close without lust, his
    lips press her neck,
The father holds his grown or ungrown son in
    his arms with measureless love, and the son
    holds the father in his arms with measureless
    love,
The white hair of the mother shines on the
    white wrist of the daughter,
The breath of the boy goes with the breath of
    the man, friend is inarm'd by friend,

The scholar kisses the teacher and the teacher
  kisses the scholar, the wrong'd made right,
The call of the slave is one with the master's call,
  and the master salutes the slave,
The felon steps forth from the prison, the insane
  becomes sane, the suffering of sick persons is
  reliev'd,
The sweatings and fevers stop, the throat that
  was unsound is sound, the lungs of the
  consumptive are resumed, the poor distress'd
  head is free,
The joints of the rheumatic move as smoothly as
  ever, and smoother than ever,
Stiflings and passages open, the paralyzed
  become supple,
The swell'd and convuls'd and congested awake
  to themselves in condition,
They pass the invigoration of the night and the
  chemistry of the night, and awake.

I too pass from the night,
I stay a while away O night, but I return to you
  again and love you.

Why should I be afraid to trust myself to you?
I am not afraid, I have been well brought
  forward by you,
I love the rich running day, but I do not desert
  her in whom I lay so long,

I know not how I came of you and I know not
    where I go with you, but I know I came well
    and shall go well.

I will stop only a time with the night, and rise
    betimes,
I will duly pass the day O my mother, and duly
    return to you.

Transpositions

LET the reformers descend from the stands
    where they are forever bawling—let an idiot
    or insane person appear on each of the stands;
Let judges and criminals be transposed—let the
    prison-keepers be put in prison—let those
    that were prisoners take the keys;
Let them that distrust birth and death lead
    the rest.

To Think of Time

TO think of—of all that retrospection,
To think of to-day, and the ages continued
  henceforward.

Have you guess'd you yourself would not
  continue?
Have you dreaded these earth-beetles?
Have you fear'd the future would be nothing
  to you?

Is to-day nothing? is the beginningless past
  nothing?
If the future is nothing they are just as surely
  nothing.

To think that the sun rose in the east—that men
  and women were flexible, real, alive—that
  every thing was alive,
To think that you and I did not see, feel, think,
  nor bear our part,
To think that we are now here and bear our part.

2

Not a day passes, not a minute or second
  without an accouchement,

Not a day passes, not a minute or second
    without a corpse.

The dull nights go over and the dull days also,
The soreness of lying so much in bed goes over,
The physician after long putting off gives the
    silent and terrible look for an answer,
The children come hurried and weeping, and
    the brothers and sisters are sent for,
Medicines stand unused on the shelf, (the
    camphor-smell has long pervaded the rooms,)
The faithful hand of the living does not desert
    the hand of the dying,
The twitching lips press lightly on the forehead
    of the dying,
The breath ceases and the pulse of the heart
    ceases,
The corpse stretches on the bed and the living
    look upon it,
It is palpable as the living are palpable.

The living look upon the corpse with their
    eyesight,
But without eyesight lingers a different living
    and looks curiously on the corpse.

3

To think the thought of death merged in the
    thought of materials,

To think of all these wonders of city and
    country, and others taking great interest in
    them, and we taking no interest in them.

To think how eager we are in building our
    houses,
To think others shall be just as eager, and we
    quite indifferent.

(I see one building the house that serves him a
    few years, or seventy or eighty years at most,
I see one building the house that serves him
    longer than that.)

Slow-moving and black lines creep over the
    whole earth—they never cease—they are the
    burial lines,
He that was President was buried, and he that is
    now President shall surely be buried.

4
A reminiscence of the vulgar fate,
A frequent sample of the life and death of
    workmen,
Each after his kind.

Cold dash of waves at the ferry-wharf, posh and
    ice in the river, half-frozen mud in the streets,

A gray discouraged sky overhead, the short last
    daylight of December,
A hearse and stages, the funeral of an old Broadway
    stage-driver, the cortege mostly drivers.

Steady the trot to the cemetery, duly rattles the
    death-bell,
The gate is pass'd, the new-dug grave is halted
    at, the living alight, the hearse uncloses,
The coffin is pass'd out, lower'd and settled, the
    whip is laid on the coffin, the earth is swiftly
    shovel'd in,
The mound above is flatted with the spades—
    silence,
A minute—no one moves or speaks—it is done,
He is decently put away—is there any thing more?

He was a good fellow, free-mouth'd, quick-
    temper'd, not bad-looking,
Ready with life or death for a friend, fond
    of women, gambled, ate hearty, drank hearty,
Had known what it was to be flush, grew low-
    spirited toward the last, sicken'd, was help'd
    by a contribution,
Died, aged forty-one years—and that was his
    funeral.

Thumb extended, finger uplifted, apron, cape,
    gloves, strap, wet-weather clothes, whip
    carefully chosen,

Boss, spotter, starter, hostler, somebody loafing
 on you, you loafing on somebody, headway,
 man before and man behind,
Good day's work, bad day's work, pet stock,
 mean stock, first out, last out, turning-in at
 night,
To think that these are so much and so nigh to
 other drivers, and he there takes no interest in
 them.

5

The markets, the government, the working-
 man's wages, to think what account they are
 through our nights and days,
To think that other working-men will make just
 as great account of them, yet we make little
 or no account.

The vulgar and the refined, what you call sin
 and what you call goodness, to think how
 wide a difference,
To think the difference will still continue to
 others, yet we lie beyond the difference.

To think how much pleasure there is,
Do you enjoy yourself in the city? or engaged in
 business? or planning a nomination and
 election? or with your wife and family?
Or with your mother and sisters? or in womanly
 housework? or the beautiful maternal cares?

These also flow onward to others, you and I
    flow onward,
But in due time you and I shall take less interest
    in them.

Your farm, profits, crops—to think how
    engross'd you are,
To think there will still be farms, profits, crops,
    yet for you of what avail?

6

What will be will be well, for what is is well,
To take interest is well, and not to take interest
    shall be well.

The domestic joys, the daily housework or
    business, the building of houses, are not
    phantasms, they have weight, form,
    location,
Farms, profits, crops, markets, wages,
    government, are none of them phantasms,
The difference between sin and goodness is no
    delusion,
The earth is not an echo, man and his life and
    all the things of his life are well-consider'd.

You are not thrown to the winds, you gather
    certainly and safely around yourself,
Yourself! yourself! yourself, for ever and ever!

7

It is not to diffuse you that you were born of
    your mother and father, it is to identify you,
It is not that you should be undecided, but that
    you should be decided,
Something long preparing and formless is
    arrived and form'd in you,
You are henceforth secure, whatever comes or goes.

The threads that were spun are gather'd, the wet
    crosses the warp, the pattern is systematic.

The preparations have every one been justified,
The orchestra have sufficiently tuned their
    instruments, the baton has given the signal.

The guest that was coming, he waited long, he
    is now housed,
He is one of those who are beautiful and happy,
    he is one of those that to look upon and be
    with is enough.

The law of the past cannot be eluded,
The law of the present and future cannot be
    eluded,
The law of the living cannot be eluded, it is
    eternal,
The law of promotion and transformation
    cannot be eluded,

The law of heroes and good-doers cannot be
eluded,
The law of drunkards, informers, mean persons,
not one iota thereof can be eluded.

8

Slow moving and black lines go ceaselessly over
the earth,
Northerner goes carried and Southerner goes
carried, and they on the Atlantic side and they
on the Pacific,
And they between, and all through the
Mississippi country, and all over the earth.

The great masters and kosmos are well as
they go, the heroes and good-doers are
well,
The known leaders and inventors and the rich
owners and pious and distinguish'd may be
well,
But there is more account than that, there is
strict account of all.

The interminable hordes of the ignorant and
wicked are not nothing,
The barbarians of Africa and Asia are not
nothing,
The perpetual successions of shallow people are
not nothing as they go.

Of and in all these things,
I have dream'd that we are not to be changed
   so much, nor the law of us changed,
I have dream'd that heroes and good-doers
   shall be under the present and past
   law,
And that murderers, drunkards, liars, shall be
   under the present and past law,
For I have dream'd that the law they are under
   now is enough.

And I have dream'd that the purpose and
   essence of the known life, the transient,
Is to form and decide identity for the unknown
   life, the permanent.

If all came but to ashes of dung,
If maggots and rats ended us, then Alarum! for
   we are betray'd,
Then indeed suspicion of death.

Do you suspect death? if I were to suspect death
   I should die now,
Do you think I could walk pleasantly and well-
   suited toward annihilation?

Pleasantly and well-suited I walk,
Whither I walk I cannot define, but I know it is
   good,

The whole universe indicates that it is good,
The past and the present indicate that it is good.

How beautiful and perfect are the animals!
How perfect the earth, and the minutest thing
   upon it!
What is called good is perfect, and what is called
   bad is just as perfect,
The vegetables and minerals are all perfect, and
   the imponderable fluids perfect;
Slowly and surely they have pass'd on to this,
   and slowly and surely they yet pass on.

9

I swear I think now that every thing without
   exception has an eternal soul!
The trees have, rooted in the ground! the weeds
   of the sea have! the animals!

I swear I think there is nothing but immortality!
That the exquisite scheme is for it, and the
   nebulous float is for it, and the cohering is for
   it!
And all preparation is for it—and identity is for
   it—and life and materials are altogether for it!
Darest Thou Now O Soul

DAREST thou now O soul,
Walk out with me toward the unknown region,

Where neither ground is for the feet nor any
    path to follow?

No map there, nor guide,
Nor voice sounding, nor touch of human hand,
Nor face with blooming flesh, nor lips, nor eyes,
    are in that land.

I know it not O soul,
Nor dost thou, all is a blank before us,
All waits undream'd of in that region, that
    inaccessible land.

Till when the ties loosen,
All but the ties eternal, Time and Space,
Nor darkness, gravitation, sense, nor any bounds
    bounding us.

Then we burst forth, we float,
In Time and Space O soul, prepared for them,
Equal, equipt at last, (O joy! O fruit of all!)
    them to fulfil O soul.

Whispers of Heavenly Death

WHISPERS of heavenly death murmur'd I hear,
Labial gossip of night, sibilant chorals,
Footsteps gently ascending, mystical breezes
    waited soft and low,
Ripples of unseen rivers, tides of a current
    flowing, forever flowing,
(Or is it the plashing of tears? the measureless
    waters of human tears?)

I see, just see skyward, great cloud-masses,
Mournfully slowly they roll, silently swelling and
    mixing,
With at times a half-dimm'd sadden'd far-off
    star,
Appearing and disappearing.

(Some parturition rather, some solemn immortal
    birth;
On the frontiers to eyes impenetrable,
Some soul is passing over.)

CHANTING THE SQUARE DEIFIC

1

CHANTING the square deific, out of the One
    advancing, out of the sides,
Out of the old and new, out of the square
    entirely divine,
Solid, four-sided, (all the sides needed,) from
    this side Jehovah am I,
Old Brahm I, and I Saturnius am;
Not Time affects me—I am Time, old, modern
    as any,
Unpersuadable, relentless, executing righteous
    judgments,
As the Earth, the Father, the brown old Kronos,
    with laws,
Aged beyond computation, yet never new, ever
    with those mighty laws rolling,
Relentless I forgive no man—whoever sins
    dies—I will have that man's life;
Therefore let none expect mercy—have the
    seasons, gravitation, the appointed days,
    mercy? no more have I,
But as the seasons and gravitation, and as all the
    appointed days that forgive not,
I dispense from this side judgments inexorable
    without the least remorse.

2

Consolator most mild, the promis'd one
    advancing,
With gentle hand extended, the mightier God
    am I,
Foretold by prophets and poets in their most
    rapt prophecies and poems,
From this side, lo! the Lord Christ gazes—lo!
    Hermes I—lo! mine is Hercules' face,
All sorrow, labor, suffering, I, tallying it, absorb
    in myself,
Many times have I been rejected, taunted, put in
    prison, and crucified, and many times shall be
    again,
All the world have I given up for my dear
    brothers' and sisters' sake, for the soul's
    sake,
Wanding my way through the homes of men,
    rich or poor, with the kiss of affection,
For I am affection, I am the cheer-bringing
    God, with hope and all-enclosing charity,
With indulgent words as to children, with fresh
    and sane words, mine only,
Young and strong I pass knowing well I am
    destin'd myself to an early death;
But my charity has no death—my wisdom dies
    not, neither early nor late,
And my sweet love bequeath'd here and
    elsewhere never dies.

3

Aloof, dissatisfied, plotting revolt,
Comrade of criminals, brother of slaves,
Crafty, despised, a drudge, ignorant,
With sudra face and worn brow, black, but in
the depths of my heart, proud as any,
Lifted now and always against whoever scorning
assumes to rule me,
Morose, full of guile, full of reminiscences,
brooding, with many wiles,
(Though it was thought I was baffled, and
dispel'd, and my wiles done, but that will
never be,)
Defiant, I, Satan, still live, still utter words, in
new lands duly appearing, (and old ones also,)
Permanent here from my side, warlike, equal
with any, real as any,
Nor time nor change shall ever change me or
my words.

4

Santa Spirita, breather, life,
Beyond the light, lighter than light,
Beyond the flames of hell, joyous, leaping easily
above hell,
Beyond Paradise, perfumed solely with mine
own perfume,
Including all life on earth, touching, including
God, including Saviour and Satan,

Ethereal, pervading all, (for without me what
  were all? what were God?)
Essence of forms, life of the real identities,
  permanent, positive, (namely the unseen,)
Life of the great round world, the sun and stars,
  and of man, I, the general soul,
Here the square finishing, the solid, I the most
  solid,
Breathe my breath also through these songs.

OF HIM I LOVE DAY AND NIGHT

OF him I love day and night I dream'd I heard
  he was dead,
And I dream'd I went where they had buried
  him I love, but he was not in that place,
And I dream'd I wander'd searching among
  burial-places to find him,
And I found that every place was a burial-place;
The houses full of life were equally full of death,
  (this house is now,)
The streets, the shipping, the places of
  amusement, the Chicago, Boston,
  Philadelphia, the Mannahatta, were as full of
  the dead as of the living,
And fuller, O vastly fuller of the dead than of
  the living;
And what I dream'd I will henceforth tell to
  every person and age,

And I stand henceforth bound to what I
    dream'd,
And now I am willing to disregard burial-places
    and dispense with them,
And if the memorials of the dead were put up
    indifferently everywhere, even in the room
    where I eat or sleep, I should be satisfied,
And if the corpse of any one I love, or if my
    own corpse, be duly render'd to powder and
    pour'd in the sea, I shall be satisfied,
Or if it be distributed to the winds I shall be
    satisfied.

YET, YET, YE DOWNCAST HOURS

YET, yet, ye downcast hours, I know ye also,
Weights of lead, how ye clog and cling at my
    ankles,
Earth to a chamber of mourning turns—I hear
    the o'erweening, mocking voice,
Matter is conqueror—matter, triumphant only,
    continues onward.

Despairing cries float ceaselessly toward me,
The call of my nearest lover, putting forth,
    alarm'd, uncertain,
The sea I am quickly to sail, come tell me,
Come tell me where I am speeding, tell me my
    destination.

I understand your anguish, but I cannot help
    you,
I approach, hear, behold, the sad mouth, the
    look out of the eyes, your mute inquiry,
Whither I go from the bed I recline on, come
    tell me,—
Old age, alarm'd, uncertain—a young woman's
    voice, appealing to me for comfort;
A young man's voice, Shall I not escape?

As If a Phantom Caress'd Me

AS if a phantom caress'd me,
I thought I was not alone walking here by the
    shore;
But the one I thought was with me as now I
    walk by the shore, the one I loved that
    caress'd me,
As I lean and look through the glimmering
    light, that one has utterly disappear'd.
And those appear that are hateful to me and
    mock me.

Assurances

I NEED no assurances, I am a man who is
    preoccupied of his own soul;

I do not doubt that from under the feet and
    beside the hands and face I am cognizant of,
    are now looking faces I am not cognizant of,
    calm and actual faces,
I do not doubt but the majesty and beauty of
    the world are latent in any iota of the world,
I do not doubt I am limitless, and that the
    universes are limitless, in vain I try to think
    how limitless,
I do not doubt that the orbs and the systems of
    orbs play their swift sports through the air on
    purpose, and that I shall one day be eligible
    to do as much as they, and more than they,
I do not doubt that temporary affairs keep on
    and on millions of years,
I do not doubt interiors have their interiors, and
    exteriors have their exteriors, and that the
    eyesight has another eyesight, and the hearing
    another hearing, and the voice another voice,
I do not doubt that the passionately-wept deaths
    of young men are provided for, and that the
    deaths of young women and the deaths of
    little children are provided for,
(Did you think Life was so well provided for,
    and Death, the purport of all Life, is not well
    provided for?)
I do not doubt that wrecks at sea, no matter
    what the horrors of them, no matter whose
    wife, child, husband, father, lover, has gone

down, are provided for, to the minutest
points,
I do not doubt that whatever can possibly
happen anywhere at any time, is provided for
in the inherences of things,
I do not think Life provides for all and for Time
and Space, but I believe Heavenly Death
provides for all.

QUICKSAND YEARS

QUICKSAND years that whirl me I know not
whither,
Your schemes, politics, fail, lines give way,
substances mock and elude me,
Only the theme I sing, the great and strong-
possess'd soul, eludes not,
One's-self must never give way—that is the final
substance—that out of all is sure,
Out of politics, triumphs, battles, life, what at
last finally remains?
When shows break up what but One's-Self is
sure?

THAT MUSIC ALWAYS ROUND ME

THAT MUSIC always round me, unceasing,
unbeginning, yet long untaught I did not hear,

But now the chorus I hear and am elated,
A tenor, strong, ascending with power and
  health, with glad notes of daybreak I
  hear,
A soprano at intervals sailing buoyantly over the
  tops of immense waves,
A transparent base shuddering lusciously under
  and through the universe,
The triumphant tutti, the funeral wailings with
  sweet flutes and violins, all these I fill myself
  with,
I hear not the volumes of sound merely, I am
  moved by the exquisite meanings,
I listen to the different voices winding in and
  out, striving, contending with fiery
  vehemence to excel each other in emotion;
I do not think the performers know themselves-
  but now I think begin to know them.

WHAT SHIP PUZZLED AT SEA

WHAT ship puzzled at sea, cons for the true
  reckoning?
Or coming in, to avoid the bars and follow the
  channel a perfect pilot needs?
Here, sailor! here, ship! take aboard the most
  perfect pilot,
Whom, in a little boat, putting off and rowing, I
  hailing you offer.

A Noiseless Patient Spider

A NOISELESS patient spider,
I mark'd where on a little promontory it stood
    isolated,
Mark'd how to explore the vacant vast
    surrounding,
It launch'd forth filament, filament, filament out
    of itself,
Ever unreeling them, ever tirelessly speeding
    them.

And you O my soul where you stand,
Surrounded, detached, in measureless oceans of
    space,
Ceaselessly musing, venturing, throwing, seeking
    the spheres to connect them,
Till the bridge you will need be form'd, till the
    ductile anchor hold,
Till the gossamer thread you fling catch
    somewhere, O my soul.

O Living Always, Always Dying

O LIVING always, always dying!
O the burials of me past and present,
O me while I stride ahead, material, visible,
    imperious as ever;

O me, what I was for years, now dead, (I lament
    not, I am content;)
O to disengage myself from those corpses of me,
    which I turn and look at where I cast them,
To pass on, (O living! always living!) and leave
    the corpses behind.

TO ONE SHORTLY TO DIE

FROM all the rest I single out you, having a
    message for you,
You are to die—let others tell you what they
    please, I cannot prevaricate,
I am exact and merciless, but I love you—there
    is no escape for you.

Softly I lay my right hand upon you, you 'ust
    feel it,
I do not argue, I bend my head close and half
    envelop it,
I sit quietly by, I remain faithful,
I am more than nurse, more than parent or
    neighbor,
I absolve you from all except yourself spiritual
    bodily, that is eternal, you yourself will surely
    escape,
The corpse you will leave will be but
    excrementitious.

The sun bursts through in unlooked-for
  directions,
Strong thoughts fill you and confidence, you
  smile,
You forget you are sick, as I forget you are
  sick,
You do not see the medicines, you do not mind
  the weeping friends, I am with you,
I exclude others from you, there is nothing to
  be commiserated,
I do not commiserate, I congratulate you.

NIGHT ON THE PRAIRIES

NIGHT on the prairies,
The supper is over, the fire on the ground burns
  low,
The wearied emigrants sleep, wrapt in their
  blankets;
I walk by myself—I stand and look at the stars,
  which I think now never realized before.

Now I absorb immortality and peace,
I admire death and test propositions.

How plenteous! how spiritual! how resume!
The same old man and soul—the same old
  aspirations, and the same content.

I was thinking the day most splendid till I saw
    what the not-day exhibited,
I was thinking this globe enough till there
    sprang out so noiseless around me myriads of
    other globes.

Now while the great thoughts of space and
    eternity fill me I will measure myself by them,
And now touch'd with the lives of other globes
    arrived as far along as those of the earth,
Or waiting to arrive, or pass'd on farther than
    those of the earth,
I henceforth no more ignore them than I ignore
    my own life,
Or the lives of the earth arrived as far as mine,
    or waiting to arrive.

O I see now that life cannot exhibit all to me, as
    the day cannot,
I see that I am to wait for what will be exhibited
    by death.

THOUGHT

AS I sit with others at a great feast, suddenly
    while the music is playing,
To my mind, (whence it comes I know not,)
    spectral in mist of a wreck at sea,

Of certain ships, how they sail from port with
    flying streamers and waited kisses, and that is
    the last of them,
Of the solemn and murky mystery about the fate
    of the President,
Of the flower of the marine science of fifty
    generations founder'd off the Northeast coast
    and going down—of the steamship Arctic
    going down,
Of the veil'd tableau—women gather'd together
    on deck, pale, heroic, waiting the moment
    that draws so close—O the moment!

A huge sob—a few bubbles—the white foam
    spirting up—and then the women gone,
Sinking there while the passionless wet flows
    on—and I now pondering, Are those women
    indeed gone?
Are souls drown'd and destroy'd so?
Is only matter triumphant?

The Last Invocation

AT the last, tenderly,
From the walls of the powerful fortress'd house,
From the clasp of the knitted locks, from the
    keep of the well-closed doors,
Let me be wafted.

Let me glide noiselessly forth;
With the key of softness unlock the locks—
    with a whisper,
Set ope the doors O soul.

Tenderly—be not impatient,
(Strong is your hold O mortal flesh,
Strong is your hold O love.)
As I Watch the Ploughman Ploughing

AS I watch'd the ploughman ploughing,
Or the sower sowing in the fields, or the
    harvester harvesting,
I saw there too, O life and death, your
    analogies;
(Life, life is the tillage, and Death is the harvest
    according.)

PENSIVE AND FALTERING

PENSIVE and faltering,
The words the Dead I write,
For living are the Dead,
(Haply the only living, only real,
And I the apparition, I the spectre.)

Thou Mother with Thy Equal Brood

THOU Mother with thy equal brood,
Thou varied chain of different States, yet one
   identity only,
A special song before I go I'd sing o'er all the
   rest,
For thee, the future.

I'd sow a seed for thee of endless Nationality,
I'd fashion thy ensemble including body and
   soul,
I'd show away ahead thy real Union, and how it
   may be accomplish'd.

The paths to the house I seek to make,
But leave to those to come the house itself.

Belief I sing, and preparation;
As Life and Nature are not great with reference
   to the present only,
But greater still from what is yet to come,
Out of that formula for thee I sing.

As a strong bird on pinions free,
Joyous, the amplest spaces heavenward cleaving,

Such be the thought I'd think of thee America,
Such be the recitative I'd bring for thee.

The conceits of the poets of other lands I'd
    bring thee not,
Nor the compliments that have served their turn
    so long,
Nor rhyme, nor the classics, nor perfume of
    foreign court or indoor library;
But an odor I'd bring as from forests of pine in
    Maine, or breath of an Illinois prairie,
With open airs of Virginia or Georgia or
    Tennessee, or from Texas uplands, or
    Florida's glades,
Or the Saguenay's black stream, or the wide
    blue spread of Huron,
With presentment of Yellowstone's scenes, or
    Yosemite,
And murmuring under, pervading all, I'd bring
    the rustling sea-sound,
That endlessly sounds from the two Great Seas
    of the world.

And for thy subtler sense subtler refrains dread
    Mother,
Preludes of intellect tallying these and thee,
    mind-formulas fitted for thee, real and sane
    and large as these and thee,
Thou! mounting higher, diving deeper than we
    knew, thou transcendental Union!

By thee fact to be justified, blended with
   thought,
Thought of man justified, blended with God,
Through thy idea, lo, the immortal reality!
Through thy reality, lo, the immortal idea!

3

Brain of the New World, what a task is thine,
To formulate the Modern—out of the peerless
   grandeur of the modern,
Out of thyself, comprising science, to recast
   poems, churches, art,
(Recast, may-be discard them, end them—
   maybe their work is done, who knows?)
By vision, hand, conception, on the background
   of the mighty past, the dead,
To limn with absolute faith the mighty living
   present.

And yet thou living present brain, heir of the
   dead, the Old World brain,
Thou that lay folded like an unborn babe within
   its folds so long,
Thou carefully prepared by it so long-haply thou
   but unfoldest it, only maturest it,
It to eventuate in thee—the essence of the by-
   gone time contain'd in thee,
Its poems, churches, arts, unwitting to
   themselves, destined with reference to thee;

Thou but the apples, long, long, long
  a-growing,
The fruit of all the Old ripening to-day in thee.

4

Sail, sail thy best, ship of Democracy,
Of value is thy freight, 'tis not the Present only,
The Past is also stored in thee,
Thou holdest not the venture of thyself alone,
  not of the Western continent alone,
Earth's resume entire floats on thy keel O ship,
  is steadied by thy spars,
With thee Time voyages in trust, the antecedent
  nations sink or swim with thee,
With all their ancient struggles, martyrs, heroes,
  epics, wars, thou bear'st the other continents,
Theirs, theirs as much as thine, the destination-
  port triumphant;
Steer then with good strong hand and wary eye
  O helmsman, thou carriest great companions,
Venerable priestly Asia sails this day with thee,
And royal feudal Europe sails with thee.

5

Beautiful world of new superber birth that rises
  to my eyes,
Like a limitless golden cloud filling the westernr
  sky,
Emblem of general maternity lifted above all,

Sacred shape of the bearer of daughters and
     sons,
Out of thy teeming womb thy giant babes in
     ceaseless procession issuing,
Acceding from such gestation, taking and giving
     continual strength and life,
World of the real—world of the twain in one,
World of the soul, born by the world of the real
     alone, led to identity, body, by it alone,
Yet in beginning only, incalculable masses of
     composite precious materials,
By history's cycles forwarded, by every nation,
     language, hither sent,
Ready, collected here, a freer, vast, electric
     world, to be constructed here,
(The true New World, the world of orbic
     science, morals, literatures to come,)
Thou wonder world yet undefined, unform'd,
     neither do I define thee,
How can I pierce the impenetrable blank of the
     future?
I feel thy ominous greatness evil as well as good,
I watch thee advancing, absorbing the present,
     transcending the past,
I see thy light lighting, and thy shadow
     shadowing, as if the entire globe,
But I do not undertake to define thee, hardly to
     comprehend thee,
I but thee name, thee prophesy, as now,
I merely thee ejaculate!

Thee in thy future,
Thee in thy only permanent life, career, thy own
unloosen'd mind, thy soaring spirit,
Thee as another equally needed sun, radiant,
ablaze, swift-moving, fructifying all,
Thee risen in potent cheerfulness and joy, in
endless great hilarity,
Scattering for good the cloud that hung so long,
that weigh'd so long upon the mind of man,
The doubt, suspicion, dread, of gradual, certain
decadence of man;
Thee in thy larger, saner brood of female,
male—thee in thy athletes, moral, spiritual,
South, North, West, East,
(To thy immortal breasts, Mother of All, thy
every daughter, son, endear'd alike, forever
equal,)
Thee in thy own musicians, singers, artists,
unborn yet, but certain,
Thee in thy moral wealth and civilization, (until
which thy proudest material civilization must
remain in vain,)
Thee in thy all-supplying, all-enclosing worship-
thee in no single bible, savior, merely,
Thy saviours countless, latent within thyself, thy
bibles incessant within thyself, equal to any,
divine as any,
(Thy soaring course thee formulating, not in thy
two great wars, nor in thy century's visible
growth,

But far more in these leaves and chants, thy
     chants, great Mother!)
Thee in an education grown of thee, in teachers,
     studies, students, born of thee,
Thee in thy democratic fetes en-masse, thy high
     original festivals, operas, lecturers, preachers,
Thee in thy ultimate, (the preparations only now
     completed, the edifice on sure foundations
     tied,)
Thee in thy pinnacles, intellect, thought, thy
     topmost rational joys, thy love and godlike
     aspiration,
In thy resplendent coming literati, thy full-
     lung'd orators, thy sacerdotal bards, kosmic
     savans,
These! these in thee, (certain to come,) to-day I
     prophesy.

6

Land tolerating all, accepting all, not for the
     good alone, all good for thee,
Land in the realms of God to be a realm unto
     thyself,
Under the rule of God to be a rule unto thyself.

(Lo, where arise three peerless stars,
To be thy natal stars my country, Ensemble,
     Evolution, Freedom,
Set in the sky of Law.)

Land of unprecedented faith, God's faith,
Thy soil, thy very subsoil, all upheav'd,
The general inner earth so long so sedulously
    draped over, now hence for what it is boldly
    laid bare,
Open'd by thee to heaven's light for benefit or
    bale.

Not for success alone,
Not to fair-sail unintermitted always,
The storm shall dash thy face, the murk of war
    and worse than war shall cover thee all over,
(Wert capable of war, its tug and trials? be
    capable of peace, its trials,
For the tug and mortal strain of nations come at
    last in prosperous peace, not war;)
In many a smiling mask death shall approach
    beguiling thee, thou in disease shalt swelter,
The livid cancer spread its hideous claws,
    clinging upon thy breasts, seeking to strike
    thee deep within,
Consumption of the worst, moral consumption,
    shall rouge thy face with hectic,
But thou shalt face thy fortunes, thy diseases,
    and surmount them all,
Whatever they are to-day and whatever through
    time they may be,
They each and all shall lift and pass away and
    cease from thee,

While thou, Time's spirals rounding, out of
    thyself, thyself still extricating, fusing,
Equable, natural, mystical Union thou, (the
    mortal with immortal blent,)
Shalt soar toward the fulfilment of the future,
    the spirit of the body and the mind,
The soul, its destinies.

The soul, its destinies, the real real,
(Purport of all these apparitions of the real;)
In thee America, the soul, its destinies,
Thou globe of globes! thou wonder nebulous!
By many a throe of heat and cold convuls'd, (by
    these thyself solidifying,)
Thou mental, moral orb—thou New, indeed
    new, Spiritual World!
The Present holds thee not—for such vast
    growth as thine,
For such unparallel'd flight as thine, such brood
    as thine,
The FUTURE only holds thee and can hold
    thee.

A Paumanok Picture

Two boats with nets lying off the sea-beach,
  quite still,
Ten fishermen waiting—they discover a thick
  school of mossbonkers—they drop the join'd
  seine-ends in the water,
The boats separate and row off, each on its
  rounding course to the beach, enclosing the
  mossbonkers,
The net is drawn in by a windlass by those who
  stop ashore,
Some of the fishermen lounge in their boats,
  others stand ankle—deep in the water, pois'd
  on strong legs,
The boats partly drawn up, the water slapping
  against them,
Strew'd on the sand in heaps and windrows, well
  out from the water, the green-back'd spotted
  mossbonkers.

Thou Orb Aloft Full-Dazzling

THOU orb aloft full-dazzling! thou hot
  October noon!
Flooding with sheeny light the gray beach sand,
The sibilant near sea with vistas far and foam,

And tawny streaks and shades and spreading
    blue;
O sun of noon refulgent! my special word to
    thee.

Hear me illustrious!
Thy lover me, for always I have loved thee,
Even as basking babe, then happy boy alone by
    some wood edge, thy touching-distant beams
    enough,
Or man matured, or young or old, as now to
    thee I launch my invocation.

(Thou canst not with thy dumbness me deceive,
I know before the fitting man all Nature yields,
Though answering not in words, the skies, trees,
    hear his voice-and thou O sun,
As for thy throes, thy perturbations, sudden
    breaks and shafts of flame gigantic,
I understand them, I know those flames, those
    perturbations well.)

Thou that with fructifying heat and light,
O'er myriad farms, o'er lands and waters North
    and South,
O'er Mississippi's endless course, o'er Texas'
    grassy plains, Kanada's woods,
O'er all the globe that turns its face to thee
    shining in space,

Thou that impartially enfoldest all, not only
    continents, seas,
Thou that to grapes and weeds and little wild
    flowers givest so liberally,
Shed, shed thyself on mine and me, with but a
    fleeting ray out of thy million millions,
Strike through these chants.

Nor only launch thy subtle dazzle and thy
    strength for these,
Prepare the later afternoon of me myself—
    prepare my lengthening shadows,
Prepare my starry nights.

From Noon to Starry Night

FACES

1

SAUNTERING the pavement or riding the
country by-road, faces!
Faces of friendship, precision, caution, suavity,
ideality,
The spiritual-prescient face, the always welcome
common benevolent face,
The face of the singing of music, the grand faces
of natural lawyers and judges broad at the
back-top,
The faces of hunters and fishers bulged at the
brows, the shaved blanch'd faces of orthodox
citizens,
The pure, extravagant, yearning, questioning
artist's face,
The ugly face of some beautiful soul, the
handsome detested or despised face,
The sacred faces of infants, the illuminated face
of the mother of many children,
The face of an amour, the face of veneration,
The face as of a dream, the face of an immobile
rock,
The face withdrawn of its good and bad, a
castrated face,

A wild hawk, his wings clipp'd by the clipper,
A stallion that yielded at last to the thongs and
   knife of the gelder.

Sauntering the pavement thus, or crossing the
   ceaseless ferry, faces and faces and faces,
I see them and complain not, and am content
   with all.

2

Do you suppose I could be content with all if I
   thought them their own finale?

This now is too lamentable a face for a man,
Some abject louse asking leave to be, cringing
   for it,
Some milk-nosed maggot blessing what lets it
   wrig to its hole.

This face is a dog's snout sniffing for garbage,
Snakes nest in that mouth, I hear the sibilant
   threat.

This face is a haze more chill than the arctic sea,
Its sleepy and wobbling icebergs crunch as they go.

This is a face of bitter herbs, this an emetic, they
   need no label,
And more of the drug-shelf, laudanum,
   caoutchouc, or hog's-lard.

This face is an epilepsy, its wordless tongue gives
    out the unearthly cry,
Its veins down the neck distend, its eyes roll till
    they show nothing but their whites,
Its teeth grit, the palms of the hands are cut by
    the turn'd-in nails,
The man falls struggling and foaming to the
    ground, while he speculates well.

This face is bitten by vermin and worms,
And this is some murderer's knife with a half-
    pull'd scabbard.

This face owes to the sexton his dismalest
    fee,
An unceasing death-bell tolls there.

3

Features of my equals would you trick me with
    your creas'd and cadaverous march?
Well, you cannot trick me.

I see your rounded never-erased flow,
I see 'neath the rims of your haggard and mean
    disguises.

Splay and twist as you like, poke with the
    tangling fores of fishes or rats,
You'll be unmuzzled, you certainly will.

I saw the face of the most smear'd and
    slobbering idiot they had at the asylum,
And I knew for my consolation what they knew
    not,
I knew of the agents that emptied and broke my
    brother,
The same wait to clear the rubbish from the
    fallen tenement,
And I shall look again in a score or two of ages,
And I shall meet the real landlord perfect and
    unharm'd, every inch as good as myself.

4

The Lord advances, and yet advances,
Always the shadow in front, always the reach'd
    hand bringing up the laggards.

Out of this face emerge banners and horses—
    O superb! I see what is coming,
I see the high pioneer-caps, see staves of runners
    clearing the way,
I hear victorious drums.

This face is a life-boat,
This is the face commanding and bearded, it
    asks no odds of the rest,
This face is flavor'd fruit ready for eating,
This face of a healthy honest boy is the
    programme of all good.

These faces bear testimony slumbering or awake,
They show their descent from the Master
  himself.

Off the word I have spoken I except not one-
  red, white, black, are all deific,
In each house is the ovum, it comes forth after a
  thousand years.

Spots or cracks at the windows do not disturb
  me,
Tall and sufficient stand behind and make signs
  to me,
I read the promise and patiently wait.

This is a full-grown lily's face,
She speaks to the limber-hipp'd man near the
  garden pickets,
Come here she blushingly cries, Come nigh to
  me limber-hipp'd man,
Stand at my side till I lean as high as I can upon
  you,
Fill me with albescent honey, bend down to me,
Rub to me with your chafing beard, rub to my
  breast and shoulders.

5

The old face of the mother of many children,
Whist! I am fully content.

Lull'd and late is the smoke of the First-day
    morning,
It hangs low over the rows of trees by the
    fences,
It hangs thin by the sassafras and wild-cherry
    and cat-brier under them.

I saw the rich ladies in full dress at the soiree,
I heard what the singers were singing so long,
Heard who sprang in crimson youth from the
    white froth and the water-blue.

Behold a woman!
She looks out from her quaker cap, her face is
    clearer and more beautiful than the sky.

She sits in an armchair under the shaded porch
    of the farmhouse,
The sun just shines on her old white head.

Her ample gown is of cream-hued linen,
Her grandsons raised the flax, and her grand-
    daughters spun it with the distaff and the
    wheel.

The melodious character of the earth,
The finish beyond which philosophy cannot go
    and does not wish to go,
The justified mother of men.

The Mystic Trumpeter

1

HARK, some wild trumpeter, some strange
  musician,
Hovering unseen in air, vibrates capricious tunes
  to-night.

I hear thee trumpeter, listening alert I catch thy
    notes,
Now pouring, whirling like a tempest round me,
Now low, subdued, now in the distance lost.

2

Come nearer bodiless one, haply in thee
    resounds
Some dead composer, haply thy pensive life
Was fill'd with aspirations high, unform'd ideals,
Waves, oceans musical, chaotically surging,
That now ecstatic ghost, close to me bending,
  thy cornet echoing, pealing,
Gives out to no one's ears but mine, but freely
  gives to mine,
That I may thee translate.

3

Blow trumpeter free and clear, I follow thee,
While at thy liquid prelude, glad, serene,
The fretting world, the streets, the noisy hours
  of day withdraw,

A holy calm descends like dew upon me,
I walk in cool refreshing night the walks of
  Paradise,
I scent the grass, the moist air and the roses;
Thy song expands my numb'd imbonded spirit,
  thou freest, launchest me,
Floating and basking upon heaven's lake.

4

Blow again trumpeter! and for my sensuous
  eyes,
Bring the old pageants, show the feudal
  world.

What charm thy music works! thou makest pass
  before me,
Ladies and cavaliers long dead, barons are in
  their castle halls, the troubadours are singing,
Arm'd knights go forth to redress wrongs, some
  in quest of the holy Graal;
I see the tournament, I see the contestants
  incased in heavy armor seated on stately
  champing horses,
I hear the shouts, the sounds of blows and
  smiting steel;
I see the Crusaders' tumultuous armies—hark,
  how the cymbals clang,
Lo, where the monks walk in advance, bearing
  the cross on high.

5

Blow again trumpeter! and for thy theme,
Take now the enclosing theme of all, the solvent
and the setting,
Love, that is pulse of all, the sustenance and the
pang,
The heart of man and woman all for love,
No other theme but love—knitting, enclosing,
all-diffusing love.

O how the immortal phantoms crowd around
me!
I see the vast alembic ever working, I see and
know the flames that heat the world,
The glow, the blush, the beating hearts of
lovers,
So blissful happy some, and some so silent, dark,
and nigh to death;
Love, that is all the earth to lovers—love, that
mocks time and space,
Love, that is day and night—love, that is sun
and moon and stars,
Love, that is crimson, sumptuous, sick with
perfume,
No other words but words of love, no other
thought but love.

6

Blow again trumpeter—conjure war's alarums.

Swift to thy spell a shuddering hum like distant
    thunder rolls,
Lo, where the arm'd men hasten—lo, mid the
    clouds of dust the glint of bayonets,
I see the grime-faced cannoneers, I mark the
    rosy flash amid the smoke, I hear the cracking
    of the guns;
Nor war alone—thy fearful music-song, wild
    player, brings every sight of fear,
The deeds of ruthless brigands, rapine,
    murder—I hear the cries for help!
I see ships foundering at sea, I behold on deck
    and below deck the terrible tableaus.

7

O trumpeter, methinks I am myself the
    instrument thou playest,
Thou melt'st my heart, my brain—thou movest,
    drawest, changest them at will;
And now thy sullen notes send darkness through
    me,
Thou takest away all cheering light, all hope,
I see the enslaved, the overthrown, the hurt, the
    opprest of the whole earth,
I feel the measureless shame and humiliation of
    my race, it becomes all mine,

Mine too the revenges of humanity, the wrongs
    of ages, baffled feuds and hatreds,
Utter defeat upon me weighs—all—the foe
    victorious,
(Yet 'mid the ruins Pride colossal stands
    unshaken to the last,
Endurance, resolution to the last.)

8

Now trumpeter for thy close,
Vouchsafe a higher strain than any yet,
Sing to my soul, renew its languishing faith and
    hope,
Rouse up my slow belief, give me some vision of
    the future,
Give me for once its prophecy and joy.

O glad, exulting, culminating song!
A vigor more than earth's is in thy notes,
Marches of victory—man disenthral'd—the
    conqueror at last,
Hymns to the universal God from universal
    man—all joy!
A reborn race appears—a perfect world, all
    joy!
Women and men in wisdom innocence and
    health—all joy!
Riotous laughing bacchanals fill'd with joy!
War, sorrow, suffering gone—the rank earth
    purged—nothing but joy left!

The ocean fill'd with joy—the atmosphere all joy!
Joy! joy! in freedom, worship, love! joy in the
    ecstasy of life!
Enough to merely be! enough to breathe!
Joy! joy! all over joy!

To a Locomotive in Winter

THEE for my recitative,
Thee in the driving storm even as now, the
    snow, the winter-day declining,
Thee in thy panoply, thy measur'd dual
    throbbing and thy beat convulsive,
Thy black cylindric body, golden brass and
    silvery steel,
Thy ponderous side-bars, parallel and
    connecting rods, gyrating, shuttling at thy
    sides,
Thy metrical, now swelling pant and roar, now
    tapering in the distance,
Thy great protruding head-light fix'd in front,
Thy long, pale, floating vapor-pennants, tinged
    with delicate purple,
The dense and murky clouds out-belching from
    thy smoke-stack,
Thy knitted frame, thy springs and valves, the
    tremulous twinkle of thy wheels,
Thy train of cars behind, obedient, merrily
    following,

Through gale or calm, now swift, now slack, yet
    steadily careering;
Type of the modern—emblem of motion and
    power—pulse of the continent,
For once come serve the Muse and merge in
    verse, even as here I see thee,
With storm and buffeting gusts of wind and
    falling snow,
By day thy warning ringing bell to sound its
    notes,
By night thy silent signal lamps to swing.

Fierce-throated beauty!
Roll through my chant with all thy lawless
    music, thy swinging lamps at night,
Thy madly-whistled laughter, echoing, rumbling
    like an earthquake, rousing all,
Law of thyself complete, thine own track firmly
    holding,
(No sweetness debonair of tearful harp or glib
    piano thine,)
Thy trills of shrieks by rocks and hills return'd,
Launch'd o'er the prairies wide, across the lakes,
To the free skies unpent and glad and strong.

O MAGNET-SOUTH

O MAGNET-SOUTH! O glistening perfumed
    South! my South!

O quick mettle, rich blood, impulse and love!
    good and evil! O all dear to me!
O dear to me my birth-things—all moving
    things and the trees where I was born—the
    grains, plants, rivers,
Dear to me my own slow sluggish rivers where
    they flow, distant, over flats of slivery sands or
    through swamps,
Dear to me the Roanoke, the Savannah, the
    Altamahaw, the Pedee, the Tombigbee, the
    Santee, the Coosa and the Sabine,
O pensive, far away wandering, I return with my
    soul to haunt their banks again,
Again in Florida I float on transparent lakes, I
    float on the Okeechobee, I cross the
    hummock-land or through pleasant openings
    or dense forests,
I see the parrots in the woods, I see the papaw-
    tree and the blossoming titi;
Again, sailing in my coaster on deck, I coast off
    Georgia, I coast up the Carolinas,
I see where the live-oak is growing, I see where
    the yellow-pine, the scented bay-tree, the
    lemon and orange, the cypress, the graceful
    palmetto,
I pass rude sea-headlands and enter Pamlico
    sound through an inlet, and dart my vision
    inland;
O the cotton plant! the growing fields of rice,
    sugar, hemp!

The cactus guarded with thorns, the laurel-tree
with large white flowers,
The range afar, the richness and barrenness, the
old woods charged with mistletoe and trailing
moss,
The piney odor and the gloom, the awful
natural stillness, (here in these dense swamps
the freebooter carries his gun, and the fugitive
has his conceal'd hut;)
O the strange fascination of these half-known
half-impassable swamps, infested by reptiles,
resounding with the bellow of the alligator,
the sad noises of the night-owl and the wild-
cat, and the whirr of the rattlesnake,
The mocking-bird, the American mimic, singing
all the forenoon, singing through the moon-
lit night,
The humming-bird, the wild turkey, the
raccoon, the opossum;
A Kentucky corn-field, the tall, graceful, long-
leav'd corn, slender, flapping, bright green,
with tassels, with beautiful ears each well-
sheath'd in its husk;
O my heart! O tender and fierce pangs, I can
stand them not, I will depart;
O to be a Virginian where I grew up! O to be a
Carolinian!
O longings irrepressible! O I will go back to old
Tennessee and never wander more.

MANNAHATTA

I WAS asking for something specific and perfect
    for my city,
Whereupon lo! upsprang the aboriginal name.

Now I see what there is in a name, a word,
    liquid, sane, unruly, musical, self-sufficient,
I see that the word of my city is that word from
    of old,
Because I see that word nested in nests of water-
    bays, superb,
Rich, hemm'd thick all around with sailships and
    steamships, an island sixteen miles long, solid-
    founded,
Numberless crowded streets, high growths of
    iron, slender, strong, light, splendidly uprising
    toward clear skies,
Tides swift and ample, well-loved by me, toward
    sundown,
The flowing sea-currents, the little islands, larger
    adjoining islands, the heights, the villas,
The countless masts, the white shore-steamers,
    the lighters, the ferry-boats, the black sea-
    steamers well-model'd,
The down-town streets, the jobbers' houses of
    business, the houses of business of the ship-
    merchants and money-brokers, the river-
    streets,

Immigrants arriving, fifteen or twenty thousand
in a week,
The carts hauling goods, the manly race of
drivers of horses, the brown-faced sailors,
The summer air, the bright sun shining, and the
sailing clouds aloft,
The winter snows, the sleigh-bells, the broken
ice in the river, passing along up or down
with the flood-tide or ebb-tide,
The mechanics of the city, the masters, well-
form'd, beautiful-faced, looking you straight
in the eyes,
Trottoirs throng'd, vehicles, Broadway, the
women, the shops and shows,
A million people—manners free and superb—
open voices—hospitality—the most
courageous and friendly young men,
City of hurried and sparkling waters! city of
spires and masts!
City nested in bays! my city!

ALL IS TRUTH

O ME, man of slack faith so long,
Standing aloof, denying portions so long,
Only aware to-day of compact all-diffused truth,
Discovering to-day there is no lie or form of lie,
and can be none, but grows as inevitably
upon itself as the truth does upon itself,

Or as any law of the earth or any natural
  production of the earth does.

(This is curious and may not be realized
  immediately, but it must be realized,
I feel in myself that I represent falsehoods
  equally with the rest,
And that the universe does.)

Where has fail'd a perfect return indifferent of
  lies or the truth?
Is it upon the ground, or in water or fire? or
  in the spirit of man? or in the meat and
  blood?

Meditating among liars and retreating sternly
  into myself, I see that there are really no liars
  or lies after all,
And that nothing fails its perfect return, and
  that what are called lies are perfect returns,
And that each thing exactly represents itself and
  what has preceded it,
And that the truth includes all, and is compact
  just as much as space is compact,
And that there is no flaw or vacuum in the
  amount of the truth—but that all is truth
  without exception;
And henceforth I will go celebrate any thing I
  see or am,
And sing and laugh and deny nothing.

A RIDDLE SONG

THAT which eludes this verse and any verse,
Unheard by sharpest ear, unform'd in clearest
    eye or cunningest mind,
Nor lore nor fame, nor happiness nor wealth,
And yet the pulse of every heart and life
    throughout the world incessantly,
Which you and I and all pursuing ever ever miss,
Open but still a secret, the real of the real, an
    illusion,
Costless, vouch-safed to each, yet never man the
    owner,
Which poets vainly seek to put in rhyme,
    historians in prose,
Which sculptor never chisel'd yet, nor painter
    painted,
Which vocalist never sung, nor orator nor actor
    ever utter'd,
Invoking here and now I challenge for my song.

Indifferently, 'mid public, private haunts, in
    solitude,
Behind the mountain and the wood,
Companion of the city's busiest streets, through
    the assemblage,
It and its radiations constantly glide.

In looks of fair unconscious babes,
Or strangely in the coffin'd dead,

Or show of breaking dawn or stars by night,
As some dissolving delicate film of dreams,
Hiding yet lingering.

Two little breaths of words comprising it,
Two words, yet all from first to last comprised
    in it.

How ardently for it!
How many ships have sail'd and sunk for it!

How many travelers started from their homes
    and neer return'd!
How much of genius boldly staked and lost for it!
What countless stores of beauty, love, ventur'd
    for it!
How all superbest deeds since Time began are
    traceable to it—and shall be to the end!
How all heroic martyrdoms to it!
How, justified by it, the horrors, evils, battles of
    the earth!
How the bright fascinating lambent flames of it,
    in every age and land, have drawn men's eyes,
Rich as a sunset on the Norway coast, the sky,
    the islands, and the cliffs,
Or midnight's silent glowing northern lights
    unreachable.

Haply God's riddle it, so vague and yet so
    certain,

The soul for it, and all the visible universe for it,
And heaven at last for it.

EXCELSIOR

WHO has gone farthest? for I would go farther,
And who has been just? for I would be the most
    just person of the earth,
And who most cautious? for I would be more
    cautious,
And who has been happiest? O I think it is I—
    I think no one was ever happier than I,
And who has lavish'd all? for I lavish constantly
    the best I have,
And who proudest? for I think I have reason to
    be the proudest son alive-for I am the son of
    the brawny and tall-topt city,
And who has been bold and true? for I would
    be the boldest and truest being of the
    universe,
And who benevolent? for I would show more
    benevolence than all the rest,
And who has receiv'd the love of the most
    friends? for I know what it is to receive the
    passionate love of many friends,
And who possesses a perfect and enamour'd
    body? for I do not believe any one possesses a
    more perfect or enamour'd body than mine,

And who thinks the amplest thoughts? for I
   would surround those thoughts,
And who has made hymns fit for the earth? for I
   am mad with devouring ecstasy to make
   joyous hymns for the whole earth.

AH POVERTIES, WINCINGS, AND SULKY RETREATS

AH poverties, wincings, and sulky retreats,
Ah you foes that in conflict have overcome me,
(For what is my life or any man's life but a
   conflict with foes, the old, the incessant war?)
You degradations, you tussle with passions and
   appetites,
You smarts from dissatisfied friendships,
   (ah wounds the sharpest of all!)
You toil of painful and choked articulations, you
   meannesses,
You shallow tongue-talks at tables, (my tongue
   the shallowest of any;)
You broken resolutions, you racking angers, you
   smother'd ennuis!
Ah think not you finally triumph, my real self
   has yet to come forth,
It shall yet march forth o'ermastering, till all lies
   beneath me,
It shall yet stand up the soldier of ultimate
   victory.

THOUGHTS

OF public opinion,

Of a calm and cool fiat sooner or later, (how
impassive! how certain and final!)

Of the President with pale face asking secretly to
himself, What will the people say at last?

Of the frivolous Judge—of the corrupt
Congressman, Governor, Mayor—of such as
these standing helpless and exposed,

Of the mumbling and screaming priest, (soon,
soon deserted,)

Of the lessening year by year of venerableness,
and of the dicta of officers, statutes, pulpits,
schools,

Of the rising forever taller and stronger and
broader of the intuitions of men and women,
and of Self-esteem and Personality;

Of the true New World—of the Democracies
resplendent en-masse,

Of the conformity of politics, armies, navies, to
them,

Of the shining sun by them—of the inherent
light, greater than the rest,

Of the envelopment of all by them, and the
effusion of all from them.

MEDIUMS

THEY shall arise in the States,

They shall report Nature, laws, physiology, and happiness,

They shall illustrate Democracy and the kosmos,

They shall be alimentive, amative, perceptive,

They shall be complete women and men, their pose brawny and supple, their drink water, their blood clean and clear,

They shall fully enjoy materialism and the sight of products, they shall enjoy the sight of the beef, lumber, bread-stuffs, of Chicago the great city.

They shall train themselves to go in public to become orators and oratresses,

Strong and sweet shall their tongues be, poems and materials of poems shall come from their lives, they shall be makers and finders,

Of them and of their works shall emerge divine conveyers, to convey gospels,

Characters, events, retrospections, shall be convey'd in gospels, trees, animals, waters, shall be convey'd,

Death, the future, the invisible faith, shall all be convey'd.

Weave in, My Hardy Life

WEAVE in, weave in, my hardy life,
Weave yet a soldier strong and full for great
    campaigns to come,
Weave in red blood, weave sinews in like ropes,
    the senses, sight weave in,
Weave lasting sure, weave day and night the wet,
    the warp, incessant weave, tire not,
(We know not what the use O life, nor know the
    aim, the end, nor really aught we know,
But know the work, the need goes on and shall
    go on, the death-envelop'd march of peace as
    well as war goes on,)
For great campaigns of peace the same the wiry
    threads to weave,
We know not why or what, yet weave, forever
    weave.

Spain, 1873–74

OUT of the murk of heaviest clouds,
Out of the feudal wrecks and heap'd-up
    skeletons of kings,
Out of that old entire European debris, the
    shatter'd mummeries,
Ruin'd cathedrals, crumble of palaces, tombs of
    priests,

Lo, Freedom's features fresh undimm'd look
forth—the same immortal face looks forth;
(A glimpse as of thy Mother's face Columbia,
A flash significant as of a sword,
Beaming towards thee.)

Nor think we forget thee maternal;
Lag'd'st thou so long? shall the clouds close
again upon thee?
Ah, but thou hast thyself now appear'd to us-
we know thee,
Thou hast given us a sure proof, the glimpse of
thyself,
Thou waitest there as everywhere thy time.

BY BROAD POTOMAC'S SHORE

BY broad Potomac's shore, again old tongue,
(Still uttering, still ejaculating, canst never cease
this babble?)
Again old heart so gay, again to you, your sense,
the full flush spring returning,
Again the freshness and the odors, again
Virginia's summer sky, pellucid blue and silver,
Again the forenoon purple of the hills,
Again the deathless grass, so noiseless soft and
green,
Again the blood-red roses blooming.

Perfume this book of mine O blood-red roses!
Lave subtly with your waters every line
  Potomac!
Give me of you O spring, before I close, to put
  between its pages!
O forenoon purple of the hills, before I close,
  of you!
O deathless grass, of you!

FROM FAR DAKOTA'S CANONS
JUNE 25, 1876

FROM far Dakota's cañons,
Lands of the wild ravine, the dusky Sioux, the
  lonesome stretch, the silence,
Haply to-day a mournful wall, haply a trumpet-
  note for heroes.

The battle-bulletin,
The Indian ambuscade, the craft, the fatal
  environment,
The cavalry companies fighting to the last in
  sternest heroism,
In the midst of their little circle, with their
  slaughter'd horses for breastworks,
The fall of Custer and all his officers and men.

Continues yet the old, old legend of our race,
The loftiest of life upheld by death,

The ancient banner perfectly maintain'd,
O lesson opportune, O how I welcome thee!

As sitting in dark days,
Lone, sulky, through the time's thick murk
    looking in vain for light, for hope,
From unsuspected parts a fierce and momentary
    proof,
(The sun there at the center though conceal'd,
Electric life forever at the center,)
Breaks forth a lightning flash.

Thou of the tawny flowing hair in battle,
I erewhile saw, with erect head, pressing ever in
    front, bearing a bright sword in thy hand,
Now ending well in death the splendid fever of
    thy deeds,
(I bring no dirge for it or thee, I bring a glad
    triumphal sonnet,)
Desperate and glorious, aye in defeat most
    desperate, most glorious,
After thy many battles in which never yielding
    up a gun or a color,
Leaving behind thee a memory sweet to
    soldiers,
Thou yieldest up thyself.

OLD WAR-DREAMS

IN midnight sleep of many a face of anguish,
Of the look at first of the mortally wounded, (of
    that indescribable look,)
Of the dead on their backs with arms extended
    wide, I dream, I dream, I dream.
Of scenes of Nature, fields and mountains,
Of skies so beauteous after a storm, and at night
    the moon so unearthly bright,
Shining sweetly, shining down, where we dig the
    trenches and gather the heaps,
I dream, I dream, I dream.

Long have they pass'd, faces and trenches and
    fields,
Where through the carnage I moved with a
    callous composure, or away from the fallen,
Onward I sped at the time—but now of their
    forms at night, I dream, I dream, I dream.

THICK-SPRINKLED BUNTING

THICK-SPRINKLED bunting! flag of stars!
Long yet your road, fateful flag—long yet your
    road, and lined with bloody death,
For the prize I see at issue at last is the world,
All its ships and shores I see interwoven with
    your threads greedy banner;

Dream'd again the flags of kings, highest borne
    to flaunt unrival'd?
O hasten flag of man—O with sure and steady
    step, passing highest flags of kings,
Walk supreme to the heavens mighty symbol—
    run up above them all,
Flag of stars! thick-sprinkled bunting!
What Best I See in Thee

To U. S. G. return'd
from his World's Tour

WHAT best I see in thee,
Is not that where thou mov'st down history's
    great highways,
Ever undimm'd by time shoots warlike victory's
    dazzle,
Or that thou sat'st where Washington sat, ruling
    the land in peace,
Or thou the man whom feudal Europe feted,
    venerable Asia swarm'd upon,
Who walk'd with kings with even pace the
    round world's promenade;
But that in foreign lands, in all thy walks with
    kings,
Those prairie sovereigns of the West, Kansas,
    Missouri, Illinois,
Ohio's, Indiana's millions, comrades, farmers,
    soldiers, all to the front,

Invisibly with thee walking with kings with even
pace the round world's promenade,
Were all so justified.
Spirit That Form'd This Scene

WRITTEN IN PLATTE CANON, COLORADO

SPIRIT that form'd this scene,
These tumbled rock-piles grim and red,
These reckless heaven-ambitious peaks,
These gorges, turbulent-clear streams, this naked
freshness,
These formless wild arrays, for reasons of their
own,
I know thee, savage spirit—we have communed
together,
Mine too such wild arrays, for reasons of their
own;
Wast charged against my chants they had
forgotten art?
To fuse within themselves its rules precise and
delicatesse?
The lyrist's measur'd beat, the wrought-out
temple's grace—column and polish'd arch
forgot?
But thou that revelest here—spirit that form'd
this scene,
They have remember'd thee.

As I Walk These Broad Majestic Days

AS I walk these broad majestic days of peace,
(For the war, the struggle of blood finish'd,
    wherein, O terrific Ideal,
Against vast odds erewhile having gloriously
    won,
Now thou stridest on, yet perhaps in time
    toward denser wars,
Perhaps to engage in time in still more dreadful
    contests, dangers,
Longer campaigns and crises, labors beyond all
    others,)
Around me I hear that eclat of the world,
    politics, produce,
The announcements of recognized things,
    science,
The approved growth of cities and the spread of
    inventions.

I see the ships, (they will last a few years,)
The vast factories with their foremen and
    workmen,
And hear the indorsement of all, and do not
    object to it.

But I too announce solid things,
Science, ships, politics, cities, factories, are not
    nothing,

Like a grand procession to music of distant
    bugles pouring, triumphantly moving, and
    grander heaving in sight,
They stand for realities—all is as it should be.

Then my realities;
What else is so real as mine?
Libertad and the divine average, freedom to
    every slave on the face of the earth,
The rapt promises and lumine of seers, the
    spiritual world, these centuries-lasting songs,
And our visions, the visions of poets, the most
    solid announcements of any.

A CLEAR MIDNIGHT

THIS is thy hour O Soul, thy free flight into the
    wordless,
Away from books, away from art, the day erased,
    the lesson done,
Thee fully forth emerging, silent, gazing,
    pondering the themes thou lovest best,
Night, sleep, death and the stars.

As the Time Draws Nigh

As the time draws nigh glooming a cloud,
A dread beyond of I know not what darkens me.

I shall go forth,
I shall traverse the States awhile, but I cannot
    tell whither or how long,
Perhaps soon some day or night while I am
    singing my voice will suddenly cease.

O book, O chants! must all then amount to but
    this?
Must we barely arrive at this beginning of
    us?—and yet it is enough, O soul;
O soul, we have positively appear'd—
    that is enough.

YEARS OF THE MODERN

YEARS of the modern! years of the
    unperform'd!
Your horizon rises, I see it parting away for
    more august dramas,
I see not America only, not only Liberty's nation
    but other nations preparing,
I see tremendous entrances and exits, new
    combinations, the solidarity of races,
I see that force advancing with irresistible power
    on the world's stage,
(Have the old forces, the old wars, played their
    parts? are the acts suitable to them closed?)

I see Freedom, completely arm'd and victorious and very haughty, with Law on one side and Peace on the other,

A stupendous trio all issuing forth against the idea of caste;

What historic dénouements are these we so rapidly approach?

I see men marching and countermarching by swift millions,

I see the frontiers and boundaries of the old aristocracies broken,

I see the landmarks of European kings removed,

I see this day the People beginning their landmarks, (all others give way;)

Never were such sharp questions ask'd as this day,

Never was average man, his soul, more energetic, more like a God,

Lo, how he urges and urges, leaving the masses no rest!

His daring foot is on land and sea everywhere, he colonizes the Pacific, the archipelagoes,

With the steamship, the electric telegraph, the newspaper, the wholesale engines of war,

With these and the world-spreading factories he interlinks all geography, all lands;

What whispers are these O lands, running ahead of you, passing under the seas?

Are all nations communing? is there going to be
  but one heart to the globe?
Is humanity forming en-masse? for lo, tyrants
  tremble, crowns grow dim,
The earth, restive, confronts a new era, perhaps
  a general divine war,
No one knows what will happen next, such
  portents fill the days and nights;
Years prophetical! the space ahead as I walk, as I
  vainly try to pierce it, is full of phantoms,
Unborn deeds, things soon to be, project their
  shapes around me,
This incredible rush and heat, this strange
  ecstatic fever of dreams O years!
Your dreams O years, how they penetrate
  through me! (I know not whether I sleep or
  wake;)
The perform'd America and Europe grow dim,
  retiring in shadow behind me,
The unperform'd, more gigantic than ever,
  advance, advance upon me.

Songs of Parting

ASHES OF SOLDIERS

ASHES of soldiers South or North,
As I muse retrospective murmuring a chant in
    thought,
The war resumes, again to my sense your shapes,
And again the advance of the armies.

Noiseless as mists and vapors,
From their graves in the trenches ascending,
From cemeteries all through Virginia and
    Tennessee,
From every point of the compass out of the
    countless graves,
In waited clouds, in myriads large, or squads of
    twos or threes or single ones they come,
And silently gather round me.

Now sound no note O trumpeters,
Not at the head of my cavalry parading on
    spirited horses,
With sabres drawn and glistening, and carbines
    by their thighs, (ah my brave horsemen!
My handsome tan-faced horsemen! what life,
    what joy and pride,
With all the perils were yours.)

Nor you drummers, neither at reveille at
    dawn,
Nor the long roll alarming the camp, nor even
    the muffled beat for burial,
Nothing from you this time O drummers
    bearing my warlike drums.

But aside from these and the marts of wealth
    and the crowded promenade,
Admitting around me comrades close unseen by
    the rest and voiceless,
The slain elate and alive again, the dust and
    debris alive,
I chant this chant of my silent soul in the name
    of all dead soldiers.

Faces so pale with wondrous eyes, very dear,
    gather closer yet,
Draw close, but speak not.

Phantoms of countless lost,
Invisible to the rest henceforth become my
    companions,
Follow me ever—desert me not while I live.

Sweet are the blooming cheeks of the
    living—sweet are the musical voices
    sounding,
But sweet, ah sweet, are the dead with their
    silent eyes.

Dearest comrades, all is over and long gone,
But love is not over—and what love, O
   comrades!
Perfume from battle-fields rising, up from the
   foetor arising.

Perfume therefore my chant, O love, immortal
   love,
Give me to bathe the memories of all dead
   soldiers,
Shroud them, embalm them, cover them all over
   with tender pride.

Perfume all—make all wholesome,
Make these ashes to nourish and blossom,
O love, solve all, fructify all with the last
   chemistry.

Give me exhaustless, make me a fountain,
That I exhale love from me wherever I go like a
   moist perennial dew,
For the ashes of all dead soldiers South or North.

THOUGHTS

1

OF these years I sing,
How they pass and have pass'd through
   convuls'd pains, as through parturitions,

How America illustrates birth, muscular youth,
  the promise, the sure fulfilment, the absolute
  success, despite of people—illustrates evil as
  well as good,
The vehement struggle so fierce for unity in
  one's-self,
How many hold despairingly yet to the models
  departed, caste, myths, obedience,
  compulsion, and to infidelity,
How few see the arrived models, the athletes,
  the Western States, or see freedom or
  spirituality, or hold any faith in results,
(But I see the athletes, and I see the results of
  the war glorious and inevitable, and they
  again leading to other results.)

How the great cities appear—how the Democratic
  masses, turbulent, willful, as I love them,
How the whirl, the contest, the wrestle of evil
  with good, the sounding and resounding,
  keep on and on,
How society waits unform'd, and is for a while
  between things ended and things begun,
How America is the continent of glories, and of
  the triumph of freedom and of the
  Democracies, and of the fruits of society, and
  of all that is begun,
And how the States are complete in themselves-
  and how all triumphs and glories are complete
  in themselves, to lead onward,

And how these of mine and of the States will in
    their turn be convuls'd, and serve other
    parturitions and transitions,
And how all people, sights, combinations, the
    democratic masses too, serve—and how every
    fact, and war itself, with all its horrors, serves,
And how now or at any time each serves the
    exquisite transition of death.

2

Of seeds dropping into the ground, of births,
Of the steady concentration of America,
    inland, upward, to impregnable and swarming
    places,
Of what Indiana, Kentucky, Arkansas, and the
    rest, are to be,
Of what a few years will show there in Nebraska,
    Colorado, Nevada, and the rest,
(Or afar, mounting the Northern Pacific to Sitka
    or Alaska,)
Of what the feuillage of America is the
    preparation for—and of what all sights,
    North, South, East and West, are,
Of this Union welded in blood, of the solemn
    price paid, of the unnamed lost ever present
    in my mind;
Of the temporary use of materials for identity's
    sake,
Of the present, passing, departing—of the
    growth of completer men than any yet,

Of all sloping down there where the fresh free
    giver the mother, the Mississippi flows,
Of mighty inland cities yet unsurvey'd and
    unsuspected,
Of the new and good names, of the modern
    developments, of inalienable homesteads,
  Of a free and original life there, of simple diet
    and clean and sweet blood,
Of litheness, majestic faces, clear eyes, and
    perfect physique there,
Of immense spiritual results future years far
    West, each side of the Anahuacs,
Of these songs, well understood there, (being
    made for that area,)
Of the native scorn of grossness and gain there,
(O it lurks in me night and day-what is gain
    after all to savageness and freedom?)

SONG AT SUNSET

SPLENDOR of ended day floating and filling me,
Hour prophetic, hour resuming the past,
Inflating my throat, you divine average,
You earth and life till the last ray gleams I sing.

Open mouth of my soul uttering gladness,
Eyes of my soul seeing perfection,
Natural life of me faithfully praising things,
Corroborating forever the triumph of things.

Illustrious every one!
Illustrious what we name space, sphere of
    unnumber'd spirits,
Illustrious the mystery of motion in all beings,
    even the tiniest insect,
Illustrious the attribute of speech, the senses, the
    body,
Illustrious the passing light—illustrious the pale
    reflection on the new moon in the western
    sky,
Illustrious whatever I see or hear or touch, to
    the last.

Good in all,
In the satisfaction and aplomb of animals,
In the annual return of the seasons,
In the hilarity of youth,
In the strength and flush of manhood,
In the grandeur and exquisiteness of old age,
In the superb vistas of death.

Wonderful to depart!
Wonderful to be here!
The heart, to jet the all-alike and innocent
    blood!
To breathe the air, how delicious!
To speak—to walk—to seize something by the
    hand!
To prepare for sleep, for bed, to look on my
    rose-color'd flesh!

To be conscious of my body, so satisfied, so
    large!
To be this incredible God I am!
To have gone forth among other Gods, these
    men and women I love.

Wonderful how I celebrate you and myself
How my thoughts play subtly at the spectacles
    around!
How the clouds pass silently overhead!
How the earth darts on and on! and how the
    sun, moon, stars, dart on and on!
How the water sports and sings! (surely it is alive!)
How the trees rise and stand up, with strong
    trunks, with branches and leaves!
(Surely there is something more in each of the
    trees, some living soul.)

O amazement of things-even the least particle!
O spirituality of things!
O strain musical flowing through ages and
    continents, now reaching me and America!
I take your strong chords, intersperse them, and
    cheerfully pass them forward.

I too carol the sun, usher'd or at noon, or as
    now, setting,
I too throb to the brain and beauty of the earth
    and of all the growths of the earth,
I too have felt the resistless call of myself.

As I steam'd down the Mississippi,
As I wander'd over the prairies,
As I have lived, as I have look'd through my
    windows my eyes,
As I went forth in the morning, as I beheld the
    light breaking in the east,
As I bathed on the beach of the Eastern Sea,
    and again on the beach of the Western Sea,
As I roam'd the streets of inland Chicago,
    whatever streets I have roam'd,
Or cities or silent woods, or even amid the
    sights of war,
Wherever I have been I have charged myself
    with contentment and triumph.

I sing to the last the equalities modern or old,
I sing the endless finales of things,
I say Nature continues, glory continues,
I praise with electric voice,
For I do not see one imperfection in the
    universe,
And I do not see one cause or result lamentable
    at last in the universe.

O setting sun! though the time has come,
I still warble under you, if none else does,
    unmitigated adoration.

As at Thy Portals Also Death

AS at thy portals also death,
Entering thy sovereign, dim, illimitable grounds,
To memories of my mother, to the divine
    blending, maternity,
To her, buried and gone, yet buried not, gone
    not from me,
(I see again the calm benignant face fresh and
    beautiful still,
I sit by the form in the coffin,
I kiss and kiss convulsively again the sweet old
    lips, the cheeks, the closed eyes in the coffin;)
To her, the ideal woman, practical, spiritual, of
    all of earth, life, love, to me the best,
I grave a monumental line, before I go, amid
    these songs,
And set a tombstone here.

My Legacy

THE business man the acquirer vast,
After assiduous years surveying results, preparing
    for departure,
Devises houses and lands to his children, bequeaths
    stocks, goods, funds for a school or hospital,
Leaves money to certain companions to buy
    tokens, souvenirs of gems and gold.

But I, my life surveying, closing,
With nothing to show to devise from its idle
    years,
Nor houses nor lands, nor tokens of gems or
    gold for my friends,
Yet certain remembrances of the war for you,
    and after you,
And little souvenirs of camps and soldiers, with
    my love,
I bind together and bequeath in this bundle of
    songs.

PENSIVE ON HER DEAD GAZING

PENSIVE on her dead gazing I heard the
    Mother of All,
Desperate on the torn bodies, on the forms
    covering the battlefields gazing,
(As the last gun ceased, but the scent of the
    powder-smoke linger'd,)
As she call'd to her earth with mournful voice
    while she stalk'd,
Absorb them well O my earth, she cried, I
    charge you lose not my sons, lose not an
    atom,
And you streams absorb them well, taking their
    dear blood,
And you local spots, and you airs that swim
    above lightly impalpable,

And all you essences of soil and growth, and you
   my rivers' depths,
And you mountain sides, and the woods where
   my dear children's blood trickling redden'd,
And you trees down in your roots to bequeath
   to all future trees,
My dead absorb or South or North—my young
   men's bodies absorb, and their precious
   precious blood,
Which holding in trust for me faithfully back
   again give me many a year hence,
In unseen essence and odor of surface and grass,
   centuries hence,
In blowing airs from the fields back again give
   me my darlings, give my immortal heroes,
Exhale me them centuries hence, breathe me
   their breath, let not an atom be lost,
O years and graves! O air and soil! O my dead,
   an aroma sweet!
Exhale them perennial sweet death, years,
   centuries hence.

CAMPS OF GREEN

NOR alone those camps of white, old comrades
   of the wars,
When as order'd forward, after a long march,
Footsore and weary, soon as the light lessens we
   halt for the night,

Some of us so fatigued carrying the gun and
    knapsack, dropping asleep in our tracks,
Others pitching the little tents, and the fires lit
    up begin to sparkle,
Outposts of pickets posted surrounding alert
    through the dark,
And a word provided for countersign, careful for
    safety,
Till to the call of the drummers at daybreak
    loudly beating the drums,
We rise up refresh'd, the night and sleep pass'd
    over, and resume our journey,
Or proceed to battle.

Lo, the camps of the tents of green,
Which the days of peace keep filling, and the
    days of war keep filling,
With a mystic army, (is it too order'd forward? is
    it too only halting awhile,
Till night and sleep pass over?)

Now in those camps of green, in their tents
    dotting the world,
In the parents, children, husbands, wives, in
    them, in the old and young,
Sleeping under the sunlight, sleeping under the
    moonlight, content and silent there at last,
Behold the mighty bivouac-field and waiting-
    camp of all,

Of the corps and generals all, and the President
    over the corps and generals all,
And of each of us O soldiers, and of each and all
    in the ranks we fought,
(There without hatred we all, all meet.)

For presently O soldiers, we too camp in our
    place in the bivouac-camps of green,
But we need not provide for outposts, nor word
    for the countersign,
Nor drummer to beat the morning drum.

THE SOBBING OF THE BELLS
(MIDNIGHT, SEPT. 19–20, 1881)

THE sobbing of the bells, the sudden death-
    news everywhere,
The slumberers rouse, the rapport of the People,
(Full well they know that message in the
    darkness,
Full well return, respond within their breasts,
    their brains, the sad reverberations,)
The passionate toll and clang—city to city,
    joining, sounding, passing,
Those heart-beats of a Nation in the night.

As They Draw to a Close

AS they draw to a close,
Of what underlies the precedent songs—of my
    aims in them,
Of the seed I have sought to plant in them,
Of joy, sweet joy, through many a year, in them,
(For them, for them have I lived, in them my
    work is done,)
Of many an aspiration fond, of many a dream
    and plan;
Through Space and Time fused in a chant, and
    the flowing eternal identity,
To Nature encompassing these, encompassing
    God—to the joyous, electric all,
To the sense of Death, and accepting exulting in
    Death in its turn the same as life,
The entrance of man to sing;
To compact you, ye parted, diverse lives,
To put rapport the mountains and rocks and
    streams,
And the winds of the north, and the forests of
    oak and pine,
With you O soul.

Joy, Shipmate, Joy!

JOY, shipmate, Joy!
(Pleas'd to my soul at death I cry,)
Our life is closed, our life begins,
The long, long anchorage we leave,
The ship is clear at last, she leaps!
She swiftly courses from the shore,
Joy, shipmate, joy.

The Untold Want

THE untold want by life and land neer granted,
Now voyager sail thou forth to seek and find.

Portals

WHAT are those of the known but to ascend
    and enter the Unknown?
And what are those of life but for Death?

These Carols

THESE carols sung to cheer my passage
    through the world I see,
For completion I dedicate to the Invisible World.

Now Finale to the Shore

NOW finale to the shore,
Now land and life final and farewell,
Now Voyager depart, (much, much for thee is
  yet in store,)
Often enough hast thou adventur'd o'er the
  seas,
Cautiously cruising, studying the charts,
Duly again to port and hawser's tie returning;
But now obey thy cherish'd secret wish,
Embrace thy friends, leave all in order,
To port and hawser's tie no more returning,
Depart upon thy endless cruise old Sailor.

So Long!

TO conclude, I announce what comes after
  me.

I remember I said before my leaves sprang at all,
I would raise my voice jocund and strong with
  reference to consummations.

When America does what was promis'd,
When through these States walk a hundred
  millions of superb persons,
When the rest part away for superb persons and
  contribute to them,

When breeds of the most perfect mothers
    denote America,
Then to me and mine our due fruition.

I have press'd through in my own right,
I have sung the body and the soul, war and peace
    have I sung, and the songs of life and death,
And the songs of birth, and shown that there
    are many births.

I have offer'd my style to every one, I have
    journey'd with confident step;
While my pleasure is yet at the full I whisper So
    long!
And take the young woman's hand and the
    young man's hand for the last time.

I announce natural persons to arise,
I announce justice triumphant,
I announce uncompromising liberty and
    equality,
I announce the justification of candor and the
    justification of pride.

I announce that the identity of these States is a
    single identity only,
I announce the Union more and more compact,
    indissoluble,
I announce splendors and majesties to make all
    the previous politics of the earth insignificant.

I announce adhesiveness, I say it shall be
    limitless, unloosen'd,
I say you shall yet find the friend you were
    looking for.

I announce a man or woman coming, perhaps
    you are the one, (So long!)
I announce the great individual, fluid as Nature,
    chaste, affectionate, compassionate, fully
    arm'd.

I announce a life that shall be copious,
    vehement, spiritual, bold,
I announce an end that shall lightly and joyfully
    meet its translation.

I announce myriads of youths, beautiful,
    gigantic, sweet-blooded,
I announce a race of splendid and savage old
    men.

O thicker and faster—(So long!)
O crowding too close upon me,
I foresee too much, it means more than I
    thought,
It appears to me I am dying.

Hasten throat and sound your last,
Salute me—salute the days once more. Peal the
    old cry once more.

Screaming electric, the atmosphere using,
At random glancing, each as I notice
    absorbing,
Swiftly on, but a little while alighting,
Curious envelop'd messages delivering,
Sparkles hot, seed ethereal down in the dirt
    dropping,
Myself unknowing, my commission obeying, to
    question it never daring,
To ages and ages yet the growth of the seed
    leaving,
To troops out of the war arising, they the tasks I
    have set promulging,
To women certain whispers of myself
    bequeathing, their affection me more clearly
    explaining,
To young men my problems offering—no dallier
    I—I the muscle of their brains trying,
So I pass, a little time vocal, visible, contrary,
Afterward a melodious echo, passionately bent
    for, (death making me really undying,)
The best of me then when no longer visible, for
    toward that I have been incessantly preparing.

What is there more, that I lag and pause and
    crouch extended with unshut mouth?
Is there a single final farewell?
My songs cease, I abandon them,
From behind the screen where I hid I advance
    personally solely to you.

Camerado, this is no book,
Who touches this touches a man,
(Is it night? are we here together alone?)
It is I you hold and who holds you,
I spring from the pages into your arms- decease
    calls me forth.

O how your fingers drowse me,
Your breath falls around me like dew, your pulse
    lulls the tympans of my ears,
I feel immerged from head to foot,
Delicious, enough.

Enough O deed impromptu and secret,
Enough O gliding present—enough O
    summ'd-up past.

Dear friend whoever you are take this kiss,
I give it especially to you, do not forget me,
I feel like one who has done work for the day to
    retire awhile,
I receive now again of my many translations,
    from my avataras ascending, while others
    doubtless await me,
An unknown sphere more real than I dream'd,
    more direct, darts awakening rays about me,
    So long!
Remember my words, I may again return,
I love you, I depart from materials,
I am as one disembodied, triumphant, dead.

MANNAHATTA

MY city's fit and noble name resumed,
Choice aboriginal name, with marvellous beauty,
 meaning,
A rocky founded island-shores where ever gayly
 dash the coming, going, hurrying sea waves.

PAUMANOK

SEA-BEAUTY! stretch'd and basking!
One side thy inland ocean laving, broad, with
 copious commerce, steamers, sails,
And one the Atlantic's wind caressing, fierce or
 gentle-mighty hulls dark-gliding in the
 distance.
Isle of sweet brooks of drinking-water—healthy
 air and soil!
Isle of the salty shore and breeze and brine!

Sands at Seventy

FROM MONTAUK POINT

I STAND as on some mighty eagle's beak,
Eastward the sea absorbing, viewing, (nothing
    but sea and sky,)
The tossing waves, the foam, the ships in the
    distance,
The wild unrest, the snowy, curling caps—that
    enbound urge and urge of waves,
Seeking the shores forever.

TO THOSE WHO'VE FAIL'D

TO those who've fail'd, in aspiration vast,
To unnam'd soldiers fallen in front on the lead,
To calm, devoted engineers—to over-ardent
    travelers—to pilots on their ships,
To many a lofty song and picture without
    recognition—I'd rear laurel-cover'd
    monument,
High, high above the rest—To all cut off before
    their time,
Possess'd by some strange spirit of fire,
Quench'd by an early death.

A Carol Closing Sixty-Nine

A CAROL closing sixty-nine- a resume-
  a repetition,
My lines in joy and hope continuing on the
  same,
Of ye, O God, Life, Nature, Freedom, Poetry;
Of you, my Land—your rivers, prairies, States—
  you, mottled Flag love,
Your aggregate retain'd entire—Of north, south,
  east and west, your items all;
Of me myself—the jocund heart yet beating in
  my breast,
The body wreck'd, old, poor and paralyzed—
  the strange inertia falling pall-like round me,
The burning fires down in my sluggish blood
  not yet extinct,
The undiminish'd faith—the groups of loving
  friends.

The Bravest Soldiers

BRAVE, brave were the soldiers (high named
  to-day) who lived through the fight;
But the bravest press'd to the front and fell,
  unnamed, unknown.

A Font of Type

THIS latent mine—these unlaunch'd voices—
    passionate powers,
Wrath, argument, or praise, or comic leer, or
    prayer devout,
(Not nonpareil, brevier, bourgeois, long primer
    merely,)
These ocean waves arousable to fury and to
    death,
Or sooth'd to ease and sheeny sun and sleep,
Within the pallid slivers slumbering.

As I Sit Writing Here

AS I sit writing here, sick and grown old,
Not my least burden is that dulness of the years,
    querilities,
Ungracious glooms, aches, lethargy,
    constipation, whimpering ennui,
May filter in my dally songs.

My Canary Bird

DID we count great, O soul, to penetrate the
    themes of mighty books,
Absorbing deep and full from thoughts, plays,
    speculations?

But now from thee to me, caged bird, to feel
    thy joyous warble,
Filling the air, the lonesome room, the long
    forenoon,
Is it not just as great, O soul?

QUERIES TO MY SEVENTIETH YEAR

APPROACHING, nearing, curious,
Thou dim, uncertain spectra—bringest thou life
    or death?
Strength, weakness, blindness, more paralysis
    and heavier?
Or placid skies and sun? Wilt stir the waters yet?
Or haply cut me short for good? Or leave me
    here as now,
Dull, parrot-like and old, with crack'd voice
    harping, screeching?

THE WALLABOUT MARTYRS

[In Brooklyn, in an old vault, mark'd by no
    special recognition, lie huddled at this
    moment the undoubtedly authentic remains
    of the stanchest and earliest revolutionary
    patriots from the British prison ships and
    prisons of the times of 1776–83, in and
    around New York, and from all over Long

Island; originally buried—many thousands
of them—in trenches in the Wallabout sands.]

GREATER than memory of Achilles or Ulysses,
More, more by far to thee than tomb of
  Alexander,
Those cart loads of old charnel ashes, scales, and
  splints of mouldy bones,
Once living men—once resolute courage,
  aspiration, strength,
The stepping stones to thee to-day and here,
  America.

THE FIRST DANDELION

SIMPLE and fresh and fair from winter's close
  emerging,
As if no artifice of fashion, business, politics, had
  ever been,
Forth from its sunny nook of shelter'd grass—
  innocent, golden, calm as the dawn,
The spring's first dandelion shows its trustful face.

AMERICA

CENTER of equal daughters, equal sons,
All, all alike endear'd, grown, ungrown, young
  or old,

Strong, ample, fair, enduring, capable, rich,
Perennial with the Earth, with Freedom, Law,
  and Love,
A grand, sane, towering, seated Mother,
Chair'd in the adamant of Time.

MEMORIES

HOW sweet the silent backward tracings!
The wanderings as in dreams—the meditation of
  old times resumed—their loves, joys, persons,
  voyages.

TO-DAY AND THEE

THE appointed winners in a long-stretch'd
  game;
The course of Time and nations—Egypt, India,
  Greece and Rome;
The past entire, with all its heroes, histories,
  arts, experiments,
Its store of songs, inventions, voyages, teachers,
  books,
Garner'd for now and thee—To think of it!
The heirdom all converged in thee!

AFTER THE DAZZLE OF DAY

AFTER the dazzle of day is gone,
Only the dark, dark night shows to my eyes the
stars;
After the clangor of organ majestic, or chorus,
or perfect band,
Silent, athwart my soul, moves the symphony
true.

ABRAHAM LINCOLN, BORN FEB. 12, 1809

TO-DAY, from each and all, a breath of
prayer—a pulse of thought,
To memory of Him—to birth of Him.

Publish'd Feb. 12, 1888.

OUT OF MAY'S SHOWS SELECTED

APPLE orchards, the trees all cover'd with
blossoms;
Wheat fields carpeted far and near in vital
emerald green;
The eternal, exhaustless freshness of each early
morning;
The yellow, golden, transparent haze of the
warm afternoon sun;

The aspiring lilac bushes with profuse purple or
  white flowers.

Halcyon Days

NOT from successful love alone,
Nor wealth, nor honor'd middle age, nor
  victories of politics or war;
But as life wanes, and all the turbulent passions
  calm,
As gorgeous, vapory, silent hues cover the
  evening sky,
As softness, fulness, rest, suffuse the frame, like
  freshier, balmier air,
As the days take on a mellower light, and the
  apple at last hangs really finish'd and
  indolent-ripe on the tree,
Then for the teeming quietest, happiest days of all!
The brooding and blissful halcyon days!
Fancies at Navesink

The Pilot in the Mist

STEAMING the northern rapids—(an old St.
  Lawrence reminiscence,
A sudden memory-flash comes back, I know not
  why,

Here waiting for the sunrise, gazing from this
    hill;)*
Again 'tis just at morning—a heavy haze
    contends with daybreak,
Again the trembling, laboring vessel veers me-
    I press through foam-dash'd rocks that almost
    touch me,
Again I mark where aft the small thin Indian
    helmsman
Looms in the mist, with brow elate and
    governing hand.

*Navesink—a sea-side mountain, lower entrance
    of New York Bay.

HAD I THE CHOICE

HAD I the choice to tally greatest bards,
To limn their portraits, stately, beautiful, and
    emulate at will,
Homer with all his wars and warriors—Hector,
    Achilles, Ajax,
Or Shakspere's woe-entangled Hamlet, Lear,
    Othello—Tennyson's fair ladies,
Metre or wit the best, or choice conceit to wield
    in perfect rhyme, delight of singers;
These, these, O sea, all these I'd gladly barter,
Would you the undulation of one wave, its trick
    to me transfer,

Or breathe one breath of yours upon my verse,
And leave its odor there.

YOU TIDES WITH CEASELESS SWELL

YOU tides with ceaseless swell! you power that
    does this work!
You unseen force, centripetal, centrifugal,
    through space's spread,
Rapport of sun, moon, earth, and all the
    constellations,
What are the messages by you from distant stars
    to us? what Sirius'? what Capella's?
What central heart—and you the pulse—vivifies
    all? what boundless aggregate of all?
What subtle indirection and significance in you?
    what clue to all in you? what fluid, vast
    identity,
Holding the universe with all its parts as one—as
    sailing in a ship?

LAST OF EBB, AND DAYLIGHT WANTING

LAST of ebb, and daylight waning,
Sented sea-cool landward making, smells of
    sedge and salt incoming,
With many a half-caught voice sent up from the
    eddies,

Many a muffled confession—many a sob and
  whisper'd word,
As of speakers far or hid.
How they sweep down and out! how they
  mutter!
Poets unnamed—artists greatest of any, with
  cherish'd lost designs,
Love's unresponse—a chorus of age's
  complaints—hope's last words,
Some suicide's despairing cry, Away to the
  boundless waste, and never again return.
On to oblivion then!
On, on, and do your part, ye burying, ebbing
  tide!
On for your time, ye furious debouche!

AND YET NOT YOU ALONE

AND yet not you alone, twilight and burying
  ebb,
Nor you, ye lost designs alone- nor failures,
  aspirations;
I know, divine deceitful ones, your glamour's
  seeming;
Duly by you, from you, the tide and light again-
  duly the hinges turning,
Duly the needed discord-parts offsetting,
  blending,

Weaving from you, from Sleep, Night, Death
    itself,
The rhythmus of Birth eternal.

PROUDLY THE FLOOD COMES IN

PROUDLY the flood comes in, shouting,
    foaming, advancing,
Long it holds at the high, with bosom broad
    outswelling,
All throbs, dilates—the farms, woods, streets of
    cities—workmen at work,
Mainsails, topsails, jibs, appear in the offing—
    steamers' pennants of smoke—and under the
    forenoon sun,
Freighted with human lives, gaily the outward
    bound, gaily the inward bound,
Flaunting from many a spar the flag I love.

BY THAT LONG SCAN OF WAVES

BY that long scan of waves, myself call'd back,
    resumed upon myself,
In every crest some undulating light or shade—
    some retrospect,
Joys, travels, studies, silent panoramas-scenes
    ephemeral,

The long past war, the battles, hospital sights,
    the wounded and the dead,
Myself through every by-gone phase—my idle
    youth—old age at hand,
My three-score years of life summ'd up, and
    more, and past,
By any grand ideal tried, intentionless, the whole
    a nothing,
And haply yet some drop within God's scheme's
    ensemble—some wave, or part of wave,
Like one of yours, ye multitudinous ocean.

Then Last Of All

THEN last of all, caught from these shores, this
    hill,
Of you O tides, the mystic human meaning:
Only by law of you, your swell and ebb,
    enclosing me the same,
The brain that shapes, the voice that chants this
    song.

Election Day, November, 1884

IF I should need to name, O Western World,
    your powerfulest scene and show,
'Twould not be you, Niagara—nor you, ye

limitless prairies—nor your huge rifts of
    canyons, Colorado,
Nor you, Yosemite—nor Yellowstone, with all its
    spasmic geyser-loops ascending to the skies,
    appearing and disappearing,
Nor Oregon's white cones—nor Huron's
    belt of mighty lakes—nor Mississippi's
    stream:—
This seething hemisphere's humanity, as now,
    I'd name—the still small voice vibrating—
    America's choosing day,
(The heart of it not in the chosen—the act itself
    the main, the quadriennial choosing,)
The stretch of North and South arous'd—sea-
    board and inland—Texas to Maine—the
    Prairie States—Vermont, Virginia, California,
The final ballot-shower from East to West—the
    paradox and conflict,
The countless snow-flakes falling—(a swordless
    conflict,
Yet more than all Rome's wars of old, or modern
    Napoleon's:) the peaceful choice of all,
Or good or ill humanity—welcoming the darker
    odds, the dross:—
Foams and ferments the wine? it serves to
    purify—while the heart pants, life glows:
These stormy gusts and winds wait precious
    ships,
Swell'd Washington's, Jefferson's, Lincoln's sails.

WITH HUSKY-HAUGHTY LIPS, O SEA!

WITH husky-haughty lips, O sea!
Where day and night I wend thy surf-beat shore,
Imaging to my sense thy varied strange
    suggestions,
(I see and plainly list thy talk and conference
    here,)
Thy troops of white-maned racers racing to the
    goal,
Thy ample, smiling face, dash'd with the
    sparkling dimples of the sun,
Thy brooding scowl and murk—thy unloos'd
    hurricanes,
Thy unsubduedness, caprices, wilfulness;
Great as thou art above the rest, thy many
    tears—a lack from all eternity in thy content,
(Naught but the greatest struggles, wrongs,
    defeats, could make thee greatest- no less
    could make thee,)
Thy lonely state—something thou ever seekist
    and seekist, yet never gain
Surely some right withheld—some voice, in
    huge monotonous rage, of freedom-lover
    pent,
Some vast heart, like a planet's, chain'd and
    chafing in those breakers,
By lengthen'd swell, and spasm, and panting
    breath,

And rhythmic rasping of thy sands and waves,
And serpent hiss, and savage peals of laughter,
And undertones of distant lion roar,
(Sounding, appealing to the sky's deaf ear—but
    now, rapport for once,
A phantom in the night thy confidant for once,)
The first and last confession of the globe,
Outsurging, muttering from thy soul's abysms,
The tale of cosmic elemental passion,
Thou tellest to a kindred soul.

DEATH OF GENERAL GRANT

AS one by one withdraw the lofty actors,
From that great play on history's stage eterne,
That lurid, partial act of war and peace-of old
    and new contending,
Fought out through wrath, fears, dark dismays,
    and many a long suspense;
All past- and since, in countless graves receding,
    mellowing.
Victor's and vanquish'd—Lincoln's and Lee's—
    now thou with them,
Man of the mighty days—and equal to the days!
Thou from the prairies!—tangled and many—
    vein'd and hard has been thy part,
To admiration has it been enacted!

RED JACKET (FROM ALOFT)

[Impromptu on Buffalo City's monument to,
  and re-burial of the old Iroquois orator,
  October 9, 1884]

UPON this scene, this show,
Yielded to-day by fashion, learning, wealth,
(Nor in caprice alone—some grains of deepest
  meaning,)
Haply, aloft, (who knows?) from distant sky—
  clouds' blended shapes,
As some old tree, or rock or cliff, thrill'd with its
  soul,
Product of Nature's sun, stars, earth direct—
  a towering human form,
In hunting-shirt of film, arm'd with the rifle, a
  half-ironical smile curving its phantom lips,
Like one of Ossian's ghosts looks down.

WASHINGTON'S MONUMENT FEBRUARY, 1885

AH, not this marble, dead and cold:
Far from its base and shaft expanding—the
  round zones circling, comprehending,
Thou, Washington, art all the world's, the
  continents entire—not yours alone, America,
Europe's as well, in every part, castle of lord or
  laborer's cot,

Or frozen North, or sultry South—the
    African's— the Arab's in his tent,
Old Asia's there with venerable smile, seated
    amid her ruins;
(Greets the antique the hero new? 'tis but the
    same—the heir legitimate, continued ever,
    The indomitable heart and arm—proofs of
    the never-broken line, Courage, alertness,
    patience, faith, the same—e'en in defeat
    defeated not, the same:)
Wherever sails a ship, or house is built on land,
    or day or night,
Through teeming cities' streets, indoors or out,
    factories or farms,
Now, or to come, or past—where patriot wills
    existed or exist,
Wherever Freedom, pois'd by Toleration, sway'd
    by Law,
Stands or is rising thy true monument.

OF THAT BLITHE THROAT OF THINE

[More than eighty-three degrees north—about a
    good day's steaming distance to the Pole by
    one of our fast oceaners in clear water—
    Greely the explorer heard the song of a single
    snow-bird merrily sounding over the
    desolation.]

OF that blithe throat of thine from arctic bleak
    and blank,
I'll mind the lesson, solitary bird—let me too
    welcome chilling drifts,
E'en the profoundest chill, as now—a torpid
    pulse, a brain unnerv'd,
Old age land-lock'd within its winter bay—
    (cold, cold, O cold!)
These snowy hairs, my feeble arm, my frozen feet,
For them thy faith, thy rule I take, and grave it
    to the last;
Not summer's zones alone—not chants of
    youth, or south's warm tides alone,
But held by sluggish floes, pack'd in the
    northern ice, the cumulus of years,
These with gay heart I also sing.

BROADWAY

WHAT hurrying human tides, or day or night!
What passions, winnings, losses, ardors, swim
    thy waters!
What whirls of evil, bliss and sorrow, stem thee!
What curious questioning glances—glints of love!
Leer, envy, scorn, contempt, hope, aspiration!
Thou portal—thou arena—thou of the myriad
    long-drawn lines and groups!
(Could but thy flagstones, curbs, facades, tell
    their inimitable tales;

Thy windows rich, and huge hotels—thy side-
walks wide;)
Thou of the endless sliding, mincing, shuffling
feet!
Thou, like the parti-colored world itself—like
infinite, teeming, mocking life!
Thou visor'd, vast, unspeakable show and
lesson!

To Get the Final Lilt of Songs

TO get the final lilt of songs,
To penetrate the inmost lore of poets—to know
the mighty ones,
Job, Homer, Eschylus, Dante, Shakespere,
Tennyson, Emerson;
To diagnose the shifting-delicate tints of
love and pride and doubt- to truly
understand,
To encompass these, the last keen faculty and
entrance-price,
Old age, and what it brings from all its past
experiences.

Old Salt Kossabone

FAR back, related on my mother's side,
Old Salt Kossabone, I'll tell you how he died:

(Had been a sailor all his life—was nearly go—
　　lived with his married grandchild, Jenny;
House on a hill, with view of bay at hand, and
　　distant cape, and stretch to open sea;)
The last of afternoons, the evening hours, for
　　many a year his regular custom,
In his great arm chair by the window seated,
(Sometimes, indeed, through half the day,)
Watching the coming, going of the vessels, he
　　mutters to himself—And now the close of all:
One struggling outbound brig, one day, baffled
　　for long—cross-tides and much wrong going,
At last at nightfall strikes the breeze aright, her
　　whole luck veering,
And swiftly bending round the cape, the
　　darkness proudly entering, cleaving, as he
　　watches,
"She's free—she's on her destination"—these
　　the last words—when Jenny came, he sat
　　there dead,
Dutch Kossabone, Old Salt, related on my
　　mother's side, far back.

THE DEAD TENOR

AS down the stage again,
With Spanish hat and plumes, and gait
　　inimitable,
Back from the fading lessons of the past, I'd call,
　　I'd tell and own,

How much from thee! the revelation of the
    singing voice from thee!
(So firm—so liquid-soft—again that tremulous,
    manly timber!
The perfect singing voice—deepest of all to me
    the lesson—trial and test of all:)
How through those strains distill'd—how the
    rapt ears, the soul of me, absorbing
    Fernando's heart, Manrico's passionate call,
    Ernani's, sweet Gennaro's.
I fold thenceforth, or seek to fold, within my
    chants transmuting,
Freedom's and Love's and Faith's unloos'd
    cantabile,
(As perfume's, color's, sunlight's correlation:)
From these, for these, with these, a hurried line,
    dead tenor,
A waited autumn leaf, dropt in the closing
    grave, the shovel'd earth,
To memory of thee.

CONTINUITIES

[From a talk I had lately with a German
    spiritualist.]

NOTHING is ever really lost, or can be lost,
No birth, identity, form—no object of the
    world.

Nor life, nor force, nor any visible thing;
Appearance must not foil, nor shifted sphere
  confuse thy brain.
Ample are time and space—ample the fields of
  Nature.

The body, sluggish, aged, cold—the embers left
  from earlier fires,
The light in the eye grown dim, shall duly flame
  again;
The sun now low in the west rises for mornings
  and for noons continual;
To frozen clods ever the spring's invisible law
  returns,
With grass and flowers and summer fruits and
  corn.

YONNONDIO

[The sense of the word is lament for the
  aborigines. It is an Iroquois term; and has
  been used for a personal name.]

A SONG, a poem of itself—the word itself a
  dirge,
Amid the wilds, the rocks, the storm and wintry
  night,
To me such misty, strange tableaux the syllables
  calling up;

Yonnondio—I see, far in the west or north, a
limitless ravine, with plains and mountains dark,
I see swarms of stalwart chieftains, medicine—
men, and warriors,
As flitting by like clouds of ghosts, they pass and
are gone in the twilight,
(Race of the woods, the landscapes free, and the
falls!
No picture, poem, statement, passing them to
the future:)
Yonnondio! Yonnondio!—unlimn'd they
disappear;
To-day gives place, and fades—the cities, farms,
factories fade;
A muffled sonorous sound, a wailing word is
borne through the air for a moment,
Then blank and gone and still, and utterly
lost.

LIFE

EVER the undiscouraged, resolute, struggling
soul of man;
(Have former armies fail'd? then we send fresh
armies- and fresh again;)
Ever the grappled mystery of all earth's ages old
or new;
Ever the eager eyes, hurrahs, the welcome-
clapping hands, the loud applause;

Ever the soul dissatisfied, curious, unconvinced
    at last;
Struggling to-day the same—battling the same.

"Going Somewhere"

MY science-friend, my noblest woman-friend,
(Now buried in an English grave—and this a
    memory-leaf for her dear sake,)
Ended our talk—"The sum, concluding all we
    know of old or modern learning, intuitions deep,
"Of all Geologies—Histories—of all
    Astronomy—of Evolution, Metaphysics all,
"Is, that we all are onward, onward, speeding
    slowly, surely bettering,
"Life, life an endless march, an endless army, (no
    halt, but it is duly over,)
"The world, the race, the soul—in space and
    time the universes,
"All bound as is befitting each—all surely going
    somewhere."

From the 1867 edition of L. of G.
Small the Theme of My Chant

SMALL the theme of my Chant, yet the greatest-
namely, One's-Self—a simple, separate person.
That, for the use of the New World, I sing.

Man's physiology complete, from top to toe, I
 sing. Not physiognomy alone, nor brain
 alone, is worthy for the Muse;—I say the
 Form complete is worthier far. The Female
 equally with the Male, I sing.
Nor cease at the theme of One's-Self. I speak
 the word of the modern, the word En-Masse.
My Days I sing, and the Lands—with interstice I
 knew of hapless War.
(O friend, whoe'er you are, at last arriving hither
 to commence, I feel through every leaf the
 pressure of your hand, which I return. And
 thus upon outjourney, footing the road, and
 more than once, and link'd together let us go.)

TRUE CONQUERORS

OLD farmers, travelers, workmen (no matter
 how crippled or bent,)
Old sailors, out of many a perilous voyage,
 storm and wreck,
Old soldiers from campaigns, with all their
 wounds, defeats and scars;
Enough that they've survived at all—long life's
 unflinching ones!
Forth from their struggles, trials, fights, to have
 emerged at all—in that alone,
True conquerors o'er all the rest.

Walt Whitman

THE UNITED STATES TO OLD WORLD CRITICS

HERE first the duties of to-day, the lessons of
   the concrete,
Wealth, order, travel, shelter, products, plenty;
As of the building of some varied, vast,
   perpetual edifice,
Whence to arise inevitable in time, the towering
   roofs, the lamps,
The solid-planted spires tall shooting to the stars.

THE CALMING THOUGHT OF ALL

THAT coursing on, whate'er men's speculations,
Amid the changing schools, theologies,
   philosophies,
Amid the bawling presentations new and old,
The round earth's silent vital laws, facts, modes
   continued.

THANKS IN OLD AGE

THANKS in old age—thanks ere I go,
For health, the midday sun, the impalpable air—
   for life, mere life,
For precious ever-lingering memories, (of you
   my mother dear—you, father—you, brothers,
   sisters, friends,)

For all my days—not those of peace alone—the
   days of war the same,
For gentle words, caresses, gifts from foreign
   lands,
For shelter, wine and meat—for sweet
   appreciation,
(You distant, dim unknown—or young or old—
   countless, unspecified, readers belov'd,
We never met, and neer shall meet—and yet our
   souls embrace, long, close and long;)
For beings, groups, love, deeds, words, books—
   for colors, forms,
For all the brave strong men—devoted, hardy
   men—who've forward sprung in freedom's
   help, all years, all lands
For braver, stronger, more devoted men—(a
   special laurel ere I go, to life's war's chosen
   ones,
The cannoneers of song and thought-the great
   artillerists—the foremost leaders, captains of
   the soul:)
As soldier from an ended war return'd—As
   traveler out of myriads, to the long procession
   retrospective,
Thanks—joyful thanks!—a soldier's, traveler's
   thanks.

Life and Death

THE two old, simple problems ever intertwined,
Close home, elusive, present, baffled, grappled.
By each successive age insoluble, pass'd on,
To ours to-day—and we pass on the same.

The Voice of the Rain

AND who art thou? said I to the soft-falling
  shower,
Which, strange to tell, gave me an answer, as
  here translated:
I am the Poem of Earth, said the voice of the
  rain,
Eternal I rise impalpable out of the land and the
  bottomless sea,
Upward to heaven, whence, vaguely form'd,
  altogether changed, and yet the same,
I descend to lave the drouths, atomies, dust-
  layers of the globe,
And all that in them without me were seeds
  only, latent, unborn;
And forever, by day and night, I give back life to
  my own origin, and make pure and beautify it
(For song, issuing from its birth-place, after
  fulfilment, wandering,
Reck'd or unreck'd, duly with love returns.)

Soon Shall the Winter's Foil Be Here

SOON shall the winter's foil be here;
Soon shall these icy ligatures unbind and melt—
    A little while,
And air, soil, wave, suffused shall be in softness,
    bloom and growth—a thousand forms shall
    rise
From these dead clods and chills as from low
    burial graves.

Thine eyes, ears—all thy best attributes—all
    that takes cognizance of natural beauty,
Shall wake and fill. Thou shalt perceive the
    simple shows, the delicate miracles of
    earth,
Dandelions, clover, the emerald grass, the early
    scents and flowers,
The arbutus under foot, the willow's yellow-
    green, the blossoming plum and cherry;
With these the robin, lark and thrush, singing
    their songs- the flitting bluebird;
For such the scenes the annual play brings on.

While Not the Past Forgetting

WHILE not the past forgetting,
To-day, at least, contention sunk entire—peace,
    brotherhood uprisen;

For sign reciprocal our Northern, Southern
   hands,
Lay on the graves of all dead soldiers, North or
   South,
(Nor for the past alone—for meanings to the
   future,)
Wreaths of roses and branches of palm.

PUBLISH'D MAY 30, 1888.
THE DYING VETERAN

[A Long Island incident—early part
of the present century.]

AMID these days of order, ease, prosperity,
Amid the current songs of beauty, peace,
   decorum,
I cast a reminiscence—(likely 'twill offend you,
I heard it in my boyhood;)—More than a
   generation since,
A queer old savage man, a fighter under
   Washington himself,
(Large, brave, cleanly, hot-blooded, no talker,
   rather spiritualistic,
Had fought in the ranks—fought well-had been
   all through the Revolutionary war,)
Lay dying—sons, daughters, church-deacons,
   lovingly tending him,

Sharping their sense, their ears, towards his
  murmuring, half-caught words:
"Let me return again to my war-days,
To the sights and scenes—to forming the line of
  battle,
To the scouts ahead reconnoitering,
To the cannons, the grim artillery,
To the galloping aids, carrying orders,
To the wounded, the fallen, the heat, the suspense,
The perfume strong, the smoke, the deafening
  noise;
Away with your life of peace!—your joys of peace!
Give me my old wild battle-life again!"

STRONGER LESSONS

HAVE you learn'd lessons only of those who
  admired you, and were tender with you, and
  stood aside for you?
Have you not learn'd great lessons from those
  who reject you, and brace themselves against
  you? or who treat you with contempt, or
  dispute the passage with you?

A PRAIRIE SUNSET

SHOT gold, maroon and violet, dazzling silver,
  emerald, fawn,

The earth's whole amplitude and Nature's
    multiform power consign'd for once to
    colors;
The light, the general air possess'd by them—
    colors till now unknown,
No limit, confine—not the Western sky alone—
    the high meridian—North, South, all,
Pure luminous color fighting the silent shadows
    to the last.

Twenty Years

DOWN on the ancient wharf, the sand, I sit,
    with a new-comer chatting:
He shipp'd as green-hand boy, and sail'd away,
    (took some sudden, vehement notion;)
Since, twenty years and more have circled round
    and round,
While he the globe was circling round and
    round,—and now returns:
How changed the place—all the old land-marks
    gone—the parents dead;
(Yes, he comes back to lay in port for good—
    to settle—has a well-fill'd purse—no do but
    this;)
The little boat that scull'd him from the sloop,
    now held in leash see,
I hear the slapping waves, the restless keel, the
    rocking in the sand,

I see the sailor kit, the canvas bag, the great box
    bound with brass,
I scan the face all berry-brown and bearded—
    the stout-strong frame,
Dress'd in its russet suit of good Scotch cloth:
(Then what the told-out story of those twenty
    years? What of the future?)

ORANGE BUDS BY MAIL FROM FLORIDA

[Voltaire closed a famous argument by claiming
    that a ship of war and the grand opera were
    proof's enough of civilization's and France's
    progress, in his day.]

A LESSER proof than old Voltaire's, yet
    greater,
Proof of this present time, and thee, thy broad
    expanse, America,
To my plain Northern hut, in outside clouds
    and snow,
Brought safely for a thousand miles o'er land
    and tide,
Some three days since on their own soil live-
    sprouting,
Now here their sweetness through my room
    unfolding,
A bunch of orange buds by mall from Florida.

Twilight

THE soft voluptuous opiate shades,
The sun just gone, the eager light dispell'd—
    (I too will soon be gone, dispell'd.)
A haze—nirwana—rest and night—oblivion.

You Lingering Sparse Leaves of Me

YOU lingering sparse leaves of me on winter-
    nearing boughs,
And I some well-shorn tree of field or orchard-
    row;
You tokens diminute and lorn—(not now the
    flush of May, or July clover-bloom—no grain
    of August now;)
You pallid banner-staves—you pennants
    valueless—you overstay'd of time,
Yet my soul-dearest leaves confirming all the rest,
The faithfulest—hardiest—last.

Not Meagre, Latent Boughs Alone

NOT meagre, latent boughs alone, O songs!
    (scaly and bare, like eagles' talons,)
But haply for some sunny day (who knows?)
    some future spring, some summer—bursting
    forth,

To verdant leaves, or sheltering shade—to
    nourishing fruit,
Apples and grapes—the stalwart limbs of trees
    emerging—the fresh, free, open air,
And love and faith, like scented roses blooming.

THE DEAD EMPEROR

TO-DAY, with bending head and eyes, thou,
    too, Columbia,
Less for the mighty crown laid low in sorrow-
    less for the Emperor,
Thy true condolence breathest, sendest out o'er
    many a salt sea mile,
Mourning a good old mana faithful shepherd,
    patriot.

Publish'd March 10, 1888.

AS THE GREEK'S SIGNAL FLAME

[For Whittier's eightieth birthday,
December 17, 1887]

AS the Greek's signal flame, by antique records
    told,
Rose from the hill-top, like applause and glory,
Welcoming in fame some special veteran, hero,
With rosy tinge reddening the land he'd served,
So I aloft from Mannahatta's ship-fringed shore,

Lift high a kindled brand for thee, Old Poet.

THE DISMANTLED SHIP

IN some unused lagoon, some nameless bay,
On sluggish, lonesome waters, anchor'd near the
    shore,
An old, dismasted, gray and batter'd ship,
    disabled, done,
After free voyages to all the seas of earth, haul'd
    up at last and hawser'd tight,
Lies rusting, mouldering.

NOW PRECEDENT SONGS, FAREWELL

NOW precedent songs, farewell—by every name
    farewell,
(Trains of a staggering line in many a strange
    procession, waggons,
From ups and downs—with intervals—from
    elder years, mid-age, or youth,)
"In Cabin'd Ships," or "Thee Old Cause" or
    "Poets to Come"
Or "Paumanok," "Song of Myself," "Calamus,"
    or "Adam,"
Or "Beat! Beat! Drums!" or "To the Leaven'd
    Soil they Trod,"
Or "Captain! My Captain!" "Kosmos,"

"Quicksand Years," or "Thoughts,"
Mother with thy Equal Brood," and many, many
  more unspecified,
From fibre heart of mine—from throat and
  tongue—(My life's hot pulsing blood,
The personal urge and form for me—not merely
  paper, automatic type and ink,)
Each song of mine—each utterance in the past—
  having its long, long history,
Of life or death, or soldier's wound, of country's
  loss or safety,
(O heaven! what flash and started endless train
  of all! compared indeed to that!
What wretched shred e'en at the best of all!)*

*The song on this page was eked out during an
  afternoon, June, 1888, in my seventieth year,
  at a critical spell of illness. Of course no
  reader and probably no human being at any
  time will ever have such phases of emotional
  and solemn action as these involve to me. I
  feel in them an end and close of all.

AN EVENING LULL

AFTER a week of physical anguish,
Unrest and pain, and feverish heat,
Toward the ending day a calm and lull comes on,
Three hours of peace and soothing rest of

brain.*

OLD AGE'S LAMBENT PEAKS

THE touch of flame—the illuminating fire—
    the loftiest look at last,
O'er city, passion, sea—o'er prairie, mountain,
    wood—the earth itself,
The airy, different, changing hues of all, in
    failing twilight,
Objects and groups, bearings, faces,
    reminiscences;
The calmer sight—the golden setting, clear and
    broad:
So much i' the atmosphere, the points of view,
    the situations whence we scan,
Brought out by them alone—so much (perhaps
    the best) unreck'd before;
The lights indeed from them—old age's lambent
    peaks.

AFTER THE SUPPER AND TALK

AFTER the supper and talk—after the day is
    done,
As a friend from friends his final withdrawal
    prolonging,
Good-bye and Good-bye with emotional lips

repeating,

(So hard for his hand to release those hands—no
   more will they meet,

No more for communion of sorrow and joy, of
   old and young,

A far-stretching journey awaits him, to return no
   more,)

Shunning, postponing severance—seeking to
   ward off the last word ever so little,

E'en at the exit-door turning—charges
   superfluous calling back—e'en as he descends
   the steps,

Something to eke out a minute additional-
   shadows of nightfall deepening,

Farewells, messages lessening—dimmer the
   forthgoer's visage and form,

Soon to be lost for aye in the darkness—loth, O
   so loth to depart!

Garrulous to the very last.

PREFACE NOTE TO 2D ANNEX
CONCLUDING L. OF G.—1891.

Had I not better withhold (in this old age
and paralysis of me) such little tags and fringe-
dots (maybe specks, stains,) as follow a long
dusty journey, and witness it afterward? I have
probably not been enough afraid of careless
touches, from the first—and am not now—nor
of parrot-like repetitions— nor platitudes and
the commonplace. Perhaps I am too democratic
for such avoidances. Besides, is not the verse-
field, as originally plann'd by my theory, now
sufficiently illustrated—and full time for me to
silently retire?—(indeed amid no loud call or
market for my sort of poetic utterance.)

In answer, or rather defiance, to that kind of
well-put interrogation, here comes this little
cluster, and conclusion of my preceding clusters.
Though not at all clear that, as here collated, it
is worth printing (certainly I have nothing fresh
to write)—I while away the hours of my 72d
year—hours of forced confinement in my den—
by putting in shape this small old age collation:

Last droplets of and after spontaneous rain,
From many limpid distillations and past
showers;
(Will they germinate anything? mere
exhalations as they all are—the land's and

sea's—America's; Will they filter to any deep
emotion? any heart and brain?)

However that may be, I feel like improving
to-day's opportunity and wind up. During the
last two years I have sent out, in the lulls of
illness and exhaustion, certain chirps—lingering-
dying ones probably (undoubtedly)—which now
I may as well gather and put in fair type while
able to see correctly—(for my eyes plainly warn
me they are dimming, and my brain more and
more palpably neglects or refuses, month after
month, even slight tasks or revisions.)

In fact, here I am these current years 1890 and
'91, (each successive fortnight getting stiffer and
stuck deeper) much like some hard-cased
dilapidated grim ancient shell-fish or time-bang'd
conch (no legs, utterly non-locomotive) cast up
high and dry on the shore-sands, helpless to move
anywhere—nothing left but behave myself quiet,
and while away the days yet assign'd, and discover
if there is anything for the said grim and time-
bang'd conch to be got at last out of inherited
good spirits and primal buoyant centre-pulses
down there deep somewhere within his gray-
blurr'd old shell...........(Reader, you must allow a
little fun here—for one reason there are too many
of the following poemets about death, &c., and
for another the passing hours (July 5, 1890) are
so sunny-fine. And old as I am feel to-day almost

a part of some frolicsome wave, or for sporting yet like a kid or kitten—probably a streak of physical adjustment and perfection here and now. I believe I have it in me perennially anyhow.)

Then behind all, the deep-down consolation (it is a glum one, but I dare not be sorry for the fact of it in the past, nor refrain from dwelling, even vaunting here at the end) that this late-years palsied old shorn and shell-fish condition of me is the indubitable outcome and growth, now near for 20 years along, of too overzealous, over-continued bodily and emotional excitement and action through the times of 1862, '3, '4 and '5, visiting and waiting on wounded and sick army volunteers, both sides, in campaigns or contests, or after them, or in hospitals or fields south of Washington City, or in that place and elsewhere—those hot, sad, wrenching times— the army volunteers, all States,—or North or South—the wounded, suffering, dying—the exhausting, sweating summers, marches, battles, carnage—those trenches hurriedly heap'd by the corpse—thousands, mainly unknown—Will the America of the future—will this vast rich Union ever realize what itself cost, back there after all?—those hecatombs of battle-deaths—Those times of which, O far-off reader, this whole book is indeed finally but a reminiscent memorial from thence by me to you?

SAIL OUT FOR GOOD, EIDOLON YACHT!

HEAVE the anchor short!
Raise main-sail and jib—steer forth,
O little white-hull'd sloop, now speed on really
    deep waters,
(I will not call it our concluding voyage,
But outset and sure entrance to the truest, best,
    maturest;)
Depart, depart from solid earth—no more
    returning to these shores,
Now on for aye our infinite free venture
    wending,
Spurning all yet tried ports, seas, hawsers,
    densities, gravitation,
Sail out for good, eidolon yacht of me!

LINGERING LAST DROPS

AND whence and why come you?

We know not whence, (was the answer,)
We only know that we drift here with the rest,
That we linger'd and lagg'd—but were waited at
    last, and are now here,
To make the passing shower's concluding drops.

Good-Bye My Fancy

GOOD-BYE* my fancy—(I had a word to say,
But 'tis not quite the time—The best of any
    man's word or say,
Is when its proper place arrives—and for its
    meaning,
I keep mine till the last.)

    *Behind a Good-bye there lurks much of the
salutation of another beginning—to me,
Development Continuity, Immortality,
Transformation, are the chiefest life-meanings of
Nature and Humanity, and are the sine qua non
of all facts, and each fact.
    Why do folks dwell so fondly on the last
words, advice, appearance, of the departing?
Those last words are not samples of the best,
which involve vitality at its full, and balance, and
perfect control and scope. But they are valuable
beyond measure to confirm and endorse the
varied train, facts, theories, and faith of the
whole preceding life.

On, on the Same, Ye Jocund Twain!

ON, on the same, Ye Jocund twain!
My life and recitative, containing birth, youth,
   mid-age years,
Fitful as motley-tongues of flame, inseparably
   twined and merged in one—combining all,
My single soul—aims, confirmations, failures,
   joys—Nor single soul alone,
I chant my nation's crucial stage, (America's, haply
   humanity's)—the trial great, the victory great,
A strange eclaircissement of all the masses past,
   the eastern world, the ancient, medieval,
Here, here from wanderings, strayings, lessons,
   wars, defeats—here at the west a voice
   triumphant—justifying all,
A gladsome pealing cry—a song for once of
   utmost pride and satisfaction;
I chant from it the common bulk, the general
   average horde, (the best sooner than the
   worst)—And now I chant old age,
(My verses, written first for forenoon life, and
   for the summer's, autumn's spread,
I pass to snow-white hairs the same, and give to
   pulses winter-cool'd the same;)
As here in careless trill, I and my recitatives, with
   faith and love,
Waiting to other work, to unknown songs,
   conditions,
On, on ye jocund twain! continue on the same!

MY 71ST YEAR

AFTER surmounting three-score and ten,
With all their chances, changes, losses, sorrows,
My parents' deaths, the vagaries of my life, the
    many tearing passions of me, the war of '63
    and '4,
As some old broken soldier, after a long, hot,
    wearying march, or haply after battle,
To-day at twilight, hobbling, answering
    company roll-call, Here, with vital voice,
Reporting yet, saluting yet the Officer over all.
Apparitions

A VAGUE mist hanging 'round half the pages:
(Sometimes how strange and clear to the soul,
That all these solid things are indeed but
    apparitions, concepts, non-realities.)

THE PALLID WREATH

SOMEHOW I cannot let it go yet, funeral
    though it is,
Let it remain back there on its nail suspended,
With pink, blue, yellow, all blanch'd, and the
    white now gray and ashy,
One wither'd rose put years ago for thee, dear
    friend;
But I do not forget thee. Hast thou then faded?

Is the odor exhaled? Are the colors, vitalities,
   dead?
No, while memories subtly play—the past vivid
   as ever;
For but last night I woke, and in that spectral
   ring saw thee,
Thy smile, eyes, face, calm, silent, loving as ever:
So let the wreath hang still awhile within my
   eye-reach,
It is not yet dead to me, nor even pallid.

An Ended Day

THE soothing sanity and blitheness of
   completion,
The pomp and hurried contest-glare and rush
   are done;
Now triumph! transformation! jubilate!*

   *NOTE.—Summer country life.—Several
years.—In my rambles and explorations I found
a woody place near the creek, where for some
reason the birds in happy mood seem'd to resort
in unusual numbers. Especially at the beginning
of the day, and again at the ending, I was sure to
get there the most copious bird-concerts. I
repair'd there frequently at sunrise-and also at
sunset, or just before . . . Once the question
arose in me: Which is the best singing, the first

or the lattermost? The first always exhilarated, and perhaps seem'd more joyous and stronger; but I always felt the sunset or late afternoon sounds more penetrating and sweeter—seem'd to touch the soul—often the evening thrushes, two or three of them, responding and perhaps blending. Though I miss'd some of the mornings, I found myself getting to be quite strictly punctual at the evening utterances.

ANOTHER NOTE.—"HE went out with the tide and the sunset," was a phrase I heard from a surgeon describing an old sailor's death under peculiarly gentle conditions.

During the Secession War, 1863 and '4, visiting the Army Hospitals around Washington, D.C., I form'd the habit, and continued it to the end, whenever the ebb or flood tide began the latter part of day, of punctually visiting those at that time populous wards of suffering men. Somehow (or I thought so) the effect of the hour was palpable. The badly wounded would get some ease, and would like to talk a little, or be talk'd to. Intellectual and emotional natures would be at their best: Deaths were always easier; medicines seem'd to have better effect when given then, and a lulling atmosphere would pervade the wards.

Similar influences, similar circumstances and hours, day-close, after great battles, even with all their horrors. I had more than once the same experience on the fields cover'd with fallen or dead.

Old, Age Ship & Crafty Death's

FROM east and west across the horizon's edge,
Two mighty masterful vessels sailers steal upon us:
But we'll make race a-time upon the seas—a
    battle—contest yet! bear lively there!
(Our joys of strife and derring-do to the last!)
Put on the old ship all her power to-day!
Crowd top-sail, top-gallant and royal studding-
    sails,
Out challenge and defiance—flags and flaunting
    pennants added,
As we take to the open—take to the deepest,
    freest waters.

To the Pending Year

HAVE I no weapon-word for thee- some
    message brief and fierce?
(Have I fought out and done indeed the battle?)
    Is there no shot left,
For all thy affectations, lisps, scorns, manifold
    silliness?
Nor for myself—my own rebellious self in thee?

Down, down, proud gorge!—though choking
  thee;
Thy bearded throat and high-borne forehead to
  the gutter;
Crouch low thy neck to eleemosynary
  gifts.

Shakspere-Bacon's Cipher

I DOUBT it not—then more, far more;
In each old song bequeath'd—in every noble
  page or text,
(Different—something unreck'd before—some
  unsuspected author,)
In every object, mountain, tree, and star—in
  every birth and life,
As part of each—evolv'd from each—meaning,
  behind the ostent,
A mystic cipher waits infolded.

Long, Long Hence

AFTER a long, long course, hundreds of years,
  denials,
Accumulations, rous'd love and joy and
  thought,
Hopes, wishes, aspirations, ponderings, victories,
  myriads of readers,

Coating, compassing, covering—after ages' and
    ages' encrustations,
Then only may these songs reach fruition.

Bravo, Paris Exposition!

ADD to your show, before you close it, France,
With all the rest, visible, concrete, temples,
    towers, goods, machines and ores,
Our sentiment waited from many million heart-
    throbs, ethereal but solid,
(We grand-sons and great-grandsons do not
    forget your grandsires,)
From fifty Nations and nebulous Nations,
    compacted, sent oversea to-day,
America's applause, love, memories and good-
    will.

Interpolation Sounds

[General Philip Sheridan was buried at the
    Cathedral, Washington, August, 1888, with
    all the pomp, music and ceremonies of the
    Roman Catholic service.]

OVER and through the burial chant,
Organ and solemn service, sermon, bending
    priests,

To me come interpolation sounds not in the
    show—plainly to me, crowding up the aisle
    and from the window,
Of sudden battle's hurry and harsh noises—
    war's grim game to sight and ear in
    earnest;
The scout call'd up and forward—the general
    mounted and his aids around him—the new-
    brought word—the instantaneous order
    issued;
The rifle crack—the cannon thud—the rushing
    forth men from their tents;
The clank of cavalry—the strange celerity of
    forming ranks—the slender bugle note;
The sound of horses' hoofs departing—saddles,
    arms, accoutrements.*

*NOTE.—CAMDEN, N.J., August 7,
1888—Walt Whitman asks the New York Herald
"to add his tribute to Sheridan:"
"In the grand constellation of five or six
names, under Lincoln's Presidency, that history
will bear for ages in her firmament as marking
the last life-throbs of secession, and beaming on
its dying gasps, Sheridan's will be bright. One
consideration soldier's example as it passes my
mind, is worth taking notice of. If the war had
continued any long time these States, in my
opinion, would have shown and proved the
most conclusive military talents ever evinced by

any nation on earth. That they possess'd a rank and file ahead of all other known in points of quality and limitlessness of number are easily admitted. But we have, too, the eligibility of organizing, handling and officering equal to the other. These two, with modern arms, transportation, and inventive American genius, would make the United States, with earnestness, not only able to stand the whole world, but conquer that world united against us."

To the Sun-Set Breeze

AH, whispering, something again, unseen,
Where late this heated day thou enterest at my
    window, door,
Thou, laving, tempering all, cool-freshing,
    gently vitalizing
Me, old, alone, sick, weak-down, melted-worn
    with sweat;
Thou, nestling, folding close and firm yet soft,
    companion better than talk, book, art,
(Thou hast, O Nature! elements! utterance to
    my heart beyond the rest—and this is of
    them,)
So sweet thy primitive taste to breathe within—
    thy soothing fingers my face and hands,
Thou, messenger—magical strange bringer to
    body and spirit of me,

(Distances balk'd—occult medicines penetrating
    me from head to foot,)
I feel the sky, the prairies vast—I feel the mighty
    northern lakes,
I feel the ocean and the forest-somehow I feel
    the globe itself swift-swimming in space;
Thou blown from lips so loved, now gone—
    haply from endless store, God-sent,
(For thou art spiritual, Godly, most of all known
    to my sense,)
Minister to speak to me, here and now, what
    word has never told, and cannot tell,
Art thou not universal concrete's distillation?
    Law's, all Astronomy's last refinement?
Hast thou no soul? Can I not know, identify
    thee?

OLD CHANTS

AN ancient song, reciting, ending,
Once gazing toward thee, Mother of All,
Musing, seeking themes fitted for thee,
Accept me, thou saidst, the elder ballads,
And name for me before thou goest each
    ancient poet.

(Of many debts incalculable,
Haply our New World's chieftest debt is to old
    poems.)

Ever so far back, preluding thee, America,
Old chants, Egyptian priests, and those of
  Ethiopia,
The Hindu epics, the Grecian, Chinese, Persian,
The Biblic books and prophets, and deep idyls
  of the Nazarene,
The Iliad, Odyssey, plots, doings, wanderings of
  Eneas,
Hesiod, Eschylus, Sophocles, Merlin, Arthur,
The Cid, Roland at Roncesvalles, the
  Nibelungen,
The troubadours, minstrels, minnesingers,
  skalds,
Chaucer, Dante, flocks of singing birds,
The Border Minstrelsy, the bye-gone ballads,
  feudal tales, essays, plays,
Shakespere, Schiller, Walter Scott, Tennyson,
As some vast wondrous weird dream-presences,
The great shadowy groups gathering around,
Darting their mighty masterful eyes forward at
  thee,
Thou! with as now thy bending neck and head,
  with courteous hand and word, ascending,
Thou! pausing a moment, drooping thine eyes
  upon them, blent with their music,
Well pleased, accepting all, curiously prepared
  for by them,
Thou enterest at thy entrance porch.

A Christmas Greeting
From a Northern Star-Group
to a Southern. 1889–90

WELCOME, Brazilian brother—thy ample place
  is ready;
A loving hand—a smile from the north—a sunny
  instant hall!
(Let the future care for itself, where it reveals its
  troubles, impedimentas,
Ours, ours the present throe, the democratic
  aim, the acceptance and the faith;)
To thee to-day our reaching arm, our
  turning neck—to thee from us the expectant
  eye,
Thou cluster free! thou brilliant lustrous one!
  thou, learning well,
The true lesson of a nation's light in the sky,
(More shining than the Cross, more than the
  Crown,)
The height to be superb humanity.

Sounds of the Winter

SOUNDS of the winter too,
Sunshine upon the mountains—many a distant
  strain
From cheery railroad train—from nearer field,
  barn, house,

The whispering air—even the mute crops,
   garner'd apples, corn,
Children's and women's tones—rhythm of many
   a farmer and of flail,
An old man's garrulous lips among the rest,
   Think not we give out yet,
Forth from these snowy hairs we keep up yet
   the lilt.

A TWILIGHT SONG

As I sit in twilight late alone by the flickering
   oak-flame,
Musing on long-pass'd war-scenes—of the
   countless buried unknown soldiers,
Of the vacant names, as unindented air's and
   sea's—the unreturn'd,
The brief truce after battle, with grim burial-
   squads, and the deep-fill'd trenches
Of gather'd from dead all America, North,
   South, East, West, whence they came up,
From wooded Maine, New-England's farms,
   from fertile Pennsylvania, Illinois, Ohio,
From the measureless West, Virginia, the South,
   the Carolinas, Texas,
(Even here in my room-shadows and half-lights
   in the noiseless flickering flames,
Again I see the stalwart ranks on—filing, rising—
   I hear the rhythmic tramp of the armies;)

You million unwrit names all, all—you dark
　　bequest from all the war,
A special verse for you—a flash of duty long
　　neglected—your mystic roll strangely gather'd
　　here,
Each name recall'd by me from out the darkness
　　and death's ashes,
Henceforth to be, deep, deep within my heart
　　recording, for many future year,
Your mystic roll entire of unknown names, or
　　North or South,
Embalm'd with love in this twilight song.

WHEN THE FULL-GROWN POET CAME

WHEN the full-grown poet came,
Out spake pleased Nature (the round impassive
　　globe, with all its shows of day and night,)
　　saying, He is mine;
But out spake too the Soul of man, proud,
　　jealous and unreconciled, Nay he is mine
　　alone;—
Then the full-grown poet stood between the
　　two, and took each by the hand;
And to-day and ever so stands, as blender,
　　uniter, tightly holding hands,
Which he will never release until he reconciles
　　the two,
And wholly and joyously blends them.

OSCEOLA

[When I was nearly grown to manhood in
    Brooklyn, New York, (middle of 1838,) I met
    one of the return'd U. S. Marines from Fort
    Moultrie, S.C., and had long talks with him—
    learn'd the occurrence below described—
    death of Osceola. The latter was a young,
    brave, leading Seminole in the Florida war of
    that time—was surrender'd to our troops,
    imprison'd and literally died of "a broken
    heart," at Fort Moultrie. He sicken'd of his
    confinement—the doctor and officers made
    every allowance and kindness possible for
    him; then the close:]

WHEN his hour for death had come,
He slowly rais'd himself from the bed on the floor,
Drew on his war-dress, shirt, leggings, and
    girdled the belt around his waist,
Call'd for vermilion paint (his looking-glass was
    held before him,)
Painted half his face and neck, his wrists, and
    back-hands.
Put the scalp-knife carefully in his belt—then
    lying down, resting moment,
Rose again, half sitting, smiled, gave in silence
    his extended hand to each and all,
Sank faintly low to the floor (tightly grasping
    the tomahawk handle,)

Fix'd his look on wife and little children—the last:
(And here a line in memory of his name and
   death.)

A VOICE FROM DEATH
(THE JOHNSTOWN, PENN., CATACLYSM,
MAY 31, 1889.)

A VOICE from Death, solemn and strange, in
   all his sweep and power,
With sudden, indescribable blow—towns
   drown'd—humanity by thousands slain,
The vaunted work of thrift, goods, dwellings,
   forge, street, iron bridge,
Dash'd pell-mell by the blow—yet usher'd life
   continuing on,
(Amid the rest, amid the rushing, whirling, wild
   debris,
A suffering woman saved—a baby safely born!)

Although I come and unannounc'd, in horror
   and in pang,
In pouring flood and fire, and wholesale elemental
   crash, (this voice so solemn, strange,)
I too a minister of Deity.

Yea, Death, we bow our faces, veil our eyes to thee,
We mourn the old, the young untimely drawn
   to thee,

The fair, the strong, the good, the capable,
The household wreck'd, the husband and the
   wife, the engulfed forger in his forge,
The corpses in the whelming waters and the mud,
The gather'd thousands to their funeral mounds,
   and thousands never found or gather'd.

Then after burying, mourning the dead,
(Faithful to them found or unfound, forgetting
   not, bearing the past, here new musing,)
A day—a passing moment or an hour—America
   itself bends low,
Silent, resign'd, submissive.

War, death, cataclysm like this, America,
Take deep to thy proud prosperous heart.

E'en as I chant, lo! out of death, and out of
   ooze and slime,
The blossoms rapidly blooming, sympathy, help,
   love,
From West and East, from South and North and
   over sea,
Its hot-spurr'd hearts and hands humanity to
   human aid moves on;
And from within a thought and lesson yet.

Thou ever-darting Globe! through Space and
   Air!
Thou waters that encompass us!

Thou that in all the life and death of us, in
    action or in sleep!
Thou laws invisible that permeate them and all,
Thou that in all, and over all, and through and
    under all, incessant!
Thou! thou! the vital, universal, giant force
    resistless, sleepless, calm,
Holding Humanity as in thy open hand, as some
    ephemeral toy,
How ill to e'er forget thee!

For I too have forgotten,
(Wrapt in these little potencies of progress, politics,
    culture, wealth, inventions, civilization,)
Have lost my recognition of your silent ever-
    swaying power, ye mighty, elemental throes,
In which and upon which we float, and every
    one of us is buoy'd.

A Persian Lesson

FOR his o'erarching and last lesson the
    greybeard sufi,
In the fresh scent of the morning in the open air,
On the slope of a teeming Persian rose-garden,
Under an ancient chestnut-tree wide spreading
    its branches,
Spoke to the young priests and students.

"Finally my children, to envelop each word,
      each part of the rest,
Allah is all, all, all—immanent in every life and
      object,
May-be at many and many-a-more removes—yet
      Allah, Allah, Allah is there.
"Has the estray wander'd far? Is the reason—
      why strangely hidden?
Would you sound below the restless ocean of
      the entire world?
Would you know the dissatisfaction? the urge
      and spur of every life;
The something never still'd—never entirely
      gone? the invisible need of every seed?

"It is the central urge in every atom,
(Often unconscious, often evil, downfallen,)
To return to its divine source and origin,
      however distant,
Latent the same in subject and in object,
      without one exception."

THE COMMONPLACE

THE commonplace I sing;
How cheap is health! how cheap nobility!
Abstinence, no falsehood, no gluttony, lust;
The open air I sing, freedom, toleration,

(Take here the mainest lesson—less from
    books—less from the schools,)
The common day and night—the common earth
    and waters,
Your farm—your work, trade, occupation,
The democratic wisdom underneath, like solid
    ground for all.

"The Rounded Catalogue Divine Complete"

[Sunday—Went this forenoon to church. A
    college professor, Rev. Dr.—, gave us a fine
    sermon, during which I caught the above
    words; but the minister included in his
    "rounded catalogue" letter and spirit, only
    the esthetic things, and entirely ignored what
    I name in the following:]

THE devilish and the dark, the dying and diseas'd,
The countless (nineteen-twentieths) low and
    evil, crude and savage,
The crazed, prisoners in jail, the horrible, rank,
    malignant,
Venom and filth, serpents, the ravenous sharks,
    liars, the dissolute;
(What is the part the wicked and the loathesome
    bear within earth's orbic scheme?)
Newts, crawling things in slime and mud, poisons,

The barren soil, the evil men, the slag and
    hideous rot.

MIRAGES

[Noted verbatin after a supper-talk outdoors in
    Nevada with two old miners.]

MORE experiences and sights, stranger, than
    you'd think for;
Times again, now mostly just after sunrise or
    before sunset,
Sometimes in spring, oftener in autumn,
    perfectly clear weather, in plain sight,
Camps far or near, the crowded streets of cities
    and the shopfronts,
(Account for it or not—credit or not—it is all true,
And my mate there could tell you the like—we
    have often confab'd about it,)
People and scenes, animals, trees, colors and
    lines, plain as could be,
Farms and dooryards of home, paths border'd
    with box, lilacs in corners,
Weddings in churches, thanksgiving dinners,
    returns of long-absent sons,
Glum funerals, the crape-veil'd mother and the
    daughters,
Trials in courts, jury and judge, the accused in
    the box,

Contestants, battles, crowds, bridges, wharves,
Now and then mark'd faces of sorrow or joy,
(I could pick them out this moment if I saw
  them again,)
Show'd to me-just to the right in the sky-edge,
Or plainly there to the left on the hill-tops.

L. OF G.'S PURPORT

NOT to exclude or demarcate, or pick out evils
  from their formidable masses (even to expose
  them,)
But add, fuse, complete, extend—and celebrate
  the immortal and the good.
Haughty this song, its words and scope,
To span vast realms of space and time,
Evolution—the cumulative—growths and
  generations.

Begun in ripen'd youth and steadily pursued,
Wandering, peering, dallying with all—war,
  peace, day and night absorbing,
Never even for one brief hour abandoning my task,
I end it here in sickness, poverty, and old age.

I sing of life, yet mind me well of death:
To-day shadowy Death dogs my steps, my
  seated shape, and has for years—
Draws sometimes close to me, as face to face.

THE UNEXPRESS'D

HOW dare one say it?
After the cycles, poems, singers, plays,
Vaunted Ionia's, India's—Homer, Shakspere—
    the long, long times' thick dotted roads, areas,
The shining clusters and the Milky Ways of
    stars—Nature's pulses reap'd,
All retrospective passions, heroes, war, love,
    adoration,
All ages' plummets dropt to their utmost depths,
All human lives, throats, wishes, brains—all
    experiences' utterance;
After the countless songs, or long or short, all
    tongues, all lands,
Still something not yet told in poesy's voice or
    print—something lacking,
(Who knows? the best yet unexpress'd and lacking.)

GRAND IS THE SEEN

GRAND is the seen, the light, to me—grand are
    the sky and stars,
Grand is the earth, and grand are lasting time
    and space,
And grand their laws, so multiform, puzzling,
    evolutionary;
But grander far the unseen soul of me,
    comprehending, endowing all those,

Lighting the light, the sky and stars, delving the
earth, sailing the sea,
(What were all those, indeed, without thee,
unseen soul? of what amount without thee?)
More evolutionary, vast, puzzling, O my soul!
More multiform far—more lasting thou than
they.

UNSEEN BUDS

UNSEEN buds, infinite, hidden well,
Under the snow and ice, under the darkness, in
every square or cubic inch,
Germinal, exquisite, in delicate lace,
microscopic, unborn,
Like babes in wombs, latent, folded, compact,
sleeping;
Billions of billions, and trillions of trillions of
them waiting,
(On earth and in the sea—the universe—the
stars there in the heavens,)
Urging slowly, surely forward, forming endless,
And waiting ever more, forever more behind.

GOOD-BYE MY FANCY!

GOOD-BYE my Fancy!
Farewell dear mate, dear love!

I'm going away, I know not where,
Or to what fortune, or whether I may ever see
 you again,
So Good-bye my Fancy.

Now for my last—let me look back a
 moment;
The slower fainter ticking of the clock is in me,
Exit, nightfall, and soon the heart-thud
 stopping.

Long have we lived, joy'd, caress'd together;
Delightful!—now separation—Good-bye my Fancy.

Yet let me not be too hasty,
Long indeed have we lived, slept, filter'd,
 become really blended into one;
Then if we die we die together, (yes, we'll
 remain one,)
If we go anywhere we'll go together to meet
 what happens,
May-be we'll be better off and blither, and learn
 something,
May-be it is yourself now really ushering me to
 the true songs, (who knows?)
May-be it is you the mortal knob really undoing,
 turning—so now finally,
Good-bye-and hail! my Fancy.

Look for these and other
HarperLargePrint books at your local bookstore

HarperLargePrint Classics
Published in deluxe paperback editions in
easy-to-read 16-point type

Pride and Prejudice, Jane Austen
A Tale of Two Cities, Charles Dickens
The Adventures of Sherlock Holmes,
   Sir Arthur Conan Doyle
This Side of Paradise, F. Scott Fitzgerald
A Room with a View, E.M. Forster
To Kill a Mockingbird, Harper Lee

Also available from HarperLargePrint

Bedside Prayers, June Cotner
Calder Pride, Janet Dailey
**How to Get What You Want and Want What
   You Have**, John Gray, Ph.D.
Mars and Venus Starting Over, John Gray,
   Ph.D.
The Anti-Aging Zone, Barry Sears, Ph.D.
Beauty Fades, Dumb Is Forever, Judy Sheindlin
A God in Ruins, Leon Uris
Little Altars Everywhere, Rebecca Wells
Worst Fears Realized, Stuart Woods

HarperLargePrint books are available
at your local bookstore,
or call 1-800-331-3761, or write:
HarperLargePrint
10 East 53rd Street, New York, New York, 10022
www.harpercollins.com